Self-efficacy in Changing Societies

Self-efficacy in Changing Societies

Edited by
Albert Bandura
Stanford University

CAMBRIDGE
UNIVERSITY PRESS

PUBLISHED BY THE PRESS SYNDICATE OF THE UNIVERSITY OF CAMBRIDGE
The Pitt Building, Trumpington Street, Cambridge, United Kingdom

CAMBRIDGE UNIVERSITY PRESS
The Edinburgh Building, Cambridge CB2 2RU, UK   http://www.cup.cam.ac.uk
40 West 20th Street, New York, NY 10011-4211, USA   http://www.cup.org
10 Stamford Road, Oakleigh, Melbourne 3166, Australia

© Cambridge University Press 1995

First published 1995
First paperback edition 1997
Reprinted 1999

Typeset in Palatino

A catalogue record for this book is available from the British Library

Library of Congress Cataloguing-in-Publication Data is available

ISBN 0-521-47467-1 hardback
ISBN 0-521-58696-8 paperback

Transferred to digital printing 2002

Contents

vi   Contents

Foreword

It has become commonplace to speak of the accelerated rate of social, economic, technological, and cultural changes that our world is undergoing. Genetic engineering, global multimedia communication, superhighways of information, and other breathtaking innovations no longer belong to the domain of science fiction. They are now part of our daily lives. Navigating between the reefs of the uncharted waters of our assailed present and daunting future is disconcerting for the best-prepared adults but even more so for the youth of our society.

Much ink has flowed on the subject of whether tomorrow's world will be a true or false El Dorado. Less effort has been invested in preparing ourselves, and particulary our youth, to cope with the extraordinary changes they face.

For this reason, I am especially pleased to introduce Albert Bandura's volume, *Self-efficacy in Changing Societies*. It is a great honor for the Johann Jacobs Foundation that the various contributions presented in this volume originated from the conference held on November 4–6, 1993, at our Communication Center, Marbach Castle (Germany), with the participation of 45 international social scientists and young scholars.

In his preface, Albert Bandura summarizes the structure of this volume, which is built around the central theme that young people's beliefs in their personal efficacy to manage the demands of rapidly changing societal conditions help them to meet these challenges.

Convinced of the fruitful applications of many of the ideas presented at the Marbach Conference on self-efficacy, the Johann Jacobs Foundation organized a follow-up policy conference on January 28–30, 1994, with the participation of some of the contributors to this volume, as well as prominent policy makers and field workers involved in youth work, particularly school systems.

It is our hope that the outcome of this policy conference, based on the inspiring ideas of Al Bandura and his colleagues, will serve as an impetus to disseminate and implement the theory of self-efficacy to develop and improve the adaptational capabilities of youth.

It only remains for me to thank Albert Bandura, the main organizer of the third Johann Jacobs Conference and editor of this volume. He communicated his vast knowledge and infectious enthusiasm with great talent to the distinguished group of speakers, panelists, and other participants, all of whom contributed to the success of the conference sponsored by our foundation. Since its inception, the foundation has been dedicated to encouraging and supporting basic research, research-informed program developments and field activities, designed to improve our understanding of human development, with particular focus on the well-being of youth in the societies in which they live.

I hope that his volume will receive the welcome it deserves, not only from specialists, but also from the general public interested in the welfare of our youth.

Klaus J. Jacobs
Chairman of the Board
Johann Jacobs Foundation

Preface

Life in the societies of today is undergoing accelerated social and technological change as well as growing global interdependence. These challenging new realities place heavy pressure on people's capabilities to exercise some control over the course their lives take. The present volume is an outgrowth of the third annual conference convened by the Johann Jacobs Foundation at Schloss Marbach to examine the impact of youths' efficacy beliefs on their modes of adaptation. The volume is structured around the central theme that youths' beliefs in their personal efficacy to manage life demands affect their psychological well-being, their accomplishments, and the direction their lives take. The various chapters analyze the diverse ways in which efficacy beliefs contribute to the selection, construction, and management of environments in adaptation under rapidly changing societal conditions.

In the introductory chapter, Bandura addresses central issues concerning the nature and function of beliefs of personal efficacy. He examines the different sources of efficacy beliefs and the psychological processes through which they exert their effects. The bulk of the chapter is devoted to the influential role played by efficacy beliefs in different spheres of human functioning. These matters concern the heavy demands on parenting efficacy under the changing structure of family systems; the principal ways in which efficacy beliefs operate as key contributors to the intellectual development of children; and the way in which such beliefs shape occupational development and pursuits and affect the quality of health and psychological well-being. Each of these issues receives detailed analysis in the various chapters in this edited volume. The chapter also examines how a sense of efficacy operates in individualistic and collectivistic social systems. It concludes with analysis of the many factors that undermine the development of collective efficacy and the ways in which people strive to regain some measure of control over conditions that affect their lives.

Human development and change is best understood by analysis of lives in time and historical contexts that present unique opportunities, challenges, constraints, and threats. In his prior classic studies, Elder documented how growing up during the Great Depression and during World War II shaped life trajectories. In his chapter in the present volume, Elder examines how economic hardships suffered by families living in rural America and in inner cities affect parents' sense of efficacy to guide their children's development. In this research, socioeconomic factors, family processes, and beliefs of personal efficacy are treated as interrelated determinants within an integrated causal structure. This chapter provides new insights on how personal agency operates within a broader network of sociostructural influences.

In his chapter, Flammer presents a developmental analysis of beliefs in one's capability to exercise control. The newborn comes without any sense of self. It must be socially constructed through transactional experiences with the environment. Flammer provides a conceptual and empirical analysis of how infants develop a sense of personal agency. Different periods of life present certain prototypic competency demands for successful functioning. The chapter traces the changes in control beliefs over the life course and in different spheres of psychosocial functioning. It also examines the impact of beliefs in personal control on the development of self-esteem and on the priorities given to different life pursuits.

The initial experiences that build a sense of agency and personal efficacy are centered in the family. Schneewind's chapter examines the impact of family practices on children's beliefs in their capabilities to produce effects. Infants who are taught to be causative are more cognitively competent in later childhood than those who have not had the benefit of early mastery experiences. Schneewind documents the long-term effects of early familial experiences on beliefs of personal efficacy in young adulthood. This chapter also addresses a number of important issues bearing on familial sources of efficacy beliefs including the impact of different family structures, the intergenerational transmission of efficacy beliefs, and the influence of the larger societal systems within which the family is embedded.

Oettingen examines how culture affects the development of personal efficacy. She compares children's self-efficacy beliefs in West Berlin, East Berlin before the unification, Russia, and the United States. These cross-cultural variations were chosen to represent individualistic and collectivistic social systems. The educational practices in East Berlin discouraged in children optimistic beliefs in personal efficacy, whereas children raised in individualistic systems had higher and more optimistic beliefs in their causative capabilities. These differences in efficacy beliefs emerged at an early phase of educational development and became pervasive. Efficacy beliefs correlate with academic achievement, although the size of the relationship varies cross-culturally. The findings of this program of cross-cultural research underscore the power of societal institutions to shape the efficacy beliefs of its youth.

Jerusalem and Mittag consider a sense of personal efficacy to be an important personal resource in human adaptation to stressful life transitions. They examine longitudinally the process of coping with stressful life transitions in the context of migration from East to West Germany before the fall of the Berlin Wall. Migrants who had a high sense of coping efficacy viewed the migratory move as a challenge to create a new life for themselves, whereas those with a low sense of efficacy perceived the move as a threat. The negative construal of the life transition produced a high level of stress and took a toll on health. In addition to the adaptive benefits of a sense of personal efficacy, social support and gainful employment helped migrants to surmount the many problems endemic to sociocultural change.

The new realities of the information era require advanced cognitive and self-management competencies to fulfill complex occupational roles and to manage the maze of demands of contemporary life. Moreover, the rapid pace of technological change and accelerated growth of knowledge are placing a premium on capability for self-directed learning throughout one's lifetime; otherwise, one's competencies quickly become outmoded. Zimmerman analyzes the processes through which children's beliefs in their capabilities to regulate their own learning and to master academic subjects set the course of their intellectual development. Such beliefs affect children's aspirations, academic motivation, level of interest in intellectual pursuits, vulnerability to scholastic anxiety, and academic accomplishments. The chapter concludes with a comparison of the conceptual and empirical distinctiveness of efficacy beliefs with related constructs designed to account for academic development.

The choices people make that affect their occupational development shape their life courses and the life-style they follow. Hackett reviews a large body of evidence showing that beliefs of personal efficacy play a key role in occupational development and pursuits. The higher the people's perceived efficacy to fulfill occupational roles, the wider the career options they seriously consider pursuing, the greater the interest they have in them, and the more successfully they perform their occupational roles.

Demographic trends indicate that societies will have to rely increasingly on the talents of women and ethnic minorities for scientific, technological, and economic attainments. Yet most women and minorities are shunning scientific and technological fields because of a low sense of efficacy for quantitative activities. Occupational socialization practices are thus at odds with the human resources societies need for their success. Hackett discusses both individual and social remedies to restricted aspirations and occupational pursuits.

People's beliefs in their efficacy also play an important promotive role in health. Life-style habits and environmental hazards contribute substantially to health status and functioning. This enables people to exercise some behavioral control over the quality of their health. Peoples' beliefs in their self-regulatory efficacy affect each of the three basic phases of personal change. These include initiation of efforts to alter health habits, mobilization of the self-influences needed to succeed, and enduring maintenance of achieved habit changes. Schwarzer and Fuchs review a large body of evidence on how a sense of personal efficacy operates in concert with other psychosocial factors to foster life-style changes that enhance health and to alter those that impair it. They propose a conceptual model that helps to predict the self-management of health-related behavior and provides guidelines on how to reduce detrimental health habits.

Abuse of addictive substances is a highly prevalent problem that exacts heavy personal and social costs. Drug abuse has been a chronic problem in the American society. Recent sociopolitical changes in Europe have ushered in a soaring narcotics trade that will produce mounting drug-related problems in European societies as well in the years ahead. Marlatt, Baer, and Quigley trace the unique role played by perceived self-regulatory efficacy in every phase of addictive behavior. These phases include the development of addictive habits, the success in overcoming them, vulnerability to relapse, and restorative coping that fosters long-term maintenance of desired changes. After people give up an addictive substance, relapses often occur even though withdrawal symptoms are no longer present to drive one to resume use of alcohol, drugs, or cigarette smoking. The challenging problem is elimination of psychological reliance on addictive substances for their positive effects or as an escapist mode of coping with difficult realities. Marlatt and his colleagues, therefore, devote considerable attention to treatment strategies designed to reduce vulnerability to relapses.

Many people contributed in various ways to this enterprise, and I am most pleased to take this opportunity to express my debt of gratitude to them. Paul Baltes planted the idea for this project. August Flammer and Ralf Schwarzer were of invaluable help in selecting the topical coverage and participants for this conference. Laszlo Nagy, President of the Johann Jacobs Foundation, provided generous administrative support embellished with touches of humor that help to make one's day. Judith Kressig skillfully bonded this international network of scholars by her organizational virtuosity and trusty fax machine. I have been unusually blessed with the masterful and dedicated assistance of Lisa Hellrich in managing the details of the conference and in preparing the manuscript for publication, for which I am profoundly grateful.

I am especially indebted to my coauthors, all of whom fulfilled the prescribed deadlines without fail despite burdensome schedules and calls for revisions that could easily evoke the wrath of authors. This remarkable level of responsiveness must be unique in the annals of edited volumes, which are notorious for their protracted gestations. As editor of this volume, it was a welcome relief to see those timeless Parkinsonian dictums refuted. I would also like to express my appreciation to the discussants and other participants who contributed to the intellectual life of the conference.

Finally, I wish to pay tribute to Klaus Jacobs, chairman of the Johann Jacobs Foundation, who has devoted considerable time and resources to promote the betterment of the lives of our youth. We owe much to his inspiring commitment.

Albert Bandura
Stanford University

Contributors

Albert Bandura, Department of Psychology, Stanford University, Stanford, CA, U.S.A.

John S. Baer, Department of Psychology, University of Washington, Seattle, WA, U.S.A.

Glen H. Elder, Jr., Life Course Studies, University of North Carolina, Chapel Hill, NC, U.S.A.

August Flammer, Psychological Institute, University of Bern, Bern, Switzerland

Reinhard Fuchs, Institut für Psychologie, Freie Universität Berlin, Berlin, Germany

Gail Hackett, Division of Psychology in Education, Arizona State University, Tempe, AZ

Matthais Jerusalem, Institut für Pädagogische Psychologie, Humboldt-Universität zu Berlin, Berlin, Germany

Alan Marlatt, Department of Psychology, University of Washington, Seattle, WA, U.S.A.

Waldemar Mittag, Institut für Pädagogische Psychologie, Humboldt-Universität zu Berlin, Berlin, Germany

Gabriele Oettingen, Center for Psychology and Human Development, Max Planck Institut für Bildungs forschung, Berlin, Germany

Lori A. Quigley, Department of Psychology, University of Washington, Seattle, WA, U.S.A.

Klaus A. Schneewind, Institut für Psychologie, Universität München, München, Germany

Ralf Schwarzer, Institut für Psychologie, Freie Universität Berlin, Berlin, Germany

Barry Zimmerman, Program in Educational Psychology, The City University of New York, New York, NY, U.S.A.

1. Exercise of personal and collective efficacy in changing societies

ALBERT BANDURA

People strive to exercise control over events that affect their lives. By exerting influence in spheres over which they can command some control, they are better able to realize desired futures and to forestall undesired ones. The striving for control over life circumstances permeates almost everything people do because it can secure them innumerable personal and social benefits. The ability to affect outcomes makes them predictable. Predictability fosters adoptive preparedness. Inability to exert influence over things that adversely affect one's life breeds apprehension, apathy, or despair. The capability to produce valued outcomes and to prevent undesired ones, therefore, provides powerful incentives for the development and exercise of personal control.

Although a strong sense of efficacy in socially valued pursuits is conducive to human attainment and well-being, it is not an unmixed blessing. The impact of personal efficacy on the nature and quality of life depends, of course, on the purposes to which it is put. For example, the lives of innovators and social reformers driven by unshakable efficacy are not easy ones. They are often the objects of derision, condemnation, and persecution, even though societies eventually benefit from their persevering efforts. Many people who gain recognition and fame shape their lives by overcoming seemingly insurmountable obstacles only to be catapulted to new social realities over which they have lesser control. Indeed, the annals of the famed and infamous are strewn with individuals who were both architects and victims of their destinies.

The vastly enhanced human power to transform the environment can have pervasive effects not only on current life, but on how future generations live out their lives. Our technical capability to render uninhabitable

1

much of the planet on which we reside attests to the growing magnitude of human power. There is much public concern over where some of the technologies we create are leading us. Voracious pursuit of self-interest not only produces effects that collectively may be detrimental in the long run, but creates special-interest gridlock that immobilizes efforts to solve socially the broader problems of society. Without commitment to shared purposes that transcend narrow self-interests, the exercise of control can degenerate into personal and factional conflicts of power. People have to be able to work together if they are to realize the shared destiny they desire and to preserve a habitable environment for generations to come.

Nature and function of efficacy beliefs

Because of the centrality of control in human lives, many theories about it have been proposed over the years (Adler, 1956; DeCharms, 1978; Rotter, 1966; White, 1959). People's level of motivation, affective states, and actions are based more on what they believe than on what is objectively the case. Hence, it is people's beliefs in their causative capabilities that is the major focus of inquiry. Much of the research generated by the various theories is tied to an omnibus measure of perceived control and devoted to the search for its psychosocial correlates. To fully understand personal causation requires a comprehensive theory that explains, within a unified conceptual framework, the origins of beliefs of personal efficacy, their structure and function, the processes through which they operate, and their diverse effects. Self-efficacy theory addresses all of these sub-processes both at the individual and collective level (Bandura, in press). By embedding the self-efficacy belief system in a broader sociocognitive theory, it can integrate diverse bodies of findings in varied spheres of functioning. The value of a theory is ultimately judged by the power of the methods it yields to produce desired changes. Self-efficacy theory provides explicit guidelines on how to develop and enhance human efficacy.

Self-efficacy in the exercise of human agency

People make causal contributions to their own psychosocial functioning through mechanisms of personal agency. Among the mechanisms of agency, none is more central or pervasive than people's beliefs of personal efficacy. Perceived self-efficacy refers to beliefs in one's capabilities to organize and execute the courses of action required to manage prospective situations. Efficacy beliefs influence how people think, feel, motivate themselves, and act. A central question in any theory of cognitive regulation of motivation, affect, and action concerns the issues of causality. Do efficacy beliefs operate as causal factors in human functioning? The findings of diverse causal tests, in which efficacy beliefs are systematically varied, are consistent in showing that such beliefs contribute significantly to human motivation and attainments (Bandura, 1992a).

Sources of efficacy beliefs

People's beliefs concerning their efficacy can be developed by four main ④ forms of influence. The most effective way of creating a strong sense of efficacy is through *mastery experiences*. They provide the most authentic ① evidence of whether one can muster whatever it takes to succeed (Bandura, 1982; Biran & Wilson, 1981; Feltz, Landers, & Raeder, 1979; Gist, 1989). Successes build a robust belief in one's personal efficacy. Failures undermine it, especially if failures occur before a sense of efficacy is firmly established. Developing a sense of efficacy through mastery experiences is not a matter of adopting ready-made habits. Rather, it involves acquiring the cognitive, behavioral, and self-regulatory tools for creating and exe- *biz* cuting appropriate courses of action to manage ever-changing life circum- *harder* stances. *in todays*

If people experience only easy successes they come to expect quick *economy* results and are easily discouraged by failure. A resilient sense of efficacy *?* requires experience in overcoming obstacles through perseverant effort. Some difficulties and setbacks in human pursuits serve a useful purpose in teaching that success usually requires sustained effort. After people become convinced they have what it takes to succeed, they persevere in the face of adversity and quickly rebound from setbacks. By sticking it out through tough times, they emerge stronger from adversity.

The second influential way of creating and strengthening efficacy beliefs is through the *vicarious experiences* provided by social models. See- ② ing people similar to themselves succeed by perseverant effort raises observers' beliefs that they, too, possess the capabilities to master comparable activities (Bandura, 1986; Schunk, 1987). By the same token, observing others fail despite high effort lowers observers' judgments of their own efficacy and undermines their level of motivation (Brown & Inouye, 1978). The impact of modeling on beliefs of personal efficacy is strongly influenced by perceived similarity to the models. The greater the assumed similarity the more persuasive are the models' successes and failures. If people see the models as very different from themselves their beliefs of personal efficacy are not much influenced by the models' behavior and the results it produces.

Modeling influences do more than simply provide a social standard against which to judge one's own capabilities. People seek proficient models who possess the competencies to which they aspire. Through their behavior and expressed ways of thinking, competent models transmit knowledge and teach observers effective skills and strategies for managing environmental demands. Acquisition of better means raises perceived self-efficacy. Undaunted attitudes exhibited by perseverant models as they cope with obstacles repeatedly thrown in their path can be more enabling to others than the particular skills being modeled.

Social persuasion is a third way of strengthening people's beliefs that they have what it takes to succeed. People who are persuaded verbally that they possess the capabilities to master given activities are likely to mobilize greater effort and sustain it than if they harbor self-doubts and dwell on personal deficiencies when problems arise (Litt, 1988; Schunk, 1989). To the extent that persuasive boosts in perceived self-efficacy lead people to try hard enough to succeed, self-affirming beliefs promote development of skills and a sense of personal efficacy.

It is more difficult to instill high beliefs of personal efficacy by social persuasion alone than to undermine them. Unrealistic boosts in efficacy are quickly disconfirmed by disappointing results of one's efforts. But people who have been persuaded that they lack capabilities tend to avoid challenging activities that can cultivate their potentialities, and they give up quickly in the face of difficulties. By constricting activities and undermining motivation, disbelief in one's capabilities creates its own behavioral validation.

Successful efficacy builders do more than convey positive appraisals. In addition to raising people's beliefs in their capabilities, they structure situations for them in ways that bring success and avoid placing people in situations prematurely where they are likely to fail often. They encourage individuals to measure their success in terms of self-improvement rather than by triumphs over others.

People also rely partly on their *physiological and emotional states* in judging their capabilities. They interpret their stress reactions and tension as signs of vulnerability to poor performance. In activities involving strength and stamina, people judge their fatigue, aches, and pains as signs of physical debility (Ewart, 1992). Mood also affects people's judgments of their personal efficacy. Positive mood enhances perceived self-efficacy; despondent mood diminishes it (Kavanagh & Bower, 1985). The fourth way of altering efficacy beliefs is to enhance physical status, reduce stress and negative emotional proclivities, and correct misinterpretations of bodily states.

It is not the sheer intensity of emotional and physical reactions that is important but rather how they are perceived and interpreted. For example, people who have a high sense of efficacy are likely to view their state of affective arousal as an energizing facilitator of performance, whereas those who are beset by self-doubts regard their arousal as a debilitator. Physiological indicators of efficacy play an especially influential role in health functioning and in activities requiring physical strength and stamina. Affective states can have widely generalized effects on beliefs of personal efficacy in diverse spheres of functioning.

Information that is relevant for judging personal efficacy, whether conveyed enactively, vicariously, persuasively, or affectively is not inherently instructive. Rather it gains its significance through cognitive processing. Therefore, the information conveyed by the different modes of influence should be distinguished from the cognitive processing by which that information is selected, weighted, and integrated into self-efficacy judgments. A host of factors, including personal, social, and situational ones, affect how efficacy-relevant experiences are interpreted (Bandura, in press). For example, the extent to which performance attainments alter perceived efficacy will depend on people's preconceptions of their capabilities, the perceived difficulty of the tasks, the amount of effort they expended, their physical and emotional state at the time, the amount of external aid they received, and the situational circumstances under which they performed. Each mode of influence is associated with a particular set of factors that have diagnostic significance in the self-appraisal of personal efficacy.

Efficacy-activated processes

Efficacy beliefs regulate human functioning through four major processes. They include cognitive, motivational, affective, and selection processes. These different processes usually operate in concert, rather than in isolation, in the ongoing regulation of human functioning.

Cognitive processes

The effects of efficacy beliefs on cognitive processes take a variety of forms. Much human behavior, being purposive, is regulated by forethought embodying valued goals. Personal goal setting is influenced by self-appraisal of capabilities. The stronger the perceived self-efficacy, the higher the goal challenges people set for themselves and the firmer is their commitment to them (Locke & Latham, 1990).

Most courses of action are initially organized in thought. People's beliefs in their efficacy shape the types of anticipatory scenarios they construct and rehearse. Those who have a high sense of efficacy visualize success scenarios that provide positive guides and supports for performance. Those who doubt their efficacy visualize failure scenarios and dwell on the many things that can go wrong. It is difficult to achieve much while fighting self-doubt.

A major function of thought is to enable people to predict events and to develop ways to control those that affect their lives. Such problem-solving skills require effective cognitive processing of information that contains many complexities, ambiguities, and uncertainties. In learning predictive and regulative rules people must draw on their knowledge to construct options, to weight and integrate predictive factors, to test and revise their judgments against the immediate and distal results of their actions, and to remember which factors they have tested and how well they have worked.

It requires a strong sense of efficacy to remain task oriented in the face of pressing situational demands, failures, and setbacks that have significant personal and social repercussions. Indeed, when people are faced with the task of managing difficult environmental demands under taxing circumstances, those who harbor a low sense of efficacy become more and more erratic in their analytic thinking and lower their aspirations, and the quality of their performance deteriorates (Wood & Bandura, 1989). In contrast, those who maintain a resilient sense of efficacy set themselves challenging goals and use good analytic thinking, which pays off in performance accomplishments.

Motivational processes

Efficacy beliefs play a key role in the self-regulation of motivation. Most human motivation is cognitively generated. People motivate themselves and guide their actions anticipatorily by the exercise of forethought. They form beliefs about what they can do. They anticipate likely outcomes of prospective actions. They set goals for themselves and plan courses of action designed to realize valued futures. They mobilize the resources at their command and the level of effort needed to succeed.

There are three different forms of cognitive motivators around which different theories have been developed. They include *causal attributions, outcome expectancies,* and *cognized goals.* The corresponding theories are attribution theory, expectancy-value theory, and goal theory, respectively. Efficacy beliefs operate in each of these types of cognitive motivation. Efficacy beliefs influence causal attributions (Alden, 1986; Grove, 1993; McAuley, 1991). People who regard themselves as highly efficacious attribute their failures to insufficient effort or adverse situational conditions, whereas those who regard themselves as inefficacious tend to attribute their failures to low ability. Causal attributions affect motivation, performance, and affective reactions mainly through beliefs of personal efficacy (Chwalisz, Altmaier, & Russell, 1992; Relich, Debus, & Walker, 1986; Schunk & Gunn, 1986).

In expectancy-value theory, motivation is regulated by the expectation that a given course of behavior will produce certain outcomes and the value placed on those outcomes. But people act on their beliefs about what they can do as well as on their beliefs about the likely outcomes of performance. The motivating influence of outcome expectancies is thus *Fail* partly governed by efficacy beliefs. There are countless attractive options people do not pursue because they judge they lack the capabilities for *before* them. The predictiveness of expectancy-value theory is substantially *trying* enhanced by including the influence of perceived self-efficacy (Ajzen & Madden, 1986; deVries, Dijkstra, & Kuhlman, 1988; Dzewaltowski, Noble, & Shaw, 1990; Schwarzer, 1992).

The capacity to exercise self-influence by goal challenges and evaluative reaction to one's own performances provides a major cognitive mechanism of motivation. A large body of evidence shows that explicit, challenging goals enhance and sustain motivation (Locke & Latham, 1990). Goals operate largely through self-influence processes rather than regulate motivation and action directly. Motivation based on goal setting involves a process of cognitive comparison of perceived performance to an adopted personal standard. By making self-satisfaction conditional on matching the standard, people give direction to their behavior and create incentives to persist in their efforts until they fulfill their goals. They seek self-satisfaction from fulfilling valued goals and are prompted to intensify their efforts by discontent with substandard performances.

Motivation based on goals or personal standards is governed by three types of self-influences (Bandura, 1991a; Bandura & Cervone, 1986). They include self-satisfying and self-dissatisfying reactions to one's performance, perceived self-efficacy for goal attainment, and readjustment of personal goals based on one's progress. Efficacy beliefs contribute to motivation in several ways: They determine the goals people set for themselves, how much effort they expend, how long they persevere in the face of difficulties, and their resilience to failures. When faced with obstacles and failures, people who distrust their capabilities slacken their efforts or give up quickly. Those who have a strong belief in their capabilities exert greater effort when they fail to master the challenge. Strong perseverance contributes to performance accomplishments.

Affective processes

People's beliefs in their coping capabilities affect how much stress and depression they experience in threatening or difficult situations, as well as their level of motivation. Perceived self-efficacy to exercise control over stressors plays a central role in anxiety arousal (Bandura, 1991b). It does so in several ways. Efficacy beliefs affect vigilance toward potential threats and how they are perceived and cognitively processed. People who believe that potential threats are unmanageable view many aspects of their environment as fraught with danger. They dwell on their coping deficiencies. They magnify the severity of possible threats and worry about things that rarely happen. Through such inefficacious thinking they distress themselves and impair their level of functioning (Lazarus & Folkman, 1984; Meichenbaum, 1977; Sarason, 1975). In contrast, people who believe they can exercise control over potential threats are neither ever watchful for threats nor conjure up disturbing thoughts about them. Sanderson, Rapee, and Barlow (1989) provide striking evidence for the power of efficacy belief to cognitively transform threatening situations into benign ones. Although subjected to the same environmental stressors, individuals who believe they can manage them remain unperturbed, whereas those who believe the stressors are personally uncontrollable view them in debilitating ways. The impact of efficacy beliefs on construal of uncertain life circumstances is also very much evident in wrenching transitions in life courses. In coping with adaptation to new societal demands, migrants with a high sense of efficacy treat it as a challenge, whereas those who distrust their coping capabilities view it as a threat (Jerusalem & Mittag, 1995).

People have to live continuously with a psychic environment that is largely of their own making. The exercise of control over ruminative, disturbing thoughts is a second way in which efficacy beliefs regulate anxiety arousal and depression. The exercise of control over one's own conscious-ness is summed up well in the proverb: "You cannot prevent the birds of worry and care from flying over your head. But you can stop them from building a nest in your hair." It is not the sheer frequency of disturbing thoughts, but the perceived inability to turn them off that is the major source of distress (Kent & Gibbons, 1987; Salkovskis & Harrison, 1984). Hence, the frequency of aversive thoughts is unrelated to anxiety when the effects of perceived thought control efficacy are removed. But per-ceived thought control efficacy predicts anxiety when variations in fre-quency of aversive thoughts are removed. Both perceived coping self-effi-cacy and thought control efficacy operate jointly to reduce anxiety and avoidant behavior (Ozer & Bandura, 1990).

The causative role of coping efficacy beliefs in human stress and anxiety is best revealed in studies in which phobics' beliefs in their coping efficacy is raised to different levels through guided mastery treatment (Bandura, 1988). They display little anxiety and autonomic arousal to threats they believe they can control. But as they cope with threats for which they dis-trust their coping efficacy, their anxiety and autonomic arousal mount. After their perceived coping efficacy is raised to the maximal level by guided mastery experiences, they manage the same threats without expe-riencing any distress, autonomic arousal, or activation of stress-related hormones.

The third way in which efficacy beliefs reduce or eliminate anxiety is by supporting effective modes of behavior that change threatening environ-ments into safe ones. Here, efficacy beliefs regulate stress and anxiety through their impact on coping behavior. The stronger the sense of effi-cacy the bolder people are in taking on problematic situations that gener-ate stress and the greater their success in shaping them more to their lik-ing. Major changes in aversive social conditions are usually achieved through the exercise of efficacy collectively rather than just individually.

A low sense of efficacy to exercise control breeds depression as well as anxiety. One route to depression is through unfulfilled aspiration. People who impose on themselves standards of self-worth they judge they cannot attain drive themselves to bouts of depression (Bandura, 1991a; Kanfer & Zeiss, 1983). A second route to depression is through a low sense of social efficacy to develop social relationships that bring satisfaction to one's life and cushion the adverse effects of chronic stressors. Social support re-duces vulnerability to stress, depression, and physical illness. Social sup-port is not a self-forming entity waiting around to buffer harried people against stressors. Rather, people have to go out and find or create supportive relationships for themselves. This requires a strong sense of social efficacy. Thus, a low sense of efficacy to develop satisfying and supportive relationships contributes to depression both directly and by curtailing development of social supports (Holahan & Holahan, 1987a, b). Supportive relationships, in turn, can enhance personal efficacy to reduce vulnerability to depression (Cutrona & Troutman, 1986; Major, Mueller, & Hildebrandt, 1985; Major et al., 1990). Supporters do so by modeling for others how to manage difficult situations, by demonstrating the value of perseverance, and by providing positive incentives and resources for efficacious coping.

The third route to depression is via thought control efficacy. Much human depression is cognitively generated by dejecting ruminative thought. A low sense of efficacy to control ruminative thought contributes to the occurrence, duration, and recurrence of depressive episodes (Kavanagh & Wilson, 1989). The weaker the perceived efficacy to turn off ruminative thoughts the higher the depression. Mood and perceived efficacy influence each other bidirectionally. A low sense of efficacy to gain the things in life that bring self-satisfaction and self-worth gives rise to depression, and depressive mood, in turn, diminishes belief in one's personal efficacy in a deepening self-demoralizing cycle. People then act in accordance with their mood-altered efficacy beliefs.

Selection processes

The discussion so far has centered on efficacy-activated processes that enable people to create beneficial environments and to exercise some control over those they encounter day in and day out. People are partly the product of their environment. Therefore, beliefs of personal efficacy can shape the courses people's lives take by influencing the types of activities and environments they choose to get into. In this process, destinies are shaped by selection of environments known to cultivate certain potentialities and life-styles. People avoid activities and environments they believe exceed their coping capabilities. But they readily undertake challenging activities and select environments they judge themselves capable of managing. By the choices they make, people cultivate different competencies, interests, and social networks that determine their life courses. Any factor that influences choice behavior can profoundly affect the direction of personal development. This is because the social influences operating in selected environments continue to promote certain competencies, values, and interests long after the efficacy decisional determinant has rendered its inaugurating effect.

The substantial body of research on the diverse effects of perceived personal efficacy can be summarized as follows: People who have a low sense of efficacy in given domains shy away from difficult tasks, which they view as personal threats. They have low aspirations and weak commitment to the goals they choose to pursue. When faced with difficult tasks, they dwell on their personal deficiencies, the obstacles they will encounter, and all kinds of adverse outcomes rather than concentrate on how to perform successfully. They slacken their efforts and give up quickly in the face of difficulties. They are slow to recover their sense of efficacy following failure or setbacks. Because they view insufficient performance as deficient aptitude, it does not require much failure for them to lose faith in their capabilities. They fall easy victim to stress and depression.

In contrast, a strong sense of efficacy enhances human accomplishment and personal well-being in many ways. People with high assurance in their capabilities in given domains approach difficult tasks as challenges to be mastered rather than as threats to be avoided. Such an efficacious outlook fosters intrinsic interest and deep engrossment in activities. These people set themselves challenging goals and maintain strong commitment to them. They heighten and sustain their efforts in the face of difficulties. They quickly recover their sense of efficacy after failures or setbacks. They attribute failure to insufficient effort or to deficient knowledge and skills that are acquirable. They approach threatening situations with assurance that they can exercise control over them. Such an efficacious outlook produces personal accomplishments, reduces stress, and lowers vulnerability to depression.

The multiple benefits of a resilient sense of personal efficacy do not arise simply from the incantation of capability. Saying something should not be confused with believing it to be so. Simply saying that one is capable is not necessarily self-convincing. Self-efficacy beliefs are the product of a complex process of self-persuasion that relies on cognitive processing of diverse sources of efficacy information conveyed enactively, vicariously, socially, and physiologically (Bandura, 1986, in press). Once formed, efficacy beliefs contribute importantly to the level and quality of human functioning.

Adaptive benefits of optimistic efficacy beliefs

Human accomplishments and positive well-being require an optimistic sense of personal efficacy. This is because ordinary social realities are strewn with difficulties. They are full of impediments, adversities, setbacks, frustrations, and inequities. People must have a robust sense of personal efficacy to sustain the perseverant effort needed to succeed. In pursuits strewn with obstacles, realists either forsake the venture, abort their efforts prematurely when difficulties arise, or become cynical about the prospects of effecting significant changes.

It is widely believed that misjudgment breeds personal problems. Certainly, gross miscalculation can get one into trouble. However, the functional value of accuracy of self-appraisal depends on the nature of the venture. Activities in which mistakes can produce costly or injurious consequences call for accurate self-appraisal of capabilities. It is a different matter where difficult accomplishments can produce substantial personal and social benefits and the costs involve one's time, effort, and expendable resources. Individuals have to decide for themselves which creative abilities to cultivate, whether to invest their efforts and resources in ventures that are difficult to fulfill, and how much hardship they are willing to endure in pursuits strewn with obstacles and uncertainties. It takes a resilient sense of efficacy to surmount the impediments and setbacks that characterize difficult undertakings.

When people err in their self-appraisal they tend to overestimate their capabilities (Taylor, 1989). This is a benefit rather than a cognitive failing or character flaw to be eradicated. If efficacy beliefs always reflected only what people could do, routinely they would remain steadfastly wedded to an overly conservative judgment of their capabilities that begets habitual performances. Under cautious self-appraisal, people rarely set aspirations beyond their immediate reach nor mount the extra effort needed to surpass their ordinary performances. Indeed, in social systems where children are punished for optimistic beliefs in their capabilities their attainments closely match their conservative view of what they come to expect of themselves (Oettingen, 1995).

An affirmative sense of efficacy contributes to psychological well-being as well as to performance accomplishments. People who experience much distress have been compared in their skills and beliefs in their capabilities with those who do not suffer from such problems. The findings show that it is often the normal people who are distorters of reality. But they display self-enhancing biases and distort in the positive direction. Thus, those who are socially anxious or prone to depression are often just as socially skilled as those who do not suffer from such problems (Glasgow & Arkowitz, 1975; Lewinsohn, Mischel, Chaplin, & Barton, 1980). But the normal ones believe they are much more adept than they really are. The nondepressed people also have a stronger belief that they exercise some control over situations that are unmanageable (Alloy & Abramson, 1988).

Social reformers strongly believe that they can mobilize the collective effort needed to bring social change. Although their beliefs are rarely fully realized they sustain reform efforts that achieve important gains. Were social reformers to be entirely realistic about the prospects of transforming social systems they would either forego the endeavor or fall easy victim to discouragement. Realists may adapt well to existing realities. But those with a tenacious self-efficacy are likely to change those realities.

Innovative achievements also require a resilient sense of efficacy. Innovations demand heavy investment of effort over a long period with uncertain results. Moreover, innovations that clash with existing preferences and practices meet with negative social reactions. Therefore, it comes as no surprise that one rarely finds realists in the ranks of innovators and great achievers. In his review of social reactions to human ingenuity, titled *Rejection*, John White (1982) provides vivid testimony that the striking characteristic of people who have achieved eminence in their fields is an inextinguishable sense of personal efficacy and a firm belief in the worth of what they are doing. This resilient self-belief system enabled them to override repeated early rejections of their work. Societies enjoy the considerable benefits of these persisters' accomplishments in the arts, sciences, and technologies.

In sum, the successful, the venturesome, the sociable, the nonanxious, the nondepressed, the social reformers, and the innovators take an optimistic view of their personal capabilities to exercise influence over events that affect their lives. If not unrealistically exaggerated, such personal beliefs foster positive well-being and human accomplishments. The influential role played by efficacy beliefs in different spheres of human functioning is reviewed in greater detail in the sections that follow.

Self-efficacy in the changing structure of family systems

The parenting role places continual heavy demands on coping efficacy. Parents not only have to deal with ever-changing challenges as their children grow older. They also have to manage interdependent relationships within the family system and social links to a host of extrafamilial social systems including educational, recreational, medical, and caregiving facilities. Parents who have a firm belief in their parenting efficacy are quite resourceful in promoting their children's competencies (Teti & Gelfand, 1991). Moreover, a strong sense of parenting efficacy serves as a protective factor against emotional strain and despondency (Cutrona & Troutman, 1986; Olioff & Aboud, 1991).

The family has been undergoing major structural changes. The number of single-parent families is on the rise. More and more women are joining the workforce either by economic necessity or personal preference. Increased longevity creates the need for purposeful pursuits that provide satisfaction and meaning to one's life over the full term of the expanded lifespan long after the offspring have left home. Hence, women are educating themselves more intensively and seeking fulfillment in career pursuits as well as in their family life. The traditional nuclear family comprising a working father and a homemaker mother is on the decline. The burden of change is falling heavily on the shoulders of women who find themselves managing the major share of the familial demands as well as the demands of their occupational roles. Societal practices lag behind the changes in familial life in dual-career marriages. The societal changes call for more equitable division of labor in the home and equality of occupational opportunities in the workplace.

There is considerable variation among working women in the types of role demands they face; in the degree to which work and family demands conflict and disruptively intrude into one another; in the level of shared responsibility for the care of children and household; in the availability of adequate child care; and in the types of stressors, satisfactions, and feelings of accomplishment women experience at home and at work. Given the wide diversity of adaptational conditions, it is not surprising that findings on the effects of managing multiple role demands are ambiguous and inconsistent. Even under similar conditions, effects differ across individuals depending on the coping resources they bring to bear in efforts to fulfill the various role demands.

Ozer (1992) presents evidence that perceived self-efficacy to manage the different aspects of multiple role demands is an influential factor in how women's lives are affected. Neither family income, heaviness of occupational workload, nor division of child care responsibility had direct effect on women's well-being or emotional strain over the dual roles. These factors operate through their effects on perceived self-efficacy. Women who have a strong sense of efficacy that they can manage the multiple demands of family and work, that they can exert some influence over their work schedule, and that they can enlist their husband's aid with different aspects of child care experience a low level of physical and emotional strain and a more positive sense of well-being. The effects of combining dual roles are usually framed in the literature negatively in terms of conditions under which it breeds discord and distress and the buffering role of protective factors. Ozer's research shows that a sense of efficacy in managing dual roles contributes to positive well-being rather than merely protecting against distress. Family income and perceived self-efficacy to enlist spousal aid with child care is also associated with lowered vulnerability to physical symptoms. However, women who are beset by self-doubts in their ability to combine the dual roles suffer both health problems and emotional strain.

Low-income families experience considerable economic hardships. Poor families have to cope not only with problems of subsistence; the communities in which they live provide meager positive resources for their children's development and expose them to dangers that can set them on a negative course of life. Yet many poor parents manage to raise their children successfully despite the adversities.

The research by Elder and his colleagues sheds light on psychosocial processes through which economic hardships alter parents' perceived efficacy which, in turn, affects how they raise their children (Elder & Ardelt, 1992; Elder, Eccles, Ardelt, & Lord, 1993). Objective economic hardship, by itself, has no direct influence on parents' perceived efficacy. Rather, objective financial hardship creates subjective financial strain. In intact households, subjective strain impairs parental efficacy by fueling marital discord. A supportive marital relationship enables parents to withstand poverty without it undermining their belief in their ability to guide their children's development.

Parents' beliefs that they can affect the course of their children's lives is a more influential contributor to beneficial guidance under disadvantaged conditions than under advantaged conditions, where resources, social supports, and neighborhood controls are more plentiful. Given the fragmentation of social life in impoverished communities and paucity of resources, parents have to turn inward for their support in times of stress. If it is lacking in the home the mounting stressors begin to overwhelm their coping efforts. For single parents, financial strain weakens parents' sense of efficacy both directly and indirectly by creating feelings of despondency. Regardless of family structure, parents who have a high sense of efficacy are active in promoting their children's competencies.

Social structural theories and psychological theories are often regarded as rival conceptions of human behavior or as representing different levels of causation. In the social cognitive theory of triadic reciprocal causation, social structural and personal determinants are integrated as cofactors within a unified causal structure. For example, if individuals cannot provide adequately for their livelihood because they lost their job during a recessionary period, their lack of money is a particular type of determinant that affects their behavior and well-being, not a determinant operating at a different level of causation. In tracing the path of influence from economic conditions through familial processes to perceived parental efficacy and child management practices, Elder and his associates advance understanding of how personal agency operates within a broader network of sociostructural influences.

Under conditions of adversity, families that have an efficacious outlook are likely to be more satisfied with and attached to their community because they believe they can change things for the better. In contrast, families that believe there is little they can do to improve the quality of life in their communities feel dissatisfied with and estranged from their communities. How families feel about their communities is, indeed, partly mediated through their sense of efficacy rather than simply reflecting the objective economic conditions in their communities (Rudkin, Hagell, Elder, & Conger, 1992). Parents who believe they can exercise some control over their everyday lives feel more positive about their communities and have less desire to move elsewhere. Economic conditions, per se, have only a weak direct effect on community satisfaction and only indirectly influence desire to move to the extent that it creates dissatisfaction with the community.

The influence of perceived familial efficacy on community attachment will vary depending on the level of economic adversity and the responsiveness of institutional systems to change. When both adversity and prospects for change are dismal, families with a high sense of efficacy are apt to move elsewhere in search of a better life. Migrants with a high sense of efficacy adapt more successfully to their new environment than those of lower perceived efficacy (Jerusalem & Mittig, 1995). A supportive partnership and gainful employment further help migrants to weather the difficult sociocultural transition.

Self-efficacy in intellectual development

Educational systems have undergone fundamental change at historic periods of social and technological transitions. Educational systems were originally designed to teach low-level skills in agricultural societies. When industrialization supplanted agriculture as the major economic enterprise, the educational system was adapted to the needs of heavy industry and manufacturing requiring rote performance. Sweeping changes in technologies are currently mechanizing many of the activities in the modern workplace that were formerly done manually. In this information era, information technology is operating automated production, information management, and service systems. These electronic technologies are run by structuring and manipulating information.

The historic transition from the industrial to the information era has profound implications for educational systems. In the past, youth who had little schooling had recourse to industrial and manufacturing jobs requiring little in the way of cognitive skills. Such options are rapidly shrinking. The new realities require cognitive and self-regulatory competencies to fulfill complex occupational roles and to manage the demands of contemporary life. Education has now become vital for an engaged and productive life.

The rapid pace of technological change and accelerated growth of knowledge are placing a premium on capability for self-directed learning. Good schooling fosters psychosocial growth that contributes to the quality of life beyond the vocational domain. A major goal of formal education should be to equip students with the intellectual tools, efficacy beliefs, and intrinsic interests to educate themselves throughout their lifetime. These personal resources enable individuals to gain new knowledge and to cultivate skills either for their own sake or to better their lives.

The efficacy-regulated processes reviewed in the preceding sections of this chapter play a key role in setting the course of intellectual development. They also influence how well preexisting cognitive skills are used in managing the demands of everyday life. There are three principal ways in which efficacy beliefs operate as an important contributor to academic development. These include students' beliefs in their efficacy to regulate their own learning and to master different academic subjects; teachers' beliefs in their personal efficacy to motivate and promote learning in their students; and faculties' collective sense of efficacy that their schools can accomplish significant academic progress.

Students' cognitive and self-regulatory efficacy

Efficacy beliefs play a vital role in the development of self-directed lifelong learners. Students' belief in their capabilities to master academic activities affects their aspirations, level of interest in intellectual pursuits, academic accomplishments, and how well they prepare themselves for different occupational careers (Hackett, 1985, 1995; Holden, Moncher, Schinke, & Barker, 1990; Schunk, 1989; Zimmerman, 1995). A low sense of efficacy to manage academic demands also increases vulnerability to scholastic anxiety. As Meece, Wigfield, and Eccles (1990) have shown, past academic successes and failures arouse anxiety through their effects on perceived self-efficacy. If failures weaken students' sense of efficacy they become anxious about scholastic demands. But if their perceived efficacy is unshaken by failures, they remain unperturbed.

One of the major advances in the study of lifelong cognitive development that carries important implications concerns the mechanisms of self-regulated learning. Until recently, the attention of the psychological discipline centered heavily on how the mind works in processing, organizing, and retrieving information. The mind as computational program became the conceptual model for the times. Research on how people process information has clarified many aspects of cognitive functioning. However, this austere cognitivism has neglected self-regulatory processes that govern human development and adaption. Effective intellectual functioning requires much more than simply understanding the factual knowledge and reasoning operations for given activities.

Meta-cognitive theorists have addressed the pragmatics of self-regulation in terms of selecting appropriate strategies, testing one's comprehension and state of knowledge, correcting one's deficiencies, and recognizing the utility of cognitive strategies (Brown, 1984; Paris & Newman, 1990). Meta-cognitive training aids academic learning. However, students do not necessarily transfer the skills spontaneously to dissimilar pursuits. Nor do they always use the meta-cognitive skills with regularity. Clearly, there is more to the process of self-regulation than meta-cognitive skills.

In social cognitive theory, people must develop skills in regulating the motivational, affective, and social determinants of their intellectual functioning as well as the cognitive aspects. This requires bringing self-influence to bear on every aspect of the learning process. Zimmerman (1990) has been the leading exponent of an expanded model of academic self-regulation. He and his colleagues have shown that good self-regulators do much better academically than do poor self-regulators.

Self-regulatory skills will not contribute much if students cannot get themselves to apply them persistently in the face of difficulties, stressors, or competing attractions. Firm belief in one's self-regulatory skills provides the needed staying power. The higher the students' beliefs in their efficacy to regulate their motivation and learning activities, the more assured they are in their efficacy to master academic subjects. Perceived academic efficacy, in turn, promotes intellectual achievement both directly and by raising academic aspirations (Zimmerman & Bandura, in press; Zimmerman, Bandura, & Martinez-Pons, 1992).

Impact of cognitive self-efficacy on developmental trajectories

Children's intellectual development cannot be isolated from the social relations within which it is embedded or from its social consequences. It must be analyzed from a sociocultural perspective. The broader developmental impact of perceived cognitive efficacy is revealed in research in which different facets of perceived self-efficacy are related to different patterns of interpersonal and emotional behavior (Caprara, Pastorelli, & Bandura, 1992). Children who have a high sense of efficacy to regulate their own learning and to master academic skills behave more prosocially, are more popular, and experience less rejection by their peers than do children who believe they lack these forms of academic efficacy. Moreover, a low sense of cognitive efficacy is associated with physical and verbal aggression and ready disengagement of moral self-sanctions from harmful conduct. The impact of children's disbelief in their academic efficacy on socially discordant behavior becomes stronger as they grow older.

Peer affiliations promote different developmental courses depending on *Childs* the types of values, standards of conduct, and life-styles that are modeled *friends* and sanctioned by those with whom one regularly associates. It is difficult for children to remain prosocially oriented and retain their emotional well-being in the face of repeated scholastic failures and snubbing by peers. Students of low social and intellectual efficacy are likely to gravitate to peers who do not subscribe to academic values and life-styles. Over time, growing self-doubts in cognitive competencies foreclose many occupational life courses, if not prosocial life paths themselves. Disengagement from academic pursuits often leads to heavy engagement in a constellation of problem behaviors (Jessor, Donovan, & Costa, 1991). Indeed, early academic deficiency is one of the leading predictors of aggressive life-styles and participation in antisocial activities (Hinshaw, 1992; Patterson, Capaldi, & Bank, 1991; Rutter, 1979). In these different ways, beliefs of cognitive efficacy can have reverberating effects on developmental trajectories well beyond the academic domain.

Collective school efficacy

The task of creating environments conducive to learning rests heavily on the talents and self-efficacy of teachers. Evidence indicates that classroom atmospheres are partly determined by teachers' beliefs in their instructional efficacy. Teachers who believe strongly in their instructional efficacy create mastery experiences for their students (Gibson & Dembo, 1984).

Those who have low assurance in their instructional efficacy generate negative classroom environments that are likely to undermine students' sense of efficacy and cognitive development.

Teachers' beliefs in their personal efficacy affect their general orientation toward the educational process as well as their specific instructional activities. Those who have a low sense of instructional efficacy favor a custodial orientation that relies on extrinsic inducements and negative sanctions to get students to study. Teachers who believe strongly in their instructional efficacy support development of students' intrinsic interests and academic self-directedness (Woolfolk & Hoy, 1990). In examining the cumulative impact, Ashton and Webb (1986) report that teachers' beliefs concerning their instructional efficacy predicts students' levels of academic achievement over the course of the academic year, regardless of their entering ability.

Many of the adverse conditions with which schools have to cope reflect the broader social and economic ills of the society that affect student educability and impair the school environment. Many teachers find themselves beleaguered day in and day out by disruptive and nonachieving students. Eventually, their low sense of efficacy to fulfill academic demands takes a stressful toll. Teachers who lack a secure sense of instructional efficacy show weak commitment to teaching, spend less time in subject matters in their areas of perceived inefficacy, and devote less overall time to academic matters (Enochs & Riggs, 1990; Evans & Tribble, 1986; Gibson & Dembo, 1984). They are especially vulnerable to occupational burnout. This graphic metaphor encompasses a syndrome of reactions to chronic occupational stressors that include physical and emotional exhaustion, depersonalization of the people one is serving, and feelings of futility concerning personal accomplishments. Chwalisz, Altmaier, and Russell (1992) provide evidence that teachers with high efficacy manage academic stressors by directing their efforts at resolving problems. In contrast, teachers who distrust their efficacy try to avoid dealing with academic problems and, instead, turn their efforts inward to relieve their emotional distress. This pattern of escapist coping contributes to occupational burnout.

Teachers operate collectively within an interactive social system, rather than as isolates. Schools in which the staffs collectively judge themselves as powerless to get difficult students to achieve academic success convey a group sense of academic futility that can pervade the entire life of the school. In contrast, schools in which staff members collectively judge themselves capable of promoting academic success imbue their schools with a positive atmosphere for development. Differences between schools in level of academic achievement are strongly related to the socioeconomic and ethnic composition of the student bodies. However, student characteristics affect school achievement in large part by altering the staff's beliefs in their collective instructional efficacy (Bandura, 1993). The higher the proportion of students from lower socioeconomic levels and of minority status, the lower the staff's collective beliefs in their efficacy to achieve academic progress, and the worse the schools fare academically. Student absenteeism, low achievement, and high turnover also take a toll on collective school efficacy.

The schools' collective sense of efficacy at the beginning of the academic year predicts the schools' level of academic achievement at the end of the year when the effects of the characteristics of the student bodies, their prior level of academic achievement, and the staff's experiential level are factored out. With staffs who firmly believe that students are motivatable and teachable, schools heavily populated with poor and minority students achieve high levels on standardized measures of academic competencies.

Impact of societal changes on school efficacy

Developed countries are experiencing mass migration of people seeking a better life. Some are fleeing the devastation of armed violence and political persecution, others are deserting disintegrating countries that were held together by authoritarian rule, and many living under impoverished and desperate circumstances are moved by televised visions of prosperity in other societies. Migratory pressures will persist or intensify as long as large economic disparities exist between nations. Rich nations pick off the most skilled and talented members of poorer nations, which only exacerbates the disparities. In addition to the international migrations, there are the extensive domestic migrations from rural to urban areas as family farms are progressively eliminated. These major societal changes are altering the demographic characteristics of school populations.

Migrants are uprooted from their culture and thrust into a foreign one where they have to learn new languages, social norms, values, worldviews, and unfamiliar ways of life, many of which may clash with their native culture. As countries become more ethnically diverse, educational systems face the difficult challenge of fulfilling their mission with students of diverse backgrounds and adequacy of academic preparation. Battles are fought over whether educators should adopt assimilationist or multicultural approaches in instructing children of migrants and refugees. To further complicate matters, cultural and racial conflicts in the larger society get played out in the educational system. We saw earlier that school staffs generally have a low sense of efficacy to educate poor and minority students and do not expect much of them academically. The more culturally diverse the composition of student bodies the poorer is the staffs' implementation of programs conducive to academic learning.

Many educational systems are modeled on some form of dual-track structure in which students pursue either an academic route or a vocational route through an apprenticeship system. Evans and Heinz (1991) found that there are really four different paths that students take within an institutionalized dual-track system. In addition to the academic and the skilled vocational pathway, there are the dropouts from apprenticeships who are on an uncertain life course and the educationally detached youth who are only marginal players in the system. Marginalized youth leave school with a high sense of futility and a bleak vocational livelihood. Youth adrift with no stake in the system breed societal problems.

Apprenticeship systems, which have fulfilled their mission well, must adapt to the rapid pace of social and technological change. The modern workplace requires efficacious individuals with versatile cognitive and self-management skills that enable them to master changing technologies throughout their vocational careers. Highly structured transitional systems offer a more secure passage to occupational careers but may allow less flexibility and room for changing directions along the way (Hurrelmann & Roberts, 1991). Systems that provide opportunities to pursue higher levels of learning create the means for continual self-renewal.

The characteristics of efficacious schools have been amply documented (Anderson, 1982; Brookover, Beady, Flood, Schweitzer, & Wisenbaker, 1979; Good & Brophy, 1986). However, there is a vast difference between knowing what makes school academically effective and being able to create them. There is no shortage of good educational models on how to build personal efficacy and cognitive competencies in disadvantaged youth (Comer, 1988; Levin, 1987, 1991). But the promise of these models is not being fully realized because of weak didactic modes of implementation. This is the vital but weakest link in the models of educational change. Educational systems operate within a sociopolitical context. It is around educational interventions that power relations get played out in ways that all too often impede change. A good model of implementation must provide effective strategies on how to reconcile conflicting interests, develop a common sense of mission and purpose, and mobilize community support for educational improvement.

Career development and pursuits

The choices people make during formative periods shape the course of their lives. Such choices determine which of their potentialities they cultivate, the types of options that are foreclosed or remain realizable over their life course, and the life-style they follow. Among the choices that affect life paths, those that center on occupational choice and development are of special import. Occupations structure a large part of people's everyday reality and provide them with a major source of personal identity and sense of self-worth. The process of structuring a personal career is not an easy one. In making career decisions, people have to come to grips with uncertainties about their capabilities, the instability of their interests, the prospects of alternative occupations, their accessibility, and the type of identity people seek to construct for themselves.

Efficacy determination of the slate of options

According to the rational model of human decision making, individuals supposedly explore a wide range of options, calculate their advantages and disadvantages, and then choose the option that maximizes expected utility. It is now well established that people do not behave like wholly rational utility maximizers. Efficacy beliefs determine the slate of options given any consideration. People do not regard options in domains of low perceived efficacy worth considering, whatever benefits they may hold. Such wholesale exclusions of large classes of options are made rapidly on perceived efficacy grounds with little thought to costs and benefits. Efficacy beliefs preempt expectancy-valence analyses. Perceived self-efficacy not only sets the slate of options for consideration, but influences other aspects of decision making. It affects the type of information that is collected and how it is interpreted and converted into means for managing environmental challenges.

Beliefs of personal efficacy play a key role in occupational development and pursuits. The higher people's perceived efficacy to fulfill educational requirements and occupational roles the wider the career options they seriously consider pursuing and the greater the interest they have in them (Betz & Hackett, 1981; Lent, Brown, & Hackett, in press; Matsui, Ikeda, & Ohnishi, 1989). People simply eliminate from consideration vocations

they believe to be beyond their capabilities. Efficacy beliefs predict vocational considerations when variations in actual ability, prior level of academic achievement, and vocational interests are controlled. People are
unlikely to invest much effort in exploring career options and their likely
benefits unless they have faith in their capabilities to reach good decisions.
Hence, the stronger the belief in decision-making efficacy the higher the
level of exploratory activity designed to aid selection of a vocation (Blustein, 1989).

People act on their beliefs of vocational efficacy as well as entertain
career options. For example, perceived self-efficacy to master scientific
knowledge predicts successful academic course work and perseverance in
scientific fields of study (Lent, Brown, & Larkin, 1984). Efficacy beliefs also
contribute to career pursuits by fostering the development of interests. As
these diverse lines of evidence reveal, occupational development is a matter of acquiring not only new skills and knowledge but also the sense of
efficacy through which innovativeness and productivity are realized.

Occupational self-efficacy and demographic changes

Wide gender disparities exist in career aspirations and pursuits. Although
women make up an increasing share of the workforce, not many of them
are choosing careers in scientific and technical fields or, for that matter, in
a variety of other occupations that have traditionally been dominated by
men. Women's disbelief in their quantitative and technical capabilities and
their career aspirations are shaped by the family, the educational system,
occupational practices, the mass media, and the culture at large (Hackett
& Betz, 1981; Jacobs, 1989). Dissuading societal norms and practices continue to lag behind the changing status of women and their growing participation in the workforce. As a result, women's potential and their contribution to the creative and economic life of society remain largely
unrealized.

The same is true of ethnic minorities, who often have to surmount both
discriminatory barriers and socioeconomic disadvantage. They too generally have a low sense of efficacy for scientific and technical careers requiring quantitative skills. While women and minorities are shunning scientific and technological fields, demographic trends indicate that societies
will have to rely increasingly on the talents of women and ethnic minorities to maintain scientific, technological, and economic viability. Societies
have to come to terms with the discordance between their occupational
socialization practices and the human resources needed for their success.

Societies that fail to develop the capabilities of all their youth jeopardize their social and economic progress.

From an interactionist perspective, solutions to restricted aspirations and occupational pursuits require both individual and social remedies. At the individual level, the different ways of creating a sense of personal efficacy can be enlisted to eliminate self-limiting psychological impediments that have become ingrained through cultural practices and to develop the competencies for exercising proactive control over one's occupational future. Remedies at the societal level require eradicating negative institutional biases that diminish educational and vocational aspirations and erect barriers to occupational opportunities and career advancement.

Health-promotive role of self-efficacy

The conception of human health and illness has undergone major changes in recent years. The traditional approaches relied on a *biomedical model*, which places heavy emphasis on infectious agents, ameliorative medications, and repair of physical impairments. The newer conception adopts a broader *biopsychosocial model* (Engel, 1977). Viewed from this perspective, health and disease are products of interactions among psychosocial and biological factors. Health is not merely the absence of physical impairment and disease. The biopsychosocial perspective emphasizes health enhancement as well as disease prevention. It is just as meaningful to speak of degrees of vitality as of degrees of impairment.

It is now widely acknowledged that people's health rests partly in their own hands. Apart from genetic endowment, physical health is largely determined by life-style habits and environmental conditions (Fuchs, 1974). People often suffer physical impairments and die prematurely of preventable health-impairing habits. Their nutritional habits place them at risk for cardiovascular diseases; sedentariness weakens cardiovascular capabilities and vitality; cigarette smoking creates a major health hazard for cancer, respiratory disorders, and heart disease; alcohol and drug abuse contribute to disabilities and loss of life; sexually transmitted diseases can produce serious health consequences; people are maimed or their lives cut short by physical violence and other activities fraught with physical risks; and dysfunctional ways of coping with stressors produce wear and tear on the body. With regard to injurious environmental conditions, industrial and agricultural practices are injecting carcinogens and harmful pollutants into the air we breathe, the food we eat, and the water we drink, all of which take a heavy toll on the body. Approximately half the deaths in the United States are caused prematurely by detrimental health habits over which people have some control (McGinnis & Foege, 1993). Changing health habits and environmental practices can thus yield large health benefits.

Perceived self-efficacy has been shown to be an important determinant of health-promotive behavior. There are two levels at which a sense of personal efficacy plays an influential role in human health. At the more basic level, people's beliefs in their capability to cope with the stressors in their lives activate biological systems that mediate health and disease. The second level is concerned with the exercise of direct control over the modifiable behavioral aspects of health and the rate of aging.

Biological effects of self-efficacy in coping with stressors

Many of the biological effects of perceived self-efficacy arise in the context of coping with acute or chronic stressors in the many transactions of everyday life. Stress has been implicated as an important contributor to many physical dysfunctions (Krantz, Grunberg, & Baum, 1985; O'Leary, 1990). Controllability is a key organizing principle regarding the nature of stress effects. It is not stressful life conditions per se but the perceived inability to manage them that produces the detrimental biological effects (Bandura, 1992b; Maier, Laudenslager, & Ryan, 1985; Shavit & Martin, 1987).

Social cognitive theory views stress reactions in terms of perceived inefficacy to exercise control over aversive threats and taxing environmental demands. If people believe they can deal effectively with potential environmental stressors they are not perturbed by them. But if they believe they cannot control aversive events they distress themselves and impair their level of functioning. The causal impact of beliefs of controlling efficacy on biological stress reactions is verified in experimental studies in which people are exposed to stressors under perceived inefficacy and after their beliefs of coping efficacy are raised to high levels through guided mastery experiences (Bandura, 1992b). Exposure to stressors without perceived efficacy to control them activates autonomic, catecholamine, and endogenous opioid systems. After people's perceived coping efficacy is strengthened they manage the same stressors without experiencing any distress, visceral agitation, or activation of stress-related hormones.

The types of biochemical reactions that have been shown to accompany a weak sense of coping efficacy are involved in the regulation of the immune system. Hence, exposure to uncontrollable stressors tends to im-

pair the function of the immune system in ways that can increase susceptibility to illness (Kiecolt-Glaser & Glaser, 1987; Maier, Laudenslager, &
Ryan, 1985; Shavit & Martin, 1987). Epidemiological and correlational
studies indicate that lack of behavioral or perceived control over environmental demands increases susceptibility to bacterial and viral infections,
contributes to the development of physical disorders, and accelerates the
rate of progression of disease (Schneiderman, McCabe, & Baum, 1992;
Steptoe & Appels, 1989). The common cold, which plagues us all, provides
but one example of the power of stress to impair resistance to viral infection (Cohen, Tyrrell, & Smith, 1991). People reporting different levels of
life stress were given nasal drops containing one of five respiratory
viruses or saline. They were then quarantined and monitored for infectious cold symptoms. The higher the life stress the higher were the rates of
respiratory infections and cold symptoms. The relationship between stress
and vulnerability to infectious illness was not altered by statistical control
for variety of other possible determinants.

Most human stress is activated in the course of learning how to exercise
control over environmental demands and while developing and expanding competencies. Stress activated in the process of acquiring coping efficacy may have very different physiological effects than stress experienced
in aversive situations with no prospect of ever gaining any self-protective
efficacy. Stress aroused while gaining coping mastery over threatening situations can enhance different components of the immune system
(Wiedenfeld et al., 1990). Providing people with the means for managing
acute and chronic stressors increases immunologic functioning (Antoni et
al., 1990; Gruber, Hall, Hersh, & Dubois, 1988; Kiecolt-Glaser et al., 1986).
There are substantial evolutionary benefits to experiencing enhanced
immunocompetence during development of coping capabilities vital for
effective adaptation. It would not be evolutionarily advantageous if acute
stressors invariably impaired immune function, because of their prevalence in everyday life. If this were the case, people would be bedridden
most of the time with infections or they would be quickly done in.

The field of health functioning has been heavily preoccupied with the
physiologically debilitating effects of stressors. Self-efficacy theory also
acknowledges the physiologically strengthening effects of mastery over
stressors. A growing number of studies are providing empirical support
for physiological toughening by successful coping (Dienstbier, 1989). The
psychosocial modulation of health functioning is concerned with the
determinants and mechanisms governing the physiologically toughening
effects of coping with stressors as well as their debilitating effects.

Self-efficacy in health-promotive behavior

Life-style habits can enhance or impair health. This enables people to exert some behavioral control over their vitality and quality of health. Efficacy beliefs affect every phase of personal change – whether people even consider changing their health habits; whether they enlist the motivation and perseverance needed to succeed should they choose to do so; and how well they maintain the habit changes they have achieved (Bandura, 1992b, in press). People's beliefs that they can motivate themselves and regulate their own behavior play a crucial role in whether they even consider changing detrimental health habits. They see little point to trying if they believe they do not have what it takes to succeed. If they make an attempt, they give up easily in the absence of quick results.

Effective self-regulation of health behavior is not achieved through an act of will. It requires development of self-regulatory skills. To build a sense of efficacy, people must develop skills on how to influence their own motivation and behavior. In such programs, they learn how to monitor the behavior they seek to change, how to set attainable subgoals to motivate and direct their efforts, and how to enlist incentives and social supports to sustain the effort needed to succeed (Bandura, 1986). Once equipped with skills and belief in their capabilities, people are better able to adopt behaviors that promote health and to eliminate those that impair it.

Habit changes are of little consequence unless they endure. Maintenance of habit change relies heavily on self-regulatory capabilities and the functional value of the behavior. Development of self-regulatory capabilities requires instilling a resilient sense of efficacy as well as imparting skills. Experiences in exercising control over troublesome situations serve as efficacy builders. This is an important aspect of self-management because if people are not fully convinced of their personal efficacy, they rapidly abandon the skills they have been taught when they fail to get quick results or suffer reverses. Studies of behavior that is amenable to change but difficult to maintain show that a low sense of efficacy increases vulnerability to relapse (Bandura, 1992b).

Lifelong health habits are formed during childhood and adolescence. Children need to learn nutritious eating patterns, recreational skills for lifelong fitness, and self-management skills to avoid substance abuse, delinquency and violence, and sexually transmitted diseases (Hamburg, 1992; Millstein, Petersen, & Nightingale, 1993). Preventive efforts are especially important because many of the patterns of behavior that can seriously compromise health typically begin in early adolescence. It is easier to prevent detrimental health habits than to try to change them after they have become deeply entrenched as part of a life-style. The biopsychosocial model provides a valuable public health tool for this purpose.

Health habits are rooted in familial practices. However, schools also have a vital role to play in promoting the health of a nation. This is the only place where all children can be easily reached regardless of their age, socioeconomic status, cultural background, or ethnicity. However, beleaguered educators do not want the additional responsibilities of health promotion and disease prevention, nor are they adequately equipped to do so even if they were willing to undertake this role. They have enough difficulties fulfilling their basic academic mission. Moreover, schools are reluctant to get embroiled in societal controversies regarding sexuality, drug use, and the various social morbidities that place youth at risk. Many educators rightfully argue that it is not their responsibility to remedy society's social ills. As long as health promotion is regarded as tangential to the central mission of schools, it will continue to be slighted.

The traditional style of health education provides students with factual information about health without attempting to change the social influences that shape and regulate health habits. These influences from peers, family members, the mass media, and the broader society are often in conflict. As a rule, school health education is long on didactics but short on personal enablement. It comes as no surprise that the informational approach alone does little to change health attitudes and behavior (Bruvold, 1993). Effective programs to promote healthy life-styles must address the social nature of health behavior and equip youth with the means to exercise control over habits that can jeopardize their health. This requires a multifaceted sociocognitive approach to the common determinants of interconnected health habits rather than piecemeal targeting of a specific behavior for change. A comprehensive approach is called for because problem behaviors usually go together as part of a distinctive life-style rather than appear in isolation. It is not indefinite holism that is being recommended but rather focus on the broad network of psychosocial influences that shape and support different health habits. Categorical funding of school health programs for specific health-risking behaviors encourages the fragmentation, often with bureaucratic impediments. When the more comprehensive approaches are grudgingly allowed into the schools they are typically implemented in a cursory fashion under time constraints that essentially strip them of their effectiveness.

The fact that schools provide an advantageous setting for health promotion and early intervention does not mean that educators must be the standard bearers for the health mission. Health promotion must be structured as part of a societal commitment that makes children's health a critical issue and provides the multidisciplinary personnel and resources needed to foster the health of its youth. This requires creating new school-based models of health promotion that operate in concert with the home, community, and the society at large. Issuing health mandates without supporting resources, explicit plans of action, and a system for monitoring progress will not beget a healthy society.

Experimentation with risky activities is not all that uncommon in the passage out of childhood status. Whether adolescents forsake risky activities after awhile or become chronically involved in them is determined by the interplay of personal competencies, self-management efficacy, and the prevailing social influences in their lives (Jessor, 1986). Some of these behaviors seriously compromise health. For example, cigarette smoking is the single most personally preventable cause of death. Alcohol and drug abuse similarly pose serious health problems. Historic sociopolitical changes in Europe have ushered in conditions that will produce mounting drug-related problems in the years ahead. Drug syndicates in South America, the Balkan states, and Southeast Asia are exploiting the relaxation of national border controls and the political chaos in Eastern Europe in a soaring narcotics trade. There is no shortage of couriers who can be easily recruited from the impoverished sectors of society. If certain drug routes are closed off, new ones are quickly created with a new set of courier recruits. Banks in countries needing foreign currency run flourishing money-laundering schemes for profits generated by the traffic in drugs and arms. Some of the proceeds from the drug trade are used to purchase arms for regional wars. In addition to the social and health problems created by drug dependency, high intravenous drug use spreads the HIV virus.

Exercise of self-directed change

Research on processes of change has added greatly to our understanding of the essential elements of effective interventions. Effective models rely on guided mastery experiences as the principal vehicle of personal change. This approach includes four major components. The first component is informational, designed to increase awareness and knowledge of health risks. However, factual information alone, much of which is usually redundant with what people already know, usually produces little change. The second component is concerned with the development of self-regulatory skills needed to translate informed concerns to effective exercise of control over health habits and the social influences that promote them. Self-regulation of motivation is especially important because many detrimental habits are immediately rewarding, whereas their injurious effects are slowly cumulative and delayed. If people are not fully convinced of their personal efficacy they undermine their efforts in difficult situations and readily abandon the skills they have been taught when they suffer reverses or fail to get quick results. Therefore, the third component of self-management is aimed at building a robust sense of efficacy by providing the participants with repeated opportunities for guided practice in applying the skills successfully in situations simulating those they are likely to encounter in their everyday life.

Personal change occurs within a network of social influences. Depending on their nature, social influences can aid, retard, or undermine efforts at personal change. The final component involves enlisting and creating social supports for desired personal changes. Many of the habits that can comprise health are subjected to social normative influences. There are two principal ways in which social norms exert a regulative influence on human behavior. Social norms convey standards of conduct. Adoption of personal standards creates a self-regulatory system that operates through internalized self-sanctions (Bandura, 1986). People behave in ways that give them self-satisfaction and refrain from behaving in ways that violate their standards because it brings self-censure. Behavior is also regulated by social sanctions. Social norms are associated with positive and negative reactions from others. Behavior that violates prevailing social norms elicits social censure or other negative consequences, whereas behavior that fulfills socially valued norms is approved and rewarded. Because of their proximity, immediacy, and prevalency, the interpersonal influences operating within one's immediate social network claim a stronger regulatory function than do general normative sanctions, which are more distal and applied only sporadically. Moreover, if the norms of one's immediate network are at odds with those of the larger group, the reactions of outsiders carry less weight, if they are not disregarded altogether.

Health-promotion programs that encompass the essential elements of the self-regulatory mastery model prevent or reduce injurious health habits, whereas those that rely mainly on providing health information are relatively ineffective (Botvin & Dusenbury, 1992; Bruvold, 1993; Jemmott, Jemmott, Spears, Hewitt, & Cruz-Collins, 1991). Comprehensive approaches that integrate school-based health programs with familial and community efforts are more successful in promoting health than if schools try to do it alone (Perry, Kelder, Murray, & Klepp, 1992; Telch, Killen,

McAlister, Perry, & Maccoby, 1982). Over the years, the models of health promotion and disease prevention have undergone three generational changes to augment their power. They began with an informational model that sought to change health habits by imparting knowledge and changing attitudes. They then added a self-regulatory skills component as an integral feature to enhance personal efficacy to manage health habits and their social determinants. The model was then further expanded to enlist social supports in the wider community for personal change.

Verification that preventive and treatment programs work in part through the self-efficacy mechanism at every phase of personal change provided conceptual guidelines on how to structure programs for success. Numerous studies of preventive and treatment programs for smoking and alcohol and drug abuse reveal that the interventions achieve their results partly by instilling and strengthening beliefs of personal efficacy. The higher people's sense of personal efficacy, the more successful they are in controlling addictive habits and social pressures to engage in them and the less vulnerable they are to slips and relapses (Bandura, in press; DiClemente, Fairhurst, & Piotrowski, in press; Marlatt, Baer, & Quigley, 1995). Should setbacks occur, efficacy beliefs determine how they are construed and managed. People who have strong belief in their efficacy tend to regard a slip as a temporary setback and reinstate control. In contrast, those who distrust their self-regulatory capabilities display a marked decrease in perceived self-efficacy after a slip and make little effort to reinstate control.

With achievement of reproductive maturity, adolescents have to learn how to manage their sexuality. Many engage in unprotected sex with multiple partners, which puts them at risk of unwanted pregnancies and sexually transmitted diseases, including HIV infection. Change programs incorporating elements of the self-regulatory mastery model enhance efficacy beliefs and reduce risky sexual behavior in adolescents (Gilchrist & Schinke, 1983; Jemmott, Jemmott, & Fong, 1992; Jemmott et al., 1991). The findings of these studies further corroborate that simply imparting sexual information without developing the self-regulative skills and sense of efficacy to exercise personal control over sexual relationships has little impact on patterns of sexual behavior.

Promoting healthful life-styles in youth reduces the need for expensive health services later in life. As people live longer minor dysfunctions at an earlier period have more time to develop into chronic diseases. Chronic disease has now become the dominant form of illness and the major cause of disability (Holman & Lorig, 1992). Unless societies keep people healthy throughout their expanded lifespan, they will be swamped with burgeoning health costs that drain resources needed for national programs. But health promotion in formative periods of life is not a priority in most societies. The excessive medicalization of the determinants of health has further downgraded socially oriented efforts to alter the behavioral and environmental factors that contribute so heavily to human health and debility. Economic necessity may eventually force a change in priorities.

Collective efficacy in policy and public health approaches

The quality of the health of a nation is a social as well as a personal matter. It requires changing the practices of social systems that have detrimental effects on health rather than solely changing the habits of individuals. Billions of dollars are spent annually on lobbying and advertising campaigns to promote the very products that jeopardize health. Environmental pollutants and hazardous workplaces similarly take a toll on health and impair the quality of life. Vigorous political battles are fought over environmental health and safety. It takes a great deal of united effort to dislodge entrenched detrimental practices. People's beliefs in their collective efficacy, therefore, play a vital role in the policy and public health perspective to health promotion and disease prevention. Such social efforts are aimed at raising public awareness of health hazards, educating and influencing policymakers, mobilizing public support for policy initiatives, and monitoring and ensuring enforcement of existing health regulations. A comprehensive approach to health protection and enhancement must provide people with the knowledge, skills, and sense of collective efficacy to mount social and policy initiatives that affect human health (Bandura, in press; Wallack, Dorfman, Jernigan, & Themba, 1993).

In getting things done collectively, perceived efficacy is concerned with people's beliefs in their joint capabilities to make health promotion a national priority, to forge divergent self-interests into a shared agenda, to enlist supporters and resources for collective action, to devise effective strategies and to execute them successfully, and to withstand forcible opposition and discouraging setbacks. We do not lack sound policy prescriptions in the field of health. What is lacking is the collective efficacy to realize them. Knowledge on how to develop and exercise collective efficacy can provide the guidelines for moving us further in enhancing the health of a nation's youth.

34   Albert Bandura

Self-efficacy in individualistic and collectivistic social systems

Some writers inappropriately equate self-efficacy with individualism and pit it against collectivism (Schooler, 1990; Seligman, 1990). Contrary to this view, a high sense of personal efficacy contributes just as importantly to group directedness as to self-directedness. In collectively oriented systems, people work together to produce the benefits they seek. Group pursuits are no less demanding of personal efficacy than are individual pursuits. Nor do people who work interdependently in collectivistic societies have less desire to be efficacious in the particular roles they perform than in individualistically oriented systems. Personal efficacy is valued not because of reverence for individualism but because a strong sense of personal efficacy is vital for successful adaptation and change regardless of whether it is achieved individually or by group members working together.

    Group achievements and social change are rooted in self-efficacy. The research of Earley (1993) attests to the cultural universality of the functional value of efficacy beliefs. In comparative studies, beliefs of personal efficacy contribute to productivity by members of collectivist cultures as they do by those raised in individualistic cultures. Societies are less homogeneous than is commonly believed. There are individualists in collectivistic societies and collectivists in individualistic societies. Efficacy beliefs function similarly in collectivistic and individualistic societies whether analyzed at the societal level or the individual level (Earley, 1994). Therefore, the way in which societies are structured does not say much about how well its members perform when the influence of their perceived efficacy and its motivational effects are factored out. The generalizability of the functional role of perceived efficacy is not confined to motivation and action. A low sense of coping efficacy is just as occupationally debilitating and stressful in collectivistic societies as in individualistic ones (Matsui & Onglatco, 1992). A collectivist society populated with members who are consumed by self-doubts about their capabilities and anticipate the futility of any effort to shape their future would be condemned to a dismal existence.

    Another common mistake is to assume that if people's lives are hampered by a low sense of efficacy the problem is exclusively an individual one and that the solution lies solely in personal change. People make causal contribution to their lives but they are not the sole determiners of their own destiny. Many other influences also contribute to the courses their lives take. Within this multicausality, people can improve their lives by exercising influence in areas over which they have some control. The more they bring their influence to bear on changeable conditions that affect their lives, the more they contribute to their own futures. If the practices of social systems impede or undermine personal development, a large part of the solution lies in changing the adverse institutional practices through the exercise of collective efficacy. Personal and social change are complementary rather than rival approaches to improving the quality of life.

Collective efficacy

Developmental life paths are intimately linked to the sociocultural environment in which people find themselves immersed. Therefore, human development and change is best understood through analyses of people's lives in time as they are shaped by the distinctive life experiences provided by the eras in which they live (Elder, 1995). The families and youth of today are going through times of drastic technological and social change that present unique opportunities, challenges, and constraints. Wrenching social changes that dislocate lives are not new in history. What is new is the accelerated pace of informational and technological change and the extensive globalization of human interdependence. These new realities place increasing demands on the exercise of efficacy. People's beliefs in their efficacy play a paramount role in how well they organize, create, and manage the circumstances that affect their life course.

Many of the challenges of life center on common problems that require people working together to change their lives for the better. The strength of families, communities, social institutions, and even nations lies partly in people's sense of collective efficacy that they can solve the problems they face and improve their lives through unified effort. People's beliefs in their collective efficacy influence the type of social future they seek to achieve, how much effort they put into it, and their endurance when collective efforts fail to produce quick results. The stronger they believe in their capabilities to effect social change the more actively they engage in collective efforts to alter national policies and practices (Marsh, 1977; Muller, 1972; Wiegman, Taal, Van den Bogaard, & Gutteling, 1992; Wollman & Stouder, 1991). Those who are beset by a low sense of efficacy are quickly convinced of the futility of effort to reform their institutional systems.

Rapidly changing conditions, some of which impair the quality of life and degrade the environment, call for wide-reaching solutions to human problems and greater commitment to unified purposes. Such changes can be achieved only through the united effort of people who have the skills, the sense of collective efficacy, and the incentives to shape the direction of their future environment. As the need for efficacious collective effort grows, so does the sense of collective powerlessness.

Underminers of collective efficacy

Many of the contemporary conditions of life undermine the development of collective efficacy. Life in the societies of today is increasingly affected by transnational interdependencies. What happens economically and politically in one part of the world can affect the welfare of vast populations elsewhere. There are no handy social mechanisms by which people can exercise reciprocal influence on transnational systems that affect their daily lives. The growing transnational interconnectedness of human life challenges the efficacy of governmental systems to exert a determining influence over their national life. As nations wrestle with the loss of controlling influence, they experience a crisis in confidence in their political leaders and institutions (Lipset, 1985). Governmental systems seem incapable of playing a major role in the economic life of the nation. Under such conditions, people strive to regain control over their own destinies by exercising influence over their local circumstances over which they have some command while expressing growing disaffection and cynicism about their centralized public institutions. Much of their effort is directed at preserving the past rather than shaping the social future. Local influence affirms personal efficacy. Not surprisingly, people have a higher sense of personal efficacy than institutional efficacy. The major challenge to leadership is to forge a collective sense of efficacy to take advantage of the opportunities of globalization while minimizing the price that progress extracts.

There are many other factors that serve to undermine the development of collective efficacy. Modern life is increasingly regulated by complex physical technologies that most people neither understand nor believe they can do much to influence. Pervasive dependence on the technologies that govern major aspects of life imposes dependence on specialized technicians. For example, the citizenry of nations that are heavily dependent on deteriorating atomic plants for their energy feel powerless to remove the potentially catastrophic hazard from their lives. The devastating consequences of mishaps do not respect national borders.

The social machinery of society is no less challenging. Layers of bureaucratic structures thwart effective social action. Collective efforts at social change are sustained in large part by the modeled successes of other reformers and by evidence of progress toward desired goals. Long delays between action and noticeable results discourage many advocates along the way. Even the more efficacious individuals, who are not easily deterred, find their efforts blunted by mazy organizational mechanisms that diffuse and obscure responsibility. Pitting oneself repeatedly against bureaucratic gauntlets eventually exacts its toll. Rather than developing the means for shaping their own future, most people grudgingly relinquish control to technical specialists and to public officials. In the metaphoric words of John Gardner, "Getting things done socially is no sport for the short winded."

Culture & mission

Effective action for social change requires merging diverse self-interests in support of common core values and goals. Disagreements among different constituencies create additional obstacles to successful collective action. Leadership increasingly faces the challenge of governing over diversity in ways that permit both autonomy for constituent communities to direct their own lives and unity through shared values and purposes (Esteve, 1992). The voices for parochial interests are typically much stronger than those for collective responsibility. It requires efficacious inspiring leadership to forge unity within diversity. The recent years have witnessed growing social fragmentation of societies into special-interest groups, each exercising its own factional power. Pluralism is taking the form of antagonistic factionalism. As a result, it is easier to get people to block courses of action than to merge them into a unified force for social change. Contentious factionalism and global market forces create perpetual structural instabilities in societies. Unbridled factionalism erodes connectedness to the larger society. In the more extreme forms of social fragmentation, countries are being dismantled with a vengeance along racial, religious, and ethnic lines. The new social realities pose increasing challenges on how to preserve identity and local control through regional autonomy within the context of growing interdependence of human life.

The scope and magnitude of human problems also affect perceived efficacy to find effective solutions for them. Profound global changes in the form of burgeoning populations, shrinking resources, ozone depletion, and mounting environmental devastation are destroying the ecosystems that sustain life. These changes are creating new realities requiring transnational remedies. Worldwide problems of growing magnitude and complexity instill a sense of paralysis that there is little people can do that would have a significant impact on such massive problems. National self-interests and the fear of infringement of sovereignty create further obsta-

cles to developing transnational mechanisms for change. Effective remedial and preventive measures call for concerted action at local, national,
and transnational levels. Local practices contribute to global effects. Each
person, therefore, has a part to play in the solution. The strategy of "Think
globally, act locally" is an effort to restore in people a sense of efficacy that
there are many things they can do to make a difference.

Team mentality

Bidirectionality of human influence

In analyzing the impediments to human endeavors, it is all too easy to
lose sight of the fact that human influence, whether individual or collective, is a two-way process rather than one that flows unidirectionally. The
imbalance of social power partly depends on the extent to which people
exercise the influence that is theirs to command. The less they bring their
influence to bear on conditions that affect their lives the more control they
relinquish to others.

Don't give your power away

The psychological barriers created by beliefs of collective powerlessness
are more demoralizing and debilitating than are external impediments.
People who have a sense of collective efficacy will mobilize their efforts
and resources to cope with external obstacles to the changes they seek. But
those convinced of their collective powerlessness will cease trying even
though changes are attainable through perseverant collective effort.

As a society, we enjoy the benefits left by those before us who collectively fought inhumanities and worked for social reforms that permit a
better life. Our own collective efficacy will in turn shape how future generations will live their lives. Considering the pressing worldwide problems that loom ahead, people can ill afford to trade efficacious endeavor
for public apathy or mutual immobilization. The times call for social initiatives that build people's sense of collective efficacy to influence conditions that shape their lives and that of future generations.

Set Example for others

References

Adler, A. (1956). (H. C. Ansbacher & R. R. Ansbacher, Eds.). *The individual psychology of Alfred Adler*. New York: Harper & Row.

Ajzen, I., & Madden, T. J. (1986). Prediction of goal-directed behavior: Attitudes,
intentions, and perceived behavioral control. *Journal of Experimental Social Psychology, 22*, 453–474.

Alden, L. (1986). Self-efficacy and causal attributions for social feedback. *Journal of
Research in Personality, 20*, 460–473.

Alloy, L. B., & Abramson, L. Y. (1988). Depressive realism: Four theoretical perspectives. In L. B. Alloy (Ed.), *Cognitive processes in depression*. New York: Guilford.

Anderson, C. S. (1982). The search for school climate: A review of the research.
Review of Educational Research, 52, 368–420.

Antoni, M. H., Schneiderman, N., Fletcher, M. A., Goldstein, D. A., Ironson, G., & Laperriere, A. (1990). Psychoneuroimmunology and HIV-1. *Journal of Consulting and Clinical Psychology, 58*, 38–49.

Ashton, P. T., & Webb, R. B. (1986). *Making a difference: Teachers' sense of efficacy and student achievement.* White Plains, NY: Longman, Inc.

Bandura, A. (1982). Self-efficacy mechanism in human agency. *American Psychologist, 37*, 122–147.

Bandura, A. (1986). *Social foundations of thought and action: A social cognitive theory.* Englewood Cliffs, NJ: Prentice-Hall.

Bandura, A. (1988). Perceived self-efficacy: Exercise of control through self-belief. In J. P. Dauwalder, M. Perrez, & V. Hobi (Eds.), *Annual series of European research in behavior therapy* (Vol. 2, pp. 27–59). Amsterdam/Lisse: Swets & Zeitlinger.

Bandura, A. (1991a). Self-regulation of motivation through anticipatory and self-regulatory mechanisms. In R. A. Dienstbier (Ed.), *Perspectives on motivation: Nebraska symposium on motivation* (Vol. 38, pp. 69–164). Lincoln: University of Nebraska Press.

Bandura, A. (1991b). Self-efficacy conception of anxiety. In R. Schwarzer & R. A. Wicklund (Eds.), *Anxiety and self-focused attention* (pp. 89–110). New York: Harwood.

Bandura, A. (1992a). Exercise of personal agency through the self-efficacy mechanism. In R. Schwarzer (Ed.), *Self-efficacy: Thought control of action* (pp. 3–38). Washington, DC: Hemisphere.

Bandura, A. (1992b). Self-efficacy mechanism in psychobiologic functioning. In R. Schwarzer (Ed.), *Self-efficacy: Thought control of action* (pp. 355–394). Washington, DC: Hemisphere.

Bandura, A. (1993). Perceived self-efficacy in cognitive development and functioning. *Educational Psychologist, 28*, 117–148.

Bandura, A. (in press). *Self-efficacy: The exercise of control.* New York: Freeman.

Bandura, A., & Cervone, D. (1986). Differential engagement of self-reactive influences in cognitive motivation. *Organizational Behavior and Human Decision Processes, 38*, 92–113.

Betz, N. E., & Hackett, G. (1981). The relationship of career-related self-efficacy expectations to perceived career options in college women and men. *Journal of Counseling Psychology, 28*, 399–410.

Biran, M., & Wilson, G. T. (1981). Treatment of phobic disorders using cognitive and exposure methods: A self-efficacy analysis. *Journal of Counseling and Clinical Psychology, 49*, 886–899.

Blustein, D. L. (1989). The role of goal instability and career self-efficacy in the career exploration process. *Journal of Vocational Behavior, 35*, 194–203.

Botvin, G. J., & Dusenbury, L. (1992). Substance abuse prevention: Implications for reducing risk of HIV infection. *Psychology of Addictive Behaviors, 6*, 70–80.

Brookover, W. B., Beady, C., Flood, P., Schweitzer, J., & Wisenbaker, J. (1979). *School social systems and student achievement: Schools make a difference.* New York: Praeger.

Brown, A. L. (1984). Metacognition, executive control, self-regulation, and other even more mysterious mechanisms. In F. E. Weinert & R. H. Kluwe (Eds.), *Metacognition, motivation, and learning* (pp. 60–108). Stuttgart: Kuhlhammer.

Brown, I., Jr., & Inouye, D. K. (1978). Learned helplessness through modeling: The role of perceived similarity in competence. *Journal of Personality and Social Psychology, 36*, 900–908.

Bruvold, W. H. (1993). A meta-analysis of adolescent smoking prevention programs. *American Journal of Public Health, 83,* 872–880.

Caprara, G. V., Pastorelli, C., & Bandura, A. (1992). *Impact of perceived academic self-efficacy on interpersonal and emotional behavior.* Unpublished manuscript, Stanford University, Stanford, CA.

Chwalisz, K. D., Altmaier, E. M., & Russell, D. W. (1992). Causal attributions, self-efficacy cognitions, and coping with stress. *Journal of Social and Clinical Psychology, 11,* 377–400.

Cohen, S., Tyrrell, D. A. J., & Smith, A. P. (1991). Psychological stress and susceptibility to the common cold. *New England Journal of Medicine, 325,* 606–612.

Comer, J. P. (1988). Educating poor minority children. *Scientific American, 259,* 42–48.

Cutrona, C. E., & Troutman, B. R. (1986). Social support, infant temperament, and parenting self-efficacy: A mediational model of postpartum depression. *Child Development, 57,* 1507–1518.

DeCharms, R. (1978). *Personal causation: The internal affective determinants of behavior.* New York: Academic Press.

deVries, H., Dijkstra, M., & Kuhlman, P. (1988). Self-efficacy: The third factor besides attitude and subjective norm as a predictor of behavioural intentions. *Health Education Research, 3,* 273–282.

DiClemente, C. C., Fairhurst, S. K., & Piotrowski, N. A. (in press). The role of self-efficacy in addictive behaviors. In J. Maddux (Ed.), *Self-efficacy, adaptation and adjustment: Theory, research and application.* New York: Plenum.

Dienstbier, R. A. (1989). Arousal and physiological toughness: Implications for mental and physical health. *Psychological Review, 96,* 84–100.

Dzewaltowski, D. A., Noble, J. M., & Shaw, J. M. (1990). Physical activity participation: Social cognitive theory versus the theories of reasoned action and planned behavior. *Journal of Sport and Exercise Psychology, 12,* 388–405.

Earley, P. C. (1993). East meets West meets Mideast: Further explorations of collectivistic and individualistic work groups. *Academy of Management Journal, 36,* 319–348.

Earley, P. C. (1994). Self or group? Cultural effects of training on self-efficacy and performance. *Administrative Science Quarterly, 39,* 89–117.

Elder, G. H. (1995). Life trajectories in changing societies. In A. Bandura (Ed.), *Self-efficacy in changing societies* (pp. 46–68). New York: Cambridge University Press.

Elder, G. H., & Ardelt, M. (1992, March). *Families adapting to economic pressure: Some consequences for parents and adolescents.* Paper presented at the Society for Research on Adolescence, Washington, DC

Elder, G. H., Jr., Eccles, J. S., Ardelt, M., & Lord, S. (1993, March). *Inner city parents under economic pressure: Perspectives on the strategies of parenting.* Paper presented at Biennial Meeting of the Society for Research on Child Development, New Orleans, LA.

Engel, G. L. (1977). The need for a new medical model: A challenge for biomedicine. *Science, 196,* 129–136.

Enochs, L. G., & Riggs, I. M. (1990). Further development of an elementary science teaching efficacy belief instrument: A preservice elementary scale. *School Science and Mathematics, 90,* 694–706.

Esteve, J. M. (1992). Multicultural education in Spain: The autonomous communities face the challenge of European unity. *Educational Review, 44,* 255–272.

Evans, E. D., & Tribble, M. (1986). Perceived teaching problems, self-efficacy, and commitment to teaching among preservice teachers. *Journal of Educational Research, 80,* 81–85.

Evans, K., & Heinz, W. R. (1991). Career trajectories in Britain and Germany. In J. Bynner & K. Roberts (Eds.), *Youth and work: Transition to employment in England and Germany* (pp. 205–228). London: Anglo-German Foundation.

Ewart, C. K. (1992). Role of physical self-efficacy in recovery from heart attack. In R. Schwarzer (Ed.), *Self-efficacy: Thought control of action* (pp. 287–304). Washington, DC: Hemisphere.

Feltz, D. L., Landers, D. M., & Raeder, U. (1979). Enhancing self-efficacy in high avoidance motor tasks: A comparison of modeling techniques. *Journal of Sport Psychology, 1,* 112–122.

Fuchs, V. (1974). *Who shall live? Health, economics, and social choice.* New York: Basic Books.

Gibson, S., & Dembo, M. H. (1984). Teacher efficacy: A construct validation. *Journal of Educational Psychology, 76,* 569–582.

Gilchrist, L. D., & Schinke, S. P. (1983). Coping with contraception: Cognitive and behavioral methods with adolescents. *Cognitive Therapy and Research, 7,* 379–388.

Gist, M. E. (1989). The influence of training method on self-efficacy and idea generation among managers. *Personnel Psychology, 42,* 787–805.

Glasgow, R. E., & Arkowitz, H. (1975). The behavioral assessment of male and female social competence in dyadic heterosexual interactions. *Behavior Therapy, 6,* 488–498.

Good, T. L., & Brophy, J. E. (1986). School effects. In M. C. Wittrock (Ed.), *Handbook of research on teaching* (3rd ed., pp. 570–602). New York: Macmillan.

Grove, J. R. (1993). Attributional correlates of cessation self-efficacy among smokers. *Addictive Behaviors, 18,* 311–320.

Gruber, B., Hall, N. R., Hersh, S. P., & Dubois, P. (1988). Immune system and psychologic changes in metastatic cancer patients using relaxation and guided imagery: A pilot study. *Scandinavian Journal of Behaviour Therapy, 17,* 25–46.

Hackett, G. (1985). The role of mathematics self-efficacy in the choice of math-related majors of college women and men: A path analysis. *Journal of Counseling Psychology, 32,* 47–56.

Hackett, G. (1995). Self-efficacy and career choice and development. In A. Bandura (Ed.), *Self-efficacy in changing societies* (pp. 232–258). New York: Cambridge University Press.

Hackett, G., & Betz, N. E. (1981). A self-efficacy approach to the career development of women. *Journal of Vocational Behavior, 18,* 326–339.

Hamburg, D. A. (1992). *Today's children: Creating a future for a generation in crisis.* New York: Times Books.

Hinshaw, S. P. (1992). Externalizing behavior problems and academic underachievement in childhood and adolescence: Causal relationships and underlying mechanisms. *Psychological Bulletin, 111,* 127–155.

Holahan, C. K., & Holahan, C. J. (1987a). Self-efficacy, social support, and depression in aging: A longitudinal analysis. *Journal of Gerontology, 42,* 65–68.

Holahan, C. K., & Holahan, C. J. (1987b). Life stress, hassles, and self-efficacy in aging: A replication and extension. *Journal of Applied Social Psychology, 17,* 574–592.

Holden, G., Moncher, M. S., Schinke, S. P., & Barker, K. M. (1990). Self-efficacy of children and adolescents: A meta-analysis. *Psychological Reports, 66,* 1044–1046.

Holman, H., & Lorig, K. (1992). Perceived self-efficacy in self-management of chronic disease. In R. Schwarzer (Ed.), *Self-efficacy: Thought control of action* (pp. 305–323). Washington, DC: Hemisphere.

Hurrelmann, K., & Roberts, K. (1991). Problems and solutions. In J. Bynner & K. Roberts (Eds.), *Youth and work: Transition to employment in England and Germany* (pp. 229–250). London: Anglo-German Foundation.

Jacobs, J. A. (1989). *Revolving doors: Sex segregation and women's careers.* Stanford, CA: Stanford University Press.

Jemmott, J. B., III, Jemmott, L. S., & Fong, G. T. (1992). Reductions in HIV risk-associated sexual behaviors among black male adolescents: Effects of an AIDS prevention intervention. *American Journal of Public Health, 82,* 372–377.

Jemmott, J. B., III, Jemmott, L. S., Spears, H., Hewitt, N., & Cruz-Collins, M. (1991). Self-efficacy, hedonistic expectancies, and condom-use intentions among inner-city black adolescent women: A social cognitive approach to AIDS risk behavior. *Journal of Adolescent Health, 13,* 512–519.

Jerusalem, M., & Mittig, W. (1995). Self-efficacy in stressful life transitions. In A. Bandura (Ed.), *Self-efficacy in changing societies* (pp. 177–201). New York: Cambridge University Press.

Jessor, R. (1986). Adolescent problem drinking: Psychosocial aspects and developmental outcomes. In R. K. Silbereisen et al. (Eds.), *Development as action in context* (pp. 241–264). Berlin: Springer-Verlag.

Jessor, R., Donovan, J. E., & Costa, F. M. (1991). *Beyond adolescence: Problem behavior and young adult development.* Cambridge, England: Cambridge University Press.

Kanfer, R., & Zeiss, A. M. (1983). Depression, interpersonal standard-setting, and judgments of self-efficacy. *Journal of Abnormal Psychology, 92,* 319–329.

Kavanagh, D. J., & Bower, G. H. (1985). Mood and self-efficacy: Impact of joy and sadness on perceived capabilities. *Cognitive Therapy and Research, 9,* 507–525.

Kavanagh, D. J., & Wilson, P. H. (1989). Prediction of outcome with a group version of cognitive therapy for depression. *Behaviour Research and Therapy, 27,* 333–347.

Kent, G., & Gibbons, R. (1987). Self-efficacy and the control of anxious cognitions. *Journal of Behavior Therapy & Experimental Psychiatry, 18,* 33–40.

Kiecolt-Glaser, J. K., & Glaser, R. (1987). Behavioral influences on immune function: Evidence for the interplay between stress and health. In T. Field, P. M. McCabe, & N. Schneiderman (Eds.), *Stress and coping across development* (Vol. 2, pp. 189–206). Hillsdale, NJ: Erlbaum.

Kiecolt-Glaser, J. K., Glaser, R., Strain, E. C., Stout, J. C., Tarr, K. L., Holliday, J. E., & Speicher, C. E. (1986). Modulation of cellular immunity in medical students. *Journal of Behavioral Medicine, 9,* 5–21.

Krantz, D. S., Grunberg, N. E., & Baum, A. (1985). Health psychology. *Annual Reviews in Psychology, 36,* 349–383.

Lazarus, R. S., & Folkman, S. (1984). *Stress, appraisal, and coping.* New York: Springer.

Lent, R. W., Brown, S. D., & Hackett, G. (1994). Toward a unifying social cognitive theory of career and academic interest, choice, and performance. *Journal of Vocational Behavior, 45,* 79–122.

Lent, R. W., Brown, S. D., & Larkin, K. C. (1984). Relation of self-efficacy expectations to academic achievement and persistence. *Journal of Counseling Psychology, 31,* 356–362.

Levin, H. M. (1987). New schools for the disadvantaged. *Teacher Education Quarterly, 14,* 60–83.

Levin, H. M. (1991). Learning from accelerated schools. *Policy perspectives.* Philadelphia: The Pew Higher Education Research Program.

Lewinsohn, P. M., Mischel, W., Chaplin, W., & Barton, R. (1980). Social competence and depression: The role of illusory self-perceptions. *Journal of Abnormal Psychology, 89,* 203–212.

Lipset, S. M. (1985). Feeling better: Measuring the nation's confidence. *Public Opinion, 2,* 6–9, 56–58.

Litt, M. D. (1988). Self-efficacy and perceived control: Cognitive mediators of pain tolerance. *Journal of Personality and Social Psychology, 54,* 149–160.

Locke, E. A., & Latham, G. P. (1990). *A theory of goal setting and task performance.* Englewood Cliffs, NJ: Prentice-Hall.

Maier, S. F., Laudenslager, M. L., & Ryan, S. M. (1985). Stressor controllability, immune function, and endogenous opiates. In F. R. Brush & J. B. Overmier (Eds.), *Affect, conditioning, and cognition: Essays on the determinants of behavior* (pp. 183–201). Hillsdale, NJ: Erlbaum.

Major, B., Cozzarelli, C., Sciacchitano, A. M., Cooper, M. L., Testa, M., & Mueller, P. M. (1990). Perceived social support, self-efficacy, and adjustment to abortion. *Journal of Personality and Social Psychology, 59,* 452–463.

Major, B., Mueller, P., & Hildebrandt, K. (1985). Attributions, expectations, and coping with abortion. *Journal of Personality and Social Psychology, 48,* 585–599.

Marlatt, G. A., Baer, J. S., & Quigley, L. A. (1995). Self-efficacy and alcohol and drug abuse. In A. Bandura (Ed.), *Self-efficacy in changing societies* (pp. 289–315). New York: Cambridge University Press.

Marsh, A. (1977). *Protest and political consciousness.* Beverly Hills: Sage.

Matsui, T., Ikeda, H., & Ohnishi, R. (1989). Relations of sex-typed socializations to career self-efficacy expectations of college students. *Journal of Vocational Behavior, 35,* 1–16.

Matsui, T., & Onglatco, M. L. (1992). Career self-efficacy as a moderator of the relation between occupational stress and strain. *Journal of Vocational Behavior, 41,* 79–88.

McAuley, E. (1991). Efficacy, attributional, and affective responses to exercise participation. *Journal of Sport and Exercise Psychology, 13,* 382–393.

McGinnis, J. M., & Foege, W. H. (1993). Actual causes of death in the United States. *Journal of the American Medical Association, 270,* 2207–2212.

Meece, J. L., Wigfield, A., & Eccles, J. S. (1990). Predators of math anxiety and its influence on young adolescents' course enrollment intentions and performance in mathematics. *Journal of Educational Psychology, 82,* 60–70.

Meichenbaum, D. H. (1977). *Cognitive-behavior modification: An integrative approach.* New York: Plenum Press.

Millstein, S. G., Petersen, A. C., & Nightingale, E. O. (1993). *Promoting the health of adolescents: New directions for the twenty-first century.* New York: Oxford University Press.

Muller, E. N. (1972). A test of a partial theory of potential for political violence. *The American Political Science Review, 66,* 928–959.

Oettingen, G. (1995). Cross-cultural perspective on self-efficacy beliefs. In A. Bandura (Ed.), *Self-efficacy in changing societies* (pp. 149–176). New York: Cambridge University Press.

O'Leary, A. (1990). Stress, emotion, and human immune function. *Psychological Bulletin, 108,* 363–382.

Olioff, M., & Aboud, F. E. (1991). Predicting postpartum dysphoria in primiparous mothers: Roles of perceived parenting self-efficacy and self-esteem. *Journal of Cognitive Psychotherapy, 5,* 3–14.

Ozer, E. M. (1992). *Managing work and family: The effects of childcare on perceived self-efficacy and the psychological health of new working mothers.* Unpublished doctoral dissertation, Stanford University, Stanford, CA.

Ozer, E. M., & Bandura, A. (1990). Mechanisms governing empowerment effects: A self-efficacy analysis. *Journal of Personality and Social Psychology, 58,* 472–486.

Paris, S. G., & Newman, R. S. (1990). Developmental aspects of self-regulated learning. *Educational Psychologist, 25,* 87–102.

Patterson, G. R., Capaldi, D., & Bank, L. (1991). An early starter model for predicting delinquency. In D. Pepler & K. H. Rubin (Eds.), *The development and treatment of childhood aggression.* Hillsdale, NJ: Erlbaum.

Perry, C. L., Kelder, S. H., Murray, D. M., & Klepp, K. (1992). Communitywide smoking prevention: Long-term outcomes of the Minnesota heart health program and the class of 1989 study. *American Journal of Public Health, 82,* 1210–1216.

Relich, J. D., Debus, R. L., & Walker, R. (1986). The mediating role of attribution and self-efficacy variables for treatment effects on achievement outcomes. *Contemporary Educational Psychology, 11,* 195–216.

Rotter, J. B. (1966). Generalized expectancies for internal versus external control of reinforcement. *Psychological Monographs, 80* (1, Whole No. 609).

Rudkin, L., Hagell, A., Elder, G. H., & Conger, R. (1992). *Perceptions of community well-being and the desire to move elsewhere.* Unpublished manuscript, University of North Carolina at Chapel Hill.

Rutter, M. (1979). Protective factors in children's responses to stress and disadvantage. In M. W. Kent & E. J. Rolf (Eds)., *Primary prevention of psychopathology. Volume III: Social competence in children* (pp. 49–74). Hanover, NH: University Press of New England.

Salkovskis, P. M., & Harrison, J. (1984). Abnormal and normal obsessions – a replication. *Behaviour Research and Therapy, 22,* 549–552.

Sanderson, W. C., Rapee, R. M., & Barlow, D. H. (1989). The influence of an illusion of control on panic attacks induced via inhalation of 5.5% carbon dioxide-enriched air. *Archives of General Psychiatry, 46,* 157–162.

Sarason, I. G. (1975). Anxiety and self-preoccupation. In I. G. Sarason & D. C. Spielberger (Eds.), *Stress and anxiety* (Vol. 2, pp. 27–44). Washington, DC: Hemisphere.

Schneiderman, N., McCabe, P. M., & Baum, A. (Eds.). (1992). *Stress and disease processes: Perspectives in behavioral medicine.* Hillsdale, NJ: Erlbaum.

Schooler, C. (1990). Individualism and the historical and social-structural determinants of people's concerns over self-directedness and efficacy. In J. Rodin, C. Schooler, & K. W. Schaie (Eds.), *Self-directedness: Cause and effects throughout the life course* (pp. 19–58). Hillsdale, NJ: Erlbaum.

Schunk, D. H. (1987). Peer models and children's behavioral change. *Review of Educational Research, 57,* 149–174.

Schunk, D. H. (1989). Self-efficacy and achievement behaviors. *Educational Psychology Review, 1,* 173–208.

Schunk, D. H., & Gunn, T. P. (1986). Self-efficacy and skill development: Influence of task strategies and attributions. *Journal of Educational Research, 79,* 238–244.

Schwarzer, R. (1992). Self-efficacy in the adoption and maintenance of health behaviors: Theoretical approaches and a new model. In R. Schwarzer (Ed.), *Self-efficacy: Thought control of action* (pp. 217–243). Washington, DC: Hemisphere.

Seligman, M. E. P. (1990). Why is there so much depression today? The waxing of the individual and the waning of the commons. In R. E. Ingram (Ed.), *Contem-*

porary psychological approaches to depression: Theory, research, and treatment (pp. 1–9). New York: Plenum.

Shavit, Y., & Martin, F. C. (1987). Opiates, stress, and immunity: Animal studies. *Annals of Behavioral Medicine, 9,* 11–20.

Steptoe, A., & Appels, A. (Eds.). (1989). *Stress, personal control and health.* New York: Wiley.

Taylor, S. E. (1989). *Positive illusions: Creative self-deception and the healthy mind.* New York: Basic Books.

Telch, M. J., Killen, J. D., McAlister, A. L., Perry, C. L., & Maccoby, N. (1982). Long-term follow-up of a pilot project on smoking prevention with adolescents. *Journal of Behavioral Medicine, 5,* 1–8.

Teti, D. M., & Gelfand, D. M. (1991). Behavioral competence among mothers of infants in the first year: The mediational role of maternal self-efficacy. *Child Development, 62,* 918–929.

Wallack, L., Dorfman, L., Jernigan, D., & Themba, M. (1993). *Media advocacy and public health: Power for prevention.* Newbury Park, CA: Sage.

White, J. (1982). *Rejection.* Reading, MA: Addison-Wesley.

White, R. W. (1959). Motivation reconsidered: The concept of competence. *Psychological Review, 66,* 297–333.

Wiedenfeld, S. A., O'Leary, A., Bandura, A., Brown, S., Levine, S., & Raska, K. (1990). Impact of perceived self-efficacy in coping with stressors on components of the immune system. *Journal of Personality and Social Psychology, 59,* 1082–1094.

Wiegman, O., Taal, E., Van den Bogaard, J., & Gutteling, J. M. (1992). Protection motivation theory variables as predictors of behavioural intentions in three domains of risk management. In J. A. M. Winnubst & S. Maes (Eds.), *Lifestyles, stress and health: New developments in health psychology* (pp. 55–70). Leiden, Netherlands: DSWO Press, Leiden University.

Wollman, N., & Stouder, R. (1991). Believed efficacy and political activity: A test of the specificity hypothesis. *The Journal of Social Psychology, 131,* 557–566.

Wood, R., & Bandura, A. (1989). Social cognitive theory of organizational management. *Academy of Management Review, 14,* 361–384.

Woolfolk, A. E., & Hoy, W. K. (1990). Prospective teachers' sense of efficacy and belief about control. *Journal of Educational Psychology, 82,* 81–91.

Zimmerman, B. J. (1990). Self-regulating academic learning and achievement: The emergence of a social cognitive perspective. *Educational Psychology Review, 2,* 173–201.

Zimmerman, B. J. (1995). Self-efficacy and educational development. In A. Bandura (Ed.), *Self-efficacy in changing societies* (pp. 202–231). New York: Cambridge University Press.

Zimmerman, B. J., & Bandura, A. (1994). Impact of self-regulatory influences on writing course attainment. *American Educational Research Journal, 31,* 845–862.

Zimmerman, B. J., Bandura, A., & Martinez-Pons, M. (1992). Self-motivation for academic attainment: The role of self-efficacy beliefs and personal goal-setting. *American Educational Research Journal, 29,* 663–676.

2. Life trajectories in changing societies

GLEN H. ELDER, JR.

Eras of rapid social change underscore important issues in the study of lives by generating problems of human dislocation and deprivation, as well as new opportunities. The extraordinary loss of life during World War II illustrates this point through a distorted sex ratio and its continuing influence on the social choices of women (Linz, 1985; Velkoff & Kinsella, 1993). Today Russian women over the age of 65 outnumber men by a factor of three to one, an imbalance that is greater than that of any other country in Europe, East or West. From 1940 to the present, the long arm of wartime mortality has shaped and limited their work and marriage options.

The historical record of the 20th century is filled with powerful changes of this kind – violent swings of the economic cycle, rapid industrial growth, population dislocations, mass migration, and political fragmentation. Such times prompt fresh thinking about life trajectories, human agency, and their relation. Indeed, contemporary thinking about such issues in the life course dates back to the changeful times of the early 20th century and especially to the pioneering work of W. I. Thomas and his monumental study with Florian Znaniecki (1918–1920), *The Polish Peasant in Europe and America*. This study investigated the migratory experience of Polish peasants as they left their rural homeland for urban centers in Europe and the United States during the late 19th and early 20th centuries. *The Polish Peasant* provides an ethnographic and historical account of vil-

I acknowledge support by the National Institute of Mental Health (MH 41327, MH 43270, and MH 48165), a contract with the U.S. Army Research Institute, a grant from the Department of Veterans Affairs Merit Review program, research support from the John D. and Catherine T. MacArthur Foundation Program for Successful Adolescent Development Among Youth in High-Risk Settings, and a Research Scientist Award (MH 00567).

lage and country life in Poland and of the immigrants' settlement in their new urban environments.

Immigrant lives embodied the dislocations and strains of their age and trajectory. They were socialized for a world that soon became only a memory. Thomas's own life history bears some resemblance to this change. He was born in 1863, grew up amid the foothills of western Virginia, and experienced mentors who opened his eyes to the possibilities of graduate study at the University of Chicago. Later on, Thomas founded a sociology program of study and research at the university that became known as the Chicago School of Sociology. The exercise of personal and social control became central in his biographical approach to human lives in changing societies.

In his writings Thomas called for a view of people's lives over time in a changing environment. Continuous life records, whether retrospective or prospective, offered such a view. He urged (Volkart, 1951, p. 593) that priority be given to "the longitudinal approach to life history." Studies should follow "groups of individuals into the future, getting a continuous record of experiences as they occur." From this perspective, the basic task should be one of studying "characters and life-organizations . . . in their dynamic concrete development."

Thomas referred to "typical lines of genesis" established by the social order but also, with Znaniecki, stressed the agentic potential of the individual. People construct their own lives by choosing options within structured situations. Seventy years later we find that many of the ideas expressed by Thomas and Znaniecki are part of an emerging life course paradigm that features the effects of changing societies and human agency.

This chapter surveys the defining elements of this paradigm and then explores what empirical studies of social change and their linking mechanisms tell us about the role of human agency in life trajectories.

The life course as an emerging paradigm

Life course theory represents a major change in how we think about and study developmental processes and human lives. It locates people in historical context and life stage, highlights the differential timing and connectedness of people's lives, and stresses the role of individuals in shaping their own lives. Broadly speaking, this perspective constitutes a new paradigm, a conceptual shift that has made temporality, contextual forces or influences, and process more salient dimensions in the social sciences.

As a multidisciplinary field of ideas and empirical observations, the paradigm draws on various conceptual streams, including biologically informed accounts of individual development (Bühler, 1935; Magnusson & Törestad, 1993); the generational tradition of life history studies (Thomas & Znaniecki, 1918–1920); the meanings of age in accounts of birth cohorts and age strata (Elder, 1975; Riley, Johnson, & Foner, 1972; Ryder, 1965); cultural and intergenerational models (Kertzer & Keith, 1984); and developmental lifespan psychology (Baltes, 1987).

My perspective tends to stress the interplay of changing lives and their changing social world. Examples include studies of economic decline and recovery, as in the Great Depression (Elder, 1974) through World War II, as well as the Great Farm Crisis of the 1980s, when economic indicators plunged by nearly 50% (Conger & Elder, 1994). In each case, the study traced adverse influences through family experience to the lives of children.

Overall, the life course can be viewed as a multilevel phenomenon, ranging from structured pathways in whole societies (Mayer, 1986; Meyer, 1988), social institutions, and complex organizations to the social trajectories of individuals and their developmental paths. Unfortunately, theories generally exist on one level or another and consequently provide little guidance for life course studies that cross levels. However, Bronfenbrenner's (1979) nested levels of the social environment, from macro- to microsystem, represent a conceptual advance in linking social change and individual lives.

In concept, the life course generally refers to the interweave of age-graded social trajectories, such as work and family, that are subject to changing conditions and future options; and to short-term transitions that extend from birth to retirement and death. Each trajectory can be thought of as a series of linked states, as in linked jobs across a work history. A change in state thus marks a transition – a transition from one job to another, for example. Transitions are always embedded in trajectories that give them distinctive meaning and form.

Unlike the single careers so widely studied in the past, the life course paradigm orients analysis to the dynamics of multiple, interlocking pathways. Strategies of planning are illustrated in the scheduling of marriage and parenthood, and in arranging family events according to the imperatives of a work career (Moen, Dempster-McClain, & Williams, 1992). Family pathways also have implications for children's developmental course, as when family economic misfortune interacts with the maturational history of adolescents to produce change in their concept of self (Ge,

Lorenz, Conger, Elder, & Simons, 1994). Histories of family discord and ineffective parenting may also be part of this picture.

Another broadening element comes from a view of the full life course, its continuities and change. With an eye to the two halves of the life course, analysis is necessarily more sensitive to the impact of early transitions for later experience. Indeed, we now see that the implications of early adult choices extend even into the later years of retirement and old age (Clausen, 1993), from the adequacy of economic resources to adaptive skills and activities. The later years and their quality of life cannot be understood in full without knowledge of the prior life course. Role sequences, whether functionally stable or unstable, clearly matter for subsequent health and adaptation.

A core assumption of the life course paradigm asserts that developmental processes and outcomes are shaped by the life trajectories people follow, whether reflective of good or bad times. Likewise, developmental trajectories also influence the choices and careers people follow. The flow of influence is reciprocal. Thus, more ambitious goals and endeavors are likely to appeal to efficacious youth and not to those lacking self-confidence (Elder, 1974, chap. 6). In turn, the progress of working toward goals of this kind tends to enhance a sense of personal agency.

The continual interplay between social and developmental trajectories has much to do with four distinctive features of the life course paradigm (Elder, in press): (1) human lives in relation to historical times and place, (2) human agency, (3) linked lives, and (4) social timing. Issues of human agency, linked lives, and timing identify mechanisms by which changing environments influence the course and substance of human lives.

Changing times and human agency

Especially in rapidly changing societies, differences in year of birth expose people to different historical worlds, with their distinctive priorities, constraints, and options. Historical effects on the life course take the form of a cohort effect when social change differentiates the life patterns of successive cohorts, such as older and younger men before World War II. History also takes the form of a period effect when the influence is relatively uniform across successive birth cohorts. However, birth year and cohort membership are merely a proxy for exposure to historical change.

Individual lives may reflect historical change, but to know whether this is so we must move beyond birth cohorts and their historical context to direct study of the changing environment. The research question should focus on the social change in question and its life course implications.

What is the process by which an institutional change, such as political reform in Eastern Europe, is expressed in particular life patterns?

To answer this question, consider some ways of linking historical effects to people's lives (Elder, 1991): the different implications for people of differences in age (their *life stage*), the interaction of prior life histories for adaptations (an *accentuation* of prior dispositions), the *situational imperatives* of the new arrangements, the effects of losing and regaining personal control (*control cycle*), and the social *interdependence of individual lives*.

From the vantage point of W. I. Thomas's theory of social and personal change (Elder, 1974, chap. 1), all transitions, whether normative or not, create a disparity between claims and resources, goals and accomplishments. The resulting loss of control over life outcomes prompts efforts to regain control; the entire process takes the form of a control cycle, a process well documented by studies of reactance behavior. Feelings of reactance occur whenever one or more freedoms or expectations are eliminated or threatened. Such emotions prompt efforts to regain or preserve control.

The Brehms (1982, p. 375) note that "it is the threat to control (which one already had) that motivates an attempt to deal with the environment. And the attempts to deal with the environment can be characterized as attempts to regain control." Bandura (in press) stresses the motivating effects of setting higher goals, achieving them, and then setting even higher goals.

Though all social transitions entail some risk of losing personal control, whether they produce this outcome or not has much to do with considerations of life stage and situational imperatives. Life stage refers to the age and social status of the person at the time of change. People of unlike age experience the same change event in different ways.

A severe economic recession would influence parents and children in different ways. Indeed, children in the Great Depression were influenced through the impact on parents (Elder, 1974, 1979). Moreover, younger children were more adversely influenced by Depression hardship than older children. Another example comes from military service and the disruptive effect of *late* mobilization after the age of 32 in World War II (Elder, Shanahan, & Clipp, 1994). Early mobilization, just after high school, had different consequences as it enlarged the benefits of servicemen in this war.

Typically, the meaning of the new situation and its imperatives depend on what people bring to it. Dispositions brought to stressful change may adversely accentuate the impact of the change. Thus, irritable men may become explosive under economic stress, and less resilient men may shatter under the stress of wartime combat (Elder & Caspi, 1990). One of the earliest cases of accentuation in the research literature comes from the pioneering research of Newcomb (1943) on women students of newly established Bennington College in rural Vermont in the 1930s. In the New Deal environment of Bennington, entering students who were relatively independent of parental influences tended to shift their social and political attitudes more toward the college norm than other students.

Linked lives and their timing

No features of the life course paradigm are more central to an understanding of changing environments in people's lives and their sense of personal efficacy than the concepts of linked lives and their timing. Studies dating back to Durkheim's (1897/1951) analysis of social integration and suicide and to Thomas and Znaniecki's (1918–1920) research on migration have stressed the interdependence of lives across the generations and among family, friends, and workmates. Interlocking social relationships structure the life course with personal constraints and become modes of self-control and agency through internalization.

All lives are socially timed and patterned according to the meanings of age, as in age grading. Studies informed by age have stressed the historical time of the person through birth year, as well as the social timing of events and transitions (Riley, Foner, & Waring, 1988).

The timing of encounters with major environmental change in a person's life has much to do with the goodness of fit between lives and new circumstances. This *life stage principle* implies that the effects of a particular social change will vary in type and relative influence across the life course and thus points to the potential complexity of interactions among historical, psychological, and biological factors. Mobilization for military service in World War II and the Korean War illustrates the role of life stage in structuring historical experience.

Consider two birth cohorts of Japanese men who grew up in the city of Shizuoka, a large metropolis south of Tokyo (Elder & Meguro, 1987). The older men (born 1918–1924) were typically mobilized into military service during World War II, a total of 78%. Nearly two thirds reported family members who had served. Four out of five also experienced an air raid and more than half claimed that their family suffered physical war damage. The younger men (born 1927–1930) were typically too young to serve, and yet they also were exposed to a high level of personal suffering in relation to wartime conditions, usually through the lives of significant others – the military service of family members, the death of a family member, and war damage to the family home.

The younger men were also mobilized out of school for work groups in factories and on farms, and thus an understanding of the war's effect in their lives requires knowledge of their workmates and work experience. Just as early work experience can accelerate movement into adult roles, the war-related work of these schoolchildren tended to accelerate their transition to marriage and parenthood. The mobilized men formed families at an earlier age than the nonmobilized, regardless of family background and level of education.

Time of entry into the armed forces represents one of the most powerful influences on how the service affected the lives of American men in the Oakland and Berkeley cohorts (Elder, 1986, 1987). The Oakland men were born at the beginning of the 1920s, the Berkeley men in 1928–1929. Early entry, shortly after high school, provided special advantages for life opportunity because it came before family obligations and major work advances, and ensured access to support for higher education on the GI Bill. In both cohorts, disadvantaged youth were more likely to be mobilized shortly after high school than other men. Disadvantage refers to a deprived family background in the 1930s, to poor school grades, and to feelings of inadequacy in adolescence.

By midlife, the inequality of veterans before the war had largely disappeared. Early entry proved to be timely for the Oakland and Berkeley men because it put them on a pathway to greater opportunity, apart from the trauma of combat. One important aspect of this trajectory entailed changes that made the early entrants more ambitious, self-directed, and disciplined (Elder, 1986). By placing men in a new setting divorced from home, military service promoted self-direction, mastery, and assertiveness at a formative point in life, when compared to later entrants or nonveterans. With its legitimate moratorium from career pressures, there was time to think through options and do fresh evaluations of future directions. The early entrants also had greater access to the GI Bill on educational benefits. In many respects, then, military service had become a timely developmental experience for a large number of children from disadvantaged homes.

To sum up, the interdependence and timing of lives represent key elements of the life course paradigm as we know it today. In combination, they provide a fruitful way of thinking about connections between lives and times as well as about the role of human agency in constructing life ways. The impact of social change is contingent on the life history people bring to the new situation, on their life stage at the time, and on the demands of the new situation.

To bring more empirical detail to these conclusions, I turn to studies of life disadvantage in hard times and their contribution to an understanding of human agency in life trajectories.

Rising above life's disadvantage: the role of personal agency

Children of disadvantage are not expected to do well in life, and yet we find that a surprising number do prosper in adulthood. This observation applies to the generations of American children who grew up in the Great Depression (Elder, 1974, 1979) and became successful members of the postwar generation, as well as to contemporary children who are growing up in dangerous inner cities (Elder, Eccles, Ardelt, & Lord, 1995) and the depressed countryside (Elder, 1992). How does this escape occur? What are the routes out of disadvantage?

One answer involves the variability of historical experience and efficacious behavior among families and children (Elder, 1974, 1979). Not all children of the Great Depression were exposed to drastic income losses, and those who were varied markedly in social and personal resources. They differed in age and maturity, and in parents with educational resources, self-confidence, and ego resilience.

Each of these resources played a role in moderating the impact of family hardship. In addition, hard-pressed families differed in how they coped with adversity. Some aggravated their plight by engaging in self-defeating adaptations, as in heavy drinking and social withdrawal, while others managed effectively through constructive actions and problem solving.

Some of these differences also appear in the family experience of inner-city youth today (Elder, Eccles, Ardelt, & Lord, 1995) and in the experiences of rural adolescents in the American Midwest (Elder, Foster, & Ardelt, 1994). I begin with themes from the Depression experience and then explore key parallels in the contemporary experience of inner-city and rural youth.

Blunting the impact of depression adversity

American children who were born at opposite ends of the 1920s did not share the same risk of developmental impairment when they entered the Great Depression with their families. In theory, the youngest children were most family dependent and thus encountered the greatest risk. By contrast, the oldest children were too young to leave school and face a dismal employment situation, and they were also too old to be highly dependent on their family and its well-being. Consistent with this life stage expectation, a longitudinal study of California children in these two age groups found confirming evidence on the cohort difference (Elder, 1974, 1979). The Oakland Growth Study members were born in 1920–1921; the Berkeley Guidance members in 1928–1929.

In both cohorts, drastic income loss sharply increased indebtedness and the curtailment of expenditures. Changes in relationship stemmed from fathers' loss of earnings and withdrawal from family roles and from family economic support. Economic loss increased the relative power and emotional centrality of mother in relation to boys and girls. Lastly, deprivation heightened parental irritability, the likelihood of marital conflicts, arbitrary and inconsistent discipline of children, and the risk of fathers' behavioral impairment through heavy drinking, demoralization, and health disabilities. All of these behaviors raised the level of stress in the family and increased the likelihood of destructive parent behavior.

Despite the similarity of these family processes in both cohorts, effects of the Depression crisis were most adverse among the younger Berkeley boys, and we focus on them for purposes of illustration (Elder, Caspi, & Van Nguyen, 1986). Family hardship came early in their lives and entailed a more prolonged deprivation experience, when compared to that of boys in the Oakland cohort.

Whether middle class or working class, the Berkeley boys from deprived families were less likely than the nondeprived to be judged hopeful, self-directed, assertive, and confident about the future. At the end of adolescence, they possessed little confidence in their goals or in their ability to achieve them. However, not all of the Berkeley boys came out of this experience with such impairments. Indeed, the data suggest that they were least likely to be influenced in this manner when they had a supportive, nurturant tie to mother; when father was not irritable, explosive, or punitive; and when the marital relationship remained strong.

The developmental risks of the Berkeley boys is in keeping with other findings that show family stressors to be most pathogenic for males in early childhood (Rutter & Madge, 1976). But why did the older Oakland boys fare much better? Consider status changes in the transition to adulthood. Three status changes seemed especially relevant to males in both cohorts – entry into higher education and its opportunities, the stabilizing significance of marriage, and a bridge to opportunities through military service.

Military service became the most important transition with its influence on courtship and marriage, as well as higher education through the GI Bill. Nine out of ten of the Oakland men entered the service for duty in World War II, and nearly three fourths of the Berkeley men also served in the military. In both groups, military service encouraged personal growth toward mature competence and higher education (Elder & Caspi, 1990). For the Berkeley males, these changes largely erased the developmental limitations of their Depression experience. Marriage, higher education, and military service encouraged the mastery experiences that were typically lacking in their own Depression households.

There is another angle that deserves consideration: a perspective on the roles children played in their Depression households. The Oakland boys were old enough to assume productive responsibilities within the household, and they did so, whereas the younger Berkeley boys were too young. During the peak years of the Depression, they were less than four or five years old.

Helpfulness and agency in depression households

The coming of hard times made the Oakland children more valuable in the family economy (Elder, 1974). They were called on to meet the increased labor and economic needs of deprived households, and a large number managed tasks in the family and earned money on paid jobs. As a rule, a portion of this money was used for family concerns. Girls tended to specialize in household chores, while boys were more likely to hold a paid job.

Boys who acquired paid jobs during the Depression became more socially independent between junior high and high school when compared to other youth, and they were judged to be more responsible on financial matters by their mothers. Adolescent jobs in the 1930s typically included odd jobs in the adult world, from clerking and waiting on tables to running errands and delivering newspapers, but employment of this kind carried the important implication that people counted on the workers – that they mattered.

Staff observers judged the working boys to be more efficacious and energetic than the nonemployed on a set of rating scales. Paid jobs were undoubtedly attractive to the industrious and a source of enhanced beliefs of self-efficacy – the flow of influence is reciprocal. A mother of one of the working boys described him as having "one driving interest after another, usually a practical one" (Elder, 1974, p. 145). With additional chores in the household, these working adolescents experienced something like the obligations of adult status. To observers who knew them well, they indeed appeared to be more adult oriented in values, interests, and activities when compared to other youth.

Deprived households in the Depression became more labor-intensive as they sought to make ends meet, and this led to roles that children could perform. The Oakland boys who took on the responsibilities of paid jobs and household chores were likely to give more thought to the future and especially to the work they would like to do. Boys who held jobs were more apt in adulthood to have a crystallized sense of their work career, when compared to other males. They also settled more quickly on a stable line of work and displayed less floundering during their 20s. Apart from education, this pattern of work had much to do with the occupational success of men who grew up in hard-pressed Oakland families during the 1930s.

These pathways out of disadvantage were followed by a good many children of the Great Depression. Do they have any relevance to contemporary American youth who are coming of age in the inner cities and countryside? To answer this question, I turn to a study of inner-city youth in the city of Philadelphia and to a panel study of midwestern boys and girls who are growing up in small towns and on farms in the north central region of Iowa.

Neither sample has reached the adult years and so we cannot know the adult trajectories they will follow. Nevertheless, there are striking similarities across this historical time, as the following accounts suggest.

Some parallels in contemporary America

Cities and the rural countryside have always been linked in major social and economic crises. Cities attract rural generations with their opportunities, whereas urban crises make rural life more appealing, prompting flows of return migrants. Today, the violence and economic deprivation of life in the inner city have fueled the outmigration of blacks from large cities in the United States (Johnson, 1994). At the same time, rich agricultural regions of the Midwest are losing their young people in extraordinary numbers. Between 10% and 20% of the residents of rural counties left Iowa in the 1980s for other regions (Lasley, 1994). A substantial number are migrating to cities.

The Philadelphia study, launched in 1991, is studying black and white parents and their young people in high and lower poverty neighborhoods of the inner city (Elder, Eccles, & Ardelt, 1994; Elder, Eccles, Ardelt, & Lord, 1995). The single wave sample includes 486 households, black

American and white American. Interviews were carried out with a parent, a child between the ages of 11 and 14, and a near older sibling. Neighborhood poverty rates vary from 10% to 63%.

The Iowa study was launched as a panel design in 1989 with 451 households in rural counties. The household participants include two parents, the target children (seventh graders in 1989), and a near sibling. Annual waves of data collection have been implemented each year from 1989 through 1992. Similar measures have been used in the two studies.

In each study, I focus on links between economic hardship and both parental behavior and children's lives.

The inner city and efficacious parents

Economic trends over the past decades have placed middle- to low-income families under increasing economic pressure as their standard of living has declined relative to that of upper-income households. This change along with high rates of violence and drug use have placed inner-city youth at considerable risk of impaired life chances and early death (Wilson, 1987). Not all inner-city children are impaired by such disadvantages, and yet we know surprisingly little about the escape routes and how they work.

In theory and research, the escape is aided by nurturing parents who maintain high standards of excellence and firm discipline. Beliefs in one's ability to make such standards a reality are relevant to pathways out of urban disadvantage, along with efforts to minimize risk and maximize opportunities outside the family. Parents may involve their children in recreational organizations and participate actively in their children's education through volunteer activities and classroom visits. They may also insist on the presence of an older person on the route home from school, such as a brother or family friend. The Philadelphia study explored these aspects of effective parent behavior, including family strategies that are both proactive and preventive within and outside the family.

The basic model linked total family income and unstable work-income to economic pressure, as indicated by felt financial strain and economic adjustments, such as cutting back on consumption. In theory, economic pressure diminishes the self-efficacy beliefs of adults as parents by increasing their feelings of emotional depression. We assumed that this effect of economic pressure would be greatest when social support is lacking, as among single-parent households and discordant marriages. On the

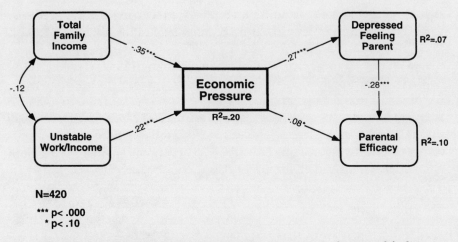

N=420

*** p< .000
  * p< .10

Figure 2.1. Influence of economic hardship on parent's depressed feelings
and efficacy (standardized coefficients).

other hand, relatively strong marriages are likely to minimize the depressive effect of hardship on the quality of parenting.

When inner-city parents believe they can make a positive difference in their children's lives and behavior, they are also likely to be engaged in preventive and proactive family strategies, both within and outside of the family. That is, efficacious parents will be engaged in combating the high risks to their children by involving them in community organizations and supervised activities.

Linking economic pressures and parental efficacy

The basic model links economic pressures and parental efficacy through variations in reported level of emotional distress. Mounting economic pressures increase the risk of depressed feelings and consequently the prospect of a diminished sense of parental effectiveness. To put this model to a test (Figure 2.1), we defined a causal sequence with total family income and unstable work-income as exogenous variables, followed by felt economic pressure (an average of two measures, financial strain and cutbacks on purchases), emotional depression (SCL-90), and a sense of parental efficacy – beliefs that the parent could make a difference in the child and his or her environment (the two scores were averaged).

As expected, the path diagram shows that depressed feelings do have a strong negative impact on a parent's sense of efficacy, and that they mediate the adverse effects of economic pressure on this outcome. Increasing levels of economic pressure increase the risk of emotional depression among black and white parents and in this manner diminish their sense of personal effectiveness as a parent. This mediational link appears in both racial groups.

Considering the limitations of our cross-sectional data, it is possible that hardship conditions might produce greater economic pressure by increasing depressed feelings; or that economic pressures might lead to a diminished sense of parental efficacy and a depressed outlook. The analytic model was reestimated with these changes in place, but the results provide no support for this arrangement. The model does not fit the data appropriately. The initial sequence still makes more sense.

Types of family structure modify the causal sequence in line with our expectations. Economic hardship and economic pressure are most predictive of depressed feelings and the absence of mastery attitudes and beliefs among single-parent households and relatively weak marriages. Hardship conditions made no difference at all on parental mood and beliefs of parenting efficacy when the marriage was strong. This protective influence occurs in part because supportive marriages are seldom coupled with depressed feelings.

What do efficacious parents do?

Are efficacious parents more engaged in family strategies, preventive and proactive, within their neighborhoods? Two types of activities index socialization strategy inside the household – the use of encouragement and collaborative activity between parent and child (labeled "work with child"). Strategies outside the home refer to efforts to involve the child in community activities, such as the YMCA and recreational groups, and to employ preventive measures, such as warnings of danger.

To discover what efficacious parents do in their neighborhoods, we computed zero order correlations between parent efficacy and the four family management strategies among black and white parents. Neighborhoods in Philadelphia are largely segregated and thus we obtained the correlations for parents in each racial group. All indications from aggregate level analyses suggest that black parents live in higher-risk neighborhoods when compared to white parents. Thus, one could argue that management strategies both in and out of the home are more required among black parents by the risks that their children experience.

The correlations in Table 2.1 show a rather striking racial difference. Black parents who rank high on personal efficacy are more likely to be involved in the use of management strategies when compared to white

Table 2.1. *Sense of parental efficacy and family management strategies, in* r *correlations*

Family Management Strategies	Correlates of Parental Efficacy		
	Black N = 264–291 r	White N = 117–128 r	Significance of Difference p
Inside Household			
Encouragement	.26	.11	.16
Work with child	.31	.05	.02
Outside Houshold			
Outside programs	.23	.11	.28
Proactive prevention	.25	.12	.22

parents. Indeed, level of personal efficacy as a parent tells very little about the use of these strategies in the white sample. Some efficacious parents may use them but others do not. The link is considerably stronger among black parents, though here too we find a number of efficacious parents who are not involved in strategies of family management. Clearly, we must know more about the particularities of neighborhood life in order to specify the connection between efficacious beliefs and actions.

Black parents rank higher on the use of family management strategies when compared to white parents, and especially in single-parent families (Elder, Eccles, & Ardelt, 1994). In particular, the single black mother tends to make greater use of community resources than white parents in this family situation. Whether single or not, black parents were devoting more effort to strategies with their sons, possibly in recognition of the neighborhood dangers to their well-being.

Philadelphia parents who feel efficacious and engaged in family management activities tend to have children who feel good about themselves and are engaged in organized activities in the community. They are less likely than other children to have problems at school. Only time will tell whether they are more likely than other inner-city children to survive neighborhood dangers and achieve a productive life.

Rural youth in a transformed world

Hard times in the inner city are mirrored in the agricultural world of youth in the Midwest. Children who were born in the early 1970s experienced the end of agricultural prosperity by the 1980s as the economy declined by a factor of a third or more (Elder, 1992). Between 1979 and 1982, construction starts and sales, among other indicators, plummeted by 40%. The significance of this change is expressed across three Iowa generations on the issue of farming. Four out of five of the grandparents in the study had farmed, and 20% of the parents continue to farm, but only seven of the young boys expressed any desire to farm when grown up.

The farm crisis of the 1980s reflected long-term forces that have increased the level of economic inequality between rural and urban worlds in the United States. These forces include the globalization of markets, the regionalization of commerce, and depopulation. A drastic devaluation of arable land in the crisis set in motion a series of adverse financial events that changed the face of rural life, sending countless families deeply into financial debt. An editorial in a small Iowa newspaper (Iowa Falls *Times-Citizen*, 1992) captured the losses of the decade:

> Rural Iowa has been damaged the most by the changing economic winds. While not broken, the rural fiber has been stretched until vacant store fronts, lost jobs, dwindling population, and decaying small towns dot the rural scene." (Conger & Elder, 1994, p. 4)

The Iowa study was designed in the 1980s to resemble major features of *Children of the Great Depression* (Elder, 1974) – in particular, by tracing the effects of economic hardship through family processes and individual adaptations to the experience of children. We focused on family processes while keeping our eyes on the larger scene of economic decline and its consequences for parents and children. Family processes became a way of thinking about the behavioral effects of this decline.

The analytic model assumes that economic hardship (low income, unstable work, and income loss) have adverse consequences for marital relations and the well-being of parents when they sharply increase the level of economic pressure. The effect of such pressure may be expressed through emotional depression and/or more conflict in marriage. In the second phase, marital discord and individual distress serve as a master link between economic pressure and ineffective parenting. Marital conflict, depressed feelings, and hostility among parents increase the risk of destructive parenting. In the third and final phase, destructive parenting links marital and individual distress with child outcomes. The assumption here is that marital conflict and ill-tempered parents have consequences for children, primarily by undermining the quality of parent behavior.

For an example of research based on this mediational model, consider a study of the Iowa boys during the seventh grade (Conger et al., 1992).

Using both observational and family member reports, we find that objective family hardship (measured by per capita income, debt to asset ratio, unstable work, and reported income loss) increased the risk of a depressed mood among mother and father through felt economic pressure. Depressed feelings made conflicted relations in marriage more likely, and consequently increased the risk of nonnurturing parental behavior in both parents. These behaviors in turn undermined the self-confidence, peer acceptance, and school performance of the boys. A similar process has been observed for girls (Conger et al., 1993).

All project research to date documents this "mediational sequence of links" and its account of economic hardship in families and life experience. Each link in the sequence plays an important role. The findings to date show remarkable correspondence to those obtained on families and adolescents in the Great Depression and in the Philadelphia project.

The trauma of farm loss

As might be expected, the most severe level of economic hardship involved families that were pushed off their land, the displaced farm families. A total of 59 of these families lost their farms during the late 1970s and early 1980s, a good many years before this study began, but they were still suffering the consequences in bouts of depression and unstable income. The wife of a man who lost his farm in 1981 observed that "it has been eight years now since we got off the farm and it's still very vivid in both of our memories." Her husband added sadly, "I still bear the wounds."

The history of economic crisis and emotional distress among displaced fathers points to notable psychological and health risks for their children. If emotional depression favors self-preoccupation, emotional distress and feelings of parent rejection should be especially common among the children of displaced parents. When compared to farm and nonfarm youth, the children from displaced farm families emerge very clearly as the high-risk group on emotional distress during the seventh grade and on the perception of rejection by father and mother. Furthermore, we find that these effects are concentrated in displaced families that ranked lowest on the emotional strength of the marriage and on the effectiveness of father's problem solving. In displaced families with strong marital bonds and effective problem solving, children held a more positive and resourceful image of self. Parents as models of mastery are clearly evident in the lives of these children.

As in the Great Depression, the children of hard-pressed families assumed more responsibilities, from unpaid chores to work on the farm and paid jobs in rural communities. Time pressures from large families and the working hours of mother, labor pressures on farms, and economic pressures jointly played a role in the work experience of the Iowa adolescents. The farm family most fully embraced the collective ethic of required helpfulness, the responsiveness of family members to the collective welfare of the family.

The contributions of farm boys in particular were valued by their parents. The more these boys earned from their projects, the more positive their parents' evaluations. By comparison, parental judgments of the working sons in nonfarm households were more often negative, reflecting the individualistic nature of work and earnings in these communities. However, the working boys in both worlds tended to describe themselves as industrious and efficacious, more so than other youth. The full significance of this work experience will not be known for some time, though it may well have shaped important disciplines that favor life success – dependability, independence, and perseverance.

Self-efficacy and the decision to migrate

When children of the farm crisis complete high school and pursue their future in the years ahead, they will enter a world that has little in common with that of their parents' adolescence after World War II. Consider a small town within the study area where the population has dropped below 800. A good many farms and young people have left the community, the local farms have expanded their acreage, and most families prefer to shop in the large cities, thereby contributing to the local business decline.

A middle-aged father and his 14-year-old son talk about the forces at work in the region (Shribman, 1991). After a long struggle, the father has decided to call it quits and give up the family farm. As he puts it, "I am tired of sitting here . . . and feeling that what I do is of no value." Not surprisingly, the boy has no desire for his father's life. As he sees it, farmers "are always in debt, they don't have any fun, they work hard and they don't get anything out of it." His plans call for college and life in the city. Judging from the Iowa study, self-efficacy and school success are likely to be distinctive of this youth's life history.

The importance of living near family or in the same community declines rather abruptly across the adolescent years of the Iowa sample.

Among farm boys and girls, identification with parents stands out as the major determinant of their desire to eventually live near parents. In the nonfarm group, those most interested in living near home were less successful in school and more attached to parents (Elder, Hagell, Rudkin, & Conger, 1993). This result is consistent with the selective nature of migration. Outmigration generally attracts the more capable members of the younger rural generation who have no prospect for life on a farm.

Is adult disenchantment with the declining quality of rural life a factor in the outmigration intentions of young people? Whatever the actual economic level and trend in particular communities, Iowa parents who regarded themselves most favorably on a sense of personal mastery were also most likely to feel satisfied with their hometown and immune to the lure of other places (Rudkin, Hagell, Elder, & Conger, 1993). For this age group, failure rather than a promising future has more to do with the desire to break local ties and move elsewhere. The process has greater kinship with structural displacement than with personal choice and agency. The Iowans who claim to have control of their lives remain positive about their communities, no doubt because they believe that they can act to improve them, no matter how diminished by economic dislocation and decline. The economic prosperity of the communities was controlled in the analysis.

Of course, feelings of personal efficacy might simply reflect or mirror community conditions and not represent a causal force in their own right relative to community satisfaction. With only cross-sectional data at hand, we have no way of ascertaining for certain whether influences flow in both directions or not. Nevertheless, the outmigration sentiments of fathers in nonfarm occupations did matter in the plans of both sons and daughters. These sentiments increased the likelihood of similar preferences across the generations. Though mothers' residential aspirations were not related to these preferences, both parents tended to characterize children with such aspirations as industrious. In farm families, fewer children held aspirations for living elsewhere, and those who did were not seen by their parents as industrious.

Conclusion

The course of human lives typically becomes problematic during eras of social transformation, a time when the ends of life frequently become obscure. Traditional beginnings through family upbringing and formal education no longer make sense in light of the changes in society. Neither custom nor contemporary rules provide adequate guidance. As noted in this chapter, problematic lives in changing times have typically attracted social inquiry and underscored the role of human agency in forming life trajectories. The life course paradigm evolved from such inquiry with its defining orientations: lives and times, linked lives and timing, and human agency in choice making.

The birth of life-course study occurred during the first decades of this century, an era of dramatic urban-industrial change. The approach became more complete as we know it today during the 1960s convergence of two strands of scholarship, one based on social relationships and the other on age and its meanings. Together, these bodies of work shaped a view of the age-graded life course, embedded in social relationships with significant others, and ever subject to social trends and influences. Once fashioned as a perspective, the life course model encouraged the study of lives in relation to social change.

This chapter explores three studies that reflect this history, with a focus on mastery experiences and models in the escape from disadvantage: (1) studies of children of the Great Depression; (2) an account of black and white inner-city children in Philadelphia; and (3) studies of rural nonfarm and farm children. The Depression studies of Americans who were born at opposite ends of the 1920s show that a successful escape from Depression hardship had much to do with their life stage when they experienced family misfortune and family adaptations. The younger children were more strongly influenced by economic hardship, especially the younger boys, but even here strong marriages and nurturant parents protected them from the full adversity of the times. In the transition to adulthood, military service played an important role in opening up career opportunities.

In Philadelphia and rural Iowa, the adverse consequences of family hardship and moderating influences closely resemble those observed among California families in the Great Depression. Among inner-city parents under economic pressure, economic hardship increased the risk of strong financial stress, depressed feelings, and a lack of personal efficacy, thereby reducing parental efforts in positive and protective experiences for their children. This causal sequence is particularly strong in single-parent households, but remains weak in families where the marriage is strong. Single black mothers, in particular, relied most heavily upon community resources.

The 1980s Great Farm Crisis forced a good many families off their farms and increased the level of family indebtedness to new and threatening levels. As in the Great Depression, lower levels of income, losses of income, and unstable work markedly increased the felt economic pressure of families, straining marriages and parent-child relations to the limit. These consequences were least severe among families with strong marriages. They were also least severe when fathers were effective problem solvers.

The Philadelphia and Iowa youth are too young for us to know about their adult lives in a world that is unlike the world of their parents. They have no control over the changes that are presently taking place, but their self-efficacy is certain to count in making choices. A sense of personal control matters most especially in social worlds that lack stability and continuity.

References

Baltes, P. B. (1987). Theoretical propositions of life-span developmental psychology: on the dynamics between growth and decline. *Developmental Psychology*, *23*, 611–626.

Bandura, A. (in press). *Self-efficacy: the exercise of control*. New York: Freeman.

Brehm, S. S., & Brehm, J. W. (1982). *Psychological reactance: a theory of freedom and control*. New York: Academic Press.

Bronfenbrenner, U. (1979). *The ecology of human development*. Cambridge, MA: Harvard University Press.

Bühler, C. (1935). The curve of life as studied in biographies. *Journal of Applied Psychology*, *19*, 405–409.

Clausen, J. A. (1993). *American lives*. New York: Free Press.

Conger, R. D., Conger, K. J., Elder, G. H., Jr., Lorenz, F. O., Simons, R. L., & Whitbeck, L. B. (1992). A family process model of economic hardship and adjustment of early adolescent boys. *Child Development*, *63*, 526–541.

Conger, R. D., Conger, K. J., Elder, G. H., Jr., Lorenz, F. O., Simons, R. L., & Whitbeck, L. B. (1993). Family economic stress and adjustment of early adolescent girls. *Developmental Psychology*, *29(2)*, 206–219.

Conger, R. D., & Elder, G. H., Jr. (1994). *Families in troubled times: adapting to change in rural America*. Hawthorne, NY: Aldine DeGruyter.

Durkheim, E. (1951). *Suicide* (J. A. Spalding & G. Simpson, Trans.). Glencoe, IL: Free Press. (Original work published 1897.)

Elder, G. H., Jr. (1974). *Children of the Great Depression: social change in life experience*. Chicago: University of Chicago Press.

Elder, G. H., Jr. (1975). Age differentiation and the life course. *Annual Review of Sociology*, *1*, 165–190.

Elder, G. H., Jr. (1979). Historical change in life patterns and personality. In P. B. Baltes & O. G. Brim, Jr. (Eds.), *Life-span development and behavior* (Vol. 2, pp. 117–159). New York: Academic Press.

Elder, G. H., Jr. (1986). Military times and turning points in men's lives. *Developmental Psychology*, *22(2)*, 233–245.

Elder, G. H., Jr. (1987). War mobilization and the life course: a cohort of World War II veterans. *Sociological Forum*, *2(2)*, 449–472.

Elder, G. H., Jr. (1991). Lives and social change. In Walter R. Heinz (Ed.), *Theoretical advances in life course research* (Vol. 1, pp. 58–86). Weinheim, Germany: Deutscher Studien Verlag.

Elder, G. H., Jr. (1992, March). Children of the farm crisis. Paper presented at the Society for Research on Adolescence, Washington, DC.

Elder, G. H., Jr. (in press). The life course paradigm: social change and individual development. In P. Moen, G. H. Elder, Jr., & K. Lüscher (Eds.), *Examining lives in context: Perspectives on the ecology of human development.* Washington, DC: APA Press.

Elder, G. H., Jr., & Caspi, A. (1990). Studying lives in a changing society: sociological and personological explorations. In A. I. Rabin, R. A. Zucker, & S. Frank (Eds.), *Studying persons and lives* (pp. 201–247). New York: Springer. (Henry A. Murray Lecture Series)

Elder, G. H., Jr., Caspi, A., & Van Nguyen, T. (1986). Resourceful and vulnerable children: family influence in hard times. In R. K. Silbereisen, K. Eyferth, & G. Rudinger (Eds.), *Development as action in context*, (pp. 167–186). Berlin: Springer-Verlag.

Elder, G. H., Jr., Eccles, J., & Ardelt, M. (1994). Inner city parents in high risk neighborhoods: their sense of agency and family strategies. Project mimeo.

Elder, G. H., Jr., Eccles, J., Ardelt, M., & Lord, S. (1995). Inner city parents under economic pressure: perspectives on the strategies of parenting. Unpublished manuscript.

Elder, G. H., Jr., Foster, E. M., & Ardelt, M. (1994). Children in the household economy. In R. D. Conger, & G. H. Elder, Jr. (Eds.), *Families in troubled times: adapting to change in rural America* (pp. 127–146). Hawthorne, NY: Aldine DeGruyter.

Elder, G. H., Jr., Hagell, A., Rudkin, L., & Conger, R. D. (1994). Looking forward in troubled times: the influence of social context on adolescent plans and orientations. In R. K. Silbereisen & E. Todt (Eds.), *Adolescence in context: the interplay of family, school, peers, and work in adjustment* (pp. 244–264). New York: Springer.

Elder, G. H., Jr., & Meguro, Y. (1987). Wartime in men's lives: a comparative study of American and Japanese cohorts. *International Journal of Behavioral Development, 10,* 439–466.

Elder, G. H., Jr., Shanahan, M. J., & Clipp, E. C. (1994). When war comes to men's lives: life course patterns in family, work, and health. *Psychology and Aging, 9(1),* 5–16.

Ge, X., Lorenz, F. O., Conger, R. D., Elder, G. H., Jr., & Simons, R. L. (1994). Trajectories of stressful life events and depressive symptoms during adolescence. *Developmental Psychology, 30,* 467–483.

Johnson, J. (1994, January). Personal communication. University of North Carolina.

Kertzer, D. I., & Keith, J. (Eds.). (1984). *Age and anthropological theory.* Ithaca, NY: Cornell University Press.

Lasley, P. (1994). Rural economic and social trends. In R. D. Conger & G. H. Elder, Jr. (Eds.), *Families in troubled times: adapting to change in rural America* (pp. 57–78). Hawthorne, NY: Aldine DeGruyter.

Linz, S. J. (Ed.). (1985). *The impact of World War II on the Soviet Union.* Totowa, NJ: Rowman and Allanheld.

Magnusson, D., & Törestad, B. (1993). A holistic view of personality: a model revisited. *Annual Review of Psychology, 44,* 427–452.

Mayer, K. U. (1986). Structural constraints on the life course. *Human Development, 29(3),* 163–170.

Meyer, J. W. (1988). The life course as a cultural construction. In Matilda W. Riley (Ed.), *Social change and the life course* (Vol. 1, pp. 49–62). Beverly Hills, CA: Sage.

Moen, P., Dempster-McClain, D., & Williams, R. M., Jr. (1992). Successful aging: A life-course perspective on women's multiple roles and health. *American Journal of Sociology, 97*, 1612–1638.

Newcomb, T. M. (1943). *Personality and social change: Attitude formation in a student community*. New York: Dryden Press.

Riley, M. W., Foner, A., & Waring, J. (1988). The sociology of age. In N. J. Smelser (Ed.), *The handbook of sociology* (pp. 243–290). Newbury Park, CA: Sage.

Riley, M. W., Johnson, M. E., & Foner, A. (Eds.). (1972). *Aging and society: a sociology of age stratification* (Vol. 3). New York: Russell Sage Foundation.

Rudkin, L., Hagell, A., Elder, G. H., Jr., & Conger, R. (1993, April). Perceptions of community well-being and the desire to move elsewhere. Paper presented at the British Psychological Association.

Rutter, M., & Madge, N. (1976). *Cycles of disadvantage: A review of research*. London: Heinemann.

Ryder, N. B. (1965). The cohort as a concept in the study of social change. *American Sociological Review, 30(6)*, 843–861.

Shribman, D. (1991, April 24). Iowa farms shrivel as the young people head for the cities. *Wall Street Journal*, pp. A7–A8.

Thomas, W. I., & Znaniecki, F. (1918–1920). *The Polish peasant in Europe and America*, Vol. 1 and 2. Urbana, IL: University of Illinois Press.

Velkoff, V., & Kinsella, K. (1993). *Aging in Eastern Europe and the former Soviet Union*. Washington, DC: Economics and Statistics Division, U.S. Department of Commerce.

Volkart, E. H. (1951). *Social behavior and personality: Contributions of W. I. Thomas to theory and social research*. New York: Social Science Research Council.

Wilson, W. J. (1987). *The truly disadvantaged: The inner city, the underclass, and public policy*. Chicago: University of Chicago Press.

3. Developmental analysis of control beliefs[1]

AUGUST FLAMMER

The developmental analysis of control beliefs serves at least three purposes – a theoretical one and two practical ones: (1) Understanding how control beliefs develop may provide insight into how they function. This is the so-called genetic approach (Baldwin, 1894; Lawler, 1978; Leont'ev, 1959; Piaget, 1947). (2) Knowledge of the developmental level at which a person is functioning fosters understanding of otherwise strange behavior. (3) Knowledge about normative developmental paths provides guidelines for the promotion of further development.

This chapter is about control beliefs and thus only indirectly about control. I distinguish among controlling (i.e., the actual regulation of a process), control (i.e., the potential to control or to regulate a process if necessary), and control belief (i.e., the subjective representation of one's capabilities to exercise control; Flammer, 1990). The focus of this contribution is on control beliefs as a mental or cognitive construct. Control beliefs are important for at least two reasons: (1) They are prerequisites for the planning, initiation, and regulation of goal-orientated actions and (2) they are part of the self-concept, where they determine to a large extent feelings of self-esteem, causing such emotional states as pride, shame, and depression. Control and control beliefs are mostly domain-specific; nevertheless there is some generality as shown in cross-domain correlations of individual differences in control beliefs.

Control beliefs are conceptualized as a composite of contingency beliefs and competence beliefs. *Contingency beliefs* are beliefs about the probability with which a certain action will lead to a certain outcome; *competence beliefs* refer to the ability to produce these actions oneself. This distinction is prevalent in several contemporary lines of research. Within his model of coping with stress, Lazarus (1966; Lazarus & Folkman, 1984) distinguishes between primary appraisal (whether a given situation is irrelevant, benign-positive, or stressful with respect to well-being) and secondary

Table 3.1. *Classical decomposition of control (beliefs)*

Lazarus	Appraisal of (successful) coping	=	Primary appraisal	+	Secondary appraisal
Bandura	Control belief	=	Response-outcome expectation	+	Efficacy expectation
E. A. Skinner	Control beliefs	=	Means-ends beliefs	+	Agency beliefs[a]
This contribution	Control beliefs	=	Contingency beliefs	+	Competence beliefs

[a] Interestingly, agency beliefs typically had higher predictability of performance than means-ends beliefs and control beliefs (e.g., Chapman, Skinner & Baltes, 1990).

appraisal (whether one has the required resources to cope with the situational demands). Correspondingly, Bandura (1977) distinguished response-outcome expectations and efficacy expectations, and E. A. Skinner (Skinner & Chapman, 1984; Skinner, Chapman, & Baltes, 1988b) introduced the notions of means-ends beliefs and agency beliefs, which taken together constitute control beliefs (Table 3.1).[2]

I will discuss the development of control beliefs on three different but interrelated dimensions: (1) the ontogenetic development of the structure of control beliefs, (2) the ontogenetic development of individual differences in the strength of control beliefs, and (3) the microgenesis of a given control belief. The first dimension describes the long-term *structural* development, the second the long-term *quantitative* development, and the third the actual or short-term emergence of a specific control belief.[3] There is a fourth interesting dimension that I will address only briefly. This deals with variations in the strength and the domains of control beliefs for different age groups and cultures.

The ontogenetic development of the control belief structure

A control belief is a personal construct of considerable complexity that is linked to environmental influences. Clearly, it is not present at birth but is gradually constructed during the lifetime of each individual. I will review the relevant literature, and for the sake of an organizational framework, I propose to decompose analytically the final product, thereby creating developmental hypotheses for its reconstruction (see Flammer, 1990). In order to provisionally test the empirical plausibility of this conceptual scheme, I will review the existing literature on the subject.

The logic of the structural composition of control beliefs

To believe in one's own control means to *self-consciously know that one is able to act in such a way that certain effects are produced*. Table 3.2 contains a proposed decomposition of this proposition and the five possible developmental steps leading to its realization.

Decomposition omits one conceptual constituent after another in a sequence that leaves the remaining composite of constituents in a form that still makes sense. Occasionally there is more than one possible omission. Although this procedure seems straightforward, there is at least one instance where an alternative is possible, that is, for the transition from (5) to (4). Instead of skipping the constituent "am able," one could just as well delete the constituent "self-consciously." Empirical research will have to verify whether or not both make sense, and if not, which is the more defensible.

To avoid repetition I will discuss this decomposition from the elementary to the complex level following the possible ontogenetic lines sketched out by the heuristic in Table 3.2.

The logical reconstruction and the ontogenetic construction of the control belief structure

I shall treat the precognitive prerequisites of control beliefs as subdevelopmental steps that lay the groundwork for my developmental theory.

- The most basic prerequisite for the establishment of a control belief is that *effects happen at all*. This prerequisite is met even by nonliving dynamic systems. For example, the mere physics of our solar system provides effects – water vaporizes and is transformed into rain, rivers erode mountains, and so forth.
- A second, less trivial prerequisite consists of *effects produced prebehaviorally by living systems at a purely physical or biochemical level*: Breathing transforms oxygen into carbon dioxide and so forth. Humans share this level of functioning with all living systems.
- Finally, a third prerequisite may be seen in *physical and chemical effects produced by behavior that is conceived of as mere reflexes and instincts*. Although such effects may alter the preconditions of further behavior through feedback processes, it is not yet implied that the organism perceives the feedback and regulates its behavior accordingly. Clearly, humans share this level of functioning with animals. As with most developmental competencies it is attained at a certain time in life and from then on remains effective. Even the actions of adults have unnoticed outcomes that are nevertheless influential.

Table 3.2. *Conceptual decomposition: From the mature control belief down to the mere production of effects*

(5) Control belief as part of the categorical self-concept	Self-consciously	knowing that	I am able	to act in such a way	that certain effects are produced.
(4) Self-awareness as the beginning of the categorical self-concept[a]	Self-consciously	knowing that	I	act(ed) in such a way	that certain effects are produced.
(3) Distinction between internal and external causes		(Consciously) knowing that	I	act(ed) in such a way	that certain effects are produced.
(2) Causal schema		Knowing (= being aware) that		certain actions	produce(d) certain effects.
(1) Event schema		Knowing (= being aware) that			certain effects happen.
- (no cognitive component)					Certain effects happen.
		Cognition	Competence		Contingency

[a] Self *concept* (Wylie, 1961) or catagorical self (Lewis & Brooks-Gunn, 1979) or "me" (Mead, 1934), as opposed to existential self (Lewis & Brooks-Gunn, 1979) or "I" (Mead, 1934).

Level 1. Functional experience: The event schema. The first noticed events in life are probably connected with one's own activities. They are not noticed as such but belong to the experience of one's own organism. This is especially true for the earliest (perceptual) "identification" of such happenings. Newborn babies accommodate their sucking behavior to the shape and the functional conditions of the mother's nipple; 3-day-old babies recognize the smell of their mother's milk; and by six days they can differentiate their mother's milk from that of other mothers (MacFarlane, 1975).

Although babies do not produce what they perceive all by themselves, they participate in this production. To a certain extent they start to regulate their behavior so as to maintain a certain set of effects. Learning takes place through contingent experiences: habituation, classical conditioning, instrumental conditioning (Janoš & Papoušek, 1977; Papoušek, 1967; Rovee-Collier & Lippsitt, 1982; Sameroff, 1968, 1971; Thoman & Ingersoll, 1993).

J. S. Watson (1966; 1967; 1971; 1979; Siqueland & DeLucia, 1969; Siqueland & Lippsitt, 1966; Watson & Ramey, 1972) showed that babies as young as 2 months old increase simple activities like moving their head or the nonnutritive sucking of a nipple if these actions move a mobile (for a review see Suomi, 1981). Apparently babies, like all humans, like the experience of behavior-event contingencies – provided the interval between the action and its effects is short (typically under 6 seconds) and both take place within a restricted domain of activities. Infants are also ready to enter into regulated interaction with their caregivers (Bruner, 1983; Papoušek & Papoušek, 1979, 1989).

This special liking for contingencies was identified and defined years ago by Karl Bühler (1919) as *"Funktionslust"* (meaning "pleasure of functioning") and by Jean Piaget (1936, 1937) as *primary circulatory reaction*. In line with Baldwin's (1894) concept of adualism, the primary circulatory reaction consists in maintaining the pleasurable state of a behavior-effect feedback loop in which the infant by chance happened to become engaged.

Research provides considerable support for the hypothesis that the experience of contingency (or noncontingency) creates expectations that become generalized to related behavior (Finkelstein & Ramey, 1977; Ramey & Finkelstein, 1978; Watson & Ramey, 1972).

Level 2. Elementary action towards an effect: The causal schema. According to Piaget, the first sign of a causal concept can be located in the *secondary circulatory reactions*. These include the initiation of the production of an effect, based on the perception of what produced that effect before. In the example of the mobile, after having experienced the contingency between the head's movement and the mobile's movement, the child sees the (non-moving) mobile as an invitation to produce the movement again. Piaget (1936) talks about a "systematic interest for causal relations" and places its onset around the end of the first half year of life. Such experiences of means–ends contingency between one's own behavior and perceptible effects have been shown to foster learning readiness and learning speed in later development (Finkelstein & Ramey, 1977; Gunnar, 1980a, b). A most interesting study by Marianne Riksen-Walraven (1978) with 9-month-old infants and their mothers has demonstrated that it is not stimulation as such (in terms of amount and variety of environmental objects) but the fact that handling objects produces contingent effects that fosters exploratory behavior and learning efficiency.[5] Automoving toys that initially frightened infants ceased to do so when the infants were able to control their movements (Gunnar, 1980a, b; Gunnar-VonGnechten, 1978). These results have important educational implications both for infant caregivers and for toy designers.

The effects discussed above are not based on the mere observation of external contingencies but rather on the basic personal activation of effects. This puts my rational decomposition in question: Are contingencies identified before and without one's own agency?

There is some interesting research about infants' perception of causal events that they have not produced by themselves. Based on Michotte's (1963) billiard ball–launching paradigm, Leslie (1982, 1984; Leslie & Keeble, 1987) had infants between 4½ and 8 months of age watch a brick moving halfway through a screen and hitting a second stationary brick in the middle of the screen, which subsequently moved out of the screen, apparently as a result of being struck. There were several types of events, for example, hit and launching ("really causal"), delayed movement of the second brick, no contact/collision between the first and the second brick but both moving in the same direction as in the first case, no collision and delay, and no collision/no reaction.

Leslie worked with the habituation-dishabituation procedure. After the infants had seen the same type of events several times, their fixation time per event rapidly decreased; they became habituated to it, that is, it lost its novelty value for the infants. After a series of events of the same type, they were shown an event of a different type that obviously had more novelty value and that resulted in prolonged fixation times, that is, the infants became dishabituated. Dishabituation turned out to be greater when the infants were habituated to the "really causal" type of event and then exposed to another type than with all other type sequences. Oakes and Cohen (1990) clearly found these effects with 10-month-old but not with 6-month-old children. Taken together with recent evidence by Cohen and Oakes (1993), the results show that infants under 6 months of age distinctly perceive various properties of objects (color, size, etc.), but not causal relations (hit and launch), whereas 10-month-old infants clearly perceive causality. Cohen and Oakes (1993) conclude that the causal schema is not an invariant cognitive module, but a cognitive schema that is gradually constructed.[6]

Is it possible that a perceptual causal schema is established without and before the establishment of a personal causal schema, that is, a schema the exclusive function of which is to classify one's own causal experiences? Or stated otherwise: Does the personal agency schema genetically precede a general causal schema, or is it a general causal schema that is eventually accommodated to a personal agency schema? The Piagetian tradition favors the first view, but Leslie's results speak in favor of the second; he is seconded in this conclusion by J. M. Mandler (1992).[7] A definite answer to this question is not yet clear, as it would have to exclude either the precedence of a personal agency schema or a general causal schema.[8]

Having identified Piaget's secondary circular reactions as prototypical level 2 actions, we are led to distinguish tertiary circular reactions as an additional level not foreseen in my conceptual analysis. I will call it "playing with causal schemata."

Level 2+. Playing with causal schemata. Tertiary circular reactions consist of arbitrarily varied actions with the apparent aim to create variations in the effect(s) or to produce a specific new effect (Piaget, 1936, p. 270). Piaget (as Hetzer in 1931) identified such actions in the object games that occur within the first months of the second year at the earliest.

Level 3. Doing by oneself: Attribution of internal causes. In the development so far, actions are aimed at specific goals or effects only because these effects are enjoyed as such and regardless of who really produced them. The distinction between *me* and *others* as the causal agents constitutes the next level of development in control beliefs. "Realization of personal agency requires both the self-observation that outcomes flow from actions and the recognition that the actions are part of oneself" (Bandura, in press, chap. 5).

Level 3 includes behavior such as refusing help and protesting against wishes and orders. It is typically introduced by talking about oneself, by calling one's own name, by talking about "I" and "me," or by repeated use of the phrase "by myself." Some authors have found such self-referential behavior already evident in 2-year-olds (Geppert & Küster, 1983; Müller, 1958). Others have found ignoring help rather than refusing help present in 1-year-old children (Klostermann, 1984, and Müller, 1984; both cit. from Lütkenhaus, Bullock, & Geppert, 1987, pp. 156–157).

Within his developmental analysis of achievement motivation, H. Heckhausen (1982, pp. 603–604) identified "centering on a self-produced outcome" as the first element of the achievement motive and "a clearer indication of achievement motivation" when such activities take the appearance of "wanting to do it oneself which . . . arises at the age of 2." A special aspect of the experience that one can personally produce and change effects is the possibility of not executing or of postponing actions. Not doing, being told not to do, and doing only when appropriate conditions are present is clearly more demanding than doing when or what one is told. Luria (1961, 1976), following the lead of Vygotsky (1934/1962), has described such events at length and demonstrated the influential role of speech in such regulation. Seen developmentally, regulative speech is initially social speech (from 1 year of age onward), which is subsequently interiorized to become overt private speech (3 to 4 years) and finally covert private speech (6 years); for similar results see Bivens and Berk (1990) and Harris (1990).

Research on delay of gratification (Mischel, 1957, 1974) has shown that the postponement of rewarding actions depends greatly on diverting attention from what is to be delayed to other things (Mischel & Mischel, 1983; Patterson & Mischel, 1976) and on happy versus sad mood (Fry, 1975). Although these experiments were conducted with school-age children, delay of gratification was repeatedly found in preschool children (Mischel, Shoda, & Rodriguez, 1989). In a recent study Shoda, Mischel, and Peake (1990) have shown that tolerance for delay of gratification in preschool years predicts the ability to cope with frustration and stress in adolescence.

Following Piaget's (1926) ideas, it is tempting to postulate an additional level between levels 3 and 4, that is, animistic (and artificialistic) thinking. However, more recent research has demonstrated that the passage through one or more of these modes of thinking is far from universal (Flammer, 1990; Valentin, 1991).

Level 4. Success and failure, a personal achievement. A success is a personal achievement that matches a personal standard. H. Heckhausen used pride and shame as indicators of success or failure respectively (Heckhausen, 1966). (For the identification of feelings of efficacy as developmental precursors of pride, see Stipek, 1983.) Heckhausen had children play with wooden blocks and construct towers to a certain height. He found that below 2½ years of age children were sometimes able to construct the tower as required, and they were apparently happy about it but not proud. Also, they often accepted their mothers' help to get the tower built. But after a certain point in life – around 2½ years of age – they did not want their mothers to steal the success from them. Joy over effects was replaced by the pride of being the producer of successes; anger over missing effects was replaced by shame about failures. These expressions of pride and shame were especially evident under competitive conditions, indicating even more clearly that personal action and success were combined: acting personally instead of relying on someone else (level 3) and achieving a personal success (or failure).

According to H. Heckhausen's (1966, 1982) research, the ontogenetic emergence of consciousness of personal success and failure occurs somewhere between 2½ and 3½ years of age.[9] Later research has demonstrated that this age may be lower with certain tasks or in certain social transactions (Bullock & Lütkenhaus, 1988; Halisch & Halisch, 1980; J. Heckhausen, 1988; Lütkenhaus, Bullock, & Geppert, 1987; for a review see Flammer, 1990, pp. 317–322). Interestingly, pride seems to emerge earlier than shame (Halisch & Halisch, 1980; H. Heckhausen, 1984; J. Heckhausen, 1988).

Level 5. Distinguishing different causes: The control belief. Empirically, the step from level 4 to level 5 may be very small. Apparently, children at level 4 not only view themselves as the personal causes of effects but also see themselves as being capable of attaining certain goals. I regard this as a generalization in the sense that children not only realize that they have produced a certain effect but that they are capable of producing that and similar effects in the future. This is a clear expression of an enduring concept of a categorical self.[10]

Empirical research has analyzed this level of the emerging distinction between causal factors that determine the outcomes of actions. These analyses largely follow Weiner's schema of causal attributions (Weiner, Frieze, Kukla, Reed, Rest, & Rosenbaum, 1971), extrapolating from causal attributions for the past outcomes to control attributions for future outcomes, that is, ability, effort, task difficulty (and powerful others), and luck. Although the differentiation may remain problematic in certain domains of achievement over the course of life, for the task domains in which children have abundant experience these differentiations are usually achieved during school years. There are two main developmental trends at this age. They include increasing differentiation of the conception of ability and the gradual reduction of a strong optimism in favor of more realism. I shall discuss the first trend here and the second later.

Level 5a. The global ability concept. The concept of ability in preschool children is typically an unstructured compound of ability, effort, visible outcome, objective feedback, and social feedback (Nicholls, 1978). When people are successful, children at this age may argue that they are smart *and* have put lot of effort into the task solution *and* were praised for the success. When they fail, they did so because they were not smart enough *and* did not work hard enough *and* were blamed for the failure. At this age, competence or smartness is seldom differentiated across performance domains like the academic or social. For example, a friend might be considered smart because he or she is neat, behaves well, and gets praised by the kindergarten teacher (Blumenfeld, Pintrich, & Hamilton, 1986; Stipek, 1981; Stipek & Tannatt, 1984; Yussen & Kane, 1985).

Level 5b. The effort concept. Around school entrance age, most children begin to focus on effort (intensity and length of work or of training) as the cause of success or failure (Nicholls, 1978). But, if questioned, they still do not explicitly distinguish effort from ability and task difficulty. This might be why the self-concept of young elementary school children is not affected much by failures. They feel they simply have to try harder (Miller, 1985; Rholes, Blackwell, Jordan, & Walters, 1980).

Level 5c. The concepts of ability and task difficulty. During the middle elementary school years, children begin to consider personal limits independent of effort (Nicholls, 1978), although – correctly – they take ability to be improvable through further development. But Kunnen (1993) found that even among 10- to 12-year-old children, many see ability as very unstable and substantially changeable within days.

A mature ability concept should logically be tied to the concept of task difficulty ("I am not able to perform tasks of great difficulty, but I am able to perform other tasks of lesser difficulty"). Nicholls has shown that a primitive task difficulty concept (e.g., the length of a song, the number of puzzle pieces) precedes a normative concept of difficulty, which is tied to whether a given person or any one of his or her classmates can solve it (Nicholls, 1980, 1984; Nicholls & Miller, 1984).[11]

Level 5d. The concept of compensation of effort and ability.   A full understanding of the compensatory relation between effort and ability is achieved only toward the end of the first decade of life (Karabenick & Heller, 1976; Kun, 1977; Kun, Parsons, & Ruble, 1974). Typical of this level is the understanding of the following interplay of ability and effort: If two persons correctly perform the same task but the first person takes more time than the second, then the first person is less able than the second. Certain authors argue that this understanding requires formal operations according to Piaget's theory of genetic epistemology (Nicholls, 1978).

It is only at level 5 in my conceptual scheme that the structure of a fully functioning control belief is achieved. This does not mean that this belief structure is attained in all domains of life, but it exists at least in those in which one has had considerable experience, such as the area of schooling. This is also the domain in which research has been largely concentrated. It is likely that educational experiences foster the differentiations described in level 5. Younger children have to learn to focus their attention and to spend enough effort on a task in order to develop a concept of effort. In the middle grades, individual differences become more consistent, perhaps through the introduction of performance grading and judgments of the probability of success in higher grades. Through these considerations the concepts of ability, task difficulty, and eventually their compensatory relations emerge.

Development of the concept of luck – luck being a counter-concept to control – has received little attention. Not surprisingly, young children include luck and effort in their concept of ability by attributing success to effort and ability even when the problem is unsolvable or solvable only by chance (Nicholls & Miller, 1985; Weisz, 1980, 1981). In the study by Skinner, Chapman, and Baltes (1988a), a decrease in luck in means-ends beliefs and in agency beliefs between the age of 7 and 12 was the most striking change of all (for comparable results see Rholes et al., 1980). Frieze and Snyder (1980) and Helmke (1993) found almost no attributions to luck in the elementary school years. It may be that young children first use the concept of luck as part of ability or smartness, then begin to realize the inappropriateness of such a concept and only then use it in an appropriate and differentiated way.

Further development?

In attaining level 5d, the control-belief structure is fully established. Speculation as to whether lawful developments beyond this level and beyond my conceptual analysis exist is tempting. I have proposed (Flammer, 1990) three further levels that describe consequences of the established control-beliefs, that is, (6) self-esteem, (7) contemplating and prioritizing values, and (8) confrontation with decrease in control. These levels most probably coexist. I therefore prefer to talk about life themes with developmentally changing priorities.

Self-esteem on the basis of personal control beliefs. The development of self-conceptions and self-esteem is probably extended over the whole lifespan. I regard the emergence of the explicit belief in personal agency producing nontrivial and valued effects as an important step in this development (Gekas & Schwalbe, 1983).

A certain amount of control over an array of possible events in life is an important condition for survival. Therefore, being good at exercising control provides physical and/or social power as well as social respect. People derive an important part of their self-esteem from the control they believe to have, as, for example, wielding social power. This is especially true in phases of life when the personal and social identity of the individual is at stake, especially in adolescence and beyond, but it is already true at school age.

Erikson (1968, p. 127) described school age identity as: "I am what I can learn to make work." Hausser (1983) related self-esteem to self-perception, the perception of personal control being one of the most important aspects of one's self-perception.

Research has repeatedly shown that when people have a choice, they prefer tasks that they believe they can perform with a high probability of success but lower than 1 (Atkinson, 1957; Stiensmeier, 1986; Strube, Lott, Lê-Xuân-Hy, Oxenberg, & Deichman, 1986; Trope, 1982). As Ruble and Flett (1988) and Boggiano, Main, and Katz (1988) have shown, this is especially true for generally successful students. The chronically unsuccessful students prefer either very easy or unrealistically difficult tasks so as to avoid unfavorable evidence about their capabilities.

Contemplating and prioritizing values. In middle adulthood most people realize that they have more control than they can really exert. Many experience stress both in not having control over important matters and in having control over too many – and possibly less important – things. Eventually most of them begin to choose, to weigh the opportunities, and to decide what seems most important to them in the long run. This is especially difficult if many highly valued personal goals are available or if several states of affairs are considered indispensable or even morally required. Tough decisions have to be made and evoke strong feelings of personal responsibility.

Confrontation with decline in control and death. As tough as the necessity of choice might be, it becomes even harder later in the course of life. Indeed with increasing age some important matters in life are less amenable to personal control. These include personal matters such as memory, physical strength, speed of information processing, influence over one's own children, and professional matters like enforced retirement, loss of political power, and so on. Of course there are still choices to be made and there is still control left, so the phrase "successful aging" (Baltes & Baltes, 1990; Baltes, Smith, Staudinger, & Sowarka, 1990) is not a euphemy. But it certainly includes among other things the serene acceptance of certain losses without falling into desperation or depression.

Most people have decades of life to prepare themselves for this last stage and even to practice it in specific areas like active elite sports, superperformances in the arts, and so forth. But it should also be noted that some people, such as the severely handicapped, are confronted very early in their lives with difficult and definitive limits.

Boundaries to personal control are omnipresent. Many of them affect unimportant matters in life; some are overcome through individual development and learning (and thus justify optimistic overestimation); some are exceedingly difficult to change and have always been there; and still others are more or less a permanent part of one's life (Flammer, 1990, pp. 144–191). There are many ways to deal with these limitations; for example, one might be despondent about one's state of affairs or accept them as part of one's life.

Rothbaum, Weisz, and Snyder (1982) proposed to distinguish a secondary from a primary mode of control. Secondary control is conceived as a strategy to change or adapt one's mind in an "attempt at understanding problems so as to derive meaning from them and to accept them" (Rothbaum et al., 1982, p. 12). While primary control seeks to change the environment to make it fit in with subjective aspirations, secondary control seeks to change subjective states (aspirations, perceptions, and interpretations) in order to make them fit in with the environment. In a strong sense, primary and secondary control are always coexistent. But the weight of secondary control processes is greater following (actual or antic- ipated) failure of primary control. Presumably there is a gradual shift from primary to secondary control over the course of life.

Band and Weisz (1988) have subsumed the following under secondary control: seeking social and spiritual support, emotion-focused crying, emotion-focused aggression, cognitive avoidance, pure cognition, and doing nothing (which clearly includes primary control as well).[12] These authors interviewed children between 6 and 12 years of age about typical reactions to stress situations. The study demonstrated a decrease in pri- mary control strategies (direct problem solving, problem-focused crying, problem-focused aggression, and problem-focused avoidance) and an increase in secondary control strategies with increasing age.

Similarly, Brandtstädter and Renner (1990) distinguished between assimilative coping (tenacious goal pursuit meaning primary control) and accommodative coping (flexible goal adjustment meaning secondary con- trol). They developed a scale to measure both types of coping. Although both modes of coping are positively correlated with high life satisfaction and low depression scores, data from a large sample of people between 34 and 63 years of age revealed a gradual shift from tenacious goal pursuit to flexible goal adjustment (see also Brandtstädter, Wentura, & Greve, 1993).

J. Heckhausen and Schulz (1993; in press) have enlarged the concept as well. In their view, secondary control is all actions targeted toward the self instead of the external world, these actions being mostly cognitive and rarely "active behavior." Based on clinical and adult developmental litera- ture, these authors strongly contend that secondary control is increasingly used over the adult course of life (to the debit of primary control), espe- cially when it comes to the advanced age level. Secondary control in terms of accepting imposed changes contributes to the well-being of old persons (Ryff, 1989).

Conclusion

The concept-analytical system as proposed in this chapter has proven to have heuristic value in that it integrates a large body of empirical findings in a coherent developmental system. Some of these findings have led to further differentiations (e.g., level 5), some related theorizing has sug- gested an additional level (i.e., level 2+), and some findings and reasoning have posed the yet unanswered question whether a general causal con- cept precedes the personal agency concept or vice versa. More im- portantly, my conceptual analysis only addresses development up to adolescence. I propose three further levels or life themes, albeit without the same analytic rigor.

Developmental conditions and strength of control beliefs: Control beliefs and developmental outcomes

The development of control beliefs has not only a structural side but also a quantitative side. Since the seminal work by Martin E. P. Seligman (Seligman, 1975; Seligman & Maier, 1967), scientists share the conviction that the subjective belief in a minimal amount of control over important matters is a necessary condition for personal well-being throughout life (e.g., Connolly, 1989). This conviction is not only shared by cognitivists and action theoreticians, but also by psychoanalysts (e.g., Broucek, 1979). A large body of empirical studies verifies this effect. Many of these studies were conducted with scales modeled after the locus of control scale (going back to Rotter, 1954, 1990), others emerged from the learned helplessness tradition (initiated by Seligman, 1975), and still others from the self-efficacy tradition (initiated by Bandura, 1977). Control beliefs have been shown to be good predictors of successful learning in school; performances in sports; marital satisfaction; health and recovery from illness; professional success and satisfaction; delay of gratification; happiness in old age; and coping with social conflicts, unemployment, and many other types of life problems like depression, withdrawal, and social passivity (for a review see Bandura, 1982, 1986, in press; Flammer, 1990; Lefcourt, 1976; Schwarzer, 1990, 1995; Syme, 1990).

Strength of control and strength of control beliefs over the lifespan

Having acquired the concept of control belief does not imply how much one believes in control over a specific state of affairs. People differ in strength of their control beliefs, and these differences also develop over time.

Human development, at least over the first several decades of life, generally increases individual control (Claes, 1981; Oléron & Soubitez, 1982). Physical conditions, psychological competencies, and social skills (e.g., power relations) enable most people to increase the number of domains in which they can exert control. Most humans are probably aware of this, but they do not take it into account when they are asked how much control they believe to have in general. As with personal satisfaction and well-being, people typically judge their personal strength of control by comparing themselves with similar people (Grant, 1988; Michalos, 1985).

The academically deficient students in a class typically remain deficient in their class, even if they make individual progress. If asked repeatedly to judge their probable performance on the same concrete school tasks, the judgment of elementary schoolchildren would mirror the actual increase of competencies over the years. But they do not consider such intra-individual changes when asked very general questions. Thus, Weisz and Stipek (1982), in a review of 33 developmental studies using 12 different locus of control scales over the elementary school age, found a slight over-all tendency in favor of the increase of internal personal control. In their review, Skinner and Connell (1986) found the cross-age data on locus of control inconsistent for childhood, but increasing from childhood to adult-hood, and virtually constant for adulthood and old age. According to more recent reviews (Gatz & Karel, 1993; Kogan, 1990; Lachman, 1986a; Lumpkin, 1986), including both cross-sectional and short-term longitudi-nal studies, the results for the adults and the older adults are not im-pressingly consistent either. Clearer patterns emerge when different con-trol domains are distinguished (Lachman, 1986b). Some but not all of the studies report a slight increase in internality between the ages of 20 and 60, and some but not all report a decrease in internality after the age of 60.

There are a few indications that control may vary over historical peri-ods, for example, increase in externality in the American 1960s (Schneider, 1971; cit. from Phares, 1978, p. 293) and in the Australian 1970s (Lange & Tiggemann, 1980), as well as increase in personal control belief in the Swiss 1980s (Grob, Flammer, & Neuenschwander, 1992), and decrease in American externality in parents aged 35 to 50 and in American grand-mothers aged 55 to 70 between 1971 and 1991 (Gatz & Karel, 1993).

Overestimation of control beliefs and the developmental value of high control beliefs

Control beliefs influence individual development. Persons high in control beliefs are not only happier with their present lives but also have a more positive outlook on their future lives (Brandtstädter, 1985, 1986, 1992; Brandtstädter, G. Krampen, & Baltes-Goetz, 1989; Brandstädter, Krampen, & Greve, 1987). They are also more likely to undertake actions that have a long-lasting bearing on their lives. Although high control beliefs raise the chances of change and development, people high in control or at least high in control beliefs may also undertake risky actions which can ad-versely affect development in the long run. This raises the question whether too much control could have adverse effects on happiness and success. Recent research has demonstrated at least two general findings concerning this issue:

1. Persons with high social power and responsibility have a higher risk of cardio-vascular diseases if they are not able to cope adequately with their challenges (Cohen & Edwards, 1989). Having too much control (and not being truly "in control of so much control") can apparently impair health and behavioral functionality.
2. Overestimating one's own share of control seems to be healthier than realistically estimating one's own control (Alloy & Abramson, 1982, 1988; Dunning & Story, 1991; Seligman, 1991; Taylor, 1989; Taylor & Brown, 1988).

First, I will consider the overestimation of control beliefs and the developmental value of high control beliefs. I will then identify conditions that foster high, stable, and generalized control beliefs.

Until recently, most theoretical lines of thinking valued the realistic estimation of life conditions and of one's competencies as the most desirable attitude in all cases (see Helmke, 1992, pp. 197–201). This appreciation has changed:

> Optimistic self-appraisals are a benefit rather than a cognitive failing to be eradicated. If self-efficacy beliefs always reflected only what people can do routinely, people would rarely fail but neither would they mount the extra effort needed to surpass their ordinary performances (Bandura, 1989, p. 732).

Whatever the mechanisms by which illusionary optimists reduce their vulnerability to depression, overestimation of control makes sense for further development. Optimism about the future includes anticipation of desirable events and self-ascribed competence to bring them about. This encourages corresponding actions that might be too difficult at first but can be developed through perseverance (Bandura, 1990; Bjorklund & Green, 1992; Taylor, 1989). Research has shown that the perception of high personal control is linked to children's motivation to explore their environment and to learn new things (Finkelstein & Ramey, 1977; Lewis & Goldberg, 1969; Ramey & Finkelstein, 1978). Helmke (1992) has shown that over a period of 1½ years students who were moderately optimistic achieved more progress in academic performance than students who were either grossly overoptimistic or unduly pessimistic.

Children. Developmental research on meta-cognition has long shown that children, especially younger ones, either grossly overestimate their capacities or underestimate the tasks and only during the middle elementary school years become more realistic (Entwistle & Hayduk, 1978; Helmke, 1993; Nicholls, 1979; Parsons & Ruble, 1977; Piaget, 1925; Skinner, Chapman, and Baltes, 1988a; and many others as documented in Stipek & MacIver, 1989, and in Helmke, 1992, pp. 202–203). It is likely that children, especially young children, often "confuse their desires and their expectations" (Stipek, 1984, p. 52; see also Schneider, 1989), an idea that fits in with the observation that preschool children have a very undifferentiated ability concept and are only beginning to consider the effect of effort. Effort allows overestimation of any magnitude, because the amount of possible effort may appear unlimited at this age. In addition, overestimation of one's own control may stem from the overestimation of contingency that characterizes both infancy and adolescence – and often also adulthood (Weisz, 1983).

Overestimation by children has been documented repeatedly (for a review see Stipek & MacIver, 1989). For illustrative purposes, I shall briefly review the (over)estimation of memory capacity (so-called metacognition of memory; Flavell & Wellman, 1977; Schneider, 1989).

If children, especially preschool children, are subjected to a memory task of a kind they know (memory span, recognition, recall) and asked how well they expect to do, they typically overestimate their actual attainments. Experience with the task corrects subsequent overestimation but typically does not eliminate it completely. Interestingly, this overestimation greatly decreases during the school years (cf. Table 3.3). One might ask whether this is due to a real developmental ceiling in these processes that the individuals gradually anticipate, or whether it is simply the scholastic experiences and the teacher's feedback that brings the optimism nearer to realism. According to research on the development of memory processes there are no reasons to expect that memory capacity reaches a ceiling toward the end of the first decade of life, not even the memory span (Schneider & Pressley, 1989). I do not know whether this is also true for general thinking of laypersons.[13]

Instead, it is likely that schooling dampens the developmental optimism. The correlation of the academic self-perception with objective school grades increases rapidly between grades two and five (MacIver, 1988; Nicholls, 1978, 1979). This is especially true if grading in school is frequent (MacIver, 1987; Rosenholtz & Rosenholtz, 1981; Simpson, 1981), highly differentiated both within the class and between performance domains (MacIver, 1988), and if it is made public (Rosenholtz & Simpson, 1984).

Achievement feedback is probably not very corrective for preschool children. One reason for this is that preschool children and children in the lower elementary grades rely much more on social feedback than on

Table 3.3. *Overestimation of one's own memory capacities from preschool to college age (in estimation/objective performance quotients)*

Study	Age Range	Nursery (N)	Kindergarten (K)	Gr. 1	Gr. 2	Gr. 3	Gr. 4	Gr. 5	Gr. 6	High School (H)	College (C)
Flavell, Friedrichs & Hoyt's (1970): Memory span	N, K, gr. 2, gr. 4	2.06	2.21		1.38		1.12				
Yussen & Levy (1975): Memory span	y. 4, y. 8, y. 20	2.47			1.22						1.06
Levin, Yussen, DeRose & Pressley (1977): Free recall	gr. 1, gr. 5, C			2.60				1.96			1.13
Levin, Yussen, DeRose & Pressley (1977): Recognition	gr. 1, gr. 5, C			0.79				0.90			0.70
Monroe & Lange (1977): Sum of all free recall tasks	preschool (5.1 yrs), gr. 2, gr. 5	1.82			1.10			1.00			
Worden & Sladewski-Awig (1982): Free recall	K, gr. 2, gr. 4, gr. 6		1.54		0.91		0.82		0.86		

objective or outcome feedback (Lewis, Wall, & Aronfreed, 1963; Spear & Armstrong, 1978; Stipek, 1987, for girls). Social feedback in preschool and in kindergarten is typically as encouraging and positive as possible, whereas in elementary school social feedback is increasingly combined with feedback about the level of academic performance and comparison with peers. Teachers' feedback becomes less and less arbitrary (Stipek & Daniels, 1988; for a review see Stipek & MacIver, 1989, pp. 532–534).

Another reason might be that schoolchildren have acquired concrete operations that enable them to coordinate different aspects. For example, they may realize that they have been weak in a ballgame but are still liked by their peers. However, this argument would imply that the overestimation of oneself and of peers is similar, which is not the case. Overestimation is typically more pronounced for oneself than for others (the so-called self-serving bias). Is it the case that control beliefs initially operate mainly in the service of self-esteem and only later guide action planning?

In a comparison of students from East and West Berlin in grades two to six, the Berlin Max-Planck researchers demonstrated that children in East Berlin had lower agency beliefs both generally and also with respect to school performance, but higher means-ends beliefs. In addition, their agency beliefs were more highly correlated with course grades (Oettingen, 1995; Oettingen, Lindenberger, & Baltes, 1992; Oettingen, Little, Lindenberger, & Baltes, in press; Stetsenko, Little, Oettingen, & Baltes, in press). Further analyses showed that the "depressive effects" on agency beliefs were mostly confined to the two thirds of the children at the lower end of the intelligence dimension (Oettingen & Little, in press). In addition, Oettingen convincingly demonstrated that the educational philosophy of the old GDR exerted considerable social pressure for realistic self-appraisal. Whether this applied to the examined classes and how this was done was not empirically assessed. But there is every reason to expect that these classes like all others received the official educational diet. Taken together with findings that control beliefs are correlated with achievement motivation (e.g., Skinner, Wellborn, & Connell, 1990), these studies document that educational systems can lower developmental optimism. The more systematic, emphatic, differentiated, and public the feedback, the greater its undermining impact. Nevertheless, this optimism does not typically become completely eradicated but only brought somewhat nearer to reality.

Overestimation with self-serving bias has also been found for motor performance but is clearly responsive to correction through performance feedback (e.g., Bjorklund, Gaultney, & Green, in press; cit. from Bjorklund & Green, 1992; Stipek & Hoffman, 1980; Stipek, Robert, & Sandborn, 1984) and for judgments of social competence (Ausubel, Schiff, & Gasser, 1952).

Skinner and Chapman (1987) propose that there are logical and empirical grounds for two seemingly contradictory hypotheses of development in childhood, that is, general increase in internality and decrease from optimism to realism. This is because the decrease in *absolute* values of internality (optimism to realism) runs parallel to a *relative* increase of internality (compared to externality). This is possible because both internality and externality decrease in absolute values.[14]

Adolescents, adults, and older adults. Some recent research has shown that overestimation of personal controllability is present among adults especially in developmentally relevant areas. J. Heckhausen (1990; see also Heckhausen & Baltes, 1991) has shown that, generally, younger, middle-aged, and older adults consider desired attributes as being more controllable than undesired ones, and that older persons (60 to 85 years) believe that undesired attributes occur later in life and are more controllable than do younger and middle-aged persons. Thus, people who are directly affected by important changes hold higher control beliefs over these changes than do persons who are not yet directly concerned with those aspects of life.

Old age clearly involves gradual decrements in capacities. Even if the control beliefs of aging people are generally higher than expected by younger people, most aging persons finally adapt their control beliefs to their objective reality (Lachman, 1983). The good news is that with most people, this "giving in" is not unduly anticipated: The majority of aging people are not so pessimistic that their fears tragically become self-fulfilling prophecies (Bandura, 1981).

If individuals are asked to compare their potential influence on developmental changes with most other people, they typically ascribe more control to themselves (Heckhausen & Krüger, 1993; Krüger & Heckhausen, 1993). This optimism is at least subjectively warranted, as the same people view their own development in later life more favorably than other people's development, both for increase and slowness of decrease in desirable attributes and for decrease and slowness of increase in undesirable attributes. In accordance with their optimism, middle-aged and old-aged people in the Heckhausen and Krüger (1993) study perceived themselves as appearing and as feeling younger than other people of their age.

Self-serving optimism has already been reported years ago (Miller & Ross, 1975; for a review see Zuckerman, 1979). As to self-ascribed control, a large sample of Swiss adolescents perceived themselves as generally having more control than their peers. This was the case for eight out of nine control domains, that is, for personal appearance, personality development, intimate relations, resolution of conflicts with parents, personal money, future working place, natural environment, and institutionalized learning opportunities. The exception was control of public matters. Not surprisingly, the few subjects feeling "less control than their peers" generally held very low control beliefs (Flammer, Grob, & Lüthi, 1987). Two years later, 1988 as compared to 1986, this self-serving optimism had even increased (Flammer, Grob, Lüthi, & Kaiser, 1989).

Studies about control illusions (Langer, 1975, 1983; Miller & Ross, 1975) are also relevant to the issue of overestimation of personal control. People believe they are exerting control even over clearly random events. As to the domains beyond control, Taylor and Brown (1988) have summarized evidence of systematic illusion phenomena with regard to self-image (most people think of themselves more positively than of most other people) and to the judgment of the future (most people believe that things will improve for them in the future, that their own future will improve more than that of others, and that undesirable events will occur to them with lower likelihood than to others). Taylor and Brown (1988) stress the findings that such illusions are positive for mental health, happiness, ability to care for others, and capacity for creative and productive work. Without mentioning possible developmental benefits, these effects may at least be regarded as important mediators for positive developmental changes.

Clearly, illusion of control can also be exaggerated. Donovan, Leavitt, and Walsh (1990), for instance, showed that persons with control illusions were more susceptible to learned helplessness in a temporarily uncontrollable environment; mothers with high control illusions were also more prone to depressed mood states (Donovan & Leavitt, 1989).

Developmental conditions for variations in control beliefs

Even if across average age groups general control beliefs do not reflect real control of and changes in control, such measurements may still reflect veridical and reliable individual differences both in control beliefs and in actual control. Again, since it is desirable to maintain a high sense of control, it is worthwhile studying the conditions under which individuals develop more or less stable beliefs in high or low control. Research so far has mainly centered on educational conditions and has rarely examined the broader ecology of socialization.

Educational practice. Many studies show that educational practices reflecting warm, supporting, sensitive, and responsive behavior result in positive attitudes and behavior in children. This is especially true for achievement motives (Heckhausen, 1991) and social attachment (e.g., Ainsworth, Blehar, Waters, & Wall, 1978; Donovan and Leavitt, 1989; Ford & Thompson, 1985). Some of these studies linking educational behavior to children's control beliefs are reviewed next.[15]

Infancy and preschool age. Interactive contingent responsiveness to infants' behavior by caregivers is an important condition for the development of high control beliefs. Skinner (1986) has demonstrated this with children between 3½ and 4½ years. Riksen-Walraven (1991) found that the girls (not the boys) in her above described sample who were allocated to the responsivity conditions at 9 to 12 months showed increased ego resiliency at the ages 7, 10, and 12. And several studies demonstrated that reported consistency of parental behavior (i.e., retrospective parental or children's reports), and retrospectively reported behavioral and attitudinal clusters like parental warmth, acceptance, and support foster later belief in internal control in children and adolescents, whereas retrospectively reported punitive and overly "controlling" behavior as well as hostile attitudes produce more belief in external control (see review in Diethelm, 1991, pp. 15–34). Similarly, observational studies have shown that contingency of parental behavior in response to infants' behavior is associated with several desirable outcomes in children and adolescents, like exploratory behavior at a very young age (Diethelm, 1991, 1992; Van Aken & Riksen-Walraven, 1992), ego resiliency (Van Aken & Riksen-Walraven, 1992), and learning efficiency.

From the Fels longitudinal study Katkovsky, Crandall, and Good (1967) reported positive correlations between parental protectiveness, affection, and approval at the age of 6 and the internality of the adolescent's locus of control at age 12. Surprisingly and hard to explain, the direction of the relations was reversed when the adolescents became young adults (Crandall & Crandall, 1983): Observed punitive, critical, and affectively negative maternal behavior between age 0 and 6 was related to the internality of the young adults' locus of control. Whether this change over the development from infancy to young adulthood is reliable or rather a yet undetected artifact remains to be investigated with new samples. Carefully planned longitudinal studies are needed with direct observation of contingent parental behavior in early infancy and measures of the children's control beliefs in subsequent years.[16]

As to further short-term investigations, there is some evidence that parental behavior that is contingent with infants' behavior later results in high control beliefs (Dunham & Dunham, 1990). Contingent turn taking between mother and infant was correlated with the level of performance on a subsequent nonsocial contingency task.

School age. Belief in high personal control over the mastery of tasks has been shown to be a strong predictor of scholastic achievement (see Zimmerman, 1995; Hackett, 1995). The concern of this chapter is whether educational practices have an impact on resultant control beliefs.

There is no doubt that repeated failure to exercise control over outcomes can create a sense of helplessness. Numerous experimental studies have used this procedure to induce helplessness, that is, by having subjects try to solve unsolvable anagrams. For some children school might indeed be a place of continuous failure.

Schunk (1989) has published numerous studies on how different types of educational practices affect children's beliefs in their academic efficacy. Among the identified factors are modeling, attribution feedback, positive incentives for accomplishments, social comparison with peer accomplishments, and so on.

An important educational asset is the guidance of casual attributions after success and after failure. Dweck (1975) had helpless children undergo an attribution retraining and found that providing successes alone was less effective than a training with a mixture of success and failure. This was true both for subsequent performance and for subsequent effort attributions.[17] Schunk (1983) demonstrated that rewards boosted control beliefs of former low control and low performance pupils, but only when they were contingent with successful performance – pity alone or sympathy for the helpless does not help! – and when the feedback was related to the pupil's own success or failure (Schunk, 1982) – encouragement alone without attainment may not be helpful either!

Reward per se is not an educational tool to be recommended. Its effects can be negative depending on whether or not it is contingent with past attainments, the subjective difficulty of the performance, and many other situational conditions (Lepper & Greene, 1975). For example, praising success on an evidently easy task raises self-confidence of younger children but lowers the confidence of older children and adults (Barker & Graham,

1987; Meyer, 1984, 1992; Meyer, Bachmann, Biermann, Hempelmann, Ploger, & Spiller, 1979). One might expect comparable effects on control beliefs.

In sum, schooling generally reduces the overestimation of control beliefs, can raise unjustifiably low control beliefs, and fosters accurate self-evaluation (Stipek, 1981). However, a strong setting of school learning sets the limitations for change, because acquired low or high control beliefs in one subject easily become generalized to other subjects that are taught by the same teacher (Dweck & Reppucci, 1973).[18] Entering a new class (i.e., having new teachers and new peers) or a new school system with a new curriculum provides opportunities to raise low control beliefs, but different and difficult transitional experiences may also undermine efficacy expectations (Midgley, Feldlaufer, & Eccles, 1989).

Personality factors. The development of individual differences in control beliefs is certainly not independent of the development of other personality characteristics. Possible factors are physical appearance, bodily constitution, intelligence, temperament, and so forth. However, there is no relevant research on this question with a developmental perspective.

Ecological and cultural factors. Ecology refers to the general living conditions in society and in a given culture, as materialized in political and other institutions, material resources, libraries, traffic systems, leisure opportunities, and so on.

Differences in control beliefs have been found among adolescents in different educational tracks by Flammer et al. (1987). Adolescents attending vocational training in Switzerland had lower control beliefs in most domains than students of the Gymnasium. This was especially so for expected control in the near future. Vocational trainees in the so-called dual system are probably confronted earlier and more directly with economical and social realities than are college students. A study by Kumpfer and Turner (1991) found relationships between school climate and self-efficacy beliefs (see also Gekas, 1989).

Another example of a specific ecology are nursing homes for permanent residents. In observing the residents' and staff's behavior, M. M. Baltes, Burgess, and Stewart (1980) found that while the residents' independent behavior was discouraged by nonresponsive behavior from the staff, dependent behavior was reinforced by dependence-supporting behavior. Although control beliefs were not measured, such practices are likely to shape control beliefs, reflecting lack of control for some but indirect control for others (Baltes, 1982, 1988; Baltes & Skinner, 1983; Baltes & Wahl, 1992; Wahl & Baltes, 1990). Other studies have demonstrated that elderly residents with opportunities to exercise control were more active, happier, and healthier (Langer & Rodin, 1976; Rodin & Langer, 1977; Schulz, 1976; Schulz & Hanusa, 1978).

Little is known about cultural differences in control beliefs. Some studies have stated that individuals in more collectivist cultures rely less on personal control and are more prone to secondary control. Such studies have been conducted with Malayan University students (Essau, 1992; Seginer, Trommsdorff, & Essau, 1993) and with Japanese mothers (Trommsdorff, 1989, based on interviews). In a quasi-replication study of Essau's (1992), using the same variant of the Response to Control-Failure Questionnaire (RCFQ) by Flammer, Züblin, and Grob (1988), Flammer (1992) found that, confronted with failure of a control attempt, Japanese adolescents as compared to Swiss adolescents were not more prone to secondary control but were more ready to relinquish personal control altogether, while the Swiss adolescents were more tenacious in primary control.

Berry and Bennett (1992) investigated Cree[19] conceptions of cognitive competence with a card sort paradigm. They found that these conceptions were opposite to the phrase "lives like a white person" and were associated with "taking time, good, hard-working, careful, patient, self-sufficient, strong developing, bush-related, and easy to see," presumably unlike "Western notions of intelligence as being fast, analytic and without social or moral dimensions" (Berry & Bennett, 1992, p. 73).

The microgenesis of control beliefs (*Aktualgenese*)

The concept of development typically applies to long-term individual development; only in a broader sense does it also include the short-term development of competence, ideas, attitudes, and so forth. Following the Gestalt psychological distinction between *Ontogenese* and *Aktualgenese*, I shall call the first ontogenesis and the second microgenesis. Microgenesis is not only a parallel to ontogenesis, but often draws upon ontogenesis.

The microgenetical question in our context is: When people are confronted with a concrete difficult task, why do they come to believe that they are able or not able to solve it?[20] Of course, people have had past experiences, they know something about task demands and about themselves. But such knowledge has to be activated, retrieved, or reconstructed from memory. And in many instances there is good reason to believe that certain people underestimate or overestimate their control despite the fact that their own valid experiences could have taught them better.

One reason for erroneous self-assessment may be found in the way people organize their knowledge in memory or in the strategies they use in searching for relevant memory contents. Williams (1988; Moore, Watts, & Williams, 1988; Williams & Broadbent, 1986; Williams & Dritschel, 1988; Williams & Scott, 1988) has been able to show that clinically depressive patients and patients with a foregoing suicide attempt react differently than average or "normal" persons if asked to recount a personal experience in response to a cue word. They were not only generally slower than "normal" persons, but specifically so in reaction to positive cues (exception: Williams, 1988); they were also less specific than "normal" persons, again especially in reaction to positive cues (see also Lloyd & Lishman, 1975).[21] This could mean that depressive and suicidal persons have less salient and less distinct encodings of positive experiences than of negative experiences and are therefore less inclined to ascribe control to themselves.

A way to examine the cognitive processes in judgment of personal control is to ask subjects why they think they are able or unable to reach certain goals. Flammer and coworkers interviewed adolescent and adult subjects about several possible tasks and challenges and eventually asked them in a seemingly casual way why they responded as they did. The results indicate that individuals most often refer to dispositional attributes. Second in frequency are references to personally experienced episodes.[22] If questioned further, the subjects indicated that they trusted more in those control beliefs for which they had referred to concrete experiences than in those based on dispositional attributes (Flammer and Kaiser, 1992; Flammer, Kaiser, Lüthi, & Grob, 1990). This in spite of the fact that they referred to dispositions more often than to experienced episodes. The latencies before the yes/no answer were shorter, when the following reference answer was episodical than when it was dispositional (Flammer & Grob, 1994).

Taken together with the finding that in the oral format the episodic answers were more frequent than in the written format, these results probably mean that individuals prefer the episodic foundation of their control beliefs but often do not have such remembered episodes at hand. Also, Güggi (in prep.) has data showing that people trust more in other people's promise of competence if they refer to repeated former experiences than if they refer either to their general abilities or to one unique experience.

Confronted with the same frame of questioning, elementary school children very often answer the why question by recounting how they would proceed or by commenting on the task. Although the proportion of such answers decreases with age, reference to motives actually increases with age (Wicki, Reber, Flammer, & Grob, 1994). This might correspond to the increased importance of effort attributions for success and failure during the school years (see the section "School Age"). It also corresponds to Flammer and colleagues (1990) and Flammer and Kaiser's (1992) findings that adolescents, in comparison to older adults, often refer to dispositions under belief in control and proportionally less under belief in no control. It seems that adolescents are still very optimistic as to their control unless they have experienced specific failures.

Another reason for spontaneously more or less accurate estimations (or reasonable overestimations) of one's own control may be found in different mood states. Positive moods raise control beliefs; negative moods lower them (Alloy, Abramson, & Viscussi, 1981; Amrhein, Salovey, & Rosenhan, 1982; Brown, 1984; Kavanagh & Bower, 1985; Salovey & Birnbaum, 1989; Wright & Mischel, 1982; but: Masters & Furman, 1966, and Underwood, Froming, & Moore, 1980, did not find a correlation between mood and locus of control). Mood may be part of a vicious circle in control perception: Failure produces disappointment and bad mood; bad mood makes failure more salient, so that the individual either avoids challenges or chooses unsolvable tasks; this produces failures and the repeated perception of one's own deficiencies.

Although the microgenesis of control beliefs is not just a parallel or an analogy of the individual development of control beliefs, it apparently draws on past experiences and development and guides and assists further development. Recall of past success and failure determines actual convictions; such remembering might be spontaneous or – in order to avoid vicious circles – therapeutically guided (Lüthi, 1990; Flammer & Scheuber-Sahli, in press; Teasdale, 1978).

Conclusion

The developmental analysis of control beliefs has addressed three facets, namely the structural facet, the quantitative and differential facet, and the microgenetic facet. The first facet included a conceptual analysis covering the first dozen years in life. The further development of control beliefs up to old age is conceptually less developed. The structural development of control beliefs is indeed concluded by adolescence, at least in certain domains, as in the educational domain. How much and under which conditions these structures transfer from one domain to another remains an open question. But even if some positive transfer occurs, there is still the need for domain-specific experiences, and this is probably what determines most of the adult development of control beliefs.

Do the three levels proposed for the adult development of control beliefs represent structural growth in the same sense as the preceding levels? In a way the answer is yes, in that they structure the consequences of the previous perception of actual control and no control. They add essential new elements in a nonarbitrary way. Although the limitation element is not completely new, most limitations in children are surmountable through effort and learning, whereas adults perceive some of them as less changeable (Flammer, 1990, pp. 162–192).

The research on the second facet, the quantitative and differential one, has been explored most extensively. The knowledge from this line of research is of evident educational and sociopolitical importance.

The least advanced research facet is the third, the microgenesis of control beliefs. In a way this is surprising because these processes are omnipresent in everyday life. Whether and why one underestimates or greatly overestimates actual control is very consequential. Teachers and psychotherapists focus much of their attention on this.

Notes

1. The author acknowledges valuable comments and/or editorial help from Françoise Alsaker, Margret M. Baltes, Albert Bandura, Nicki Crick, Jeannine Dumont, Alexander Grob, Gay Ladd, Serge Mühlethaler, Rolf Reber, Emma Smith, Urs Tschanz, and Werner Wicki.
2. Comparable distinctions have also been proposed by Weisz and Stipek (1982): Contingency judgment + Competence judgment = perceived control; Gurin and Brim (1984): Judgment of system responsiveness + judgment of personal efficacy = sense of control; and Ford and Thompson (1985): Perceptions of control + perceptions of competence = personal agency beliefs.
3. The German Gestalt psychologists distinguished the *Ontogenese* (ontogenesis, meaning long-term individual development) from the *Aktualgenese* (the actual and short-term emergence, or microgenesis, of a mental entity, i.e., a Gestalt).
4. By consciousness in this context I mean that a person deliberately attributes the predicate of doing or being able to do to himself or herself in the sense of the categorical self. What is done consciously may be recalled on the basis of retrieval from memory and not only by retrospective inference. I equate the mere knowing that one is able to act in such a way that certain effects are produced with "feeling of control."
5. However, later data within this longitudinal study showed no correlations between the children's exploratory competence at 30 months and their exploratory competence at 12 months nor with their mothers' sensitivity (Meij & Riksen-Walraven, 1992).
6. A careful study by Spangler, Bräutigam, and Stadler (1984) deserves to be mentioned here. These authors observed 14 infants between the ages of 14 and 17 months intensively and described behavior categories that represent further differentiations of my

levels 2, 2+, and 3. The individual sequence of the first appearance of each category was almost perfect, that is overall:

1. short action for immediate short effect (e.g., clapping two wooden blocks) = Level 2(+)
2. continued action for continued effect (e.g., pulling wooden duck on a string) = Level 2(+)
3. action for later effect (e.g., throwing a ball) = Level 2(+)
4. seemingly planned action without consideration of the effect (e.g., filling a bucket with sand) = Level 2+
5. planned action with consideration of the effect (e.g., building and correcting a wooden pyramid) = Level 2+
6. actions with reference to personal origin (i.e., refusing help, showing what is achieved) = Levels 3 and 4.

7. Kaye's (1982) data also favor the view that personal agency comes after the general causal schema. He had 6-month-old infants learn to retrieve objects hidden behind screens by observing adult models. Having acquired the skill through observation, the infants generalized it to other objects and transferred the action from one hand to another. However, these findings may be indicative only of the microgenesis of specific schemata, not of the very first agency schema.

8. Correctly inferring contingency is not a simple process applicable to any contingent relation. There is a long cognitive pathway from simple perception of two temporally contingent events to complicated logical structures of dependency (Shaklee & Goldston, 1988; Shaklee, Holt, Elek, & Hall, 1988; Weisz, 1983).

9. H. Heckhausen (1982, p. 606) identified the "attribution of the outcome of an action to one's own competence and self-evaluation of competence" as emerging after age 3 as the 2nd level (or "characteristic") of his developmental theory of achievement motivation. This corresponds to the levels 4 and 5 of my scheme.

10. Clearly, more primitive "self-concepts" arise earlier in life, depending on the definition of self-concept (e.g., Stern, 1985).

11. Heinz Heckhausen (1982, p. 608 ff.) postulated "distinguishing between degrees of task difficulty and personal competence," which according to him is achieved by the 5th year as the 3rd level or "characteristic" in his analysis. His 4th level or "characteristic" consists of "distinguishing between the causal concepts of ability and effort." The remaining 8 levels or "characteristics" of H. Heckhausen's (1982) analysis are of special interest to motivation and are therefore not documented here.

12. The secondary control concept was rather heterogeneous from the beginning: Rothbaum et al. (1982) included predictive, illusionary, vicarious, and interpretive secondary control. Although some researchers have narrowed the concept by focusing on the postfailure control strategy of discounting the missed goal and highlighting a related higher-order goal that is presumably preserved and even better served through the failure at hand (Essau, 1992; Flammer et al., 1988), others have made it even broader (Band & Weisz, 1988; Heckhausen & Schulz, in press).

13. This raises the question whether a social representation of the developmental ceiling to memory exists, maybe specifically for memory span. However, the data in Table 3.3 does not show such a differentiation between different types of memory processes.

14. However, there seems to be a problem with the scale, because internality and externality combined are exhaustive and their sum should therefore remain constant. There is also a problem with the validity of this finding, because it rests on means-ends belief data and not on agency data. Internality of agency remained more or less constant in the Skinner, Chapman, and Baltes (1988a) study (effort decreasing, ability increasing), and externality of agency too did not markedly change (luck decreasing, powerful other increasing). Although one could conclude that the controllability judgments (i.e.,

means-ends judgments) decrease, one cannot conclude from this study that personal agency judgments or personal control judgments decrease during the normal school years.

Again, this does not exclude the fact that control indeed increases, but the control beliefs probably do not. Control beliefs are probably relative to what one thinks everyone else is able to control and relative to what one thinks is controllable at all (cf. comparative results with happiness and well-being).

15. There are many educational studies investigating control beliefs as independent variables. In contrast to most other contributions, the focus here is on control beliefs as dependent variables.

16. I know of one such prospective study done in Fribourg and Hamburg; what is reported so far covers only the first year of the subjects' lives and clearly does not tap control *beliefs* yet (Diethelm, 1991). There were positive correlations between contingency of parental behavior in the 2nd month and exploratory behavior and fearlessness of unknown adults in the 12th month of life.

17. Although the changes in the Intellectual Achievement Responsibility Scale – a control belief – like measure by Crandall, Katkovsky, and Crandall (1965) – were inconsistent, I take the positive effects on effort attributions as an indicator of a possible increase in control belief. Persistence in trying to solve a task is clearly correlated with high control beliefs (Lütkenhaus, 1987). For a comparable study see Chapin and Dyck (1976).

18. Again, the dependent measures were only performances and not control beliefs.

19. The Cree are a group of native Indians living in northern Ontario.

20. An additional question would be why people are interested in finding out whether they are able to master a given task. I skip this interesting literature (e.g., Atkinson, 1957; Boggiano, Main, & Katz, 1988; Klonowicz & Zawadzka, 1988; Stiensmeier, 1986; Strube, Lott, Lê-Xuân-Hy, Oxenberg, & Deichman, 1986; Trope, 1982; for a review see Flammer, 1990, pp. 199–202).

21. It must be added that extension studies did not yield the same results neither with adolescents with generally low control beliefs within the "normal" population range (Flammer & Rheindorf, 1991) nor with clinically depressive adolescents (Avramakis & Joray, 1991). The last investigation did yield generally less specific answers in depressive adolescents, but neither pronouncedly less specific nor slower to positive cues.

22. Surprisingly, in three investigations with a total of 661 subjects and 10 answers each there were almost no references to models, about 1 out of 100.

References

Ainsworth, M. D. S., Blehar, M., Waters, E., & Wall, S. (1978). *Patterns of attachment.* Hillsdale, NJ: Erlbaum.

Alloy, L. B., & Abramson, L. Y. (1982). Learned helplessness, depression, and the illusion of control. *Journal of Personality and Social Psychology, 42,* 1114–1126.

Alloy, L. B., & Abramson, L. Y. (1988). Depressive realism: Four theoretical perspectives. In L. B. Alloy (Ed.), *Cognitive processes in depression: Treatment, research and theory* (pp. 223–265). New York: Guilford.

Alloy, L. B., Abramson, L. Y., & Viscussi, D. (1981). Induced mood and the illusion of control. *Journal of Personality and Social Psychology, 41,* 1129–1140.

Amrhein, J., Salovey, P., & Rosenhan, D. L. (1982). Joy and sadness generate attributional vulnerability in men. Unpublished manuscript. Stanford University.

Atkinson, J. W. (1957). Motivational determinants of risk-taking behavior. *Psychological Review, 64,* 359–372.

100   August Flammer

Ausubel, D., Schiff, H., & Gasser, E. (1952). A preliminary study of the developmental trends in socioempathy: Accuracy of perception of own and others'
sociometric status. *Child Development, 23,* 111–128.

Avramakis, J., & Joray, M. (1991). Bereichsspezifische Kontrollattributionen und
autobiographisches Gedächtnis bei Jugendlichen mit depressiver Stimmung
[Domain-specific control attributions and autobiographical memory in depressive adolescents]. Lizentiatsarbeit. University of Berne.

Baldwin, J. M. (1894). *The development of the child and of the race.* New York: Macmillan.

Baltes, M. M. (1982). Environmental factors in dependency among nursing home
residents: A social ecology analysis. In T. A. Wills (Ed.), *Basic processes in helping
relationships* (pp. 405–425). New York: Academic.

Baltes, M. M. (1988). The etiology and maintenance of dependency in the elderly:
Three phases of operant research. *Behavior Therapy, 19,* 301–319.

Baltes, M. M., Burgess, R. L., & Stewart, R. B. (1980). Independence and dependence in self-care behaviors in nursing home residents: An operant-observa-
tional study. *International Journal of Behavioral Development, 3,* 498–500.

Baltes, M. M., & Skinner, E. A. (1983). Cognitive performance deficits and hospital-
ization: Learned helplessness, instrumental passivity, or what? Comment to
Raps, Peterson, Jonas, and Seligman. *Journal of Personality and Social Psychology,
45,* 1013–1016.

Baltes, M. M., & Wahl, H. W. (1992). The dependency-support script in institutions:
Generalization to community settings. *Psychology and Aging, 7,* 409–418.

Baltes, P. B., & Baltes, M. M. (Eds.). (1990). *Successful aging.* Cambridge: Cambridge
University Press.

Baltes, P. B., Smith, J., Staudinger, U. M., & Sowarka, D. (1990). Wisdom: One facet
of successful aging? In M. Perlmutter (Ed.), *Late life potential* (pp. 63–81). Washington, DC: The Gerontological Society of America.

Band, E. B., & Weisz, J. R. (1988). How to feel better when it feels bad: Children's
perspectives on coping with everyday stress. *Developmental Psychology, 24,*
247–269.

Bandura, A. (1977). Self-efficacy: Toward a unifying theory of behavioral change.
Psychological Review, 84, 191–215.

Bandura, A. (1981). Self-referent thought: a developmental analysis of self-efficacy.
In J. Flavell & L. Ross (Eds.), *Social cognitive development: Frontiers and possible
futures* (pp. 200–239). Cambridge: Cambridge University Press.

Bandura, A. (1982). Self-efficacy mechanism in human agency. *American Psychologist, 37,* 122–147.

Bandura, A. (1986). *Social foundations of thought and action: A social cognitive theory.*
Englewood Cliffs, NJ: Prentice-Hall.

Bandura, A. (1989). Regulation of cognitive processes through perceived self-efficacy. *Developmental Psychology, 25,* 729–735.

Bandura, A. (1990). Conclusion: Reflections on nonability determinants of competence. In R. J. Sternberg & J. Kolligian (Eds.), *Competence considered* (pp. 315–
362). New Haven, CT: Yale University Press.

Bandura, A. (in press). *Self-efficacy: The exercise of control.* New York: Freeman.

Barker, G., & Graham, S. (1987). Developmental study of praise and blame as attributional cues. *Journal of Educational Psychology, 79,* 62–66.

Berry, J. W., & Bennett, J. A. (1992). Cree conceptions of cognitive competence.
International Journal of Psychology, 27, 73–88.

Bjorklund, D. F., Gaultney, J. F., & Green, B. L. (in press). "I watch, therefore, I can
do": The development of meta-imitation over the preschool years and the

advantage of optimism in one's imitative skills. In M. L. Howe & R. Pasnak (Eds.), *Emerging themes in cognitive development* (Vol. 2). New York: Springer.

Bjorklund, D. F., & Green, B. L. (1992). The adaptive nature of cognitive immaturity. *American Psychologist, 47,* 46–54.

Bivens, J. A., & Berk, L. E. (1990). A longitudinal study of the development of elementary school children's private speech. *Merrill Palmer Quarterly, 36,* 443–463.

Blumenfeld, P., Pintrich, P., & Hamilton, V. (1986). Children's concept of ability, effort, and conduct. *American Educational Research Journal, 23,* 95–104.

Boggiano, A. K., Main, D. S., & Katz, P. A. (1988). Children's preference for challenge: The role of perceived competence and control. *Journal of Personality and Social Psychology, 54,* 134–141.

Brandtstädter, J. (1985). Entwicklungsbezogene Handlungsorientierungen und Emotionen im Erwachsenenalter [Development-related action orientation and emotions in adults]. *Zeitschrift für Entwicklungspsychologie und Pädagogische Psychologie, 17,* 41–52.

Brandtstädter, J. (1986). Personal self-regulation of development: Cross-sequential analyses of development-related control beliefs and emotions in the age range from 30 to 60 years. Research report. Trier, Germany: Universität Trier.

Brandtstädter, J. (1992). Personal control over development: Some developmental implications of self-efficacy. In R. Schwarzer (Ed.), *Self-efficacy: Thought control of action* (pp. 127–145). Washington, DC: Hemisphere.

Brandtstädter, J., Krampen, G., & Baltes-Goetz, B. (1989). Kontrollüberzeugungen im Kontext persönlicher Entwicklung [Control beliefs related to personal development]. In G. Krampen (Ed.), *Diagnostik von Attributionen und Kontrollüberzeugungen* (pp. 155–171). Göttingen, Germany: Hogrefe.

Brandtstädter, J., Krampen, G., & Greve, W. (1987). Personal control over development: Effects on the perception and emotional evaluation of personal development in adulthood. *International Journal of Behavioral Development, 10,* 99–120.

Brandtstädter, J., & Renner, G. (1990). Tenacious goal pursuit and flexible goal adjustment: Explication and age-related analysis of assimilative and accommodative strategies of coping. *Psychology and Aging, 5,* 58–67.

Brandtstädter, J., Wentura, D., & Greve, W. (1993). Adaptive resources of the aging self: Outlines of an emergent perspective. *International Journal of Behavioral Development, 16,* 323–349.

Broucek, F. (1979). Efficacy in infancy: A review of some experimental studies and their possible implications for clinical theory. *International Journal of Psychoanalysis, 60,* 311–316.

Brown, J. (1984). Effects of induced mood on causal attributions for success and failure. *Motivation and Emotion, 8,* 343–353.

Bruner, J. (1983)). *Child's talk: Learning to use language.* New York: Norton.

Bühler, K. (1919). *Abriss der geistigen Entwicklung des Kindes* [Outline of the mental development of a child]. Leipzig, Germany: Quelle & Meyer.

Bullock, M., Lütkenhaus, P. (1988). The development of volitional behavior in the toddler years. *Child Development, 59,* 664–674.

Chapin, M., & Dycke, D.G. (1976). Persistence in children's reading behavior as a function of N length and attribution retraining. *Journal of Abnormal Psychology, 85,* 511–515.

Claes, M. (1981). L'évolution de l'attribution des causes des succès et des échecs au cours de la scolarité [The evolution of the causal attribution of successes and failures over the school biography]. *Revue de Psychologie Appliquée, 31,* 275–294.

Cohen, L. B., & Oakes, L. M. (1993). How infants perceive a simple causal event. *Developmental Psychology, 29,* 421–433.

Cohen, S., & Edwards, J. (1989). Personality characteristics as moderators of the relationship between stress and disorder. In R. Neufeld (Ed.), *Advances in the investigation of psychological stress* (pp. 235–283). New York: Wiley.

Connolly, J. (1989). Social self-efficacy in adolescence: Relations with self-concept, social adjustment, and mental health. *Canadian Journal of Behavioral Science, 21,* 258–269.

Crandall, V., & Crandall, B. W. (1983). Maternal and childhood behaviors as antecedents of internal-external control perceptions in young adulthood. In H. M. Lefcourt (Ed.), *Research with the locus of control-construct: Vol. I. Assessment methods* (pp. 53–103). New York: Academic.

Crandall, V., Katkovsky, W., & Crandall, V. J. (1965). Children's belief in their own control of reinforcements in intellectual-academic achievement situations. *Child Development, 36,* 91–109.

Diethelm, K. (1991). *Mutter-Kind-Interaktion. Entwicklung von Kontrollüberzeugungen* [Mother-child interaction. Development of control beliefs]. Bern, Switzerland: Huber.

Diethelm, K. (1992). Frühe Mutter-Kind-Interaktion und die Entwicklung kompotenten Verhaltens [Early mother-child interaction and the development of competent behavior]. *Vierteljahresschrift für Heilpädagogik und ihre Nachbarwissenschaften, 61,* 83–91.

Donovan, W. L., & Leavitt, L. A. (1989). Maternal self-efficacy and infant attachment: Integrating physiology, perceptions, and behavior. *Child Development, 60,* 460–472.

Donovan, W. L., Leavitt, L. A., & Walsh, R. O. (1990). Maternal self-efficacy: Illusory control and its effect on susceptibility to learned helplessness. *Child Development, 61,* 1638–1647.

Dunham, P., & Dunham, F. (1990). Effects of mother-infant social interaction on infants' subsequent contingency task performance. *Child Development, 61,* 785–783.

Dunning, D., & Story, A. L. (1991). Depression, realism, and the overconfidence effect: Are the sadder wiser when predicting future actions and events? *Journal of Personality and Social Psychology, 61,* 521–532.

Dweck, C. S. (1975). The role of expectations and the alleviation of learned helplessness. *Journal of Personality and Social Psychology, 31,* 674–685.

Dweck, C. S., & Reppucci, N. D. (1973). Learned helplessness and reinforcement responsibility in children. *Journal of Personality and Social Psychology, 25,* 109–116.

Entwistle, D., & Hayduk, L. (1978). *Too great expectations: The academic outlook of young children.* Baltimore, MD: The Johns Hopkins University Press.

Erikson, E. H. (1968). *Identity: Youth and crisis.* New York: Norton (dt. Jugend und Krise. Weinheim, Germany: Klett-Cotta, 1981).

Essau, C. (1992). *Primary-secondary control and coping: A cross-cultural comparison.* Regensburg, Germany: Roderer.

Finkelstein, N. W., & Ramey, C. (1977). Learning to control the environment in infancy. *Child Development, 48,* 806–819.

Flammer, A. (1990). *Erfahrung der eigenen Wirksamkeit* [Experiencing one's own efficacy]. Bern, Switzerland: Huber.

Flammer, A. (1992). Secondary control in an individual-centered and in a group-centered culture. In W. Meeus, M. De Goede, W. Kox, & K. Hurrelmann (Eds)., *Adolescence, careers, and cultures* (pp. 131–141). Berlin: De Gruyter.

Flammer, A., & Grob, A. (1994). Kontrollmeinungen, ihre Begründungen und Autobiographie [Control beliefs, their justification, and autobiography]. *Zeitschrift für Experimentelle und Angewandte Psychologie, 41*, 17–38.

Flammer, A., Grob, A., & Lüthi, R. (1987). Kontrollattributionen bei Jugendlichen [Control attributions in adolescents]. Research Report. Bern, Switzerland: Universität Bern.

Flammer, A., Grob, A., Lüthi, R., & Kaiser, F. G. (1989). Kontrollattributionen und Wohlbefinden von Schweizer Jugendlichen [Control attributions and well-being in Swiss adolescents]. Research Report Nr. 1989-4. Bern, Switzerland: University of Bern Department of Psychology.

Flammer, A., & Kaiser, F. G. (1992). Kontrollmeinung und Selbstwissen bei Jugendlichen [Control-belief and self-knowledge among adolescents]. Research Report Nr. 1992-2. Bern, Switzerland: University of Bern.

Flammer, A., Kaiser, F. G., Lüthi, R., & Grob, A. (1990). Kontrollmeinungen und Selbstwissen [Control beliefs and self-knowledge]. *Schweizerische Zeitschrift für Psychologie, 49*, 159–172.

Flammer, A., & Rheindorf, E. (1991). Control-belief and selective recall from autobiography. *Archives de psychologie, 59*, 125–142.

Flammer, A. & Scheuber-Sahli, E. (in press). Selective recall as intervention to modify control-beliefs in an achievement setting. *Swiss Journal of Psychology.*

Flammer, A., Züblin, C., & Grob, A. (1988). Sekundäre Kontrolle bei Jugendlichen [Secondary control in adolescents]. *Zeitschrift für Entwicklungspsychologie und Pädagogische Psychologie, 20*, 239–262.

Flavell, J., Friedrichs, A., & Hoyt, J. (1970). Developmental changes in memorization processes. *Cognitive Psychology, 1*, 324–340.

Flavell, J., & Wellman, H. (1977). Metamemory. In R. V. Kail & J. W. Hagen (Eds.), *Perspectives on the development of memory and cognition* (pp. 3–33). Hillsdale, NJ: Erlbaum.

Ford, M. E., & Thompson, R. A. (1985). Perceptions of personal agency and infant attachment: Toward a lifespan perspective on competence development. *International Journal of Behavioral Development, 8*, 377–406.

Frieze, I. H., & Snyder, H. L. (1980). Children's belief about the causes of success and failure in school settings. *Journal of Educational Psychology, 72*, 186–196.

Fry, P. S. (1975). Affect and resistance to temptation. *Developmental Psychology, 11*, 466–472.

Gatz, M., & Karel, M. H. (1993). Individual change in perceived control over 20 years. *International Journal of Behavioral Development, 16*, 305–322.

Gekas, V. (1989). The social psychology of self-efficacy. *Annual Review of Sociology, 15*, 291–316.

Gekas, V., & Schwalbe, M. L. (1983). Beyond the looking-glass self: Social structure and efficacy-based self-esteem. *Social Psychology Quarterly, 46*, 77–88.

Geppert, U., & Küster, U. (1983). The emergence of "wanting to do it oneself": A precursor of achievement motivation. *International Journal of Behavioral Development, 3*, 355–369.

Grant, B. T. (1988). Quality of life and visual impairment: Coping strategies and adaptation procedures. Unpublished doctoral dissertation, University of Melbourne, Australia.

Grob, A., Flammer, A., & Neuenschwander, M. (1992). Kontrollattributionen und Wohlbefinden von Schweizer Jugendlichen III [Control attributions and well-being in Swiss adolescents III]. Research Report Nr. 1992-4. Bern, Switzerland: University of Bern Department of Psychology.

Güggi, S. (in prep.). Confidence in control beliefs. Dissertation. Bern, Switzerland: University of Bern Department of Psychology.

Gunnar, M. R. (1980a). Contingent simulation: A review of its role in early development. In S. Levine & H. Ursin (Eds.), *Coping and health* (pp. 101–119). New York: Plenum.

Gunnar, M. R. (1980b). Control, warning signals, and distress in infancy. *Developmental Psychology, 16,* 281–289.

Gunnar-VonGnechten, M. R. (1978). Changing a frightening toy into a pleasant toy by allowing the infant to control its action. *Developmental Psychology, 14,* 157–162.

Gurin, P., & Brim, O. G. (1984). Change in self in adulthood: The example of sense of control. In P. B. Baltes & O. G. Brim (Eds.), *Life-span development and behavior* (Vol. 6) (pp. 282–234). New York: Academic.

Hackett, G. (1995). Self-efficacy and career choice and development. In A. Bandura (Ed.), *Self-efficacy in changing societies* (pp. 232–258). New York: Cambridge University Press.

Halisch, C., & Halisch, F. (1980). Kognitive Voraussetzungen frühkindlicher Selbstbewertungsreaktionen nach Erfolg und Misserfolg. *Zeitschrift für Entwicklungspsychologie und Pädagogische Psychologie, 12,* 193–212.

Harris, K. R. (1990). Developing self-regulated learners: The role of private speech and self-instructions. Special Issue: Self-regulated learning and academic achievement. *Educational Psychologist, 25,* 35–49.

Hausser, K. (1983). *Identitätsentwicklung* [Development of identity]. Stuttgart: utb.

Heckhausen, H. (1966). Die Entwicklung des Erlebens von Erfolg und Misserfolg [The development of the experience of success and failure]. *Bild der Wissenschraft, 7,* 547–553.

Heckhausen, H. (1982). The development of achievement motivation. In W. W. Hartup (Ed.), *Review of child development research* (Vol. 6) (pp. 600–668). Chicago: University of Chicago Press.

Heckhausen, H. (1984). Emergent achievement behavior: Some early developments. In J. G. Nicholls (Ed.), *The development of achievement motivation* (Vol. 3) (pp. 1–37). Greenwich, CT: JAI Press.

Heckhausen, H. (1991). *Motivation and action.* New York: Springer.

Heckhausen, J. (1988). Becoming aware of one's competence in the second year: Developmental progression within the mother-child dyad. *International Journal of Behavioral Development, 11,* 305–326.

Heckhausen, J. (1990). Entwicklung im Erwachsenenalter aus der Sicht junger, mittelalter und alter Erwachsener [Development in adult age viewed from young, middle-aged and old adults]. *Zeitschrift für Entwicklungspsychologie und Pädagogische Psychologie, 22,* 1–21.

Heckhausen, J., & Baltes, P. B. (1991). Perceived controllability of expected psychological change across adulthood and old age. *Journal of Gerontology: Psychological Sciences, 46,* 165–173.

Heckhausen, J., & Krüger, J. (1993). Developmental expectations for the self and most other people: Age grading in three functions of social comparison. *Developmental Psychology, 29,* 539–548.

Heckhausen, J., & Schulz, R. (1993). Optimisation by selection and compensation: Balancing primary and secondary control in life span development. *International Journal of Behavioral Development, 16,* 287–303.

Heckhausen, J., & Schulz, R. (in press). A life-span theory of control. *Psychological Review.*

Helmke, A. (1992). *Selbstvertrauen und schulische Leistungen* [Self-confidence and academic achievements]. Göttingen, Germany: Hogrefe.

Helmke, A. (1993). Achievement-related motives, self-evaluations, causal attributions and school experiences of third graders. In F. E. Weinert & W. Schneider (Eds.), *The Munich Longitudinal Study on the Genesis of Individual Competencies (LOGIC), Report No. 9* (pp. 111–133). Munich: Max-Planck-Institute for Psychological Research.

Hetzer, H. (1931). *Kind und Schaffen* [Child and creation]. Jena, Germany: Gustav Fischer.

Janoš, O., & Papoušek, H. (1977). Acquisition of appetitional and palpebral conditioned reflexes by the same infants. *Early Human Development, 1,* 91–97.

Karabenick, J., & Heller, K. (1976). A developmental study of effort and ability attributions. *Developmental Psychology, 12,* 559–560.

Katkovsky, W., Crandall, V., & Good, S. (1967). Parental antecedents of children's beliefs in internal-external control of reinforcements in intellectual achievements situations. *Child Development, 38,* 765–776.

Kavanagh, D. J., & Bower, G. H. (1985). Mood and self-efficacy: Impact of joy and sadness on perceived capabilities. *Cognitive Therapy and Research, 9,* 507–525.

Kaye, K. (1982). *The mental and social life of babies: How parents create persons.* Chicago: University of Chicago Press.

Klonowicz, T., & Zawadzka, G. (1988). Reactivity and personal control over stimulation supply. *European Journal of Personality, 2,* 1–10.

Klostermann, M. (1984). Selbermachenwollen bei Kindern in Abhängigkeit vom Schwierigkeitsgrad [Wanting to do by oneself in children in reference to degree of difficulty]. Unpublished master's thesis, Ruhr-Universität, Bochum, Germany.

Kogan, N. (1990). Personality and aging. In J. E. Birren & K. W. Schaie (Eds.), *Handbook of the psychology of aging* (3rd ed.) (pp. 330–346). New York: Academic.

Krüger, J., & Heckhausen, J. (1993). Personality development across the adult life span: Subjective conceptions vs. cross-sectional contrasts. *Journal of Gerontology: Psychological Sciences, 48,* P100 – P108.

Kumpfer, K. L., & Turner, C. W. (1991). The social ecology model of adolescent substance abuse: Implications for prevention. *International Journal of the Addictions, 25,* 435–463.

Kun, A. (1977). Development of magnitude-covariation and compensation schemata in ability and effort attributions of performance. *Child Development, 48,* 862–873.

Kun, A., Parsons, J., & Ruble, D. (1974). Development of integration processes using ability and effort information to predict outcome. *Developmental Psychology, 10,* 721–732.

Kunnen, S. (1993). Attributions and perceived control over school failure in handicapped and non-handicapped children. *International Journal of Behavioral Development, 16,* 113–125.

Lachman, M. E. (1983). Perceptions of intellectual aging: Antecedent or consequence of intellectual functioning? *Developmental Psychology, 19,* 482–498.

Lachman, M. E. (1986a). Locus of control in aging research: A case for multidimensional and domain-specific assessment. *Psychology and Aging, 1,* 34–40.

Lachman, M. E. (1986b). Personal control in later life: Stability, change, and cognitive correlates. In M. M. Baltes & P. B. Baltes (Eds.), *The psychology of control and aging* (pp. 207–236). Hillsdale, NJ: Erlbaum.

Lange, R., & Tiggemann, M. (1980). Changes within the Australian population to more external control beliefs. *Australian Psychologist, 15,* 495–497.

Langer, E. J. (1975). The illusion of control. *Journal of Personality and Social Psychology*, *32*, 311–328.

Langer, E. J. (1983). *The psychology of control*. London: Sage.

Langer, E. J., & Rodin, J. (1976). The effects of choice and enhanced personal responsibility for the aged: A field experiment in an institutional setting. *Journal of Personality and Social Psychology*, *34*, 191–198.

Lawler, J. (1978). Dialektische Philosophie und Entwicklungspsychologie: Hegel und Piaget über Widerspruch. In K. Riegel (Ed.), *Zur Ontogenese dialektischer Operationen* (pp. 7–29). Frankfurt: Suhrkamp.

Lazarus (1966). *Psychological stress and the coping process*. New York: McGraw-Hill.

Lazarus, R. S., & Folkman, S. (1984). *Stress, appraisal and coping* (6th ed). New York: Springer.

Lefcourt, H. M. (Ed.). (1976). *Locus of control: Current trends in theory and research*. New York: Wiley.

Leont'ev, A. N. (1959). *Probleme der Entwicklung des Psychischen* [Problems of the psychic development]. Königstein: Anthenäum.

Lepper, M. R., & Greene, D. (1975). Turning play into work: Effects of adult surveillance and extrinsic rewards on children's intrinsic motivation. *Journal of Personality and Social Psychology*, *31*, 479–486.

Leslie, A. M. (1982). The perception of causality in infants. *Perception*, *11*, 173–186.

Leslie, A. M. (1984). Spatiotemporal continuity and the perception of causality in infants. *Perception*, *13*, 287–305.

Leslie, A. M., & Keeble, S. (1987). Do six-month-olds perceive causality? *Cognition*, *25*, 265–288.

Levin, J. R., Yussen, S. R., DeRose, T. M., & Pressley, M. (1977). Developmental changes in assessing recall and recognition memory capacity. *Developmental Psychology*, *13*, 608–615.

Lewis, M., & Brooks-Gunn, J. (1979). *Social cognition and the acquisition of self*. New York: Plenum.

Lewis, M., & Goldberg, S. (1969). Perceptual-cognitive development in infancy: A generalized expectancy model as a function of the mother-infant interaction. *Merrill-Palmer Quarterly*, *15*, 81–100.

Lewis, M., Wall, M., & Aronfreed, J. (1963). Developmental change in the relative values of social and nonsocial reinforcement. *Journal of Experimental Psychology*, *66*, 133–137.

Lloyd, G. G., & Lishman, W. A. (1975). Effect of depression on the speed of recall of pleasant and unpleasant experiences. *Psychological Medicine*, *5*, 173–180.

Lumpkin, J. R. (1986). The relationship between locus of control and age: New evidence. *Journal of Social Behavior and Personality*, *1*, 245–252.

Luria, A. R. (1961). *The role of speech in the regulation of normal and abnormal behavior*. New York: Basic.

Luria, A. R. (1976). *Cognitive development: Its cultural and social foundations*. Cambridge, MA: Harvard University Press.

Lüthi, R. (1990). Der Einfluss von Erfahrungen und Erinnerungen auf den Aufbau und die Veränderung von Selbstkognitionen [The influence of experiences and their recall on the construction and change of self-cognition]. Unpublished doctoral dissertation, University of Berne.

Lütkenhaus, P. (1987). Preschoolers' feelings of competence, its function for persistence and its relation to social experiences. Paper presented to the ISSBD Conference in Tokyo, Japan.

Lütkenhaus, P., Bullock, M., & Geppert, U. (1987). Toddlers' action: Knowledge, control and the self. In F. Halisch & J. Kuhl (Eds.), *Motivation, intention and volition* (pp. 145–161). Berlin: Springer.

MacFarlane, J. (1975). Olfaction in the development of social preferences in the human neonate. In M. Hofer (Ed.), *Parent-infant interaction* (pp. 103–117). Amsterdam: Elsevier.

MacIver, D. (1987). Classroom factors and student characteristics predicting students' use of achievement standards during ability self-assessment. *Child Development, 58*, 1258–1271.

MacIver, D. (1988). Classroom environments and the stratification of pupils' ability perception. *Journal of Educational Psychology, 80*, 494–504.

Mandler, J. M. (1992). How to build a baby: II. Conceptual primitives. *Psychological Review, 99*, 587–604.

Masters, J., & Furman, W. (1966). Effects of affective states on noncontingent outcome expectancies and beliefs in internal or external control. *Developmental Psychology, 12*, 481–482.

Mead, G. H. (1934). *Mind, self, and society: From standpoint of a social behaviorist.* Chicago: Chicago University Press.

Meij, J., & Riksen-Walraven, J. (1992). Stability of children's competence motivation from 12 to 30 months in relation to patterns of change in maternal sensitivity. Paper presented at the Vth European Conference on Developmental Psychology in Sevilla, Spain.

Meyer, W. U. (1984). Das Konzept von der eigenen Begabund [The concept of one's own ability]. *Psychologische Rundschau, 35*, 136–150.

Meyer, W. U. (1992). Paradoxical effects of praise and criticism on perceived ability. *European Review of Social Psychology, 3*, 259–283.

Meyer, W. U., Bachmann, M., Biermann, V., Hempelmann, P., Ploger, F. O., & Spiller, H. (1979). The informational value of evaluative behavior: Influence of praise and blame on perceptions of ability. *Journal of Educational Psychology, 71*, 259–268.

Michalos, A. (1985). Multiple discrepancies theory (MDT). *Social Indicators Research, 16*, 347–413.

Michotte, A. (1963). *The perception of causality.* London: Methuen.

Midgley, C., Feldlaufer, H., & Eccles, J. S. (1989). Change in teacher efficacy and student self- and task-related beliefs in mathematics during the transition to junior high school. *Journal of Educational Psychology, 81*, 247–258.

Miller, A. (1985). A developmental study of the cognitive basis of performance impairment after failure. *Journal of Personality and Social Psychology, 49*, 529–538.

Miller, D. T., & Ross, M. (1975). Self-serving biases in the attribution of causality: Fact or fiction? *Psychological Bulletin, 82*, 213–225.

Mischel, H. N., & Mischel, W. (1983). The development of children's knowledge of self-control strategies. *Child Development, 54*, 603–619.

Mischel, W. (1957). Preference for delayed reinforcement. *Journal of Abnormal Social Psychology, 56*, 57–61.

Mischel, W. (1974). Processes in delay of gratification. In L. Berkowitz (Ed.), *Advances in experimental social psychology* (Vol. 7) (pp. 249–292). New York: Academic.

Mischel, W., Shoda, Y., & Rodriguez, M. L. (1989). Delay of gratification in children. *Science, 244*, 933–938.

Monroe, E. K., & Lange, G. (1977). The accuracy with which children judge the composition of their free recall. *Child Development*, *48*, 381–387.

Moore, R. G., Watts, F. N., & Williams, J. M. G. (1988). The specificity of personal memories in depression. *British Journal of Clinical Psychology*, *27*, 275–276.

Müller, A. (1958). Ueber die Entwicklung des Leistungsanspruchsniveaus. [On the development of the performance aspiration level]. *Zeitschrift für Psychologie*, *162*, 238–353.

Müller, L. (1984). Selbermachenwollen bei Kleinkindern, wenn der erwachsene Spielpartner vorübergehend den Tätigkeitsvollzug an sich ziehen will. [Wanting to do by one-self in situations where the adult partner wants to do part of the job for a given while]. Unpublished master's thesis, Ruhr-Universität, Bochum, Germany.

Nicholls, J. G. (1978). The development of the concepts of effort and ability, perception of academic attainment, and the understanding that difficult tasks require more ability. *Child Development*, *49*, 800–814.

Nicholls, J. G. (1979). Development of perception of own attainment and causal attributions for success and failure in reading. *Journal of Educational Psychology*, *71*, 94–99.

Nicholls, J. G. (1980). The development of the concept of difficulty. *Merrill-Palmer Quarterly*, *26*, 271–281.

Nicholls, J. G. (1984). Conceptions of ability and achievement motivation. In A. Ames & C. Ames (Eds.), *Research on motivation in education: Vol. 1. Student motivation* (pp. 39–73). New York: Academic.

Nicholls, J. G., & Miller, A. T. (1984). Development and its discontents: The differentiation of the concept of ability. In J. G. Nicholls (Ed.), *Advances in motivation and achievement: Vol. 3. The development of achievement motivation* (pp. 185–218). Greenwich, CT: JAI.

Nicholls, J. G., & Miller, A. T. (1985). Differentiation of the concepts of luck and skill. *Developmental Psychology*, *21*, 76–82.

Oakes, L. M., & Cohen, L. B. (1990). Infant perception of a causal event. *Cognitive Development*, *5*, 193–207.

Oettingen, G., Lindenberger, U., & Baltes, P. B. (1992). Sind die schulleistungsbezogenen Ueberzeugungen Ostberlin'er Kinder entwicklungshemmend? [Do the school achievement related beliefs of East Berlin children prevent development?]. *Zeitschrift für Pädagogik*, *38*, 299–324.

Oettingen, G., & Little, T. D. (1993). Intelligenz und Selbstwirksamekeitsurteile bei ost- und Westberliner Schulkindern. [Influence of age, gender, agency, and connotations on the self-evaluation of the locus of control in school-age children]. *Zeitschrift für Socialpsychologie*.

Oettingen, G., Little, T. D., Lindenberger, U., & Baltes, P. B. (in press). Causality, agency, and control beliefs and their association with school performance in East versus West Berlin children: A natural experiment on the role of context. *Journal of Personality and Social Psychology*.

Oléron, P., & Soubitez, M. C. (1982). Influence des variables age, sexe, agent et connotation sur l'évaluation du "locus of control" par des enfants d'âge scolaire. *Revue de Psychologie Appliquée*, *32*, 91–104.

Papoušek, H. (1967). Experimental studies of appetitional behavior in human newborns and infants. In H. W. Stevenson, E. H. Hess, & H. L. Rheingold (Eds.), *Early behavior: Comparative developmental approaches* (pp. 249–277). New York: Wiley.

Papoušek, H., & Papoušek, M. (1979). Early ontogeny of human social interaction: Its biological roots and social dimensions. In M. Von Cranach, K. Foppa, W.

Lepenies, & D. Ploog (Eds.), *Human ethology: Claims and limits of a new discipline* (pp. 456–478). Cambridge, MA: Cambridge University Press.

Papoušek, H., & Papoušek, M. (1989). Stimmliche Kommunikation im frühen Säuglingsalter als Wegbereiter der Sprachentwicklung [Vocal communication in early infancy as promoter of language development]. In H. Keller (Ed.), *Handbuch der Kleinkindforschung* (pp. 465–490). Berlin: Springer.

Parsons, J., & Ruble, D. (1977). The development of achievement-related expectancies. *Child Development, 48,* 1075–1079.

Patterson, C. J., & Mischel, W. (1976). Effects of temptation-inhibiting and task-facilitating plans on self-control. *Journal of Personality and Social Psychology, 33,* 209–217.

Phares, E. J. (1978). Locus of control. In H. London & J. E. Exner (Eds.), *Dimensions of personality* (pp. 263–304). New York: Wiley.

Piaget, J. (1925). De quelques formes primitives de causalité chez l'enfant. [On some primitive forms of causality in the child]. *Année psychologique, 26,* 31–71.

Piaget, J. (1926). *La représentation de monde chez l'enfant* [The child's representation of the world]. Paris: Alcan.

Piaget, J. (1936). *La naissance de l'intelligence chez l'enfant* [The birth of infant intelligence]. Neuchâtel, France: Delachaux et Niestlé.

Piaget, J. (1937). *La construction due réel chez l'enfant* [The child's construction of the real]. Neuchâtel, France: Delachaux et Niestlé.

Piaget, J. (1947). *Psychologie de l'intelligence.* [Psychology of intelligence]. Paris: Colin.

Ramey, C. T., & Finkelstein, N. W. (1978). Contingent stimulation and infant competence. *Journal of Pediatric Psychology, 3,* 89–96.

Rholes, W., Blackwell, J., Jordan, C., & Walters, C. (1980). A developmental study of learned helplessness. *Developmental Psychology, 16,* 616–624.

Riksen-Walraven, J. M. (1978). Effects of caregiver behavior on habituation rate and self-efficacy in infants. *International Journal of Behavioral Development, 1,* 105–130.

Riksen-Walraven, M. (1991). Die Entwicklung kindlicher Kompetenz im Zusammenhang mit sozialer Unterstützung [Development of infants' competence as a function of social support]. In Mönks, F. J., & Lehwald, G. (Eds.), *Neugier, Erkundung und Begabund bei Kleinkindern* (pp. 77–92). Basel, Germany: Reinhardt.

Rodin, J., & Langer, E. J. (1977). Long-term effects of a control-relevant intervention with the institutionalized aged. *Journal of Personality and Social Psychology, 35,* 897–903. Erratum to Rodin & Langer: *Journal of Personality and Social Psychology, 36,* 462.

Rondal, J. A. (1976). Investigation of the regulatory power of the impulsive and meaningful aspects of speech. *Genetic Psychology Monographs, 94,* 3-33.

Rosenholtz, S. J., & Rosenholtz, S. H. (1981). Classroom organization and the perception of ability. *Sociology of Education, 54,* 132–140.

Rosenholtz, S. J., & Simpson, C. (1984). The formation of ability conceptions: Developmental or social construction? *Review of Educational Research, 54,* 31–63.

Rothbaum, F. M., Weisz, J. R., & Snyder, S. S. (1982). Changing the world and changing the self: a two-process model of perceived control. *Journal of Personality and Social Psychology, 42,* 5–37.

Rotter, J. B. (1954). *Social learning and clinical psychology.* Englewood Cliffs, NJ: Prentice-Hall.

Rotter, J. B. (1990). Internal versus external control of reinforcement. *American Psychologist, 45,* 489–493.

Rovee-Collier, C. K., & Lippsitt, L. P. (1982). Learning, adaptation and memory in the newborn. In P. M. Stratton (Ed.), *Psychobiology of the human newborn* (pp. 147–190). New York: Wiley.

Ruble, D. N., & Flett, G. L. (1988). Conflicting goals in self-evaluative information seeking: Developmental and ability level analyses. *Child Development, 59,* 97–106.

Ryff, C. D. (1989). In the eye of the beholder: Views of psychological well-being among middle-aged and older adults. *Psychology and Aging, 4,* 195–210.

Salovey, P., & Birnbaum, D. (1989). Influence of mood on health-relevant cognitions. *Journal of Personality and Social Psychology, 57,* 539–551.

Sameroff, A. J. (1968). The components of sucking in the newborn. *Journal of Experimental Child Psychology, 6,* 607–623.

Sameroff, A. J. (1971). Can conditioned responses be established in the newborn infant? *Developmental Psychology, 5,* 411–442.

Schneider, J. M. (1971). College students' belief in personal control, 1966–1970. *Journal of Individual Psychology, 27,* 188.

Schneider, W. (1989). *Zur Entwicklung des Meta-Gedächtnisses bei Kindern* [On the development of meta-memory in children]. Bern, Switzerland: Huber.

Schneider, W., & Pressley, M. (1989). *Memory development between 2 and 20.* New York: Springer.

Schulz, R. (1976). Effects of control and predictability on the physical and psychological well-being of the institutionalized aged. *Journal of Personality and Social Psychology, 33,* 563–573.

Schulz, R., & Hanusa, B. H. (1978). Long-term effects of control and predictability enhancing interventions: Findings and ethical issues. *Journal of Personality and Social Psychology, 36,* 1194–1201.

Schunk, D. H. (1982). Effects of effort attributional feedback on children's perceived self-efficacy and achievement. *Journal of Educational Psychology, 74,* 548–556.

Schunk, D. H. (1983). Reward contingencies and the development of children's skills and self-efficacy. *Journal of Educational Psychology; 1983, 75,* 511–518.

Schunk, D. H. (1989). Self-efficacy and cognitive skill learning. In C. Ames & R. Ames (Eds.), *Research on motivation in education: Vol. 3. Goals and cognitions* (pp. 13–44). San Diego: Academic.

Schwarzer, R. (Ed.), (1990). *Gesundheitspsychologie* [Psychology of health]. Göttingen, Germany: Hogrefe.

Seginer, R., Trommsdorff, G., & Essau, C. (1993). Adolescent control beliefs: Cross-cultural variations of primary and secondary orientations. *International Journal of Behavioral Development, 16,* 243–260.

Seligman, M. E. P. (1975). *Helplessness: On depression, development and death.* San Francisco: Freeman.

Seligman, M. E. P. (1991). *Learned optimism.* New York: Knopf.

Seligman, M. E. P., & Maier, S. F. (1967). Failure to escape traumatic shock. *Journal of Experimental Psychology, 74,* 1–9.

Shaklee, H., & Goldston, D. (1988). Development in causal reasoning. Information sampling and judgment rule. *Cognitive Development, 4,* 269–281.

Shaklee, H., Holt, P., Elek, S., & Hall, L. (1988). Covariation judgment: Improving rule use among children, adolescents, and adults. *Child Development, 59,* 755–768.

Shoda, Y., Mischel, W., & Peake, P. K. (1990). Predicting adolescent cognitive and self-regulatory competencies from preschool delay of gratification: Identifying diagnostic conditions. *Developmental Psychology, 26,* 978–986.

Simpson, C. (1981). Classroom structure and the organization of ability. *Sociology of Education*, 54, 120–129.

Siqueland, E. R., & DeLucia, C. A. (1969). Visual reinforcement of non-nutritive sucking in human infants. *Science*, 165, 1144–1146.

Siqueland, E. R., & Lippsitt, L. P. (1966). Conditioned head-turning behavior in newborns. *Journal of Experimental Child Psychology*, 3, 356–376.

Skinner, E.A., (1986). The origins of young children's perceived control: Mother contingent and sensitive behavior. *International Journal of Behavioral Development*, 9, 359–382.

Skinner, E.A., & Chapman, M. (1984). Control beliefs in an action perspective. *Human Development*, 77, 129–133.

Skinner, E. A., & Chapman, M. (1987). Resolution of a developmental paradox: How can perceived internality increase, decrease, and remain the same across middle childhood? *Developmental Psychology*, 23, 44–48.

Skinner, E. A., Chapman, M., & Baltes, P. B. (1988a). Children's belief about control, means-ends, and agency: Developmental differences during middle childhood. *International Journal of Behavioral Development*, 11, 369–388.

Skinner, E.A., Chapman, M., & Baltes, P. B. (1988b). Control, means-ends, and agency beliefs: A new conceptualization and its measurement during childhood. *Journal of Personality and Social Psychology*, 54, 117–133.

Skinner, E. A., & Connell, J. P. (1986). Control understanding: Suggestions for a developmental framework. In M. Baltes & P. B. Baltes (Eds.), *The psychology of aging and control* (pp. 35–69). Hillsdale, NJ: Erlbaum.

Skinner, E. A., Wellborn, J. G., & Connell, J. P. (1990). What it takes to do well in school and whether I've got it: A process model of perceived control and children's engagement and achievement in school. *Journal of Educational Psychology*, 82, 22–32.

Spangler, G., Bräutigam, I., & Stadler, R. (1984). Handlungsentwicjlung in der frühen Kindheit und ihre Abhängigkeit von der kognitiven Entwicklung und der emotionalen Erregbarkeit des Kindes [Action development in early infancy as a function of the cognitive development and the emotional arousability]. *Zeitschrift für Entwicklungspsychologie und Pädagogische Psychologie*, 16, 181–193.

Spear, P., & Armstrong, S. (1978). Effects of performance expectancies created by peer comparison as related to social reinforcement, task difficulty, and age of child. *Journal of Experimental Child Psychology*, 25, 254–266.

Stern, D. N. (1985). *The interpersonal world of the infants*. New York: Basic Books.

Stetsenko, A., Little, T., Oettingen, G., & Baltes, P. B. (in press). Agency, control, and means-ends beliefs in Moscow children: How similar are they with the beliefs of Western children? *Developmental Psychology*.

Stiensmeier, J. (1986). Wichtigkeit und Kontrollerleben als Bedingungen von Lageorientierung [Importance and experience of controllability as conditions of state orientation]. *Archiv für Psychologie*, 138, 127–138.

Stipek, D. (1981). Children's perceptions of their own and their class-mates' abilities. *Journal of Educational Psychology*, 73, 404–410.

Stipek, D. (1983). A developmental analysis of pride and shame. *Human Development*, 26, 42–54.

Stipek, D. (1984). Young children's performance expectations: Logical analysis or wishful thinking? In J. G. Nicholls (Ed.), *The development of achievement motivation* (pp. 33–56). Greenwich, CT: JAI.

Stipek, D. (1987). Emotional responses to objective and normative performance feedback. *Journal of Applied Developmental Psychology*, 8, 183–195.

Stipek, D., & Hoffman, J. (1980). Development of children's performance-related judgments. *Child Development, 51,* 912–914.

Stipek, D., & MacIver, D. (1989). Developmental change in children's assessment of intellectual competence. *Child Development, 60,* 521–538.

Stipek, D., Robert, T., & Sandborn, M. (1984). Preschool-age children's performance expectations for themselves and another child as a function of the incentive value of success and the salience of past performance. *Child Development, 55,* 1983–1989.

Stipek, D., & Tannatt, L. (1984). Children's judgments of their own and their peers' academic competence. *Journal of Educational Psychology, 76,* 75–84.

Stipek, D. J., & Daniels, D. H. (1988). Declining perceptions of competence: A consequence of changes in the child or in the educational environment? *Journal of Educational Psychology, 80,* 352–356.

Strube, M. J., Lott, C. L., Lê-Xuân-Hy, G. M., Oxenberg, J., & Deichman, A. K. (1986). Self-evaluation of abilities: Accurate self-assessment versus biased self-enhancement. *Journal of Personality and Social Psychology, 51,* 16–25.

Suomi, S. J. (1981). The perception of contingency and social development. In M. E. Lamb & L. R. Sherrod (Eds.), *Infant social cognition* (pp. 177–203). Hillsdale, NJ: Erlbaum.

Syme, S. L. (1990). Control and health: An epidemiological perspective. In J. Rodin, C. Schooler, & K. W. Schaie (Eds.), *Self-directedness: Cause and effects throughout the life course* (pp. 213–229). Hillsdale, NJ: Erlbaum.

Taylor, S. E. (1989). *Positive illusions: Creative self-deception and the healthy mind.* New York: Basic Books.

Taylor, S. E., & Brown, J. D. (1988). Illusion and well-being: A social psychological perspective on mental health. *Psychological Bulletin, 103,* 193–210.

Teasdale, J. D. (1978). Effects of real and recalled success on learned helplessness and depression. *Journal of Abnormal Psychology, 87,* 155–164.

Thoman, E. B., & Ingersoll, E. W. (1993). Learning in premature infants. *Developmental Psychology, 29,* 692–700.

Trommsdorff, G. (1989). Sozialisation und Werthaltungen im Kulturvergleich [Socialization and value orientation in cross-cultural comparison]. In G. Trommsdorff (Ed.), *Sozialisation im Kulturvergleich* [Socialization and cross-cultural comparison]. (pp. 97–121). Stuttgart: Enke.

Trope, Y. (1982). Self-assessment and task performance. *Journal of Experimental Social Psychology, 18,* 201–215.

Underwood, B., Froming, W. J., & Moore, B. S. (1980). Mood and personality: A search for the causal relationship. *Journal of Personality, 48,* 15–23.

Valentin, P. (1991). Weltbilder von Kinern und Jugendlichen: Eine entwicklungspsychologische Perspektive [Mental representations of the word in children and adolescents]. Unpublished doctoral dissertation, University of Bern, Switzerland.

Van Aken, M. A. G., & Riksen-Walraven, J. M. (1992). Parental support and the development of competence in children. *International Journal of Behavioral Development, 15,* 101–123.

Vygotsky, L. S. (1962). *Thought and Language.* (transl. by E. Hartman & G. Vakar). Cambridge, MA: Massachusetts Institute of Technology Press. (Original work published 1934)

Wahl, H. W., & Baltes, M. M. (1990). Die soziale Umwelt alter Menschen: Entwicklungsanregende oder -hemmende Pflegeinteraktionen? [The social environment of old people: Development supporting or development inhibiting interactions with care persons?]. *Zeitschrift für Entwicklungspsychologie und Pädagogische Psychologie, 22,* 266–283.

Watson, J. S. (1966). The development and generalization of "contingency awareness" in early infancy: Some hypotheses. *Merrill-Palmer Quarterly, 12*, 123–135.

Watson, J. S. (1967). Memory and "contingent analysis" in infant learning. *Merrill-Palmer Quarterly, 13*, 55–76.

Watson, J. S. (1971). Cognitive perceptual development in infancy. *Merrill-Palmer Quarterly, 18*, 139–152.

Watson, J. S. (1979). Perception of contingency as a determinant of social responsiveness. In E. G. Thoman (Ed.), *Origins of the infant's social responsiveness* (pp. 33–64). Hillsdale, NJ: Erlbaum.

Watson, J. S., & Ramey, C. T. (1972). Reactions to response-contingent stimulation in early infancy. *Merrill-Palmer Quarterly, 18*, 219–227.

Weiner, B., Frieze, I. H., Kukla, A., Reed, L., Rest, S., & Rosenbaum, R. M. (1971). *Perceiving the causes of success and failure.* New York: General Learning Press.

Weisz, J. R. (1980). Developmental change in perceived control: Recognizing noncontingency in the laboratory and perceiving it in the world. *Developmental Psychology, 16*, 385–390.

Weisz, J. R. (1981). Illusory contingency in children at the state fair. *Developmental Psychology, 17*, 481–489.

Weisz, J. R. (1983). Can I control it? The pursuit of veridical answers across the life-span. In P. B. Baltes & O. G. Grim (Eds.), *Life-span development and behavior* (Vol. 5) (pp. 233–300). New York: Academic.

Weisz, J. R., & Stipek, D. J. (1982). Competence, contingency, and the development of perceived control. *Human Development, 25*, 250–281.

Wicki, W., Reber, R., Flammer, A., & Grob, A. (1994). Begründung der Kontrollmeinung bei Kindern und Jugendlichen [Justification of control beliefs by children and adolescents]. *Zeitschrift für Entwicklungspsychologie und Pädagogische Psychologie.*

Williams, J. M. G. (1988). General and specific autobiographical memory and emotional disturbance. In M. M. Gruneberg, P. E. Morris, & R. N. Sykes (Eds.), *Practical aspects of memory: Volume 1. Memory in everyday life* (pp. 295–300). New York: Wiley.

Williams, J. M. G., & Broadbent, K. (1986). Autobiographical memory in suicide attempters. *Journal of Abnormal Psychology, 95*, 144–149.

Williams, J. M. G., & Dritschel, B. H. (1988). Emotional disturbance and the specificity of autobiographical memory. *Cognition and Emotion, 2*, 221–234.

Williams, J. M. G., & Scott, J. (1988). Autobiographical memory in depression. *Psychological Medicine, 18*, 689–695.

Worden, P. E., & Sladewski-Awig, L. J. (1982). Children's awareness of memorability. *Journal of Educational Psychology, 74*, 341–350.

Wright, J., & Mischel, W. (1982). The influences of affect on cognitive social learning person variables. *Journal of Personality and Social Psychology, 43*, 901–914.

Wylie, R. (1961). *The self concept.* Lincoln: University of Nebraska Press.

Yussen, S., & Kane, P. (1985). Children's conception of intelligence. In S. W. Yussen (Ed.), *The growth of reflection in children* (pp. 207–241). New York: Academic.

Yussen, S., & Levy, V. (1975). Developmental changes in predicting one's own span of short-term memory. *Journal of Experimental Child Psychology, 19*, 502–508.

Simmerman, B. (1995). Self-efficacy and educational development. In A. Bandura (Ed.), *Self-efficacy in changing societies* (pp. 202–231). New York: Cambridge University Press.

Zuckerman, M. (1979). Attribution of success and failure revisited, or: The motivational bias is alive and well in attribution theory. *Journal of Personality, 47*, 245–287.

4. Impact of family processes on control beliefs

KLAUS A. SCHNEEWIND

The focus of this chapter is on the structural and process-oriented aspects of family life that are expected to have an influence on children's and adolescents' acquisition of control beliefs or, more specifically, on the development of self-efficacy and outcome expectations. After dealing with some theoretical and assessment issues, I will review available research on this topic with a special emphasis on parenting and relevant conditions that influence the parenting process. In addition, I will occasionally intersperse some results from my own research to illustrate in somewhat greater detail how I have tried to address various questions pertaining to this topic. Finally, after demonstrating that a fuller understanding of the development of personal control beliefs makes it necessary to include influences that are beyond the family system, I will briefly comment on an integrative model that might serve as a guide for further research in this field.

Self-efficacy and other control-related constructs

Recent theorizing in the behavioral and social sciences underscores the need for overarching principles concerning factors that motivate and guide human behavior. Among these approaches, Bakan's (1966) seminal work on the "duality of human existence" and his two concepts of "communion" and "agency" have become quite popular in recent years (e.g., McAdams, 1988; Wiggins, 1991). In McAdam's (1988, p. 12) words:

> Agency refers to the organism's striving to consolidate its individuality, to separate from other organisms, to master the surroundings, to assert, protect, and expand the self. Communion, on the other

I would like to extend my gratitude to Albert Bandura for his scholarly comments and stylistic help in preparing this chapter.

hand, refers to the organism's striving to lose its individuality by merging with others and the surrounding environment, to partici- pate in a "larger organism" of which it is part, to surrender the self through contact, openness, and cooperation.

It should not go unmentioned, though, that the roots of these concepts date back to the presocratic Greek philosopher Empedokles, who distin- guished between "love" and "strife" as two basic "cosmic forces . . . explaining the possibility of change and of growth and decay, respec- tively" (Röd, 1976, p. 148).

For the human being these seemingly very broad concepts might be conceived as "integrative themes in lives" (McAdams, 1985) expressing themselves in varying ways depending on the contexts and developmen- tal status of the individual person. Moreover, the integrative nature of these concepts implies that they encompass motivational, emotional, cog- nitive, and actional components, all of which can be thought to be interre- lated aspects of the intrapersonal system. At the same time both concepts represent developmentally changing phenonema that, depending on people's transactions with their environment, especially in times of crisis and transition, challenge people to restructure their balance and to find corresponding behavioral expressions (Schneewind, 1994). Although I will concentrate in the present chapter on human agency as it is affected by family structure and socialization, it should be emphasized that both life themes are intrinsically interwoven aspects of human life.

The motivational component of human agency can be seen in a person's basic need to control and master the environment (e.g., Harter, 1978; White, 1959). Flammer (1990, p. 115) speaks of an "innate basic need for control" (*Kontrollgrundbedürfnis*) that, depending on particular goals that become salient in the person's life course, is channeled into a multitude of specific needs for control (*Kontrollbedürfnisse*). Thus, the various control needs are always goal-oriented and manifest themselves in specific con- trol behaviors that are mediated and accompanied by corresponding cog- nitive and emotional processes, that is, control beliefs and control feelings or emotions.

As a consequence of the "cognitive revolution" in psychology, control beliefs or expectancies became a major theoretical and research issue. Especially since Rotter (1966, p. 1) introduced his concept of "generalized expectancies for internal versus external control of reinforcement" (usu- ally referred to as "locus of control") as part of his social learning theory of personality (Rotter, 1954), a vast amount of research has been accumulated (e.g., Krampen, 1989a; Strickland, 1989; Rotter, 1990). Rotter's concept of locus of control refers to the perception of self as a more or less outcome-controlling agent. However, perceptions of the self as a more or less competent agent remain unspecified, although they are usually implied. Bandura's (1977) influential theoretical paper on self-efficacy led to more conceptual clarity by introducing two kinds of expectations about the self: outcome expectations, which are "the person's estimate that a given behavior will lead to certain outcomes," and efficacy expectations, which refer to a person's belief "that one can successfully execute the behavior required to produce the outcomes" (Bandura, 1977, p. 193). In the meantime an impressive number of research studies attest to the theoretical and empirical importance of the self-efficacy construct (for reviews see Bandura, 1986, 1989).

In addition, several theoretically similar but differently labeled concepts have been introduced. Among these are, for instance, Weisz and Stipek's (1982) distinction between *contingency judgments* and *competence judgments* as essential components of perceived control; Ford and Thompson's (1985) *perceptions of control* and *perceptions of competence*, which both contribute to what they call *personal agency beliefs*; Skinner, Chapman, and Baltes' (1988) theoretical model comprising *means-ends beliefs*, *agency beliefs*, and *control beliefs*, the latter representing the individual's convictions of the self as an outcome controlling agent independent of means. In a similar vein, a research program that I started in 1982 to assess personal control orientations in children and adolescents was based on an action-theoretic approach distinguishing between *goal control* and *means control* as two interrelated components of *personal control* (Schneewind, 1987a, 1987b; Schneewind & Wünsche, 1985).

Another "cognate of personal control" (Peterson & Stunkard, 1992) is the concept of *explanatory style*, which essentially is a reformulation of Seligman's (1975) learned helplessness model in terms of attibution theory (e.g., Peterson, 1991). Theoretically, however, explanatory style refers to past-oriented attributions of success and failure in attempting to attain particular goals, whereas personal control beliefs deal with future-oriented expectations concerning a person's more or less effective coping with upcoming challenges. Thus, although explanatory style and personal control might refer to interacting aspects of a person's cognitive system, it makes much sense to keep both constructs clearly distinct at the conceptual level.

It should also be mentioned that, from a developmental perspective, the assumption of differentially operating outcome and self-efficacy expectancies implies a relatively high level of cognitive functioning, that is, rather elaborate cognitive representations of self and nonself, means and ends, knowledge of goals, and so on (e.g., Diethelm, 1991; Flammer, 1990; Weisz & Stipek, 1982). Thus, for instance, Earl (1987, p. 421) postulated a more general concept called self-trust that he defined as "the faith (belief plus action) in one's ability to fulfill a perceived task." According to Earl, self-trust operates at the intersection of the pre-conscious and conscious level and is instigated by rather vaguely perceived external cues ("hunches"). In addition, self-trust precedes the decision to engage in specific goal-directed behaviors that are mediated by efficacy and outcome expectations. Usually these behaviors become actualized with a high degree of flexiblity and tenacity in pursuing a particular goal. Viewed this way, self-trust seems to have much in common with recent concepts of modern attachment theory, which is based on the assumption that secure attachments lead to a positive model of the self (e.g., Bartholomew, 1990), thus pointing to the more "communal" antecedents of agency beliefs.

Assessment self-efficacy within the family context

Although, as already mentioned, the concept of self-efficacy is rather popular in present-day psychology, the amount of research focusing upon familial antecedents of the development of self-efficacy beliefs is amazingly scarce. This holds especially true if one keeps to the more precise definition of efficacy expectations or competence beliefs as mediating cognitive variables within a more general control-theoretic paradigm.

Because the main focus of the present contribution is on familial antecedents of self-efficacy, one important theoretical and empirical question is how self-efficacy expectations become socialized within the family context. More specifically, one of the central questions is how and to what extent parents contribute to the development and consolidation of self-efficacy beliefs in their offspring. This leaves us with the problem of assessing self-efficacy in children, which is an especially difficult task if the children are still on a preverbal level.

One way to circumvent this problem is to look at the development of "contingency awareness" in infants as it has been done by Watson and his colleagues in a series of ingenious experiments (e.g., Finkelstein & Ramey, 1977; Watson, 1966; Watson & Ramey, 1972.). In Switzerland, Perrez and his coworkers have further developed this approach by focusing on the relation of objective behavior-outcome contingencies and subjective contingency perceptions, which are thought to be early precursors of control beliefs (e.g., Diethelm 1991; Perrez, 1989; Perrez, Ackermann, & Diethelm, 1983). It should be noted, however, that in Bandura's terminology, contingency perceptions are roughly equivalent to what he calls outcome expectations. Thus, at best, contingency perceptions are implying that something like a self-efficacy mechanism is operating as a mediating variable.

Things become somewhat easier when children can be asked directly to report on how self-efficacious they feel with respect to different goal domains like academic achievements, social competence, or physical fitness. Several instruments are available to assess these perceived competencies among which Harter's (1982) Perceived Competence Scale for Children (PCSC) is perhaps most salient (for German adaptations see, Asendorpf & van Aken, 1993; Wünsche & Schneewind, 1989). Other assessment devices are Skinner, Chapman, and Baltes' (1988) Control, Agency, Means-Ends Inventory (CAMI), which separates self-efficacy, control, and causality beliefs. For my own instrument, called Diagnosis of Personal Control (DPK), a questionnaire and a playboard version (the latter especially designed for younger children) is available (Schneewind, 1987a, 1987b, 1989a; Schneewind, Wünsche, & Pausch, 1989). As already mentioned above, the DPK enables one to assess beliefs about *goal control*. This is defined as children's knowledge of important and substitutable means to attain particular goals in academic, social, or physical domains, and "means control" of the extent to which children believe that these goal-relevant means are actually available and can be influenced by them. Incidentally, means control turned out to be substantially higher correlated across goal domains with Harter's (1982) corresponding subscales of her PCSC ($r = .43$) than goal control ($r = .24$), thus attesting not only to the construct validity of the means control parameter in our model but also to the relevance of distinguishing between these two components of personal control orientations (Schneewind, 1987a).

In other research contexts, as in the realm of children's social behavior, specific assessment devices using questionnaires or situational scenarios have been designed to measure how easy or hard it is for children to execute particular prosocial or aggressive acts to handle certain conflicts in peer relationships. This is a rather straightforward operationalization of domain- and situation-specific self-efficacy expectations. In addition, in some of these studies outcome expectancies have also been assessed using the same format, that is, children are asked to estimate the extent to which their interventions will be successful to resolve the social conflict (e.g. Cuddy & Frame, 1991; Wheeler & Ladd, 1982; Perry, Perry & Rasmussen, 1986; Pettit, Harrist, Bates, & Dodge, 1991; Wheeler & Ladd, 1982).

At the adult level, several assessment instruments are available to measure generalized or specific self-efficacy beliefs. In Germany, for example,

Schwarzer and his research group have developed a number of questionnaire scales to assess specific perceived academic competencies as well as more general beliefs of self-efficacy (Jerusalem & Schwarzer, 1986; Schwarzer & Jerusalem, 1989).

Shifting our focus from the child to the parent, it is of particular interest in the present context whether generalized and specific parental self-efficacy beliefs have an impact on the child. Among the latter, parenting efficacy as measured by parents' conviction to carry out competently necessary child-rearing activities is of special importance. It can be argued that such beliefs mediate actual parenting behavior, which, among other developmental outcomes, might influence the child's own self-efficacy and control beliefs (for corresponding studies see, e.g. Bugenthal & Shennum, 1984; Cutrona & Troutman, 1986; Teti & Gelfand, 1991). Some of the measures that have been used are, for instance, Johnston and Mash's (1989) Parenting Sense of Competence (PSOC) scale; Abidin's (1986) Sense of Competence Scale as part of his Parenting Stress Index (PSI); Campis, Layman, and Prentice-Dunn's (1986) Parental Locus of Control Scale (PLCS), which contains a Parenting Efficacy factor; Gross and Rocissano's (1988) Toddler Care Questionnaire (TCQ); Teti and Gelfand's (1991) Maternal Self-Efficacy Scale; and our own Parenting Competence Scale (PCS), which has been devised as an individual (mother, father) and parental team measure to assess perceived competencies in handling infants and toddlers (Schneewind, Knopp, Schmidt-Rinke, Sierwald, & Vierzigmann, 1989).

From a family systems perspective it can be argued that it is not only parenting efficacy that, via corresponding parental behavior, has an impact on the child's development but also perceived couple efficacy, that is, the spouses' mutual belief that they can manage their relationship in a constructive and competent way. Besides strengthening the spousal bond, couple efficacy can be conceived as a major prerequisite for effective parenting, which, in turn, feeds back to the marital system (e.g., Belsky, 1990). Not much research has addressed this particular issue. As a consequence, corresponding assessment instruments are largely missing, except for a few scales like the Miller Marital Locus of Control Scale (Miller, Lefcourt, & Ware, 1983) or our own Perceived Couple Competence Scale (Schneewind et al., 1989).

If I now turn to the familial correlates and antecedents of self-efficacy I will not refer to self-efficacy or competence expectations in only their strict conceptual sense. Rather, because of the paucity of empirical studies that are truly faithful to the definition of self-efficacy and its theoretically equivalent constructs, I will also include studies bearing on other aspects of self-related cognitive representations within a control-theoretic paradigm, especially personal agency or control beliefs.

Family structure and control beliefs

Considering the variables that are more distal indicators of family functioning, some studies address the relationship between particular structural aspects of the family like sibling position, family completeness, and family size with children's or parents' control orientations. Krampen (1982a, 1994) and Carton and Nowicki (in press) have provided valuable summaries of this type of research.

Sibling position

With respect to sibling ordinal position several studies have shown that single and first-born children display more internal control beliefs than later-born children (e.g., Crandall, Katkovsky, & Crandall, 1965; Hoffman & Teyber, 1979; Krampen, 1982b). This difference has usually been explained in terms of first-borns being ascribed more responsibility and receiving more extended and intensive attention by their parents than their later-born siblings, thus providing more opportunties for experiencing behavior-outcome contingencies. Furthermore, in some studies also significant sibling-sex interactions and sibling spacing effects have been reported (e.g., Hoffman & Teyber, 1979; Marks, 1973). However, like the effects of sibling position, the interaction effects are rather small in terms of explained variance.

Family completeness

In some studies, parental loss, especially father absence, which is an important indicator of family completeness, is reported to have an impact on children's control beliefs. Children living in single-parent, mother-headed families tend to show a higher external control orientation (e.g., Duke & Lancaster, 1976; Hetherington, 1972;). More fine-grained analyses, however, reveal that other variables like age and sex of the child, cause of father absence (death or divorce), or time elapsed since father loss have differential effects on the children's control orientations. Thus, boys tend to report higher external control beliefs than girls, especially if the cause of father absence is death (Parish & Copeland, 1980), although these differences disappear when the time interval of father loss is taken into account (Parish, 1981).

Although some studies have documented higher external control beliefs as a consequence of parental divorce (e.g., Lancaster & Richmond, 1983; Parish & Boyd, 1983), others were not able to corroberate these findings (e.g., Hainline & Feig, 1978; Parish, 1981). In at least one study parental divorce was related to internal control expectancies in a sample of third- and fifth-graders (Kalter, Alpern, Spence, & Plunkett, 1984).

More specifically, parenting efficacy does not seem to be differentially related to marital status, that is, married versus divorced/separated, as Luster and Kain (1987) have shown in their analysis of a large sample of 3,000 parents in the United States. However, it should be noted that studies usually compare averages of children's level of control in complete versus incomplete families. Differential analyses underscore the importance of considering the impact of potentially moderating variables as, for example, post-divorce conflict among ex-spouses or children's emotional adjustment to divorce (e.g., Kurdek, Blisk, & Siesky, 1981; Kurdek & Blisk, 1983; Slater & Haber, Kurdek & Blisk, 1986; Reisel, 1984). Thus, Reisel (1986) found that only those children who lost their fathers due to divorce and showed pronounced signs of emotional disturbance to the divorce were more externally controlled. This is but one example of the necessity to conduct more elaborate process and outcome analyses on the differential effects of divorce (e.g., Amato, 1993; Kurdek, 1993). In addition, it should be noted that global measures of perceived efficacy may mask relationships that are revealed by more sensitive domain-specific measures.

Family size

Another aspect of family structure that has been related to efficacy or control beliefs is family size. Walter and Ziegler (1980) found that external control beliefs, especially in last-born children, increase with the number of children in the family. Parental efficacy was not related to family size in Luster and Kain's (1987) study, whereas Ladd and Price (1986) report a significant albeit small correlation between the parents' perceived difficulty with child-rearing tasks in the social domain and family size. Again, it is difficult to draw reasonably valid conclusions from these studies because family size might be confounded with a host of other influences (e.g., the family's socioeconomic status, racial background, etc.). More process-oriented aspects of family life, therefore, need to be taken into account.

In sum, the available evidence on the relation between distal indicators of family structure and children's control beliefs or parental efficacy expectations reveals that the effects are either small or inconsistent. In any case, more subtle psychological processes within the family context may mediate the rather extended explanatory gap between family structure and personal control orientations. It is to these mediating variables that I turn next.

Parental influences on children's control beliefs

Based on the assumptions of social learning theory it has long been hypothesized that, due to their early onset, duration, and intensity, parental child-rearing practices have an important influence on the development and shaping of children's control orientations. The benefits of internal control beliefs, at least for the Western culture, have been well documented in numerous studies (e.g., Krampen, 1982a; Lefcourt, 1976; Mielke, 1982; Phares, 1976; Rotter, 1990; Strickland, 1989). It is therefore of special interest to examine parental child-rearing practices that supposedly strengthen internal control beliefs and their positive consequences on children's further personality development. Rotter (1966, p. 24), for example, has argued that "the consistency and treatment by parents" might be essential antecedents of generalized control expectations in children. Empirical evidence has, indeed, accumulated corroborating this hypothesis. More importantly, specific aspects of parenting practices have been shown to be especially important contributors to the development of children's control beliefs (for reviews see Carton & Nowicki, in press; Diethelm, 1991; Krampen, 1982a, 1994).

Parental correlates of children's control beliefs

The finding concerning the relationship between parenting and children's internal as opposed to external control beliefs appears to be quite consistent: Parents providing a *stimulating family environment* (e.g., Bradley & Caldwell, 1979; Nowicki & Schneewind, 1982; Schneewind, 1982, 1989b), being consistently and contingently *responsive* to their children's behavior (e.g., Davis & Phares, 1969; Diethelm, 1991; Schneewind & Pfeiffer, 1978; Skinner, 1986; Yates, Kennelly, & Cox, 1975), emphasizing early *independence training* (e.g., Chance, 1970; Chandler, Wolf, Cook, & Dugovics, 1980; Meyer & Wacker, 1970; Wichern & Nowicki, 1976), engaging *autonomy granting* and *less intrusive interactions* (e.g., Gordon, Nowicki, & Wichern, 1981; Lehwald, 1991; Loeb, 1975), using *less hostile* and *more inductive disci-*

plinary techniques (e.g., Davis & Phares, 1969; Krampen, 1989b; Tolor & Jalowiec, 1968; Whitbeck, 1987), and relating to the child in a *warm and emotionally supportive way* (e.g., Krampen, 1989b; MacDonald, 1971; Nowicki & Segal, 1974; Schneewind & Pfeiffer, 1978; Yates, et al., 1975) tend to have children with a more internal control orientation. Conversely, parents who provide less stimulation, who are less responsive and more authoritarian, intrusive, overprotective, rejecting, or neglectful are more likely to have children with an external control orientation.

These summary findings are based on diverse types of studies using (a) cross-sectional versus longitudinal designs, (b) self-report versus observational data, (c) maternal versus paternal child-rearing practices, (d) present versus retrospective reports of parental behavior, (e) boys versus girls ranging in age from infancy to adolescence, and to a lesser degree (f) generalized versus domain-specific control expectations, (g) uni- versus multidimensional measures of control beliefs, and (h) intra- versus cross-cultural comparisons. It should be mentioned, however, that observational and longitudinal studies are clearly underrepresented. In addition, most of the studies are based on mother-child relations, thus falling short of a more complex family systems perspective. More specific control orientations referring to particular goal domains are also understudied, as are intra- and intercultural variations of control beliefs.

Longitudinal evidence on parenting antecedents of children's control beliefs

Of particular importance are longitudinal and controlled intervention studies because, unlike cross-sectional correlational designs, they help to shed more light on the status of parenting behavior as antecedents of personal control. As to possible early precursors of personal control, it has been suggested that studying the development of "contingency awareness" during infancy (e.g., Finkelstein & Ramey, 1977; Watson & Ramey, 1972) might be particularly promising. In a recent Swiss longitudinal study, Diethelm (1991) found that the more 2-month-old infants elicited or received more contingent stimulation from their parents the greater was their exploratory behavior of their inanimate and social environments when they were 1 year old.

Similarly, Riksen-Walraven (1978) in a well-designed Dutch intervention study demonstrated that 9-month-old infants whose primary caregivers were trained to provide responsive stimulation for their children explored their environment more intensively, showed more positive affect while doing so, and learned experimentally induced behavior-outcome contingencies more rapidly. Moreover, Riksen-Walraven (1978, p. 128) observed that her intervention program not only had an impact on the children's active exploration of their environment but also influenced the parent's efficacy expectations:

> As the parent sees that his [sic] acts have effect, he builds up the expectation that he is effective in influencing the infant's behavior, and, hence, will be motivated to be more responsive towards his child. Once changed by the program, the parents' expectation remains stable, because it gives rise to behavior which, by its consequences, confirms that expectation.

Thus, both the development of infants' contingency awareness and the parents' efficacy expectations can be fostered by specific parent-child transactions at the infant age. More importantly, the long-term impact of these early intervention-induced changes were at least partially demonstrated in a 12-year follow-up assessment (Riksen-Walraven, 1991).

On the whole, however, longitudinal studies that extend into later developmental phases are extremely rare. In fact, in their critical review on the antecedents of locus of control, Carton and Nowicki (in press) found just two relevant studies. Whereas the short-term longitudinal study by Krampen (1989b) basically confirmed that parental practices contribute to children's control orientations, the results of a long-term study by Crandall and Crandall (1983) differed from the usual pattern in several respects. Mothers of young adults were observed to be more critical, rejecting, and less affectionate than when their children were in their preschool years. But they put as much emphasis on independence training as has been found in other studies. There has been much speculation about the unexpected relationship found in the Crandall and Crandall study. Besides the usual methodological reservations (e.g., small sample size, questionable psychometric properties of assessment instruments), the study focused on mother-child relations only, thus omitting the possible influences of other family members, especially fathers, on children's development of personal control.

Our own as yet unpublished study tested 200 German families in 1976 when their children were 9 to 14 years old and then retested them in 1992. We measured the parents' and children's control beliefs as well as various aspects of parenting style (Schneewind, Beckmann, & Hecht-Jackl, 1985), that is, parental child-rearing goals, attitudes, and practices as perceived by the parents and the children respectively (Schneewind & Ruppert,

1992). The cross-sectional findings based on the 1976 measurement wave essentially corroborated the previously found pattern of child-rearing influence on children's internal versus external control orientations (e.g., Schneewind, 1982, 1985, 1989b; Schneewind, Beckmann, & Engfer, 1983; Schneewind & Pfeiffer, 1978).

We now briefly present some of the findings on the predictive relationship of individual differences in parenting practices as perceived by their children in 1976 to their generalized self-efficacy beliefs as measured 16 years later when they were young adults ranging in age from 25 to 30 years. Generalized self-efficacy was measured with the Jerusalem and Schwarzer (1986) short version of their corresponding scale, which assesses mainly people's confidence to master difficult and unforeseen problems in their lives. In hierarchical multiple regression analyses, 16% of the variance in generalized efficacy of males and 12% of the variance in females was predicted by the children's perceived parental behavior assessed in 1976. Of particular interest, however, is that the configuration of parental predictors is quite different for males and females. For male adults, those who during their childhood experienced a close and warm relationship with their fathers and a somewhat demanding and task-oriented, albeit nonrejecting, relationship with their mothers developed higher confidence in their general problem-solving efficacy. In addition, high interparental congruence, especially the use of rewarding and punishing disciplinary techniques, also contributes to the young men's generalized self-efficacy. In contrast, self-efficacious adult women experienced more pressure from their fathers to fulfill parental values like demonstrating status, achievement striving, and educational attainment when they were young girls. Their mothers tended to rely on psychological influence, such as appealing to the daughters' sympathy, to make them comply with their mothers' wishes.

From the results of this long-term prospective study it seems, then, that the parental antecedents of generalized self-efficacy expectations are differently patterned across gender. In addition, although internal locus of control and self-efficacy are only moderately correlated on the adult level, boys show more continuity than girls in the parental correlates of control beliefs. In fact, the correlates of parenting practices with internal locus of control measured in 1976 were quite similar for boys and girls. For the sons the more salient child-rearing variables (e.g., paternal closeness) by and large retained their prognostic value across time whereas there were some marked changes for girls. For example, the use of maternal psychological methods of influence was a positive predictor of internality in young adulthood although it was negatively related to an internal control orientation in childhood. We do not know why these gender-specific changes occurred. We can only speculate that in our society highly self-efficacious and presumably successful young women might have to adopt a "male" perspective for which they are better prepared by achievement-related parental demands, especially by their fathers.

Besides these gender-specific parental antecedents of young adults' generalized self-efficacy beliefs, we found a small but longitudinally consistent relationship between children's earlier perceptions of their family as providing a stimulating environment (i.e., greater variety of common recreational activities, higher cultural orientation, more social contacts with nonfamily members) and their control beliefs as young adults. Although the predictive correlation explains only about 4% of the variance in young adults' control beliefs, this relation holds equally for both sexes and for generalized self-efficacy as well as locus of control. In addition, these results repeat earlier cross-sectional findings for children and adolescents, at which time considerably stronger relations were obtained between a stimulating family climate and internal control beliefs in the context of emotionally supportive and flexibly organized family relationships (e.g., Nowicki & Schneewind, 1982; Schneewind, 1982, 1989b). In any case, these findings are fully in accord with theoretical conjectures, assuming that variety and responsiveness in the family environment is an important prerequisite for the development of individual efficacy and control beliefs.

Intergenerational transmission of control beliefs: The modeling hypothesis

Another issue that has been addressed in several studies concerns the possible modeling effects on intergenerational transmission of control beliefs. This is usually tested by the level of correlation between parental and children's control beliefs. Several studies failed to confirm the modeling hypothesis for children at the preschool level (e.g., Galejs, Hegland, & King, 1985; Schave & Fox, 1986). However, moderate positive intergenerational correlations have been found for older children and adolescents (e.g., Lifshitz & Ramot, 1978; Ollendick, 1979; Whitbeck, 1987). Such findings lend some support to the notion that control orientations may be transmitted from one generation to the other via modeling.

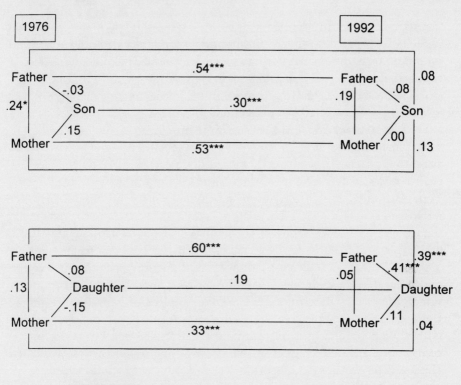

Figure 4.1. Stabilities and intrafamilial correlations of locus of control for sons (N = 96) and daughters (N = 98); time interval: 17 years.

Longitudinal data on the modeling issue are virtually nonexistent. However, we were able to test this notion in our 16 year longitudinal study on personality and family development (Schneewind & Ruppert, 1992). Figure 4.1 presents the long-term stabilities as well as intra- and intergenerational correlations of generalized internal versus external control orientations of our male and female subjects. Central orientations were measured by German adaptations of Nowicki's children and adult versions of his locus of control scale (Nowicki & Duke, 1974; Nowicki & Strickland, 1973; Rinke & Schneewind, 1978).

As shown in Figure 4.1, locus of control is moderately stable over time, especially for parents. But the intrafamilial correlations do not confirm the modeling hypothesis at either measurement point. The one notable exception is that, over time, daughters seem to have adopted their fathers' control orientation, thus lending some support to the "male view" hypothesis for internally controlled young women.

What is still lacking, however, are more fine-grained analyses to explain how particular familial processes contribute either directly via specific parenting practices or indirectly via modeling to children's acquisition of their control beliefs. One of the few studies shedding some light on this issue examined the child-rearing antecedents of children's efficacy and outcome expectations in handling peer conflicts by prosocial and assertive versus aggressive strategies (Pettit, Harrist, Bates, & Dodge, 1991). The children's social behavior was assessed on the basis of teacher ratings assuming that the children's actual social behavior in the school setting was mediated by their corresponding efficacy and outcome expectations, which in turn are determined by specific patterns of parent-child interactions.

With respect to aggression, coercive and intrusive mother-child interactions led to children's higher self-efficacy for aggressive tactics, which fostered greater readiness to resort to aggression in peer relationships. Moreover, further analyses revealed that efficacy expectations were crucial mediators of children's aggressiveness in peer relations. However, a similar causal sequence was not obtained for prosocial or assertive behavior. Although the results of this study provide only partial support of the impact of specific patterns of mother-child interactions on the child's control beliefs and their links to behavior, this type of theoretically informed empirical research can advance our understanding of the processes that contribute to the transmission of interpersonal style within the family context.

Antecedents of parenting efficacy

Another line of theorizing and research concerns parental beliefs about their parenting role, especially in light of renewed interest in how parental beliefs translate into actual parental practices (e.g., Goodnow & Collins, 1990; Miller, 1988). Parenting efficacy constitutes a special aspect of parental belief systems focusing on the beliefs that parents have the capabilities to manage the tasks of nurturing and socializing their children. Mothers who believe that they can influence their infants' performances in specific developmental tasks are more involved and stimulating when interacting with them (e.g., Parks & Smeriglio, 1986; Smeriglio & Parks, 1983). Similarly, Tulkin (1977) reported that compared to working-class mothers, middle-class mothers who engaged in more verbal interactions with their infants and provided them with a greater variety of stimulation expressed stronger beliefs in their ability to influence the development of their children. On the negative side, Bugenthal and Shennum (1984) found that parents who are low on parenting efficacy tend to become more irritated when interacting with an unresponsive child than parents with a high confidence in their parenting competence. In the realm of child abuse, it was found that abusive and neglectful mothers reported more unrealistic expectations for their children (Azar, Robinson, Hekimian, & Twentyman, 1984) and described themselves as being less satisfied and efficacious as parents than nonabusive mothers (Mash, Johnston, & Kovitz, 1983).

A few studies have also looked at possible antecedents and the moderating role played by perceived parenting efficacy in relation to actual parenting competence (e.g., Cutrona & Troutman, 1986; Donovan & Leavitt, 1989; Teti & Gelfand, 1991; Teti, Gelfand, & Pompa, 1990). In particular, Teti and Gelfand (1991) were able to demonstrate that observed maternal competence, even after controlling for a number of other factors like sociodemographic status, maternal depression, spousal support, and difficulty of infant temperament, was still related to maternal parenting efficacy, thus supporting the relevance of perceived self-efficacy as a mediating variable in the parenting process.

Again, these studies are based on cross-sectional designs and thus make it difficult to disentangle the direction of causation. Infant difficulty, for example, might either be an antecedent or consequence of parenting efficacy. To test this hypothesis longitudinally on the transition to parenthood my colleagues and I applied our Parenting Competence Scale (PCS) to a sample of 48 parents to be 1 month before the birth of their first child and again 3 months and 9 months after they became parents. In addition, as an indicator of infant difficulty we collected data on the perceived child soothability scale as part of a more comprehensive instrument to assess individual differences in infant temperament (Schneewind et al., 1989) when the infants were 3 and 9 months old. The resulting cross-lagged correlations between parenting competence and infant soothability are shown in Figure 4.2.

From the results presented in Figure 4.2 it becomes evident that for both sexes parenting competence is quite stable over time, including prebirth measurement. Moreover, keeping Kenny's (1979) caveats concerning the causal interpretation of cross-lagged correlations in mind, the data sug-

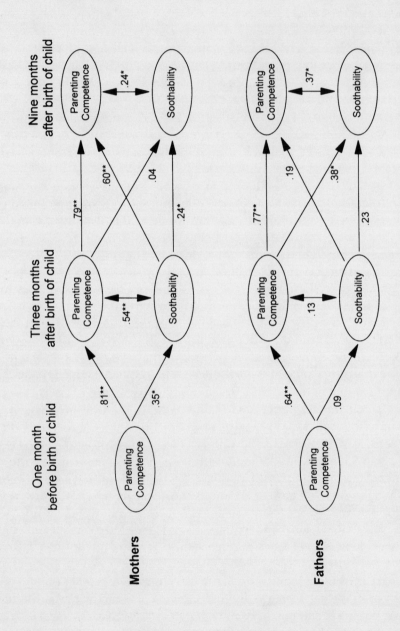

One month before birth of child

Three months after birth of child

Nine months after birth of child

Mothers

.81** .35*

.54** .79** .60** .04 .24*

Fathers

.64*** .09

.13 .77** .19 .38* .23 .37*

Figure 4.2. Cross-lagged correlations for mother's and father's parenting competence with infant's soothability (N = 48).

gest that in early infancy the mothers' parenting efficacy is influenced by their babies' soothability rather than the other way around. For the fathers, however, the data clearly do not support a causal relation between parenting efficacy and infant soothability. One plausible explanation is that, in our sample, fathers had limited opportunities for extended interaction with their children because they were all working full time.

Further evidence on familial antecedents of individual differences in parenting efficacy is rather scarce. In one study, Gross, Rocissano, and Roncoli (1989) found that prior child care experience and, for preterm births only, birth order of the child were strong predictors of maternal parenting confidence during toddlerhood. More directly, Simons and his colleagues in a series of recent studies based on the Iowa Youth and Families Project (e.g., Simons, Beaman, Conger, & Chao, 1993; Simons, Whitbeck, Conger, & Wu, 1991) found that the quality of grandparents' parenting (i.e., harsh discipline or supportiveness) is related to the parents' own discipline and what the authors call parenting impact beliefs, which, in turn, influence their actual child-rearing practices.

In our Options of Young Couples Project (Schneewind et al., 1992) we were interested in determining whether the parenting efficacy of young couples expecting their first child ($N = 48$) could be predicted from their retrospectively reported experience with their own mothers and fathers during childhood. We assumed that perceived quality of parenting, closeness to parents, quality of the parents' marital relationship, and several subtly conveyed parental "delegations" (e.g., pursuing a life-style with or without children) might be predictive of the young parents' own parenting efficacy.

Using stepwise multiple regression analysis we found that 27% of the variance in young fathers' parenting efficacy and 18% of the variance of young mothers' parenting efficacy could be explained by the family-of-origin variables. However, the most predictive aspects of former family relationships differed markedly across the sexes. For the young fathers, a combination of two maternal delegations (i.e., focusing on a successful work career and at the same time assuring the continuity of family tradition) contributed most to their own parenting confidence. But the young mothers' parenting efficacy depended more on the quality of parenting they received during their childhood. Interestingly, however, the combination of high maternal but low paternal parenting competence along with a closer relationship with the mother than with the father was the most salient predictor of the young mothers' parenting efficacy. Thus it seems that young fathers derive their sense of parenting competence primarily from rather abstract and subtle maternal delegations, whereas young mothers rely more on their parents as models of good parenting. In particular, it appears that perceived parenting and relationship deficits of their fathers might have motivated the daughters to seek their parenting competence in their mothers.

In sum, the available evidence on the antecedents and consequences of parenting efficacy highlight its relevance as an important mediating factor in parent-child transactions. It should be noted, however, that from infancy through adolescence and even beyond, changing developmental tasks require quite different competencies on the part of the parents in caring for and relating to their children. Thus, for example, a mother who at an early developmental stage of her child is firmly convinced that she has the necessary competencies to care for her infant and actually behaves as a responsive and loving mother might be overwhelmed by the demands and problems of her child during the transition to puberty. Therefore, knowledge of age-appropriate developmental tasks and functionally related parenting practices appear to be crucial prerequisites for parents' developmentally synchronized adaptation of their sense of parenting competence. This is a promising field for further research and preventive intervention.

Perceived couple efficacy in the family context

Individual differences in parenting efficacy might not only be determined by the parents' familial experience but also by a host of other influences, especially the couple's relationship. There is ample research evidence that strained marital relationships are associated with a less effective parenting style (for reviews see Belsky, 1981, 1990). To explain this finding it has been suggested that for parents who live in a disharmonious relationship it might be particularly difficult to build a strong and efficient coparenting alliance (e.g., Gable, Belsky, & Crnic, 1992). Interestingly, however, most of the reseach has focused on the assessment of feelings, attitudes, conflicts, and behaviors in couple relationships without paying much attention to control beliefs that might also have an impact on the quality of couple interaction and satisfaction, as has been documented in several studies (e.g., Brandtstädter, Krampen, & Heil, 1986; Constantine & Bahr, 1981; Hohmann, 1988). In fact, high couple efficacy (i.e., a couple's confidence in being able to handle problems and disagreements in a mutually satisfying way) might be a protective factor in coping with potentially stressful events, whereas low couple efficacy might make the couple more vulnerable to stress, which can undermine further development for efficacy.

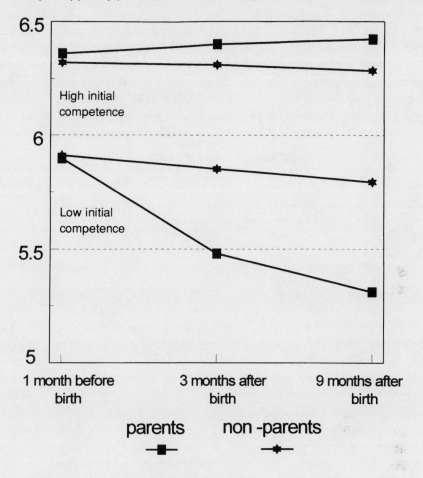

Figure 4.3. Development of parents and non-parents' couple competence with high and low initial couple competence.

We tested this hypothesis in a quasi-experimental longitudinal design, in which the development of young parents with their first child is contrasted with the development of a comparable group of nonparents. Couple efficacy was assessed for both groups using our Couple Competence Scale (Schneewind et al., 1989) 1 month before birth of the first child in the parent group, then 10 months later, and finally a year later. In addition, at the prebirth assessment we divided each of the parent and nonparent groups in two subgroups, one with high and the other one with low couple efficacy expectations. The changes in couple efficacy were then measured across time. The results of this study are shown in Figure 4.3.

Assuming, as many researchers do, that the transition to parenthood is a major stress-inducing event in early family development, we expected that the parent subgroup with initially low couple efficacy scores would decline in their couple competence over time. As can be seen from Figure 4.3 this hypothesis is clearly confirmed. Moreover, the results show that the high couple efficacy groups, regardless of whether they are parents or nonparents, stably remain at a high level of couple competence over the 2-year period.

The development and consequences of couple efficacy beliefs warrants greater research attention, especially within a family systems approach, where personal, couple, and parenting control orientations might operate as a set of interrelated expectancies that guide the process of family socialization.

Beyond the family: The larger developmental context of control beliefs

So far we have dealt mainly with family structure and intrafamilial processes as antecedents or correlates of efficacy and control beliefs. However, as Bronfenbrenner (1979, 1986) has aptly shown us in his conceptual analysis of hierarchically ordered developmental systems, the family is a microsystem that is related to other microsystems (e.g., school or peer group) and at the same time embedded into larger societal systems like the economic, subcultural, and cultural system. We have already seen that social class has a major influence on parenting efficacy which, in turn, is related to parental child-rearing practices and children's developmental outcomes (e.g., Luster & Kain, 1987; Tulkin, 1977). It is here where an integration of psychological and sociological theorizing provides a broader perspective on the acquisition and development of personal control orientations.

One hypothesis that has repeatedly been espoused by sociologists contends that there is a strong linkage between social class and parental values, which then determine the parents' child-rearing practices. Specifically, it has been shown that the lower the parents' socioeconomic status, the more likely they are to value conformity to external authority. As a consequence, they tend to put more emphasis on parental values like obedience and good manners, which are enforced with strict and constraining disciplinary techniques. On the other hand, it has been documented that parents of higher socioeconomic status favor values like self-direction and self-responsibility. This, in turn, is reflected in the parents' greater child support and their preference for inductive disciplinary techniques (e.g., Gecas, 1979; Kohn, 1979).

In a recent study, Luster, Rhodes, and Haas (1989) have replicated these findings. More importantly, however, they have also shown that the link between parental values and child-rearing practices is mediated by specific parental beliefs concerning the appropriateness and effectiveness of corresponding parenting practices. Such beliefs include spoiling the child by being too responsive and affectionate or talking and reading to the child, based on the belief that verbal stimulation promotes children's cognitive development. Such parental beliefs refer to outcome expectancies of particular parenting practices tied to specific parental goals like rearing an unspoiled child or having an intelligent child, characteristics that the parents might regard as functionally relevant for integrating the child into the larger society.

Particular parenting outcome beliefs do not necessarily imply corresponding efficacy beliefs or competent performance of the parenting behavior. Thus, parents might be convinced that talking and reading a lot to their children promotes their cognitive development, but nevertheless may not take the time or have the patience to engage in such activities. Certain parental beliefs, like avoiding affection and responsiveness in order to prevent the child from being spoiled, might impair the development of a close and warm parent-child relationship even though the parents are certain they could be more affectionate. Thus, more fine-grained analyses are required to clarify the interplay of social class–related parental goals, parenting outcome and efficacy beliefs, and parenting practices in guiding their children's development.

Some of the critics of social class as an explanatory factor in socialization research have argued that it is a rather distal social address variable that needs to be further specified in terms of actual conditions of life (e.g., Bertram, 1981; Bronfenbrenner, 1979; Vaskovics, 1982). Thus, for example, the parents' particular occupational experiences and institutional opportunities and restraints shape their personality and intrafamilial behavior more directly than traditional social class indicators such as income, education, or occupational status.

In an effort to test this hypothesis in the intrafamilial transmission of generalized control beliefs, we constructed a causal model in which a restricted ecocontext along with monotonous and less self-directed experiences at the workplace lead to a less active and more controlling family climate and to a more externally controlled personality structure of the parents. Furthermore, we hypothesized that the particular constellation of an unstimulating and controlling family environment and parents' generalized external control beliefs work together to produce an authoritarian

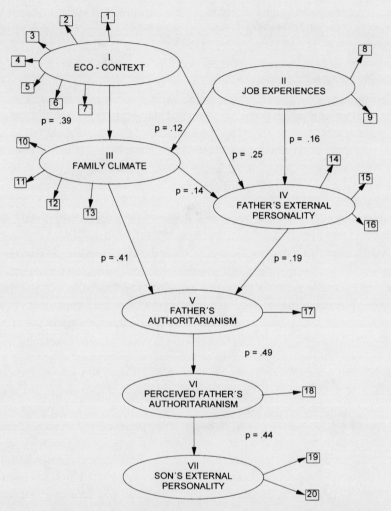

Figure 4.4. Intra- and extrafamilial influences on the manifestation of an external personality (from Schneewind, 1989c, p. 203).

parenting style. If it is perceived as such by the children, they are likely to develop external control beliefs as part of their personality structure.

Using Wold's (1979) partial least square version of a structural equation model we tested the causal sequence as specified in our theoretical model with a sample of 285 father-son dyads (age of sons: 9 to 14 years). Figure 4.4 presents the results of this analysis (Schneewind, 1989c).

As can be seen from the flow of path coefficients, the findings lend some support to our causal model. Specifically, 19% of the variance of sons' internal versus external personality structure could be explained by the model. It should be kept in mind, however, that these results are based on cross-sectional data and thus do not allow for a dynamic-transactional analysis of possible reciprocal influences. Moreover, the model is oriented more toward structure rather than process, thus omitting the subtle interplay of parental values, parental efficacy and outcome expectancies, and parenting behavior.

Finally, it should not go unmentioned that in all the studies that we have reviewed thus far the way control beliefs have been conceptualized is reflective of the self-centered value system of the Western world. As Rothbaum, Weisz, and Snyder (1982, p. 8) have pointed out, "the individual's ability to change the environment to fit the self's needs" is particularly salient in the Western value system. In contrast to this concept of control, which they call primary control, the same authors have focused on another aspect of control, called secondary control, which refers to a person's ability to adjust his or her needs to existing reality. However, this does not necessarily preclude that secondary control might be highly functional in pursuing collectivistic goals and thus contribute to the development of collective efficacy. Cross-cultural research has shown that primary control beliefs are typical for societies with an individualistic (Western world) value system, whereas secondary control beliefs are more dominant in societies with a collectivistic (Eastern world) value system (e.g., Weisz, Rothbaum, & Blackburn, 1984). It has been documented that differences in the global societal value system are reflected in corresponding parent-child relations. By contrasting child-related expectations of German and Japanese parents, Trommsdorff (1989), for example, could show that German parents, who are said to belong to an individualistic (i.e., more agency-oriented) society, put more emphasis on their children's independence, coping with parent-child conflicts, and learning through sanctions. Japanese parents, who supposedly represent a collectivistic (i.e., more communion-oriented) society, expected their children to be more submissive, learn through imitation, and stay in a harmonious relationship with their parents. Such behavior might well be a necessary prerequisite for the children's later adaptation to work life. Moreover, quite in accordance with theoretical predictions, it turned out that the German children scored higher on primary control beliefs while the Japanese children displayed more secondary control beliefs.

In sum, cultural and subcultural value systems guide concrete parental expectations that are deemed functionally relevant for the child's adaptation and integration into a given society. Different value systems, however, do not offset the theoretical and empirical importance of the parents' efficacy and outcome beliefs in pursuing what appears to be their main task as parents, that is, to prepare their children to become accepted members of the society they belong to.

Conclusion: An integrative model for studying control beliefs within the family context

In considering the research evidence reviewed in the preceding sections a more comprehensive picture of how control beliefs develop within the family gradually took shape. Focusing solely on family structure or parent-child relations is too narrow an approach for an adequate understanding of how children acquire and expand their personal control beliefs. Therefore, a more comprehensive conceptualization of the processes that influence children's acquistion and development of control beliefs within the family context is presented in Figure 4.5.

Without going much into the detail, I will briefly comment on the basic reasoning that led to this conceptual model. To begin with, parental child-rearing goals are of crucial importance in determining the parents' efficacy and outcome expectations and subsequently their actual behavior when they tackle the difficult developmental tasks of giving support, direction, and guidance to their children to help them find their place in society. However, parental goals are tied to particular cultural and subcultural values that the parents experienced while they went through their own socialization. In addition, the parents' socialization was influenced by the opportunities and constraints inherent in the specific material and social conditions of life that were and maybe still are characteristic of their life space. More specifically, the place parents found themselves in society and all the corresponding experiences shaped their repertoire of goals, beliefs, and behaviors in dealing with their children. In addition to the overall pattern of the parents' prevalent material and social conditions of life, specific features of family structure and family relationships as well as couple and interparental relationships impinge on the parenting process.

With regard to the children it is important to view their transactions with their parents as an active, self-constructing process. This involves active internal representation of events and progressive construction and elaboration of personal goals, belief systems, and corresponding behaviors. The same holds true, of course, for other socialization influences to which children are exposed. It is one of the subtle challenges for parents to adjust their parenting practices to the child's developmental status, thus

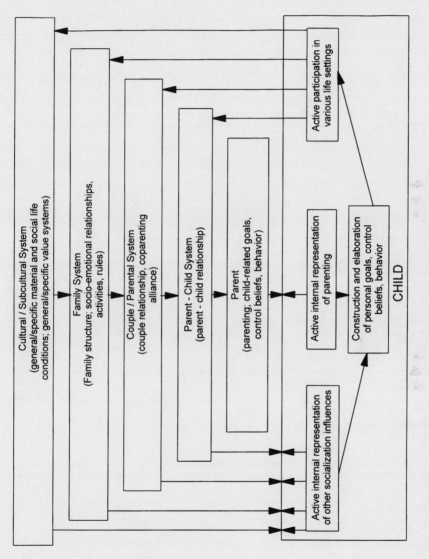

Figure 4.5. An integrative model for studying control beliefs within the family context.

140   Klaus A. Schneewind

instilling and guiding their children's internal processes that gradually enable them to participate as independent but also interdependent selves in various settings within the social system. As developing children continually participate in these settings they actively construct and integrate particular self-related cognitions into their self-system. Self-efficacy and outcome expectations may be conceived as a special class of such self-related cognitions that, depending on the child's level of cognitive functioning, become elaborated and help guide the course of children's further self-development.

The implications of this model are specific enough, but sufficiently open to invite further research addressing the important question of how family processes mediate between society and the developing self-system.

References

Abidin, R. R. (1986). *Parenting Stress Index: Manual.* Charlottesvile, VA: Pediatric Psychology Press.
Amato, P. R. (1993). Children's adjustment to divorce: Theories, hypotheses and empirical support. *Journal of Marriage and the Family, 55*, 23–38.
Asendorpf, J., & van Aken, M. A. G. (1993). Deutsche Versionen der Selbstkonzeptskalen von Harter [German versions of Harter's self-concept scales]. *Zeitschrift für Entwicklungspsychologie und Pädagogische Psychologie, 25*, 64–86.
Azar, S. T., Robinson, D. R., Hekimian, E., & Twentyman, C. T. (1984). Unrealistic expectations and problem-solving ability in maltreating and comparison mothers. *Journal of Consulting and Clinical Psychology, 52*, 687–691.
Bakan, D. (1966). *The duality of human existence: Isolation and communion in Western man.* Boston: Beacon Press.
Bandura, A. (1977). Self-efficacy: Toward a unifying theory of behavioral change. *Psychological Review, 84*, 191–215.
Bandura, A. (1986). *Social foundation of thoughts and actions: A social cognitive theory.* Englewood Cliffs, NJ: Prentice-Hall.
Bandura, A. (1989). Human agency in social cognitive theory. *American Psychologist, 44*, 1175–1184.
Bartholomew, K. (1990). Avoidance of intimacy: An attachment perspective. *Journal of Social and Personal Relationships, 7*, 147–178.
Belsky, J. (1981). Early human experience: A family perspective. *Developmental Psychology, 17*, 3–23.
Belsky, J. (1990). Children and marriage. In F. D. Fincham & T. N. Bradbury (Eds.), *The psychology of marriage* (pp. 172–200). New York: The Guilford Press.
Bertram, H. (1981). *Sozialstruktur und Sozialisation: Zur mikroanalytischen Analyse von Chancenungleichheit* [Social structure and socialization: A microanalytic analysis of inequality of opportunities]. Neuwied, Germany: Luchterhand.
Bradley, R. H., & Caldwell, B. M. (1979). Home environment and locus of control. *Journal of Clinical Child Psychology, 8*, 107–111.
Brandtstädter, J., Krampen, G., & Heil, F. E. (1986). Personal control and emotional evaluation of development in partnership relations during adulthood. In M.

M. Baltes & P. B. Baltes (Eds.), *The psychology of aging and control* (pp. 265–296). Hillsdale, NJ: Erlbaum.

Bronfenbrenner, U. (1979). *The ecology of human development: Experiments by nature and design.* Cambridge, MA: Harvard University Press.

Bronfenbrenner, U. (1986). Ecology of the family as a context of human development. *Developmental Psychology, 22,* 723–742.

Bugenthal, D. B., & Shennum, W. A. (1984). "Difficult" children as elicitors and targets of adult communication patterns: An attributional-behavioral transactional analysis. *Monographs of the Society for Research in Child Development, 49* (1), Serial No. 205.

Campis, L. K., Layman, R. D., & Prentice-Dunn, S. (1986). The Parental Locus of Control Scale: Development and validation. *Journal of Clinical Child Psychology, 15,* 260–267.

Carton, J. S., & Nowicki, S. (in press). Antecedents of individual differences in locus of control of reinforcement: A critical review. *Genetic Psychological Monographs.*

Chance, J. E. (1972). Academic correlates and maternal antecedents of children's belief in external or internal control of reinforcements. In J. B. Rotter, J. E. Chance, & E. J. Phares (Eds.), *Applications of a social learning theory of personality* (pp. 168–179). New York: Holt, Rinehart & Winston.

Chandler, T. A., Wolf, F. M., Cook, B., & Dugovics, D. (1980). Parental correlates of locus of control in fifth graders: An attempt at experimentation in the home. *Merrill-Palmer Quarterly, 26,* 183–195.

Constantine, J. A., & Bahr, S. J. (1981). Locus of control and marital stability. *Journal of Divorce, 4,* 11–22.

Crandall, V. C., & Crandall, B. W. (1983). Maternal and childhood behaviors as antecedents of internal-external control perceptions in young adulthood. In H. M. Lefcourt (Ed.), *Research with the locus of control construct: Vol. 2. Developments and social problems* (pp. 53–103). New York: Academic.

Crandall, V. C., Katkovsky, W., & Crandall, V. J. (1965). Children's belief in their own control of reinforcements in intellectual-academic achievement situations. *Child Development, 36,* 91–109.

Cuddy, M. E., & Frame, C. (1991). Comparison of aggressive and nonaggressive boys' self-efficacy and outcome expectancy beliefs. *Child Study Journal, 21,* 135–152.

Cutrona, C. E., & Troutman, B. R. (1986). Social support, infant temperament, and parenting self-efficacy: A mediational model of post-partum depression. *Child Development, 57,* 1507–1518.

Davis, W. L., & Phares, E. J. (1969). Parental antecedents of internal-external control of reinforcement. *Psychological Reports, 24,* 427–436.

Diethelm, K. (1991). *Mutter-Kind-Interaktion. Entwicklung von ersten Kontrollüberzeugungen* [Mother-child interaction. Development of early control beliefs]. Bern, Switzerland: Huber.

Donovan, W. L., & Leavitt, L. A. (1989). Maternal self-efficacy and infant attachment: Integrating physiology, perceptions, and behavior. *Child Development, 60,* 460–472.

Duke, M. P., & Lancaster, W. (1976). A note on locus of control as a function of father absence. *Journal of Genetic Psychology, 129,* 335–336.

Earl, W. L. (1987). Creativity and self-trust: A field study. *Adolescence, 22,* 419–432.

Finkelstein, N. W., & Ramey, C. (1977). Learning to control the environment in infancy. *Child Development, 48,* 806–819.

Flammer, A. (1990). *Erfahrung der eigenen Wirksamkeit* [Experience of one's own effi-cacy]. Bern, Switzerland: Huber.

Ford, M. E., & Thompson, R. A. (1985). Perception of personal agency and infant attachment: Toward a life-span perspective of competence development. *International Journal of Behavioral Development, 8*, 377–406.

Gable, S., Belsky, J., & Crnic, K. (1992). Marriage, parenting and child development: Progress and prospects. *Journal of Family Psychology, 5*, 276–294.

Galejs, I., Hegland, S. M., & King, A. (1985). Social agents and the development of locus of control in young children. *Journal of Genetic Psychology, 146*, 181–187.

Gecas, V. (1979). The influence of social class on socialization. In W. R. Burr, R. Hill, F. I. Nye, & I. L. Reiss (Eds.), *Contemporary theories about the family* (Vol. 1, pp. 365–404). New York: Free Press.

Goodnow, J. J., & Collins, W. A. (1990). *Development according to parents: The nature, causes, and consequences of parents' ideas*. Hillsdale, NJ: Erlbaum.

Gordon, D. A., Nowicki, S., & Wichern, F. (1981). Observed maternal and child behaviors in a dependency-producing task as a function of children's locus of control orientation. *Merrill-Palmer Quarterly, 27*, 43–71.

Gross, D., & Rocissano, L. (1988). Maternal confidence in toddlerhood: Its measurement for clinical practice and research. *Nurse Practitioner, 13*, 19–29.

Gross, D., Rocissano, L., & Roncoli, M. (1989). Maternal confidence during toddlerhood: Comparisons of preterm and fullterm groups. *Research in Nursing and Health, 12*, 1–9.

Hainline, L., & Feig, E. (1978). Correlates of childhood father absence in college-aged women. *Child Development, 49*, 37–42.

Harter, S. (1978). Effectance motivation reconsidered: Toward a developmental model. *Human Development, 21*, 34–64.

Harter, S. (1982). The perceived competence scale for children. *Child Development, 53*, 87–97.

Hetherington, E. M. (1972). Effects of fathers' absence on personality development in adolescent daughters. *Developmental Psychology, 7*, 313–326.

Hoffman, J. A., & Teyber, E. C. (1979). Some relationships between sibling age space and personality. *Merrill-Palmer Quarterly, 25*, 77–80.

Hohmann, P. M. (1988). *Kontrolle und Zufriedenheit in Beziehungen* [Control and satisfaction in relationships]. Munich: Profil.

Jerusalem, M., & Schwarzer, R. (1986). Selbstwirksamkeit [Self-efficacy]. In R. Schwarzer (Ed.), *Skalen zur Befindlichkeit und Persönlichkeit* [Scales for measuring states and personality]. (Forschungsbericht 5, pp. 15–18). Berlin: Freie Universität.

Johnston, C., & Mash, E. J. (1989). A measure of parenting satisfaction and efficacy. *Journal of Clinical Child Psychology, 2*, 167–175.

Kalter, N., Alpern, D., Spence, R., & Plunkett, J. W. (1984). Locus of control in children of divorce. *Journal of Personality Assessment, 48*, 410–414.

Kenny, D. A. (1979). *Correlation and causality*. New York: Wiley.

Kohn, M. L. (1979). The effects of social class on parental values and practices. In D. Reiss & H. A. Hoffman (Eds.), *The American family: Dying or developing* (pp. 45–68). New York: Plenum.

Krampen, G. (1982a). *Differentialpsychologie der Kontrollüberzeugungen* [Differential psychology of control beliefs]. Göttingen: Hogrefe.

Krampen, G. (1982b). Schulische und familiäre Entwicklungsbedingungen von Kontrollüberzeugungen [School and familial conditions for developing control beliefs]. *Schweizerische Zeitschrift für Psychologie und ihre Anwendungen, 41*, 16–35.

Krampen, G. (1989a). Diagnostik von Attributionen und Kontrollüberzeugungen: Theorien, Geschichte, Probleme [Diagnosis of attributions and control beliefs; Theories, history, problems]. In G. Krampen (Ed.), *Diagnostik von Attributionen und Kontrollüberzeugungen* [Diagnosis of attributions and control beliefs] (pp. 3–19). Göttingen: Hogrefe.

Krampen, G. (1989b). Perceived childrearing practices and the development of locus of control in early adolescence. *International Journal of Behavioral Development, 12,* 177–193.

Krampen, G. (1994). Kontrollüberzeugungen in der Erziehung und Sozialisation [Control beliefs in education and socialization]. In K. A. Schneewind (Ed.), *Psychologie der Erziehung und Sozialisation: Enzyklopädie der Psychologie. Pädagogische Psychologie* [Psychology of education and socialization. Encyclopedia of psychology. Educational psychology] (Vol. 1, pp. 375–402). Göttingen: Hogrefe.

Kurdek, L. A. (1993). Issues in proposing a general model of the effects of divorce on children. *Journal of Marriage and the Family, 55,* 39–41.

Kurdek, L. A., & Blisk, D. (1983). Dimensions and correlates of mothers' divorce experience. *Journal of Divorce, 6,* 1–24.

Kurdek, L. A., Blisk, D., & Siesky, A. E. (1981). Correlates of children's long-term adjustment to their parents' divorce. *Developmental Psychology, 17,* 565–579.

Ladd, G. W., & Price, J. M. (1986). Promoting children's cognitive and social competence: The relation between parents' perceptions of task difficulty and children's perceived and actual competence. *Child Development, 57,* 446–460.

Lancaster, W. W., & Richmond, B. D. (1983). Perceived locus of control as a function of father absence, age and geographic location. *Journal of Genetic Psychology, 143,* 51–56.

Lefcourt, H. M. (1976). *Locus of control.* Hillsdale, NJ: Erlbaum.

Lehwald, G. (1991). Früherfassung und Frühförderung von Begabungen: Methodische Probleme, empirische Befunde, praktische Konsequenzen [Early assessment and support of abilities: Methodical problems, empirical findings, practical consequences]. In F. J. Mönks & G. Lehwald (Eds.), *Neugier, Erkundung und Begabung bei Kleinkindern* [Curiosity, exploration, and ability in early childhood] (pp. 135–144). Munich: Reinhardt.

Lifshitz, M., & Ramot, L. (1978). Toward a framework for developing children's locus of control orientation. *Child Development, 49,* 85–95.

Loeb, R. C. (1975). Concomitants of boys' locus of control examined in parent-child interactions. *Developmental Psychology, 11,* 353–358.

Luster, T., & Kain, E. L. (1987). The relation between family context and perception of parental efficacy. *Early Child Development and Care, 29,* 301–311.

Luster, T., Rhoades, K., & Haas, B. (1989). The relation between parental values and parenting behavior: A test of the Kohn hypothesis. *Journal of Marriage and the Family, 51,* 139–147.

MacDonald, A. P. (1971). Internal-external locus of control: Parental antecedents. *Journal of Consulting and Clinical Psychology, 37,* 141–147.

Marks, E. (1973). Sex, birth order, and belief about personal power. *Developmental Psychology, 6,* 184.

Mash, E. J., Johnston, C., & Kovitz, K. (1983). A comparison of the mother-child interactions of physically abused and nonabused children during play and task situations. *Journal of Clinical Child Psychology, 12,* 337–346.

McAdams, D. P. (1985). *Power, intimacy, and the life story: Personological inquiries into identity.* New York: The Guilford Press.

144 Klaus A. Schneewind

McAdams, D. P. (1988). Personal needs and personal relationships. In S. W. Duck (Ed.), *Handbook of personal relationships* (pp. 7–22). London: Wiley & Sons.

Meyer, B. U., & Wacker, A. (1970). Die Entstehung der erlebten Selbstverantwortlichkeit in Abhängigkeit vom Zeitpunkt der Erziehung [The development of perceived self-responsibility depending on the timing of educational practices]. *Archiv für Psychologie, 122*, 24–39.

Mielke, R. (Ed.). (1982). *Interne/externe Kontrollüberzeugung* [Internal/external control belief]. Bern, Switzerland: Huber.

Miller, P., Lefcourt, H. M., & Ware, E. (1983). The construction and development of the Miller Marital Locus of Control Scale. *Canadian Journal of Behavioral Science, 15*, 266–279.

Miller, S. A. (1988). Parents' beliefs about children's cognitive development. *Child Development, 59*, 259–285.

Nowicki, S., & Duke, M. P. (1974). A locus of control scale for college as well as non-college adults. *Journal of Personality Assessment, 38*, 136–137.

Nowicki, S., & Schneewind, K. A. (1982). Relation of family climate variables to locus of control in German and American students. *Journal of Genetic Psychology, 141*, 277–286.

Nowicki, S., & Segal, W. (1974). Perceived parental characteristics, locus of control orientation, and behavioral correlates of locus of control. *Developmental Psychology, 10*, 33–37.

Nowicki, S., & Strickland, B. R. (1973). A locus of control scale for children. *Journal of Consulting and Clinical Psychology, 40*, 148–154.

Ollendick, D. G. (1979). Parental locus of control and the assessment of children's personality characteristics. *Journal of Personality Assessment, 43*, 401–405.

Parish, T. S. (1981). The relationship between years of father absence and locus of control. *Journal of Genetic Psychology, 138*, 301–302.

Parish, T. S., & Boyd, D. A. (1983). Locus of control as related to family backround and marital status. *Journal of Genetic Psychology, 143*, 287–288.

Parish, T. S., & Copeland, T. F. (1980). Locus of control and father loss. *Journal of Genetic Psychology, 136*, 147–148.

Parks, P. L., & Smeriglio, V. L. (1986). Relationships among parenting knowledge, quality of stimulation in the home and infant development. *Family Relations, 35*, 411–416.

Perrez, M. (1989). Diagnostik von Kontingenzerfahrungen in der frühen Kindheit [Diagnosis of contingency awareness in early childhood]. In G. Krampen (Ed.), *Diagnostik von Attributionen und Kontrollüberzeugungen* [Diagnosis of attributions and control beliefs] (pp. 172–185). Göttingen, Germany: Hogrefe.

Perrez, M., Ackermann, E. & Diethelm, K. (1983). Die Bedeutung der sozialen Kontingenzen für die Entwicklung des Kindes im ersten Lebensjahr [The importance of social contingencies for the child's development in the first year of life]. *Verhaltensmodifikation, 4*, 114–129.

Perry, D. E., Perry, L. C., & Rasmussen, P. (1986). Cognitive social learning mediators of aggression. *Child Development, 57*, 700–711.

Peterson, C. (1991). The meaning and measurement of explanatory style. *Psychological Inquiry, 2*, 1–10.

Peterson, C., & Stunkard, A. J. (1992). Cognates of personal control: Locus of control, self-efficacy, and explanatory style. *Applied and Preventive Psychology, 1*, 111–117.

Pettit, G. S., Harrist, A. W., Bates, J. E., & Dodge, K. A. (1991). Family interaction, social cognition and children's subsequent relationships with peers at Kindergarten. *Journal of Social and Personal Relationships, 8*, 383–402.

Phares, E. J. (1976). *Locus of control in personality.* Morristown, NJ: General Learning Press.

Reisel, B. (1986). *Scheidung aus der Perspektive des Kindes* [Divorce from the child's perspective]. Unpublished dissertation, University of Vienna.

Riksen-Walraven, M. (1978). Effects of caregiver behavior on habituation rate and self-efficacy in infants. *International Journal of Behavioral Development, 1,* 105–130.

Riksen-Walraven, M. (1991). Die Entwicklung kindlicher Kompetenz im Zusammenhang mit sozialer Unterstützung [The development of children's competence in relation to social support]. In F. J. Mönks & G. Lehwald (Eds.), *Neugier, Erkundung und Begabung bei Kleinkindern* [Curiosity, exploration and ability in early childhood] (pp. 77–92). Munich: Reinhardt.

Rinke, R., & Schneewind, K. A. (1978). LOC-E und LOC-K: *Zwei Fragebogen zur Erfassung internaler versus externaler Kontrollüberzeugungen bei Erwachsenen und Kindern* [Two questionnaires for assessing internal versus external control beliefs in adults and children]. Arbeitsbericht 26 aus dem Projekt Eltern-Kind-Beziehungen. Munich: Universität München.

Röd, W. (1976). *Die Philosophie der Antike 1: Von Thales bis Demokrit* [Philosophy of the Antique 1. From Thales to Demokrit]. Munich: Beck.

Rothbaum, F. M., Weisz, J. R., & Snyder, S. S. (1982). Changing the world and changing the self: A two-process model of perceived control. *Journal of Personality and Social Psychology, 42,* 5–37.

Rotter, J. B. (1954). *Social learning and clinical psychology.* Englewood Cliffs, NJ: Prentice-Hall.

Rotter, J. B. (1966). Generalized expectancies for internal versus external control of reinforcement. *Psychlogical Monographs, 80* (1) (whole No. 609), 1–28.

Rotter, J. B. (1990). Internal versus external control of reinforcement. *American Psychologist, 45,* 489–493.

Schave, B., & Fox, F. (1986). Similarities and differences between six-year-old identical and fraternal twins and their parents on measures of locus of control and moral development. *Educational Research Quarterly, 11,* 49–56.

Schneewind, K. A. (1982). Familiäre Aspekte der Selbstverantwortlichkeit [Familial aspects of self-responsibility]. In R. Mielke (Ed.), *Interne/externe Kontrollüberzeugungen* [Internal/external control beliefs] (pp. 199–221). Bern, Switzerland: Huber.

Schneewind, K. A. (1985). Entwicklung personaler Kontrolle im Kontext der Familie [Development of personal control within the context of the family]. In W. F. Kugemann, S. Preiser, & K. A. Schneewind (Eds.), *Psychologie und komplexe Lebenswirklichkeit* [Psychology and the complexity of real life] (pp. 201–233). Göttingen, Germany: Hogrefe.

Schneewind, K. A. (1987a). *Validierung eines Instruments zur Diagnostik personaler Kontrolle bei Kindern (DPK-K)* [Validation of an instrument for the Diagnosis of Personal Control in Children (DPC-C)]. Abschlussbericht an die Deutsche Forschungsgemeinschaft. Munich: Universität München.

Schneewind, K. A. (1987b). Personale Kontrolle: Zur Theorie und Empirie eines zentralen psychologischen Konstrukts [Personal control: Theoretical and empirical contributions to a focal psychological construct]. In W. Maiers & M. Markard (Eds.), *Kritische Psychologie als Subjektwissenschaft* [Critical psychology as science of the subject] (pp. 177–191). Berlin: Campus.

Schneewind, K. A. (1989a). Conceptualization and validation of an action-theoretic model of personal control. In J. P. Forgas & J. M. Innes (Eds.), *Recent advances in*

146   Klaus A. Schneewind

social psychology: An international perspective (pp. 441–447). North Holland: Elsevier Science Publishers B.V.

Schneewind, K. A. (1989b). Eindimensionale Skalen zur Erfassung von Kontrollüberzeugungen bei Erwachsenen und Kindern [Unidimensional scales for assessing control beliefs in adults and children]. In G. Krampen (Ed.), *Diagnostik von Attributionen und Kontrollüberzeugungen* [Diagnosis of attributions and control beliefs] (pp. 80–92). Göttingen, Germany: Hogrefe.

Schneewind, K. A. (1989c). Contextual approaches to family systems research: The macro-micro puzzle. In K. Kreppner & R. M. Lerner (Eds.), *Family systems and life-span development* (pp. 197–221). Hillsdale, NJ: Erlbaum.

Schneewind, K. A. (1994). Persönlichkeitsentwicklung im Kontext von Erziehung und Sozialisation [Personality development in the context of education and socialization]. In K. A. Schneewind (Ed.), *Psychologie der Erziehung und Sozialisation: Enzyklopädie der Psychologie. Pädagogische Psychologie* [Psychology of education and socialization. Encyclopedia of Psychology. Educational Psychology] (Vol. 1, pp. 197–225). Göttingen, Germany: Hogrefe.

Schneewind, K. A., Beckmann, M., & Engfer, A. (1983). *Eltern und Kinder* [Parents and children]. Stuttgart: Kohlhammer.

Schneewind, K. A., Beckmann, M., & Hecht-Jackl, A. (1985). *Familiendiagnostisches Testsystem* [Family diagnostic test system]. Forschungsberichte aus dem Institutsbereich Persönlichkeitspsychologie und Psychodiagnostik. Munich: Universität München.

Schneewind, K. A., Knopp, V., Schmidt-Rinke, M., Sierwald, W., & Vierzigmann, G. (1989). *Optionen der Lebensgestaltung junger Ehen und Kinderwunsch. Materialband 1* [Options of young couples and their desire to have children. Documentation volume 1]. Munich: Universität München.

Schneewind, K. A., & Pfeiffer, P. (1978). Elterliches Erziehungsverhalten und kindliche Selbstverantwortlichkeit [Parenting and children's self-responsibility]. In K. A. Schneewind & H. Lukesch (Eds.), *Familiäre Sozialisation* [Family socialization] (pp. 190–205). Stuttgart: Klett-Cotta.

Schneewind, K. A., & Ruppert, S. (1992). *Projekt Eltern-Kind-Beziehungen/Nachuntersuchung: Materialband* [The parent-child relations project followup: Documentation volume 1]. Munich: Universität München.

Schneewind, K. A., Vaskovics, L. A. (1992). *Optionen der Lebensgestaltung junger Ehen und Kinderwunsch* [Options of young couples and their desire to have children]. Stuttgart: Kohlhammer.

Schneewind, K. A., & Wünsche, P. (1985). Diagnostik personaler Kontrolle bei Kindern (DPK): Theoretische Grundlegung und erste empirische Befunde [Diagnosis of personal control in children (DPC): Theory and first empirical findings]. In L. Montada (Ed.), *Bericht über die 7. Tagung Entwicklungspsychologie in Trier* [Proceedings of the 7th conference on developmental psychology in Trier] (p. 297). Trier, Germany: Universitätsverlag.

Schneewind, K. A., Wünsche, P., & Pausch, H. P. (1989). Zur mehrdimensionalen Diagnostik personaler Kontrollüberzeugungen und Attributionen bei Kindern und Jugendlichen [Multidimensional diagnosis of personal control beliefs and attributions in children and adolescents]. In G. Krampen (Ed.), *Diagnostik von Attributionen und Kontrollüberzeugungen* [Diagnosis of attributions and control beliefs] (pp. 146–154). Göttingen, Germany: Hogrefe.

Schwarzer, R., & Jerusalem, M. (1989). Erfassung leistungsbezogener und allgemeiner Kontroll- und Kompetenzerwartungen [Assessment of achievement-related and general control- and competence expectancies]. In G. Krampen (Ed.), *Diagnostik von Attributionen und Kontrollüberzeugungen* [Diagnosis of attributions and control beliefs] (pp. 127–133). Göttingen, Germany: Hogrefe.

Seligman, M. E. P. (1975). *Helplessness: On depression, development, and death.* San Francisco: Freeman.

Simons, R. L., Beaman, J., Conger, R. D., & Chao, W. (1993). Childhood experience, conception of parenting, and attitudes of spouse as determinants of parental behavior. *Journal of Marriage and the Family, 55*, 91–106.

Simons, R. L., Whitbeck, L. B., Conger, R. D., & Wu, C. (1991). Intergenerational transmission of harsh parenting. *Developmental Psychology, 27*, 159–171.

Skinner, E. A. (1986). The origins of young children's perceived control: Mother contingent and sensitive behavior. *International Journal of Behavioral Development, 9*, 359–382.

Skinner, E. A., Chapman, M., & Baltes, P. B. (1988). Control, means-ends and agency beliefs: A new conceptualization and its measurement during childhood. *Journal of Personality and Social Psychology, 54*, 117–133.

Slater, E. J., & Haber, J. D. (1984). Adolescent adjustment following divorce as a function of familial conflict. *Journal of Consulting and Clinical Psychology, 52*, 920–921.

Smeriglio, V. L., & Parks, P. L. (1983). Measuring mothers' perceptions about the influence of infant caregiving practices. *Child Psychiatry and Human Development, 13*, 237–244.

Strickland, B. R. (1989). Internal-external control expectancies: From contingency to creativity. *American Psychologist, 44*, 1–12.

Teti, D. M., & Gelfand, D. M. (1991). Behavioral competence among mothers of infants in the first year: The mediational role of maternal self-efficacy. *Child Development, 62*, 918–929.

Teti, D. M., Gelfand, D. M., & Pompa, J. (1990). Depressed mothers' behavioral competence with their infants: Demographic and psychosocial correlates. *Development and Psychopathology, 2*, 259–270.

Tolor, A., & Jalowiec, J. E. (1968). Body boundary, parental attitudes, and internal-external expectancy. *Journal of Consulting and Clinical Psychology, 32*, 206–209.

Trommsdorff, G. (1989). Sozialisation und Werthaltungen im Kulturvergleich [Socialization and values in a cross-cultural perspective]. In G. Trommsdorff (Ed.), *Sozialisation im Kulturvergleich* [Socialization in a cross-cultural perspective] (pp. 97–121). Stuttgart: Enke.

Tulkin, S. R. (1977). Social class differences in maternal and infant behavior. In H. Leiderman, S. R. Tulkin, & S. Rosenfeld (Eds.), *Culture and infancy* (pp. 495–537). New York: Academic.

Vaskovics, L. A. (1982). Sozialökologische Einflussfaktoren familialer Sozialisation [Socio-ecological influences on familial socialization]. In L. A. Vaskovics (Ed.), *Umweltbedingungen familialer Sozialisation* [Environmental conditions of familial socialization] (pp. 1–24). Stuttgart: Enke.

Walter, D. A., & Ziegler, C. A. (1980). The effects of birth order on locus of control. *Bulletin of the Psychonomic Society, 15*, 293–294.

Watson, J. S. (1966). The development and generalization of "contingency awareness" in early infancy: Some hypotheses. *Merrill-Palmer Quarterly, 12*, 123–135.

Watson, J. S., & Ramey, C. T. (1972). Reaction to response-contingent stimulation in early infancy. *Merrill-Palmer Quarterly, 18*, 119–127.

Weisz, J. R., Rothbaum, F. M., & Blackburn, T. C. (1984). Standing out and standing in. The psychology of control in America and Japan. *American Psychologist, 39*, 955–969.

148   Klaus A. Schneewind

Weisz, J. R., & Stipek, D. J. (1982). Competence, contingency and undevelopment of perceived control. *Human Development, 25*, 250–281.

Wheeler, V. A., & Ladd, G. W. (1982). Assessment of children's self-efficacy for social interactions with peers. *Developmental Psychology, 18*, 795–805.

Whitbeck, L. B. (1987). Modelling efficacy: The effect of perceived parental efficacy on the self-efficacy of early adolescents. *Journal of Early Adolescence, 7*, 175–177.

White, R. W. (1959). Motivation reconsidered: The concept of competence. *Psychological Review, 66*, 297–333.

Wichern, F., & Nowicki, S. (1976). Independence training practices and locus of control orientation in children and adolescents. *Developmental Psychology, 12*, 77.

Wiggins, J. S. (1991). Agency and communion as conceptional coordinates for the understanding and measurement of interpersonal behavior. In D. Cicchetti & W. Grove (Eds.), *Thinking clearly about psychology: Essays in honor of Paul Everett Meehl* (pp. 89–113). Minneapolis: University of Minnesota Press.

Wold, H. (1979). *Model construction and evaluation when theoretical knowledge is scarce.* Cahier 79.01 du département d'économetrie. Geneva: Faculté des sciences économiques et sociales, Université de Genève.

Wünsche, P., & Schneewind, K. A. (1989). Entwicklung eines Fragebogens zur Erfassung von Selbst- und Kompetenzeinschätzungen bei Kindern [Development of questionnaire for assessing children's self- and competence judgements] (FSK-K). *Diagnostica, 35*, 217–235.

Yates, R., Kennelly, K., & Cox, S. (1975). Perceived contingency of parental reinforcements, parent-child relations and locus of control. *Psychological Reports, 36*, 139–146.

5. Cross-cultural perspectives on self-efficacy

GABRIELE OETTINGEN

The present chapter addresses three major issues. First, we analyze how culture might affect the various sources of self-efficacy belief systems. For this purpose, the dimensions of cultural diversity specified by Hofstede (1980, 1991; see also Triandis, 1989) and their impact on the sources of self-efficacy information in family and school contexts are examined. Second, we compare children's self-efficacy beliefs in East and West Berlin, Moscow, and Los Angeles based on data from an ongoing research project coordinated by G. Oettingen, T. D. Little, and P. B. Baltes. The results demonstrate cross-cultural variations in efficacy beliefs that are congruent with differences in efficacy-relevant influences hypothesized to be operating in each culture's school contexts. Third, we discuss the critical question of whether self-efficacy effects on cognition, affect, and motivation are universal across cultures. We speculate on the type of research that would be needed to demonstrate universality, which raises issues of individual versus collective efficacy.

Culture and the sources of self-efficacy information

Bandura (1977, in press) specifies four information sources that people use in forming their sense of personal efficacy. The most important source is *performance experiences*. Successes build a sense of self-efficacy; failures weaken it. Repeated early failures especially may have the most adverse effect if they cannot be discounted as due to lack of effort or unfavorable circumstances. Failures are less detrimental if people have already developed a strong sense of self-efficacy through early frequent successes. Successes achieved in the face of adversities are particularly beneficial. A strong sense of efficacy acquired in one area of functioning may transfer to other areas, thus creating a general sense of personal efficacy (Bandura, 1977, 1986).

Other people's attainments can also influence self-efficacy formation. First, models provide a standard of judging one's capabilities. Most achievements – for example, school grades – are judged relatively, and one's own capability is inferred by comparing one's attainments to those of one's peers (Festinger, 1954). Second, even without personal performance experiences, individuals may infer their self-efficacy by observing the successes and failures of others. Thus, through *vicarious experience*, the successes of similar others raise one's own sense of efficacy, whereas their failures lead to lowered levels. Observers may derive a boost in self-efficacy even from competent models who are dissimilar simply because they transmit knowledge, skills, and strategies that enhance competencies.

Competent people can also influence self-efficacy beliefs through active influence attempts. Such *verbal persuasion* can be particularly effective when the communicator is endowed with trustworthiness, expertise, and attractiveness (Hovland & Weiss, 1952; Petty & Cacioppo, 1986). If, however, the communicator's appraisals portray the target person as unrealistically efficacious, failure experiences will quickly erase any temporary boost in self-efficacy.

A final source of efficacy information is provided by one's *physical and emotional reactions*. For example, a low level of arousal while coping with a difficult or threatening course of action would indicate an assured sense of efficacy. Conversely, high states of perturbing emotional arousal are likely to be interpreted as self-inefficacy. With regard to physical states, the experience of pain and fatigue may be viewed as a sign of inefficacy. Mood states such as depression also affect judgment of personal efficacy. People judge themselves as efficacious in positive moods and as inefficacious in depressed moods (Kavanagh & Bower, 1985). It is important to note that the interpretation of somatic and emotional states with regard to self-efficacy judgments is complex. People take into account the experienced level of activation as well as their knowledge of how performances have been affected by emotional arousal in different past situations (see Bandura, 1977, 1986).

Although there are four potential sources of efficacy information, people may not always have access to all of them. The opportunity for vicarious experiences, for example, may be limited because there are few competent models from whom one can learn. Moreover, individuals may sample selectively and weight and integrate the information available in their preferred manner. The persuasive efforts of others (e.g., therapists) may be discounted in light of one's own deferent performances. Conversely, one may readily embrace positive verbal persuasions and disregard negative performance experiences.

These considerations imply that forming beliefs of personal efficacy is a complex process of self-appraisal which entails selecting, weighting, and integrating information from multiple sources. It is in this appraisal process that culture may play its influential role. Culture may affect not only the type of information provided by the various sources, but also which information is selected and how it is weighted and integrated in people's self-efficacy judgments.

How should we conceptualize this role of culture? We assume that culture reveals its effect on self-efficacy beliefs by affecting the fundamental systems and institutions of virtually all human societies: the family, the school, the workplace, and the community. Everyday conduct in these different contexts provides information for one's self-efficacy in different kinds of pursuits. Understanding how cultures affect everyday conduct in these major societal systems can help to clarify how people's self-efficacy appraisals vary across cultures. We will first examine the crucial dimensions on which cultures differ.

Dimensions of cultural differences

Culture may be conceived of as "the collective programming of the mind which distinguishes the members of one human group from another" (Hofstede, 1980, p. 25). This definition suggests that value systems constitute one major source of cultural differences. It has long been argued that cultures differ primarily in their system of values (Inkeles & Levinson, 1969). Recent attempts to investigate empirically these differences have identified a small number of crucial cultural dimensions (Hofstede, 1980, 1991; Triandis, 1989). Hofstede (1980, 1991) analyzed cultural value systems in matched samples of employees belonging to the same multinational business in more than 40 countries. He identified four dimensions of cultural differences, which he defined as follows:

(a) *Individualism/Collectivism.* Collectivist cultures promote the view that people belong to in-groups that demand lasting loyalty from which members cannot easily free themselves. In return, people receive protection from the in-group. In contrast, individualist cultures promote the view that people look primarily after their own welfare and their immediate family's interests. They value an autonomous definition of the self and individual goals more than group goals (see also Triandis, McCusker, & Hui, 1990).

(b) *Power distance*. In cultures with large disparity in power, people are expected to accept inequality in power. This is especially true for the less powerful members of the culture. People in cultures with small power distance value a more equal distribution of power.

(c) *Uncertainty avoidance.* People in cultures of strong uncertainty avoidance are easily distressed by new, unstructured, unclear, or unpredictable situations. They try to avoid such situations by maintaining strict codes of conduct and a belief in absolute truths. Members of such cultures tend to be compulsive, security seeking, intolerant, aggressive, and emotional. In contrast, people in cultures of weak uncertainty avoidance tend to be relaxed, tolerant, risk accepting, contemplative, and unaggressive.

(d) *Masculinity/Femininity*. A masculine culture strives for a maximal distinction between men and women. Men are expected to strive for material success, to be assertive, ambitious, and competitive, whereas women are expected to be successful in serving the communal side of life, such as caring for children and the weak. Women are not expected to take on professional jobs. In contrast, feminine cultures also value men who care for the nonmaterial aspects of life and women who obtain professional and technical jobs. In higher education men and women tend to pursue studies in the same subjects, whereas in masculine societies different subjects are "proper" for men and women.

Similar dimensions of differences in cultural values have been highlighted by other researchers (e.g., Markus & Kitayama, 1991; Triandis, 1989). Returning to the question of how culture affects self-efficacy appraisals, we turn next to an analysis of how the various dimensions might express themselves in major societal systems and institutions, such as the family and the school.

Cultural differences and self-efficacy appraisal

Sources of efficacy may vary in three ways: First, some sources may be more *prevalent* than others. For example, in societies that are rigidly segregated by gender, women may have less exposure to male models and vice versa. Second, even when sources are equally prevalent they may take different *forms*. For example, in collectivist systems children get feedback on how their in-group performed as well as on their individual performance, whereas in individualist systems children get feedback only on their personal performance. Third, sources might differ in how they are *valued*. For example, emphasizing individual attainments should be prized more in individualist systems than in collectivist systems.

Individualism/collectivism. Hofstede (1989, 1991; see also Triandis, 1989; Triandis et al., 1990) claims that families in cultures high on collectivism teach their children to love and respect the needs of their in-group. In school, children pursue performance goals demonstrating required competencies more than learning goals of expanding one's competencies (Ames, 1992; Dweck & Leggett, 1988), and they create a social reality that makes their performance outcomes noticeable to their collective. In cultures high on individualism, children are expected to learn how to learn. Performance outcomes are seen as instrumental to achieving self-actualization and the realization of one's individual potential. This striving does not cease when the needs of the in-group are satisfied. Rather, there is a constant attempt to realize one's individual potential through the pursuit of personal goals.

Children in individualist cultures should focus their self-appraisals of efficacy on information concerning their personal performance attainments (e.g., improvements or declines; see Rosenholtz & Rosenholtz, 1981). In contrast, in collectivist cultures the evaluation by in-group members should be the most important source of efficacy information, with modeling by other in-group members also being influential. Whereas children in individualist cultures may be more in tune with their private emotional states, children socialized in collectivist cultures should be more responsive to the preference of their in-group and thus emotions are used more strategically (Markus & Kitayama, 1991). Accordingly, emotional states should be a more immediate and thereby more prominent source for the self-efficacy appraisals of children raised in individualist systems than in collectivist systems (i.e., idiocentric versus allocentric orientations, respectively; see Triandis, 1989; Triandis, Leung, Villareal, & Clack, 1985).

Consider an example. Youth who approach the end of schooling have to assess their self-efficacy for different occupations in making career decisions (Betz & Hackett, 1986; Lent & Hackett, 1987). If becoming a banker is considered an appropriate option, people will appraise their efficacy for performing the banker role. A youngster in an individualist culture would give heavy weight to past performances in relevant academic domains. Affective reactions to images of being a banker might also be considered. For a youth in a collectivist culture, the self-appraisal of efficacy would center on the in-group's belief that the person has the capabilities to become a successful banker, and whether other members of the in-group might have higher talent for this occupation. The differential preference for sources of efficacy information by youths raised in individualist versus collectivist systems should be most pronounced when the goal pursuit in question is fully individualist (e.g., promoting one's personal potential) or fully collectivist (e.g., promoting one's in-group potential), respectively.

Power distance. Hofstede's (1986, 1991) ideas on how power distance or power disparity affects family and school life focus on young people's relation to authority. In a culture with large power differential, children are taught to obey their parents and to treat them as superiors. Education is teacher-centered (see Stipek, 1988), in which students expect teachers to control the educational activities. The study material is supposed to reflect the wisdom of the educational personnel, who are not to be contradicted or criticized. Parents are expected to support the teachers. In contrast, in cultures with small power differential, children are encouraged to express their views freely in the family and to treat parents as equals. Education in school is child-centered (see Stipek, 1988, 1991). Teachers expect students to initiate communication, speak up and criticize, and to find their own direction and pace of learning. The study material can, in principle, be obtained from any competent person. Parents are expected to side with the students.

The teacher is a powerful influence agent under conditions of large power differential. When children assess their self-efficacy in school, their appraisals should be largely the product of teachers' evaluations and actions. Accordingly, children would tend to judge their capabilities in terms of teachers' evaluations. Peers who serve as models are also perceived through the eyes of teachers. Since teachers are endowed with many attributes of successful influence agents (e.g., expertise, power), their evaluative feedback should carry heavy weight in children's self-appraisals of their own capabilities. With respect to affective states, emotional distress over poor academic performance would contribute a sense of inefficacy. Unquestioned authority of teachers may heighten negative emotional arousal. Thus, children's emotional states should become a prevalent informational source for self-efficacy judgments.

For children in cultures of low power differential things are quite different. Because children are allowed to exert influence on their direction and contents of learning, they largely become the creators of their performance history. Accordingly, evaluating past performance means sampling information comparatively free of authorities' influences (e.g., teachers, parents, peer group heroes). The impact of authority is further diminished because the verbalized evaluations of teachers in such cultures are not given undue weight. Finally, children's vicarious experiences regarding peer performances and interpretation of emotional states are comparatively less affected by the force of teacher or parent evaluations because of their lesser influence.

It appears, then, that children in cultures with small power differential are offered more opportunities to operate as "origins" than as "pawns" (de Charms, 1968; Deci, Vallerand, Pelletier, & Ryan, 1991; Ryan & Stiller, 1991). Accordingly, we expect the described differences in the appraisal of self-efficacy to be particularly pronounced when children evaluate their performances on projects they have chosen for themselves (e.g., to learn about Miro's paintings by employing various self-chosen strategies) as compared to children in cultures of large power differential, who pursue projects structured by authorities (e.g., learn about Miro's paintings by use of an assigned book).

Uncertainty avoidance. Hofstede (1986, 1991) speculates that in families of cultures with strong uncertainty avoidance, foreign influences are experienced as a source of high threat and stress, while familiarity and predictability are calming. In both family and school settings, emotional reactions are accepted and self-righteousness is prevalent. Teachers are expected to have all the right answers and to speak in a formal manner (Stroebe, 1976), and intellectual disagreement is interpreted as a personal offense. Students adapt to highly structured, unidimensional teaching strategies (Rosenholtz & Rosenholtz, 1981; Rosenholtz & Simpson, 1984), where materials and assignments are predefined and instructions are detailed. Students and teachers desire rules and readily embrace them.

In contrast, members of families in cultures with weak uncertainty avoidance are curious about new and foreign experiences, are unperturbed about facing new problems, and respond reflectively rather than emotionally to ambiguities (see also Sorrentino, Raynor, Zubek, & Short, 1990). Teachers are not expected to know all things. They use plain language, take intellectual disagreements as challenges, and seek parents' opinions and ideas. Students deal effectively with multidimensional teaching strategies (Rosenholtz & Rosenholtz, 1981; Rosenholtz & Simpson, 1984), which entail only partially structured learning materials, general instructions, and flexible, individualized pacing.

Children socialized in schools of strong uncertainty avoidance can look back on a fully designed performance history, since the highly structured teaching leaves few ambiguities. Regular and frequent performance feedback on the same assignments for all students in a given classroom produces precise rank ordering of one's own ability. The monolithic structure and social ranking serve as powerful influences in facilitating a precise appraisal of one's performance-based self-efficacy. Students know exactly where they stand in the social comparative judgment of their own efficacy. Moreover, the verbal communications of the important persuaders (i.e., teachers, parents, and peers) are phrased unambiguously and reflect a high degree of social consensus. The experience of negative emotional states in dealing with new or unfamiliar activities reinforces a low sense of efficacy. Negative emotional states arising from unfavorable peer comparisons provide further reminders of personal inefficacy. Surpassing one's peers in the social ranking generates positive emotional states that tend to enhance self-appraisals of efficacy.

Children raised in families and schools that show less uncertainty avoidance face more ambiguity when it comes to appraising their efficacy. Performance feedback and social ranking by performance attainment is less certain and less possible because of individualized instruction. Hence, inferences from performance attainments as well as from vicarious experiences provide leeway for personal self-evaluation. This permits self-enhancing attributions and judgments of capability (Abramson, Seligman, & Teasdale, 1978; Bandura, 1986; Taylor, 1989; Taylor & Brown, 1988). In addition, the less authoritative social evaluations can be used in one's own service. Similarly, emotional states should be a less telling source for self-efficacy judgments. This is because ambiguity is more of a challenge than a threat. These effects should be particularly pronounced when children in strong uncertainty-avoidant cultures strive for certainty-oriented goals (e.g., becoming a civil clerk) and children in weak uncertainty-avoidant contexts strive for uncertainty-oriented goals (e.g., becoming a scientist).

Masculinity-Femininity. In masculine societies families stress achievement and competition. In school, teachers single out high-achieving students as the ideal and highlight students' academic successes. Students are competitive, publicize their successes, and regard their failures as calamities. Subject matters that are instrumental to promoting professional careers are valued, and studying academic subjects that in sex-typed societies are labeled feminine is seen as irrelevant for men. In societies that are more feminine, families stress social interrelatedness and try to solve conflicts through compromises (e.g., countries high on femininity include Denmark, Norway, and Sweden). In school, the norm is set by the average student, students' social adaptation is valued, and academic failure is not taken too seriously. The choice of academic subjects is determined by intrinsic interests, and men feel free to pursue subjects traditionally regarded as feminine.

Male children in masculine societies face stiff performance competition. Therefore, they are sensitive of how others are performing in appraising their own self-efficacy. Successes that exceed those of their competitors and praise of personal accomplishments in comparison to others increase self-efficacy. The emotional states stemming from personal comparison are weighted most heavily. In feminine cultures, performance attainments should affect self-efficacy judgments, regardless of gender or whether they surpass those of others or fall below them. Again, the different cultural effects on self-efficacy appraisals should be particularly pronounced for male children in masculine cultures when pursuing careers stereotyped as masculine (e.g., becoming a broker) and for children in feminine cultures who choose traditionally feminine vocational pursuits (e.g., becoming a social worker), respectively.

Summary. The preceding discussion has analyzed how cultural differences might promote different self-efficacy appraisals. We have relied primarily on the salient cultural dimensions singled out by Hofstede (1980), and have used his speculations (Hofstede, 1991) on how cultural variations on these dimensions might be manifested in the social practices of familial and education systems. These notions suggested ways in which cultural variations impact on self-efficacy appraisals.

Cultural orientations are not dichotomous, and the cultural dimensions discussed do not operate *in unisono*, as the preceding discussion might imply. These various dimensional properties should be conceived of as continuous variables operating in concert. Each given culture is characterized by a score on each of these dimensions (see Hofstede's 1980 study with employees of IBM in 40 different countries). Furthermore, the dimension of individualism/collectivism correlates positively and substantially with power distance; that is, the more individualist a society is, the smaller it is in power differential. However, this correlation disappears when national wealth is partialed out. Uncertainty avoidance and masculinity/feminity are neither interrelated nor related to wealth.

A complete empirical analysis of the link between culture and self-efficacy appraisals would require selection of cultures representing the relevant dimensions. One would then observe social transactions in family and school settings of the different cultures to verify that they in fact differ in the expected ways. The social transactions are considered to be mediators of cultural effects on self-appraisals. Finally, one would assess the self-efficacy appraisals of the children.

At the Max Planck Institute for Human Development and Education, we chose a more parsimonious test of the effects of culture on self-efficacy appraisal. We selected several cultures that vary in their cultural orientation and at the same time are known to have created school systems differing in the respective features. More specifically, we assessed children's self-efficacy beliefs concerning their perceived academic capabilities in East Berlin, West Berlin, Moscow, and Los Angeles.

Empirical analysis of the link between culture and self-efficacy

Comparative analysis of East Berlin and West Berlin school systems

Before the fall of the Berlin wall, the school systems in East Berlin and West Berlin differed in four major ways (DDR: Schule im Aufbruch, 1990; Giessmann, 1990; Klier, 1990; Waterkamp, 1990). They included: (a) the role of the in-group, (b) respect for and power of teachers, (c) standardization of learning and teaching strategies, and (d) degree of social comparison.

In East Berlin, frequent teacher and peer evaluations were given both verbally and nonverbally in front of the entire "class collective" throughout the school day (Schnabel, 1977; Tautz, 1978; Weck, 1981; Witzlack, 1986). Teachers were expected to evaluate their students publicly at parent-teacher assemblies, at parents' workplaces, at meetings of the state-run youth organizations (i.e., Pioneers, Free German Youth; Waterkamp, 1990), or at other occasions outside the classroom. Public grading began at the first grade level. In addition to this early, pervasive, and differentiated performance feedback, teaching strategies in East Berlin were group-oriented and unidimensional. In all schools at given grade levels in the former GDR (East Germany), children received exactly the same materials, class assignments, and pace of studying, regardless of the children's preferences or potential, thereby enhancing evaluative social comparisons of performance attainments. Moreover, teachers were expected to adhere strictly to the prescribed curriculum, assignments, and pace of teaching, and were discouraged to accommodate the specific interests and needs of the individual children (Waterkamp, 1988, 1990).

The East Berlin educational practices were part of the general political program guided by official party doctrine aimed at educating (and reeducating) "harmoniously developed socialistic personalities" (Waterkamp, 1990, p. 263). Accordingly, one central goal of the educational philosophy in East Berlin was to foster in all students the ability to evaluate themselves "adequately" in the sense of adopting the authorities' (e.g., the teachers') evaluations of students' competence and personality attributes (Franz, 1987). An "open and honest" atmosphere in the class-collective, grounded on accurate self- and peer evaluations, was considered to be essential for the successful development of an independent and responsible personality and of the collective (Falkenhagen, 1989; Finck, 1989; Franz, 1982, 1987, 1989; Krause, 1989; Wiese, 1989; see also Waterkamp, 1990). Teaching adequate self-evaluation was a primary objective for the teacher, the parents, and the class-collective. Finally, characteristics such as quietness and honesty were regarded as desirable, whereas feelings of "knowing better" and "superiority" were considered undesirable in children's personality development (Weck, 1981).

From time to time, students had to undergo "learning conferences," in which, after being required to publicly evaluate themselves, good students were praised by the teacher and the class-collective, whereas weak students had to explain remorsefully why they had failed and how they planned to avoid future failure (see also Franz, 1982; Schnabel, 1977; Tautz, 1978; Weck, 1981). Such personal revelations were then evaluated by both teachers and the class-collective. Moreover, every student was expected to feel responsible for the successes and failures of his or her in-group or class-collective (for similar regulations in Russia, see Bronfenbrenner, 1970).

In West Berlin, neither were public self-evaluations used, nor was performance feedback in the form of grades given until the end of the second grade. Privacy concerning students' grades was emphasized, though it could not be guaranteed. Children's performance records were kept in the schools, not to be discussed in public. Teaching strategies were less unidimensional (i.e., materials, assignments, and pacing were more individualized), and teachers were allowed to respect the individual needs of their students to a greater extent than in East Berlin. These differences in type of performance feedback and teaching strategies between the school systems of East Berlin and West Berlin were also reflected in different educational goals. In West Berlin there was no explicit educational goal of accurate self-evaluation. Rather, the educational philosophy focused on conveying factual knowledge to the children, and avoided influencing children to adopt an absolute truth or any other state-defined value system (Waterkamp, 1987, 1990).

Differences in self-efficacy beliefs

Clearly, in the East German school system, cultural values related to collectivism, large power differential, strong uncertainty avoidance, and masculine-oriented achievement striving were more strongly modeled and promoted than in the West Berlin school system. For these reasons we predicted that East Berlin children would appraise their efficacy differently than would West Berlin schoolchildren. Specifically, we expected East Berlin children to have a lower sense of personal efficacy and to be more congruent in their judgments with their teachers' evaluations.

The commencement of school means that, for the first time, children have their performance attainments judged by a teacher, and find themselves compared to their classmates. School systems high on collectivism and power differential tend to make children's self-appraisals dependent on the opinions of in-group members (e.g., class-collective) and authorities (e.g., teachers). If, in addition, an orientation toward uncertainty avoidance and masculine strivings prevails, authorities and in-group members concur in making children classify themselves unambiguously in accord with the status assigned to them in the class-collective, thereby fostering adequate self-appraisals.

Adopting adequate self-appraisals should be a problem, however, particularly for students who are comparatively less intelligent. Given that children enter school with illusory optimism regarding their capabilities (Stipek, 1984, 1988), less intelligent students are more frequently confronted with performance feedback that contradicts their naive optimism. Accordingly, entering school implies for children with low intelligence that they will have to discard their initial positive self-views and adopt a critical self-evaluation reflecting their inefficacy. In the course of acknowledging a sense of personal inefficacy, failure feedbacks will more readily be accepted as accurate.

For intelligent children things are quite different, because the performance feedback they experience is largely consistent with their initial naive optimism. As a consequence, entering school does not imply a correction of their self-views. Highly intelligent children will thus establish a robust sense of efficacy regarding their school performances. Disparate failure experiences will not be integrated in these self-efficacy beliefs, as they are simply dismissed.

In school contexts where differentiated, unambiguous, and public performance feedback as well as unidimensional teaching strategies are practiced at the outset of schooling, children of low intelligence should be less able to escape the correction of their naive optimism than those in school contexts that practice delayed, undifferentiated, ambiguous, and private performance feedback on multidimensional teaching activities. In contrast, for the self-efficacy judgment of highly intelligent children, feedback procedures and teaching strategies practiced in a given school context should carry less weight. Because these children receive predominantly positive performance feedback, correction of optimistic self-views is not much of an issue. It is not surprising, then, that the East German educational goal of teaching students adequate self-evaluation focused mainly on the low-performing students. It was acknowledged that these students should find it especially difficult to adopt an accurate self-view (see Franz, 1987; Schnabel, 1977; Weck, 1981).

These considerations imply that the differences in school context between East and West Berlin affect the self-appraisal of less intelligent children only. More specifically, East Berlin children of low intelligence should possess a weaker sense of self-efficacy than West Berlin children of low intelligence, whereas East and West Berlin children of high intelligence should not differ in their relatively strong self-efficacy. In addition, East Berlin children of low intelligence should conform more readily to their teachers' evaluations than their West Berlin counterparts, whereas no differences between East and West Berlin were expected for highly intelligent children.

In June 1990, before the unification of the two Germanies, Oettingen, Little, Lindenberger, and Baltes (1994) assessed the efficacy beliefs and school grades in 313 East Berlin children drawn from two schools. Students were sampled from grades two to six (i.e., 8 to 12 years of age). Data were compared to those of an age-matched study conducted 1 year later with 527 children of West Berlin. We administered the short form of the Control, Agency and Means-Ends Interview (CAMI; Little, Oettingen, Stetsenko, & Baltes, 1994a; Oettingen et al., 1994; Skinner, Chapman, & Baltes, 1988). Fifty-eight items assess (1) causality beliefs reflecting children's judgments on what causes good or poor school performance, (2) control beliefs, which measure children's evaluation of the extent to which they can influence their school performance, and (3) efficacy (agency) beliefs, which concern children's judgments as to whether they have access to the means that influence academic performance (i.e., effort, ability, luck, teachers' assistance). The 4-point response scale for all items ranged from "never" to "always." Efficacy belief items include: "I can really pay attention in class" (effort); "I'm pretty smart at school even without working very hard" (ability). These efficacy beliefs (also called agency beliefs) combine beliefs about means concerning effort, ability, and luck as a second-order factor and teachers' assistance as a first-order factor (Little et al., 1993). The factorial structure of the CAMI measure shows equivalent factor loadings and covariances across seven cultures, includ-

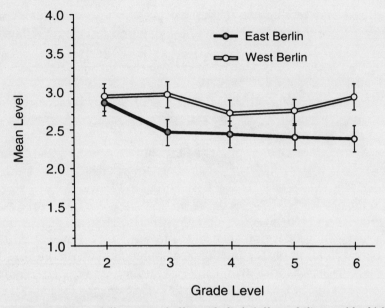

Figure 5.1. Mean differences of efficacy beliefs (effort, ability, and luck) by grade level in East and West Berlin children. Nonoverlapping error bars mean $p < .05$ (from Oettingen et al., 1994).

ing East and West Berlin, Moscow, and Los Angeles (Little et al., 1994a), indicating that it is a valid and reliable instrument across cultures. In contrast to the flexible conceptualization of efficacy beliefs, which may be applied to any type of performance (see Bandura, in press), agency beliefs refer to discrete a priori defined means (e.g., access to effort, ability, but also to the entity of luck) relevant in the school performance domain. In our various samples of children in middle childhood, agency beliefs pertaining to luck form one factor with those pertaining to effort and ability, indicating that children of this age group perceive having access to luck as an issue of their personal control.

East Berlin children had a lower sense of academic efficacy than West Berlin children on all aspects of personal agency. That is, they believed themselves to have lesser capability to exert effort in school, to be less smart, to attract less luck, and to attain less help of their teachers (Oettingen et al., 1994). The lower perceived efficacy of East Berlin children begins in the third grade and is pervasive for the rest of the school years (Figure 5.1).

Moreover, East Berlin children showed higher correlations between their efficacy beliefs and course grades than did West Berlin children, indi-

Table 5.1. *Efficacy beliefs and course grades by grade level*

Grade Level	East Berlin	West Berlin
2	.79**	.61
3	.74**	.60
4	.72	.77
5	.75*	.67
6	.88**	.83

*$p \leq$ .01
**$p \leq$ .001
Source: Oettigen et al., 1994

cating the impact of a consensual construction of competence in the East Berlin school system. As early as in the second grade level the correlations were r = .79 for East Berlin students and r = .61 for West Berlin students (see Table 5.1). The congruence between efficacy beliefs and course grades for East Berlin children (overall r = .77) is considerably higher than the correlations for American children (r's about .30), as reported by Skinner, Wellborn, and Connell (1990), using a similar instrument.

The differential mean levels (Figure 5.2) between East and West Berlin children are mainly due to children at the lower levels of intellectual functioning, as assessed with the RAVEN matrices (Oettingen & Little, 1993). Highly intelligent children in East and West Berlin do not differ significantly in their self-efficacy judgments, whereas significantly lower scores are observed in East as compared to West Berlin children in the low and medium intelligence groups.

The difference between East and West Berlin children in their readiness to conform to their teachers' evaluations is also moderated by the children's intelligence. For East Berlin children who ranked in the lower third of intelligence, more than 80% of the variance in efficacy beliefs was explained by course grades (see Figure 5.3). This was 40% more than in the comparable West Berlin group. For the children of medium intelligence the difference was 16%, whereas no difference in explained variance was observed for the high intelligence group. This pattern of results cannot be explained by differences in variance of teacher evaluations (course grades) or agency beliefs, because the variances of these variables did not differ between groups of different intelligence (RAVEN scores) across and within East and West Berlin.

Correlations between efficacy beliefs and course grades increase with intelligence within the West Berlin sample (see Figure 5.3). This is in line

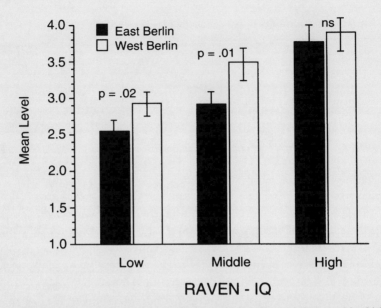

Figure 5.2. Mean differences of efficacy beliefs (effort, ability, and luck) by tripartite RAVEN-IQ in East and West Berlin children. Nonoverlapping error bars mean $p < .05$ (from Oettingen & Little, 1993).

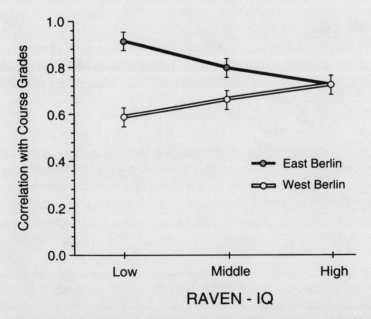

Figure 5.3. Correlations of efficacy beliefs (effort, ability, and luck) with course grades by tripartite RAVEN-IQ in East and West Berlin children. Nonoverlapping error bars mean $p < .05$ (from Oettingen & Little, 1993).

with findings of a meta-analysis by Mabe and West (1982) and the common observation in the Western literature that positive performance feedback is more readily accepted than negative performance feedback (for summaries, see Taylor, 1989; Taylor & Brown, 1988). In contrast, in East Berlin, where accurate self-evaluation was the explicit educational goal, the less intelligent children accepted their negative social evaluation more readily than the more intelligent children accepted their positive evaluation. Apparently, the East Berlin school context was successful in forcing less intelligent students to turn their initial performance optimism into a more negative self-view.

Implications for East and West Berlin children

Low efficacy beliefs undermine motivation, generate negative affect, and impair cognitive functioning. For example, people with low self-efficacy beliefs give up more readily in the face of difficulties, experience more anxiety, are less effective in using problem-solving strategies, and have lower aspirations (Bandura, 1986, 1991, in press; Betz & Hackett, 1986; Multon, Brown, & Lent, 1991; Pintrich & De Groot, 1990; Schunk, 1991; Wood & Bandura, 1989).

Accordingly, East Berlin children should be more handicapped by motivational and affective problems linked to a low sense of efficacy than their West Berlin peers. The high correlations between efficacy beliefs and course grades in East Berlin also suggest negative consequences of having to judge one's capabilities in accordance with teacher and group evaluations. From the beginning of their schooling, East Berlin children believe they are capable of achieving only as much as their teachers' opinions suggest.

This is especially true for children functioning at the lower level of intelligence. They are the ones who would really need the motivational and affective benefits of a positive sense of efficacy. The unusually high correlation of $r = .90$ between efficacy beliefs and academic performance in the less intelligent East Berlin children suggests a strong negative prognosis of low future performance, which considerably narrows their developmental plasticity (Baltes, 1987).

The unification of East and West Germany requires acculturation for the East Berlin children (Berry, 1990), because they are adopting the West German culture system. In their transition from school to work, East Berlin youngsters, especially those at lower levels of intellectual functioning, may be handicapped by a weaker sense of efficacy than their West Berlin competitors. Moreover, they may be less resilient in dealing with failures, because failures readily validate their low self-appraisals of their capabilities.

Our results also suggest implications for the social interactions between East and West Berliners in the workplace. Misunderstandings might arise if East Berliners interpret the positive expression of personal efficacy by West Berliners as presumptuousness and arrogance (*Besserwessi*), whereas West Berliners might tend to interpret the realistic self-appraisals of East Berliners as inappropriate pessimism. This stereotype is voiced in the West German popular press, which complains about the chronic motivational deficits of former East German citizens.

From an ethnocentric West German point of view there is good reason to be optimistic about effective acculturation of East Germans to the West German society. Our data suggest that a school system issuing repeated criticism of optimistic self-appraisal can get students to give up their naive optimism regarding their personal capabilities. When such undermining school practices are discontinued, which is currently occurring by adoption of the West Berlin school system in the East Berlin schools, the children are more likely to maintain their positive beliefs in their potential.

Such a West German ethnocentric view might lead one to overlook the fact that the type of self-efficacy appraisals engaged in East Berlin children had some social advantages for managing life in former East Germany. If people evaluated themselves adequately, they were engaging in a socially desired and valued self-appraisal strategy. Indeed, children who evaluated themselves adequately were rewarded with positions of leadership in the class-collective (Waterkamp, 1988), whereas voicing an optimistic sense of personal efficacy brought social censure (Maron, 1992; Weck, 1981). The motivational and cognitive benefits of a strong sense of personal efficacy might thus have incurred social costs.

Comparison of efficacy beliefs in East Berlin and Moscow children

East Berlin had imported the socialistic philosophy of education from the Soviet Union. In accord with Hofstede's view (1991) that culture manifests itself in societal institutions, we assumed that East Berlin and Moscow school systems would show – albeit following the same educational philosophies – subtle differences reflecting the cultural value differences between Russia and East Germany (Stetsenko, Little, Oettingen, & Baltes, in press).

In the former Soviet Union, both Soviet educational scientists and teachers concurred with the politicians' complaints in the 1980s, that the educational and political rules were insufficiently obeyed and not effectively implemented in daily school life. They argued that educational goals and regulations were formally adopted and implemented just as a showcase (e.g., see Ligachev, 1989). At the same time, youngsters in the upper school grades frequently complained about their "lack of independence and excessive petty tutelage by teachers" (Kon, 1989, p. 60). Moreover, Russian youths commonly disregard school regulations and enjoy making fun of teachers (Elkonin & Dragunova, 1967; Kon, 1989). This picture of everyday school life fits in with the disrespect for authority and disobedience expressed in Russian fairy tales, novels, and proverbs (e.g., "The sky is high and the Tsar is far!"). In Hofstede's terms, this type of disrespect presents a picture of high power distance (see Polivanova, 1992) that is responded to in a resistant way. In other words, the climate of cultural institutions is characterized by rebellion against the authorities' high power pressures. The school context with its tradition of making fun of teachers is a case in point. In addition, the Russian political developments of the past decade indicate an increased readiness for societal change, which should be accompanied by a value change toward low uncertainty avoidance.

East Germans, on the other hand, are not known to have rebelled against the high power distance expressed in their cultural institutions. Rather, they responded by dependence, that is, they respected authorities and readily conformed to their power pressures. East Berlin's Prussian tradition of submissively dealing with authorities may have prevented resistant counterreactions. In addition, East Germany was the last country of the Eastern bloc to start experimenting with societal change. This indicates that avoiding uncertainty was valued highly in East Germany. Indeed, East Germans waited for the Russians to give allowance and then readily accepted West German influences and regulations.

Therefore, children in Moscow, being embedded in a cultural context of lower power differential (because of counterdependence) and lower uncertainty avoidance than children in East Berlin, should score comparatively higher on self-efficacy and lower on conformity with teacher evaluations. In 1990 we (Little, Oettingen, Stetsenko, & Baltes, 1994b; Oettingen, Little, Stetsenko, & Baltes, 1993; Stetsenko et al., in press) assessed the self-efficacy beliefs of more than 500 children grades two to six of two Moscow schools. The mean levels of self-efficacy beliefs were higher in the Moscow children than in the East Berlin children, with differences beginning in the third grade and extending to higher school years. Specifically, the Moscow children were more confident in being able to mobilize effort, being smart, and having luck on their side. The correlations between efficacy beliefs and course grades were lower in Moscow (r's in the .50s vs. in the .70s in East Berlin; Stetsenko et al., in press), indicating a lower conformity to the teachers' competence evaluations in the Moscow than in the East Berlin children. These findings further suggest that cultural characteristics – in this case power differential and uncertainty avoidance – influence children's self-appraisals of efficacy in school settings.

Comparison of efficacy beliefs in Los Angeles and West Berlin children

The effect of cultural variations in educational practices on appraisal of self-efficacy was also evident in a study comparing more than 600 children from two Los Angeles schools with our West Berlin sample (Little et al., 1994b). In the past decades, educational philosophy in the United States favored school environments that provide opportunities for children to develop and express their unique potentials (Ames, 1992; Stipek, 1988, 1991). Accordingly, a unidimensional instruction was moderated in favor of multidimensional teaching. Today, multidimensional teaching practices are widely used in American schools. Students have much choice as to what they want to learn (e.g., the subjects of art, math, physics, languages), how they want to go about it (e.g., materials used, grouping), and the pace at which they do so. Individualized education makes a clear-cut ranking of students difficult. Moreover, precise information on where one actually stands among one's peers does not seem to be a major concern of teachers, parents, and students.

The everyday school life is in accord with Hofstede's (1980) finding that the United States is more individualistic than West Germany, the reverse being true for the dimension of uncertainty avoidance. Indeed, the self-efficacy beliefs of Los Angeles children were higher than those of the West Berlin children. At the same time, the correlations between efficacy beliefs and course grades were lower in Los Angeles than in West Berlin (r's in the .40s vs. in the .60s in West Berlin; Little et al., 1994b; Little, Oettingen, Stetsenko, & Baltes, 1993). This suggests that individualist, weak uncertainty-avoidant cultures might promote more optimistic beliefs of personal efficacy and less comformity with performance evaluations by teachers than in collectivist, strong uncertainty-avoidant cultures.

It seems possible that the observed differences between Los Angeles and West Berlin may also originate from cultural differences in power distance. After all, a multidimensional teaching style requires a different teacher-student relationship than does a unidimensional teaching style.

Indeed, for schools in the United States, Stipek (1988, 1991) postulates a change in teacher-student relations away from teacher-centered toward child-centered school practices. Assuming that these changes have been implemented to a higher degree in the Los Angeles sample than in the West Berlin sample, the observed differences in self-efficacy may also be the result of differences in power distance between teachers and students in Los Angeles (lower power distance) as compared to West Berlin (higher power distance). Although Hofstede views the United States, and in particular West Germany, as adhering to low power distance, it is likely that the West German educational system values power differentials more highly than the American system. Indeed, the high power differential characteristic of the West German university system survived the many reforms aimed at changing an autocratic professor-student relationship. Finally, there are recent complaints about an overemphasis of laissez-faire teaching practices in U.S. schools.

Summary. Of the four cultural samples, East Berlin children demonstrated the most pessimistic beliefs of personal efficacy and showed the highest conformity with teachers' performance evaluations. Descriptive accounts of the educational practices of the East Berlin school system reflect high collectivism, large power differential, strong uncertainty avoidance, and an emphasis on social comparison. The most optimistic self-efficacy beliefs and the least pressure for social construction of competence characterized the Los Angeles schoolchildren, who are embedded in a school system with high levels of individualism and weak ambiguity avoidance. The West Berlin and Moscow children fell in between in their level of perceived efficacy and conformity with teachers' evaluations.

Are the beneficial effects of high self-efficacy universal?

Strong efficacy beliefs lead to greater persistence in the face of difficulties, reduce fear of failure, improve problem-focused analytic thinking, and raise aspirations – at least, this is what has been shown in Western cultures (see Bandura, 1989, in press). But are the beneficial effects of a strong sense of personal efficacy universal? That is, do they generalize across cultures irrespective of the different values to which various cultures subscribe? There is reason to believe that they are indeed universal, because they are founded in basic psychological principles and mechanisms common to human agency in general.

On first sight, however, achieving equivalence across culture in the assessment of self-efficacy seems hardly feasible. The *public* expression of high personal efficacy beliefs may incur social costs and these social costs may differ across cultures. Goffman's (1955, 1959) writings on self-presentation point out that allowing others to save face facilitates social interaction. Moderating one's expressions of efficacy in public reduces the risk that others will feel less efficacious in comparison (i.e., lose face). Cultures that stress interpersonal harmony (see Markus & Kitayama, 1991; Rosenberger, 1992) should discourage expressing high self-efficacy beliefs publicly. This may go so far that even the expression of satisfaction over personal accomplishments is suppressed. Stipek, Weiner, and Li (1989) report that the Chinese are less likely than Americans to claim their own successful efforts as a source of pride. Kitayama and Markus (1990) found in Japanese subjects that feeling pride (as well as feeling superior, puffed up) is associated with feelings of indebtedness, shame, and guilt.

But do we have to conclude from these findings that people in cultures stressing interrelatedness will chronically fail to report on their "true" sense of personal efficacy, because they succumb to the cultural norm to be self-effacing? We caution against this conclusion. As Hofstede's descriptions of cultures imply, people in collectivist cultures focus on promoting the interrelatedness between in-group but not out-group members. The described self-effacing expression of efficacy feelings should therefore solely apply to interactions between in-group members. Collectivist individuals should feel no qualms expressing a strong sense of efficacy to members of out-groups. As Espinoza and Garza (1985) observed, collectivist individuals in point of fact fiercely compete with out-group members, even more so than individualists. In a standard testing situation, therefore, collectivist individuals should truly report on their self-efficacy feelings as they are not dealing with their in-group. It is not surprising, then, that Matsui and his colleagues find in Japan the same self-efficacy effects on career aspirations (Matsui, Ikeda, & Ohnishi, 1989; Matsui & Onglatco, 1991) and coping with stress (Matsui & Onglatco, 1992) as observed in the United States.

The most frequent criticism of the assumption that self-efficacy effects are universal, however, is the following: Self-efficacy would by definition relate to feelings of a single individual's personal efficacy; therefore, the postulated beneficial effects of self-efficacy on a person's goal pursuit are to hold only in individualist cultures. But there is no reason to believe that individuals from collectivist cultures do not form personal goals. According to Hofstede, it is the content of the goals that is different between individualist and collectivist cultures. Whereas individualist persons (i.e., idiocentrics; Triandis, 1989) prefer to set goals for themselves that relate to self-actualization, collectivist individuals (i.e., allocentrics) prefer to set goals for themselves that relate to promoting the welfare of their in-group. For both types of goals, it should be the self-efficacious individuals who make good progress toward realizing their goals, whereas the individuals plagued by self-doubt should be less effective.

This does not imply that collectivist and individualist society members feel equally efficacious in individualistic as compared to in-group work settings. Actually, Earley (1993) observed that members of collectivist cultures felt more self-efficacious in an in-group work setting than members of individualist cultures, whereas the reverse was true for an individualistic work setting. More important, however, Earley found that the assessed level of self-efficacy was a highly valid predictor of performance for both types of work conditions (i.e., individualistic vs. collectivistic) for both types of people (i.e., individualists vs. collectivists). This latter finding further supports the assumption that self-efficacy effects on performance are universal.

Conclusion remarks

Cross-cultural research on self-efficacy beliefs clarify how efficacy beliefs originate under different social and institutional practices. It points to the power of societal institutions, which, in culturally determined ways, modify prevalence, form, and evaluation of different sources of self-efficacy information. The research reported in this chapter analyzed how societal educational institutions differentially affect self-efficacy appraisals of children in East Berlin, West Berlin, Moscow, and Los Angeles. Cross-cultural research also needs to be extended to the effects of the social practices in the family, the community, and the workplace on self-efficacy appraisals. The links between cultural differences and their expression in these various institutions have yet to be established empirically. Finally, available evidence indicates that efficacy beliefs have similar effects on human functioning across cultures.

References

Abramson, L. Y., Seligman, M. E. P. , & Teasdale, J. D. (1978). Learned helplessness in humans: Critique and reformulation. *Journal of Abnormal Psychology, 87*, 49–74.

Ames, C. (1992). Classrooms: Goals, structures, and student motivation. *Journal of Educational Psychology, 84*, 261–271.

Baltes, P. B. (1987). Theoretical propositions of life-span developmental psychology: On the dynamics between growth and decline. *Developmental Psychology, 23*, 611–626.

Bandura, A. (1977). Self-efficacy: Toward a unifying theory of behavioral change. *Psychological Review, 84,* 191–215.

Bandura, A. (1986). *Social foundations of thought and action: A social cognitive theory.* Englewood Cliffs, NJ: Prentice Hall.

Bandura, A. (1989). Human agency in social cognitive theory. *American Psychologist, 44,* 1175–1184.

Bandura, A. (1991). Self-regulation of motivation through anticipatory and self-reactive mechanisms. In R. A. Dienstbier (Ed.), *Nebraska symposium on motivation: Perspectives on motivation.* (Vol. 38, pp. 69–164). Lincoln: University of Nebraska Press.

Bandura, A. (in press). *Self-efficacy: The exercise of control.* New York: Freeman.

Berry, J. W. (1990). Psychology of acculturation. In J. J. Berman (Ed.), *Nebraska symposium on motivation: Cross-cultural perspectives.* (Vol. 37, pp. 201–234). Lincoln: University of Nebraska Press.

Betz, N. E., & Hackett, G. (1986). Applications of self-efficacy theory to understanding career choice behavior. *Journal of Social and Clinical Psychology, 4,* 279–289.

Bronfenbrenner, U. (1970). *Two worlds of childhood.* New York: Sage.

DDR: Schule im Aufbruch [East Germany: School awakening]. [Special issue] (1990). *Pädagogik, 3.*

de Charms, R. (1968). *Personal causation: The internal affective determinants of behavior.* New York: Academic.

Deci, E. L., Vallerand, R. J., Pelletier, L. G., & Ryan, R. M. (1991). Motivation and education: The self-determination perspective. Special issue: Current issues and new directions in motivational theory and research. *Educational Psychologist, 26,* 325–346.

Dweck, C. S., & Leggett, E. L. (1988). A social-cognitive approach to motivation and personality. *Psychological Review, 95,* 256–273.

Earley, P. C. (1993). East meets West meets Mideast: Further explorations of collectivistic and individualistic work groups. *Academy of Management Journal, 36,* 319–348.

Elkonin, D., & Dragunova, T. (1967). *Age-related and individual characteristics of early adolescents.* Moscow: Prosveshenije.

Espinoza, J. A., & Garza, T. (1985). Social group salience and inter-ethnic cooperation. *Journal of Experimental Social Psychology, 21,* 380–392.

Falkenhagen, H. (1989). Selbstbewusstsein, Selbstregulation und Selbstreflexion [Self-esteem, self-regulation, and self-reflection]. *Erziehungwissenschaftliche Forschung, 13,* 83–90.

Festinger, L. (1954). A theory of social comparison processes. *Human Relations, 7,* 117–140.

Finck, W. (1989). Zu einigen Selbstparametern bei Schülern mit unterschiedlichem Lernverhalten [On some self-related parameters in school children differing in learning behavior]. *Erziehungswissenschaftliche Forschung, 13,* 101–110.

Franz, S. (1982). *Entwicklung der Selbsteinschätzung bei Schülern* [Development of self-evaluation in school children]. Berlin: Volk und Wissen.

Franz, S. (1987). *Unsere Schüler zur Selbsteinschätzung befähigen* [Teaching self-evaluation to our students]. Berlin: Volk und Wissen.

Franz, S. (1989). Anforderungsbezogene Selbsteinschätzung bei Abiturstufenschülern und Studenten [Task-related self-evaluation in high school and university students]. *Erziehungswissenschaftliche Forschung, 13,* 48–59.

Giessmann, B. (1990). Die FDJ an den Schulen der DDR – Chancen und Grenzen der Funktionswahrnehmung ["Free German Youth" Organization in schools in the GDR – Chances and limitations in achieving its political functions].

Zeitschrift für Sozialisationsforschung und Erziehungssoziologie (1. Beiheft), 91–104.

Goffman, E. (1955). On Facework. *Psychiatry, 18,* 213–231.

Goffman, E. (1959). *The presentation of self in everyday life.* Garden City, NJ: Doubleday.

Hofstede, G. (1980). *Culture's consequences: International differences in work-related values.* Beverly Hills, CA: Sage.

Hofstede, G. (1986). Cultural differences in teaching and learning. *International Journal of Intercultural Relations, 10,* 301–320.

Hofstede, G. (1989). Sozialisation am Arbeitsplatz aus kulturvergleichender Sicht [Socialization at the workplace from a cross-cultural perspective]. In G. Trommsdorff (Ed.), *Sozialisation im Kulturvergleich* [Socialization across culture] (pp. 156–173). Stuttgart: Enke.

Hofstede, G. (1991). *Cultures and organizations: Software of the mind.* London: McGraw-Hill.

Hovland, C. I., & Weiss, W. (1952). The influence of source credibility on communication effectiveness. *Public Opinion Quarterly, 15,* 635–650.

Inkeles, A., & Levinson, D. J. (1969). National character: The study of model personality and sociocultural systems. In G. Lindsey & E. Aronson (Eds.), *The handbook of social psychology* (2nd ed., Vol. 4). Reading, MA: Addison-Wesley.

Kavanagh, D. J., & Bower, G. H. (1985). Mood and self-efficacy: Impact of joy and sadness on perceived capabilities. *Cognitive Therapy and Research, 9,* 507–525.

Kitayama, S., & Markus, H. (1990, August). *Culture and emotion: The role of other-focused emotions.* Paper presented at the 98th Annual Convention of the American Psychological Association, Boston.

Klier, F. (1990). *Lüg Vaterland: Erziehung in der DDR* [Lie fatherland: Education in the GDR]. Munich: Kindler.

Kon, I. S. (1989). The psychology of independence. *Soviet Education, 31,* 57–64.

Krause, C. (1989). Zur Genese des Selbstbildes im Kindes- und Jugendalter – Ergebnisse und Probleme einer Längsschnittuntersuchung [The development of the self-image in childhood and adolescence – Results and problems of a longitudinal investigation]. *Erziehungswissenschaftliche Forschung, 13,* 7–30.

Lent, R. W., & Hackett, G. (1987). Career self-efficacy: Empirical status and future directions. *Journal of Vocational Behavior, 30,* 347–382.

Ligachev, E. (1989). On the course of restructuring the education system and the party's tasks in carrying it out. *Soviet Education, 31,* 6–68.

Little, T. D., Oettingen, G., Stetsenko, A., & Baltes, P. B. (1993, July). *School performance-related beliefs across political system and culture: A comparison of children in East-, West-Berlin, Moscow, Prague, and Los Angeles.* Paper presented at the 3rd European Congress of Psychology, Tampere, Finland.

Little, T. D., Oettingen, G., Stetsenko, A., & Baltes, P. B. (1994a). *A cross-cultural validity assessment of the revised control, agency, and means-ends interview (CAMI) using mean and covariance structures (MACS) analyses.* Tech. Rep. No. 1. Berlin: Max Planck Institute for Human Development and Education.

Little, T. D., Oettingen, G., Stetsenko, A., & Baltes, P. B. (1994b). *Children's school performance-related beliefs: How do American children compare to German and Russian children?* Unpublished manuscript.

Mabe III, P. A., & West, S. G. (1982). Validity of self-evaluation of ability: A review and meta-analysis. *Journal of Applied Psychology, 67,* 280–296.

Markus, H. R., & Kitayama, S. (1991). Culture and the self: Implications for cognition, emotion, and motivation. *Psychological Review, 98,* 224–253.

Maron, M. (1992). Zonophobie. *Kursbuch, 109,* 91–96.

Matsui, T., Ikeda, H., & Ohnishi, R. (1989). Relations of sex-typed socializations to career self-efficacy expectations of college students. *Journal of Vocational Behavior, 35*, 1–16.

Matsui, T., & Onglatco, M. L. (1991). Instrumentality, expressiveness, and self-efficacy in career activities among Japanese working women. *Journal of Vocational Behavior, 39*, 241–250.

Matsui, T., & Onglatco, M. L. (1992). Career self-efficacy as a moderator of the relation between occupational stress and strain. *Journal of Vocational Behavior, 41*, 79–88.

Multon, K. D., Brown, S. D., & Lent, R. W. (1991). Relation of self-efficacy beliefs to academic outcomes: A meta-analytic investigation. *Journal of Counseling Psychology, 38*, 30–38.

Oettingen, G., & Little, T. D. (1993). Intelligenz und Selbstwirksamkeitsurteile bei Ost- und Westberliner Schulkindern [Intelligence and performance-related self-efficacy beliefs in East and West Berlin children]. *Zeitschrift für Sozialpsychologie, 24*, 186–197.

Oettingen, G., Little, T. D., Lindenberger, U., & Baltes, P. B. (1994). Causality, agency, and control beliefs in East versus West Berlin children: A natural experiment on the role of context. *Journal of Personality and Social Psychology, 66*, 579–595.

Oettingen, G., Little, T. D., Stetsenko, A., & Baltes, P. B. (1993, March). *School performance-related beliefs across political system and culture: A comparison of children in East Berlin, West Berlin, Moscow and Los Angeles.* Paper presented at the 60th Biennial Meeting of the Society for Research on Child Development, New Orleans.

Petty, R. E., & Cacioppo, J. T. (1986). *Communication and persuasion: Central and peripheral routes to attitude change.* New York: Springer.

Pintrich, P. R., & De Groot, E. V. (1990). Motivational and self-regulated learning components of classroom academic performance. *Journal of Educational Psychology, 82*, 33–40.

Polivanova, K. N. (1992). The modern situation in primary education in Russia. In A. Tjeldvoll (Ed.), *Education in East/Central Europe: Report of the Oslo Seminar* (pp. 225–231). New York: Graduate School of Education Publications.

Rosenberger, N. R. (Ed.). (1992). *Japanese sense of self.* Cambridge, England: Cambridge University Press.

Rosenholtz, S. J., & Rosenholtz, S. H. (1981). Classroom organization and the perception of ability. *Sociology of Education, 54*, 132–140.

Rosenholtz, S. J., & Simpson, C. (1984). The formation of ability conceptions: Developmental trend or social construction? *Review of Educational Research, 54*, 31–63.

Ryan, R. M., & Stiller, J. (1991). The social contexts of internalization: Parent and teacher influences on autonomy, motivation, and learning. In M. L. Maehr & P R. Pintrich (Eds.), *Advances in motivation and achievement* (Vol. 7, pp. 115–149). Greenwich, CT: JAI.

Schnabel, G. (1977). *Die Selbst- und Fremdeinschätzung: Wesentliche Mittel der Charakterentwicklung* [Self- and other evaluations: Critical means for character development]. Pädagogische Lesung. Berlin: Deutsches Institut für internationale pädagogische Forschung.

Schunk, D. H. (1991). Self-efficacy and academic motivation. Special issue: Current issues and new directions in motivational theory and research. *Educational Psychologist, 26*, 207–231.

Skinner, E. A., Chapman, M., & Baltes, P. B. (1988). Control, means-ends, and agency beliefs: A new conceptualization and its measurement during childhood. *Journal of Personality and Social Psychology, 54*, 117–133.

Skinner, E. A., Wellborn, J. G., & Connell, J. P. (1990). What it takes to do well in school and whether I've got it: A process model of perceived control and children's engagement and achievement in school. *Journal of Educational Psychology, 82*, 22–32.

Sorrentino, R. M., Raynor, J. O., Zubek, J. M., & Short, J.-A. C. (1990). Personality functioning and change. Informational and affective influences on cognitive, moral, and social development. In E. T. Higgins & R. M. Sorrentino (Eds.), *Handbook of motivation and cognition: Foundations of social behavior* (Vol. 2, pp. 193–228). New York: Guilford.

Stetsenko, A., Little, T. D., Oettingen, G., & Baltes, P. B. (in press). Agency, control, and means-ends beliefs about school performance in Moscow children: How similar are they to beliefs of Western children? *Developmental Psychology*.

Stipek, D. J. (1984). The development of achievement motivation. In R. Ames & C. Ames (Eds.), *Research on motivation in education: Student motivation* (Vol. 1, pp. 145–174). Orlando, FL: Academic.

Stipek, D. J. (1988). *Motivation to learn: From theory to practice.* Englewood Cliffs, NJ: Prentice Hall.

Stipek, D. J. (1991). Characterizing early childhood education programs. *New Directions for Child Development, 53*, 47–55.

Stipek, D., Weiner, B., & Li, K. (1989). Testing some attribution-emotion relations in the People's Republic of China. *Journal of Personality and Social Psychology, 56*, 109–116.

Stroebe, W. (1976). Is social psychology really that complicated? A review of Martin Irle's Lehrbuch der Sozialpsychologie. *European Journal of Social Psychology, 6*, 509–511.

Tautz, D. (1978). *Erfahrungen bei der Befähigung der Schüler zur realen Selbsteinschätzung* [Experiences with teaching schoolchildren to realistically self-evaluate]. Pädagogische Lesung. Berlin: Deutsches Institut für internationale pädagogische Forschung.

Taylor, S. E. (1989). *Positive illusions: Creative self-deception and the healthy mind.* New York: Basic Books.

Taylor, S. E., & Brown, J. D. (1988). Illusion and well-being: A social psychological perspective on mental health. *Psychological Bulletin, 103*, 193–210.

Triandis, H. C. (1989). The self and social behavior in differing cultural contexts. *Psychological Review, 96*, 506–520.

Triandis, H. C., Leung, K., Villareal, M. J., & Clack, F. L. (1985). Allocentric versus idiocentric tendencies: Convergent and discriminant validation. *Journal of Research in Personality, 19*, 395–415.

Triandis, H. C., McCusker, C., & Hui, C. H. (1990). Multimethod probes of individualism and collectivism. *Journal of Personality and Social Psychology, 59*, 1006–1020.

Waterkamp, D. (1987). *Handbuch zum Bildungswesen der DDR* [Handbook of the educational system of the GDR]. Berlin: Berlin Verlag.

Waterkamp, D. (1988). "Achtung Sammeln": Disziplin in der Schule der DDR ["Attention: Assemble": Discipline in the school of the GDR]. In G. Helwig (Ed.), *Schule in der DDR* (pp. 37–64). Cologne, Germany: Wissenschaft und Politik.

176   Gabriele Oettingen

Waterkamp, D. (1990). Erziehung in der Schule [Education in the school]. In Bundesministerium für innerdeutsche Beziehungen (Ed.), *Vergleich von Bildung und Erziehung in der Bundesrepublik Deutschland und in der Deutschen Demokratischen Republik* (pp. 261–277). Cologne, Germany: Wissenschaft und Politik.

Weck, H. (1981). *Bewertung und Zensierung* [Evaluation and grading]. Berlin: Volk und Wissen.

Wiese, H. (1989). Zur Selbsteinschätzung bei Schülern 5. und 6. Klassen bezüglich ihrer Lernmotivation [On self-evaluative judgments of fifth and sixth graders with respect to their learning motivation]. *Erziehungswissenschaftliche Forschung, 13*, 117–123.

Witzlack, G. (1986). *Verhaltensbewertung und Schülerbeurteilung* [Evaluating behavior and judging students]. (3rd ed.) Berlin: Volk und Wissen.

Wood, R., & Bandura, A. (1989). Impact of conceptions of ability on self-regulatory mechanisms and complex decision-making. *Journal of Personality and Social Psychology, 56*, 407–415.

6. Self-efficacy in stressful life transitions

MATTHIAS JERUSALEM AND
WALDEMAR MITTAG

During the revolutionary events in East Germany in 1989, more than 300,000 citizens left that country and moved to West Germany. As a result of this exodus, more than 50,000 migrants settled in West Berlin. Some came via the West German embassies in Warsaw, Prague, or Budapest, or fled the country under other dubious and dangerous conditions. A larger number crossed the border after the fall of the Berlin Wall on November 9, 1989. The aim of our program of research was to investigate psycho-emotional and health-related adaptation processes within a subgroup of these migrants, that is, young adults. The focus centers on two research issues, both of which concern the contribution of perceived self-efficacy to adaptation processes. The first issue is concerned with whether general self-efficacy beliefs are affected by this stressful life transition. The stressors include the environmental constraints in the new country, unemployment, and lack of social support. The second issue examined the extent to which interindividual differences in stress appraisals, emotional states, and health can be predicted by general beliefs in personal efficacy, employment status, and partnership status as an indicator of access to social support. In this context, self-efficacy is conceived of not as a domain-specific or situation-specific cognition but as a traitlike general sense of confidence in one's own capabilities to master different types of environmental demands.

The decision to leave or flee one's country and home has far-reaching and severe consequences. According to stress theory, such a migratory action can be considered as the onset of a nonnormative critical life transition. As with other critical events (such as accidents, losses, divorce, illness, etc.) the resultant psychological crisis may have a profound impact on personality development, psychosocial functioning, and well-being (Cohen, 1988; Johnson, 1986; Montada, Filipp, & Lerner, 1992). It is not only necessary to cope with daily hassles, especially crowded living conditions in camps or makeshift living facilities, but also with the threat of long-term unemployment and the need to find or cultivate new social networks. Thus, the migrants are disadvantaged not only by higher situational demands than previously, but also by their heightened vulnerability to stress because they have to deal with loss of their jobs and social support from former colleagues, friends, and relatives.

According to the cognitive-relational stress theory (Lazarus, 1991; Lazarus & Folkman, 1987), people's psychological adaptation to new circumstances may be either facilitated or impeded depending on contextual factors. These factors include personal resources or vulnerabilities on the one hand and environmental resources or constraints on the other. In encounters with stressors, resources, vulnerabilities, and constraints influence stress appraisals, coping strategies, and subjective well-being. Strong resources and weak constraints foster adaptive coping strategies that mediate better psychological and physical well-being than weak resources and severe constraints (Hobfoll, 1989; Jerusalem, 1993; Jerusalem & Schwarzer, 1989, 1992). In the research reported here, perceived self-efficacy, employment, and partnership serve as resources in the adaptational process.

Perceived self-efficacy and adaptation

In the context of stressful life transitions, general beliefs of efficacy may serve as a personal resource or vulnerability factor (Bandura, 1986, 1991, 1992; Jerusalem, 1990a, 1993; Schwarzer, 1992). People with a high sense of perceived efficacy trust their own capabilities to master different types of environmental demands. They tend to interpret demands and problems more as challenges than as threats or subjectively uncontrollable events. High perceived efficacy enables individuals to face stressful demands with confidence, feel motivated by physiological arousal, and judge positive events as caused by effort and negative events as due primarily to external circumstances. In these different ways, a generalized belief in one's efficacy serves as a resource factor that should buffer against distressing experiences fostering positive "eustress" perceptions instead. In contrast, individuals who are characterized by low perceived efficacy are prone to self-doubts, anxiety arousal, threat appraisals of events and perceptions of coping deficiencies when confronted with difficult situations and demands. Moreover, previous research on anxiety and self-related cognitions has demonstrated that a low sense of coping efficacy leaves people vulnerable to aversive experiences because they tend to worry, have weak task-specific competence expectancies, interpret physiological arousal as indicative of anxiety, regard social feedback as evaluations of personal value, and feel more personally responsible for failure than for success (Brown & Siegel, 1988; Carver & Scheier, 1988; Jerusalem, 1990b; Sarason, 1988; Schwarzer, 1986; Wine, 1982). Distress appraisals under a low sense of efficacy are accompanied by strong negative emotional reactions and somatic complaints, whereas more favorable cognitive interpretations of difficult situations under a high sense of efficacy protect against psychological and physical harm.

Like other traitlike personal characteristics, weak self-efficacy expectancies have numerous causes. A history of failures, lack of supportive feedback, and an unfavorable attributional style of one's successes and failures by parents, teachers, and peers may lead to the development of a tendency to scan the environment for potential dangers ("sensitizing"), to appraise demands as threatening, and to cope with problems in dysfunctional ways. Although general self-efficacy is conceived of as a trait, it is changeable, especially in response to critical life events by young adults whose sense of efficacy is not yet as elaborated and stabilized as in older persons. Thus, changes in the beliefs of personal efficacy might be expected for young migrants when faced with dramatic shifts in their living conditions. These sociocultural transitions provide totally different starting points for coping with life demands, new and unfamiliar environmental opportunities and constraints, societal values and individual skills to manage them.

Within this stressful transitional adaptation to the new societal living conditions, self-efficacy can function as a personal resource protecting against deleterious experiences, negative emotions, and health impairment. Perceived efficacy itself can undergo changes as a result of cumulative experiences in coping with complex demands in the new environment.

Environmental constraints and adaptation

In addition to personal resources, environmental constraints are considered as antecedents of the adaptational dynamics. Among the many daily hassles that confront migrants are included some major stressors that significantly threaten the quality of life. For example, migrants have lost their jobs as well as their former social networks. Because employment and social integration serve as protective resources in coping with stressful demands, a lack or impairment of these resources creates personal vulnerabilities to the adverse effects of unfavorable environmental conditions.

Employment provides income for one's livelihood and a source of respect in a Western society characterized by high material and economical values. Thus, the impact of unemployment on personal well-being goes beyond direct economic costs. Lack or loss of gainful employment creates insecurity regarding one's future life perspective. Although unemployment can have variable effects, studies generally report impairment of psychological and physical well-being for the majority of the unemployed, especially those in long-term unemployment (Dooley & Catalano, 1988; Feather, 1990; Mortimer, 1991; Schwefel, Svensson, & Zöllner, 1987; Warr, 1987). Young people are especially vulnerable to such detrimental psychological consequences because they still are striving to gain an established and valued position within the society. Unemployment for them means jeopardizing a hopeful perspective toward the future. The stressful quality of unemployment is mostly attributable to a weakened ability to exercise control over one's life because of financial hardships or disruption of social networks, lowered aspirations, a lot of time without meaningful activities to break up each day, and reduced opportunities for social contacts. An enduring status of unemployment requires continuous adaptational efforts – instrumental actions to eliminate the jobless state as well as emotional coping to alleviate the distressing experiences of unemployment (Lazarus, 1991). For migrants, unemployment following relocation appears to be a universal phenomenon not entirely under personal control. Thus, problem-focused behaviors such as searching or qualifying for a job may be seen as of limited value. Instead, efforts are focused more on coping strategies for managing emotional distress, particularly in the case of extended unemployment. The long-term psychological consequences of unemployment may be feelings of discouragement, hopelessness, and despondency as well as lowered self-worth and health impairment. Kelvin and Jarrett (1985) contend that these adverse effects are exacerbated by social comparison processes because working people may perceive the chronically unemployed as inherently inadequate.

A stabile *social network* is a structural prerequisite to feeling socially integrated and emotionally accepted (Duck, 1990; Lin, Dean, & Ensel, 1986; Sarason, Sarason, & Pierce, 1990; Schwarzer & Leppin, 1992; Veiel & Baumann, 1992). *Social integration* refers to the mere number of social relationships one has with relatives, friends, colleagues, and the frequency of contacts with them. *Social support* refers to the function and quality of beneficial social relationships. *Perceived support* represents the anticipation of supportive action if needed, whereas *received support* reflects the actual help provided by others in actual social encounters. A general sense that one is loved and cared for by others, and that these others would help if really needed, contributes to psychological and physical well-being. During a stressful life transition the perceived availability of social supports might also help to reduce stress appraisals insofar as the balance between threat and coping assets may be more favorable. Social support might also operate as a proactive influence strengthening coping efficacy that diminishes the threat value of potential stressors (Bandura, 1992). However, after support is sought, discrepancies between expectation and actuality may occur. Support received may differ from support expected, either because members of the social network do not respond appropriately, or because the amount of available support was underestimated. The most common and important source of support is an intimate partner with whom one shares one's dwelling and everyday life.

Partnership can expand social networks and create stronger social embeddedness because two people usually have a wider range of social ties than does any one individual. Moreover, a stable partnership might instill higher confidence in the trustworthiness and the supportiveness of an intimate partner. Interpersonal commitments to support each other may also lead to an actual increase in the amount of help given when needed. For these reasons, partnership should be a prominent predictor of stress, emotional states, and health. People living with an intimate partner should suffer less from distressful experiences, and they should benefit from a more positive psychological and physical well-being than those who are alone and have no one to turn to in time of need.

The complex stressor of migration

Resource factors may influence psychological and physical well-being through different mechanisms. Self-efficacy, employment, and partner support, respectively, may each have either a general benign effect on well-being or may alleviate stress and its consequences. In the former case, resources have a direct effect, whereas in the latter instance, resources serve as a buffer or moderator between stressful events and their consequences. Strong efficacy beliefs might buffer stress effects caused by unemployment or a lack of a close partner. Employment and partner support may have a positive long-term influence by strengthening perceived efficacy or at least alleviating some of the negative effects of a weak sense of efficacy. Resources can differ in psychological significance, making perceived efficacy a dominant predictor and environmental conditions subordinate, or vice versa. Moreover, beneficial and detrimental effects may depend partly on gender, since both the importance of employment and social support may differ for men and women (Feather, 1990; Schwarzer & Leppin, 1992). Last but not least, resource factors might be confounded with each other at the onset of the adaptation process already. For example, rapid reemployment after migration might be a consequence of high perceived efficacy and respective coping effectiveness, or employed people might be more attractive as social partners than unemployed ones. Such interdependencies must be considered before using separate resource factors as predictors of stress, emotional reactivity, and health evaluations.

In accord with these theoretical considerations, the present research examined individual differences in stress appraisals, anxiety, and subjective health as a function of perceived self-efficacy, employment status, and partner support. It was expected that, over time, high self-efficacious migrants would report more favorable appraisals and well-being than low self-efficacious migrants. Unemployed persons should perceive more stressors and experience more anxiety and health complaints than employed persons. Those having access to a supportive partner should function better than those living alone. A further issue of interest concerns the impact of radical social changes on a general sense of personal efficacy and the effects of employment status and/or supportive partnerships on changes in perceived self-efficacy. No hypotheses were advanced concerning the interdependencies of personal resources, the occurrence of buffer or main effects, and the significance of gender differences in effects of migration.

Analysis of coping with life transitions

In early November 1989, before the opening of the Berlin Wall, a longitudinal study was launched to gain better understanding of the adaptation processes of refugees and migrants from East Germany. The longitudinal study included assessments at three points in time. The first wave of assessment took place around December 1989; data for the second wave were obtained in the summer of 1990; and the third wave assessment was conducted in the summer of 1991. The participants were East German migrants who left their country between August 1989 and February 1990. Although the sample consisted of 235 migrants, the present analysis is confined to migrants who were searching for a job because of the theoretical importance of the effects of involuntary unemployment. Housewives and students were excluded. This subsample comprised 124 young adults, 55 females, and 69 males between 18 and 30 years of age with a median age of 25 years. Perceived self-efficacy, employment status, partnership, anxiety, and health indicators were measured by questionnaires at all three points in time. Stress appraisals were assessed only at the second and third point in time.

Assessment of variables

Generalized self-efficacy was measured by a German 10-item self-efficacy scale (Jerusalem & Schwarzer, 1986), based on Bandura's (1977) self-efficacy theory. The reliability and predictive validity was verified in prior studies (Jerusalem & Schwarzer, 1989, 1992; Mittag & Schwarzer, 1993). Sample items include "No matter what comes my way, I am usually able to handle it," "I remain calm when facing difficulties because I can rely on my coping abilities."

Employment status was assessed at the three points in time by a single item on whether the person was employed or unemployed. Employment status was categorized in three separable groups: (a) jobless at all points in time, (b) jobless at the beginning but employed at Time 3, and (c) employed at all points in time.

Based on a differentiated family status measure (married, single with or without partner, etc.), the participants were categorized into two *partnership* groups: one group who had a partner at all points in time ("partner"), the other group who were without a partner at all points in time ("no partner").

Cognitive appraisals were measured by three short psychometric scales assessing perceived challenge, threat, and loss. The *Challenge* scale consisted of three items, such as "My present life situation is exciting because I am always confronted with new demands." *Threat* was measured by a four-item scale containing statements such as "I worry that I cannot manage the many new demands." *Loss* was represented by four items. A sample item is: "I am discouraged because since my migration everything has become even worse."

Anxiety was assessed by a short subscale of four items from the German version of the State Trait Personality Inventory (STPI; Hodapp, Schwarzer, Schwenkmezger, Laux, & Spielberger, 1988). A sample item is: "I get tense and restless when I think of all my worries and problems."

Health complaints were measured by 24 items referring to physical complaints such as exhaustion, heart and gastric complaints, and rheumatic pains (Brähler & Scheer, 1983). In addition, subjects were asked to judge their current *subjective health state* on a 4-point Likert scale ("poor," "moderate," "good," "excellent").

Before conducting the detailed statistical analyses, a check of interdependencies among the resource factors yielded no significant correlation coefficients: For both women and men, perceived self-efficacy, employment status, and partnership turned out to be independent of each other. To investigate longitudinal adaptation processes, two types of data analyses were conducted. In a first step, separate analyses of variance with repeated measures were computed to evaluate longitudinal changes in perceived self-efficacy as a function of employment status and partnership, respectively. Second, analyses of covariance with repeated measures were performed to examine effects of the resource factors of perceived self-efficacy, employment status, and partnership on stress appraisals, anxiety, and health complaints over time. To control for possible gender differences, gender was included as a covariant.

Longitudinal changes in self-efficacy

Regarding self-efficacy, neither the sample mean nor the separate means for different employment status and partnership subgroups changed over time. Moreover, at all points in time, the environmental resource factors also did not account for any interindividual differences in perceived self-efficacy level. The findings were the same for men as for women. In brief, for the group as a whole, perceived self-efficacy turned out to be stable over time and was unaffected by employment status, partnership, or gender. However, as we shall see next, migrants varied in their perceived self-efficacy, which had a strong impact on the quality of their adaptation.

Resources and adaptation processes

To investigate the impact of employment status, partnership, and perceived self-efficacy (at Time 1) on the level and change in adaptation, three-way analyses of covariance were performed. By median split of the self-efficacy scores participants were categorized into "low self-efficacy" and "high self-efficacy" subgroups. Employment status and partnership were categorized as previously noted. To retain sufficient cell sizes, and in consideration of the empirical independence among the three resource factors, each analysis was conducted with only two predictors at a time.

Repeated measures of the dependent variables constituted the within-subjects factors: stress appraisals of challenge, threat, and loss at the last two points in time, and anxiety, subjective health state, and health complaints at all points in time. Migrants who were unemployed at point 1 in time but successfully applied for a job before point 3 in time ("employed at T3") with respect to all dependent variables ranged between the remaining two employment status groups.

To illustrate most clearly the effects caused by employment status the figures contain only the two extreme groups, that is, "always employed" versus "always jobless" young adults. The role of gender is only reported when it emerges as a significant factor. In all but one of the analyses, perceived self-efficacy, employment status, and partnership had significant effects on challenge appraisal, perceived threat, and loss. Figure 6.1 displays the differences for appraisal of challenge at Time 2 and Time 3 as a function of self-efficacy and partnership. Migrants who expressed a strong sense of efficacy viewed their social change more as a challenge than did those of low perceived efficacy. Migrants who had a partner were more inclined to view the change as a challenge than were migrants without a partner. Employment status did not account for any differences in appraisal of challenge at any point in time.

Threat appraisals were affected by all resource factors. Main effects were found for perceived self-efficacy, partnership, and employment status. The effects of perceived efficacy and partnership are depicted in Figure 6.2. Migrants without a close partner viewed their environment as more threatening than those who had the benefit of a partner. Regardless of partnerships, migrants of low perceived efficacy felt more threatened than those of high perceived efficacy. Threat increased slightly for young migrants living without a partner, whereas threat perceptions clearly decreased when migrants had the support of a partner. With regard to employment status, unemployed migrants felt much more threatened than those who were employed. The former group also suffered from higher threat compared to those who had found a job during the period of the study. Over all employment statuses, high self-efficacious persons reported significantly less threat than low self-efficacious persons. In general, males felt more threatened than females. Concerning loss appraisals, exactly the same patterns of relationships were obtained as with threat appraisals.

Analyses of anxiety yielded significant effects of perceived self-efficacy and time indicating a general decline in level of anxiety. However, changes over time were moderated by partnership. Migrants who had a

186

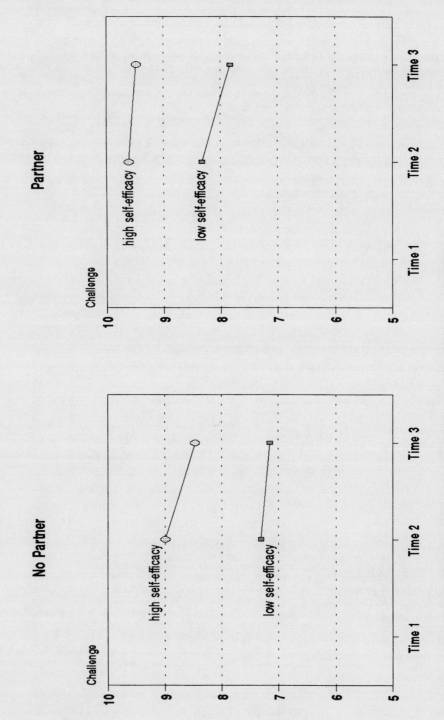

Figure 6.1. Perceived challenge as a function of perceived personal efficacy and partnership.

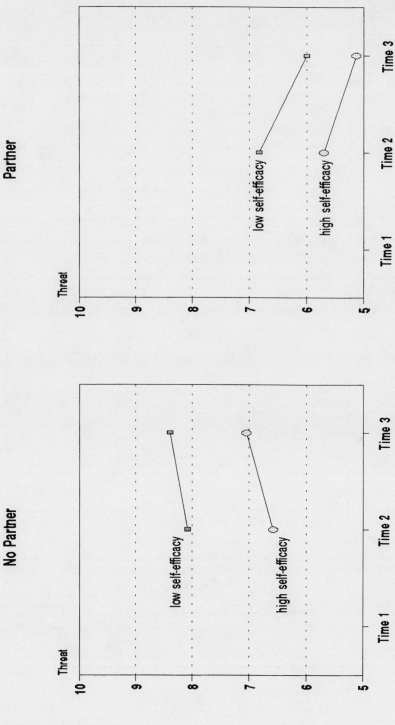

Figure 6.2. Perceived threat as a function of perceived personal efficacy and partnership.

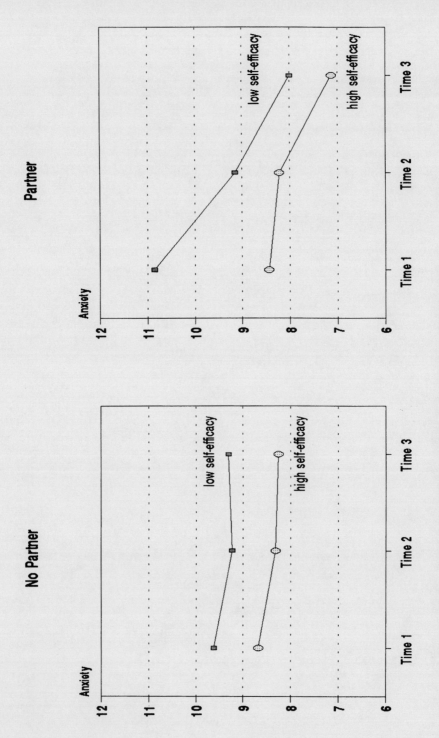

Figure 6.3. Level of anxiety as a function of perceived personal efficacy and partnership.

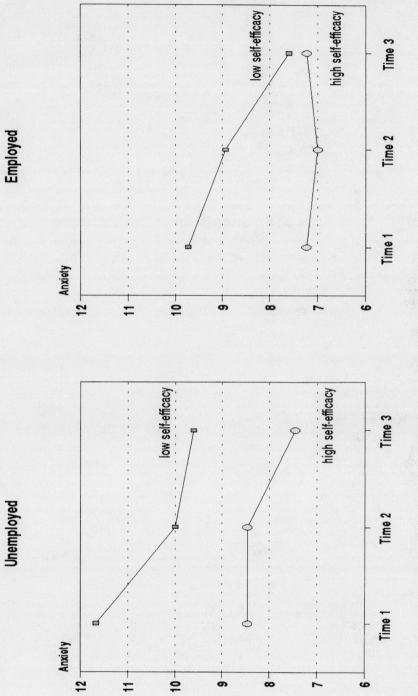

Figure 6.4. Level of anxiety as a function of perceived personal efficacy and employment.

high sense of efficacy felt less anxious than those with low perceived efficacy. Partnership did not have an overall effect. However, migrants who had a close partner became less anxious over time, particularly those of low self-efficacy, but those who had no partner did not experience any decline in anxiety over time (see Figure 6.3).

Figure 6.4 shows anxiety level as a function of perceived self-efficacy and employment status. Apart from the main effect of perceived self-efficacy and the general decrease of anxiety over time, there is a statistical tendency for the unemployed to experience more anxiety than the employed. A theoretically interesting result was found within the group of migrants who were always employed: Initially those with low perceived efficacy reported considerably higher anxiety than their high efficacy counterparts; but at the last point in time the groups no longer differed in this respect. This is mainly due to the decline over time in anxiety for the low self-efficacy group, whereas the high self-efficacy migrants maintained their lower level of anxiety over time.

The effects of perceived efficacy and employment status on subjective health state are shown in Figure 6.5. The highly efficacious migrants reported better current health than did migrants of low perceived self-efficacy. This effect is most evident for long-term unemployed migrants, whereas for the employed ones, perceived self-efficacy seemed to play a minor role in subjective health. There was also a tendency for the "always employed" migrants to be in better health than the "always jobless" ones. Partnership did not exert an unqualified effect on health. Over time, a general improvement in health took place. However, partnership interacted with perceived efficacy. This interactive effect is shown in Figure 6.6. Low self-efficacious migrants with a close partner report an improvement in health over time, whereas those without a partner did not change for the better.

Figure 6.7 shows the level of health complaints over time as a function of employment status and self-efficacy. High perceived self-efficacy was associated with fewer health complaints. Over time, these differences remain much larger in the long-term unemployed than in the always employed group of young migrants. Indeed, the long-term employed even attained comparably favorable health complaints scores in high and low efficacy groups alike. Partnership had no main effect but interacted with perceived self-efficacy over time. Self-inefficacious migrants with partners reported a decrease in health complaints, whereas those without partners reported a decline in health complaints only if they had a high sense of personal efficacy.

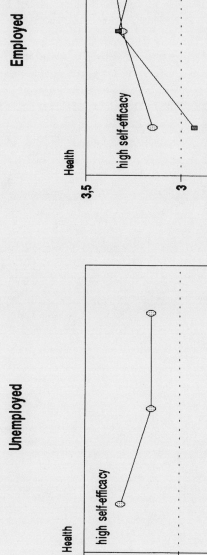

Figure 6.5. Health status as a function of perceived personal efficacy and employment.

192

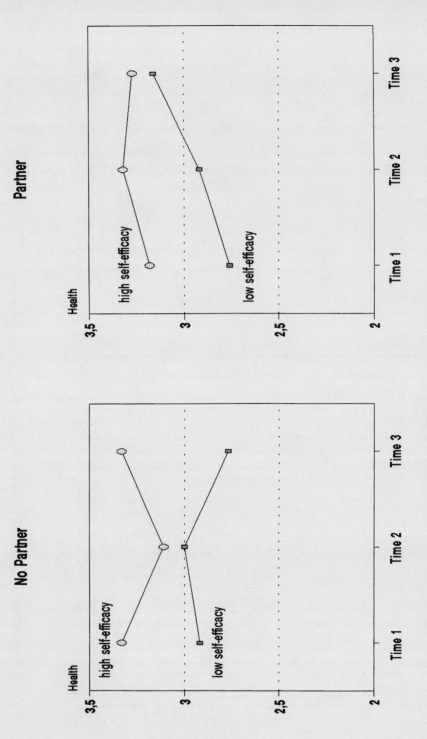

Figure 6.6. Health status as a function of perceived personal efficacy and partnership.

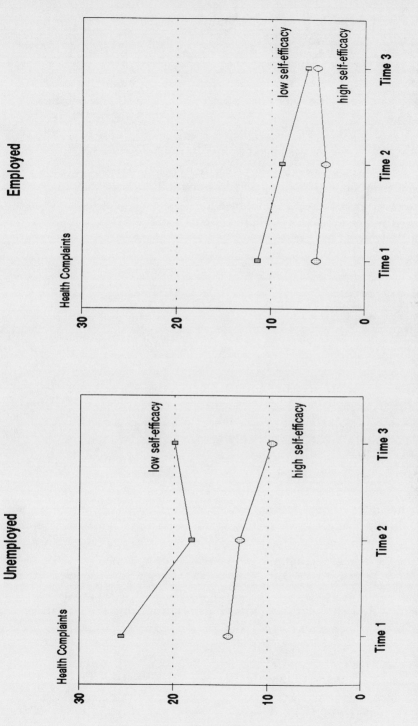

Figure 6.7. Health complaints as a function of perceived personal efficacy and employment.

193

In sum, the findings taken as a whole demonstrate that appraisal of challenges and threats in the new social realities, anxiety, and subjective health are influenced by both personal and environmental resources. Long-term unemployment or having no close partner for a long time was associated with more negative stress appraisals, higher levels of anxiety and a worse health state. Migrants who had a high sense of efficacy felt more challenged than threatened by the social changes in their lives. They reported less anxiety and better health than those of low self-efficacy. Self-efficacy as a personal resource also seemed to buffer the negative effects of stressful environmental circumstances. A general sense of efficacy emerged as a dominant overall predictor, whereas the importance of environmental predictors varied depending on the aspect of adaptation being assessed.

Summary remarks

This research investigated the adaptation processes of young East German migrants and refugees during a stressful life transition of almost two years after their move to the West as a reaction to the collapse of the Eastern system. A key issue concerned the role of a generalized sense of efficacy to exercise control over the new and stressful life conditions in this adaptational process. Social resources in the form of employment and close partnerships were evaluated as predictors of the adaptation dynamics.

The migrants studied were relatively young. Despite their age, they had already formed a rather stable trait of general self-efficacy that was not much affected by the stress of migration, employment, and partnership status. This stability under substantial environmental change may be interpreted in several ways. One possibility is that self-beliefs are crystallised by adolescence or young adulthood and remain resistant to later environmental influences. An alternative explanation is that youth who have left their communities in search of a better life continue to believe in their ultimate capability to succeed. If youths leave countries permitting little leeway to exercise personal control, they may retain a sense of efficacy if they have some success in making things happen in their new environment even though the adaptation involves many stressors. Realistic anticipations of future barriers, possible setbacks, and generally difficult circumstances, in conjunction with perceived advantage of being young and the intention to build up a new life, may sustain beliefs of personal efficacy. Another possibility for the apparent stability reflects the level at which beliefs of personal efficacy are measured. Global measures of perceived control may fail to detect changes revealed by domain-specific measures because they may mask variations across domains of functioning and different individuals (Lachmann, 1986). Moreover, this stability of personal efficacy is confined to the time period observed in this study. It is possible that in the long run repeated failures to cope with the demands of the new environment would eventually take a toll on perceived self-efficacy.

It is interesting to note that perceived self-efficacy, employment status, and partnership are not interrelated. General efficacy does not seem to be an asset on the job market nor an advantage in attracting an intimate partner. Being employed or not and living with a close partner does not affect the personal belief system. Partnership also does not facilitate job hunting, and whether young migrants are jobless or employed is irrelevant for whether they live alone or with a partner. The general nature of the efficacy measure may provide one explanation. Perceived self-efficacy to find gainful employment has been shown to be a good predictor of who succeeds in finding a meaningful job (Kanfer & Hulin, 1985; van Ryn & Vinokur, 1992). Another possible explanation for this somewhat unexpected result is that objective constraints to getting a job are so severe that neither perceived efficacy nor support of a partner may help to reach that goal. However, this may change with time. Long-term unemployment might weaken generalized self-efficacy beliefs, and weak beliefs might lead to less persistence in job hunting or even resignation and inactivity, which in turn can reduce the chances of securing employment. Similar interrelations may occur in due time regarding partnerships. The crucial question could be how long it takes for unemployment and/or living alone to affect self-worth and self-beliefs.

Perceived self-efficacy proved to be a powerful personal resource regarding the impact of migration stress on cognitive appraisals as well as on psychological and physical well-being. Perceived self-efficacy had strong effects on all the aspects of adaptation that were assessed. Highly self-efficacious migrants perceived the demands in their new life more as challenges and less as threats. They experienced lower anxiety, better health, and fewer health complaints than low self-efficacious migrants. The latter group was prone to view the social change as threatening and stressful, one that took a toll on their physical well-being. A strong sense of personal efficacy seems to reduce the likelihood of negative appraisals of stressful life demands, and, as a consequence, it provides protection against emotional distress and health impairments.

With regard to environmental factors, employment status also seems to play an important role in the process of psychological adaptation. Particularly, migrants who remained jobless over two years felt more distressed and anxious and expressed more health complaints than those who were employed all along. Thus, long-term unemployment is a risk factor that increases vulnerability to stress. This adverse effect applies particularly to young migrants and newcomers who have to start afresh, to strive to build a secure means of livelihood, and to become accepted within the new society. Employment is central to fulfilling these aims. To be without a job means to remain an outsider. Partnership is a second environmental predictor that accounted only for interindividual differences in cognitive appraisals: Migrants who had a close partner for support viewed their new environment more as a challenge than a threat or loss than those who lived alone all along. Other effects emerged in a time lag. Over time, partnered migrants displayed more favorable trends in threat, loss, and anxiety than did those without a close partner. Although moderated by self-efficacy, similar trends appeared for health complaints. These results suggest that the direct stress-protective value of a partner's support might be restricted to appraisals of demands and coping options that in turn may serve as mediators of indirect support effects on well-being that become manifest later. Of course, this is rather speculative because the quality of relationships and the extent to which partners actually offered support were not evaluated.

Gender differences were found in threat and loss appraisals only. Females reported less threat and loss experiences than males. Gender did not interact with employment status and/or partnership in this respect. Although no gender-specific hypotheses were advanced, it is noteworthy that the psychological significance of unemployment did not differ with respect to gender. One might argue that in a society with gender-specific roles of employed men on the one hand and housewives on the other, employment might be less important for women than for men. As a consequence, men should be more stressed by unemployment than women. The lack of gender differences regarding impact of unemployment could be due to the vocational status of the female population in former East Germany. In contrast to the lower employment rate of women in many Western countries, 80% to 90% of the females had been employed in their home country. Due to their socialization, previous vocational experience, and its significance for personal and social standing, employment could be highly valued and very important for these women. As a consequence, unemployment means a loss of former resources, which affects them just as much as their male counterparts. Nor were any gender differences found with regard to partnership. This finding contradicts the social support literature, which portray women as not more supportive but more dependent on social support than men. Possible reasons for this conflicting result might be the limitations of the network measure taken to assess support. Another possibility is that the migrants' common high insecurity in the new society makes close partnership for males as important as it does for females.

Considering all three predictors together deepens our understanding of the psychological dynamics of adaptation to marked life transitions. Not only were different risk groups of migrants identified, but developmental trends and mutual buffer mechanisms become evident. When ranking the subgroups according to their appraisals of stressors, at all points in time the most unfavorable perceptions of challenge, threat, and loss were found for low self-efficacious subjects who had no partner or were unemployed. The same detrimental pattern for migrants with prevailing weak resources emerged regarding their psychological and physical well-being. It is the multiple handicap of weak personal resources and strong environmental constraints that makes these young migrants most vulnerable to emotional distress and health impairments. In contrast to the vulnerability of this high-risk group, migrants characterized by multiple resources, that is, those with high perceived self-efficacy, a job, and a supportive partner, benefit substantially from this constellation of factors. They achieved the most favorable adaptation. The remaining groups characterized by different patterns of resources experience levels of stress and impairment of well-being between the two extreme groups of multiple high resources and multiple vulnerabilities, respectively. A comparison of the relative standing of each group illustrates the especially strong psychological impact produced by multiple risk conditions: The group with the highest personal and social resources experienced better adaptational outcomes than those with fewer resources and considerably better than those with very limited resources.

Subgroups of distinguishable risk conditions also differ with regard to stress dynamics. For example, in threat appraisals partnership is the decisive factor for change over time: Threat and loss perceptions change for the better if a partner is available, and for the worse if not. Different patterns also appear for anxiety and health complaints. Although both indicators of negative well-being generally decrease over time, a supportive relationship contributes to this beneficial change. Anxiety levels of migrants without a supportive partner remain stable; the anxiety of those living with a partner declines over time. The reduction in anxiety is greater for the low than for the high self-efficacy group. A supportive partner seems not only to further positive emotional changes but, over time, may also serve as a buffer that alleviates negative impact of weak generalized beliefs.

A similar stress-buffering influence is exerted by perceived self-efficacy concerning the impact of unemployment on subjective health status. For employed migrants, perceived self-efficacy does not differentiate reported health status. For the unemployed ones, however, high self-efficacy beliefs buffer detrimental influences of unemployment on health. To a lesser degree perceived self-efficacy also seems to reduce the negative consequences of a lack of a supportive partner on health complaints. These complex interrelations underline the need to consider different resources and constraints simultaneously to gain full understanding of the determinants and dynamics of migration stress.

From a theoretical point of view, personal resources and environmental constraints differ somewhat in their influence on the adaptation process. Generalized self-efficacy beliefs serve as key moderators for the impact of environmental demands on stress experiences as represented by cognitive appraisals and well-being in managing the difficult circumstances of a major life transition that all migrants must face. A high sense of efficacy makes life subjectively less stressing, whereas low self-efficacy is accompanied by strong distress. Employment status and partnership, in contrast, are not clear moderators, but they are personal risk conditions that change the life situation itself and thereby intensify or lower stress, independent of general beliefs.

To a large extent, the empirical findings are in accord with the theoretical expectations. However, certain limitations of this research should be acknowledged. Assessment of health status relied on subjective reports. Stress appraisals were assessed only at two points in time. Therefore, nothing can be said about initial interindividual differences in appraisals or whether developmental trends occur that may already begin at the outset. Finally, the design implicitly assumes a causal influence of environmental constraints on negative appraisals and affects. Although this direction is highly reasonable, it cannot be ruled out that the causality operates in the opposite direction. For example, feeling anxious and sick can be a justification for not searching for a job or a reason for not being hired. On the other hand, healthy and psychologically stable individuals usually have a better chance of finding a job and of staying employed.

Despite some limitations, there is no doubt that for the young migrants strong self-efficacy beliefs, employment, and a supportive partnership serve as protective resources against unfavorable appraisals of environmental stress, emotional disturbance, and health impairment. Regarding the validity and generalizability of these effects, the empirical evidence is most convincing for the importance of perceived self-efficacy as a personal resource in adaptation and change. Its overall effects surpass those of environmental factors. Generalizations about employment and partner support, however, are more qualified. Employment was assessed only as a dichotomous variable that does not consider job quality, job satisfaction, contract conditions, and other conditions of work. In the case of partnership, its psychological relevance might become more evident if indicators such as perceived and received social support, its subjective evaluation, size of the social network, and the qualitative character of social relationships or of social support were considered as well.

The major strength of the present study can be seen in its ecological validity in assessing adaptation in a natural life setting longitudinally. It is also the only available panel study of psychological changes in East German migrants. It is necessary, however, to take into account some peculiarities of the East Germans observed here that make their psychosocial situation quite different from that of migrants in other cultural settings. With regard to West Germans, East German immigrants have the same language, cultural heritage, and perhaps even close relatives. Compared with these commonalities, migration presents more formidable problems to migrants who confront barriers of language, cultural patterns, ethnic differences, and hostility as intruders. It certainly requires a very resistant sense of efficacy to surmount these multiple barriers. For that reason, the generalizability of the findings needs to be tested with other migrant groups adapting to different cultural milieus.

References

Bandura, A. (1977). Self-efficacy: Toward a unifying theory of behavioral change. *Psychological Review, 84*, 191–215.

Bandura, A. (1986). *Social foundations of thought and action: A social cognitive theory.* Englewood Cliffs, NJ: Prentice-Hall.

Bandura, A. (1991). Self-efficacy conception of anxiety. In R. Schwarzer & R. A. Wicklund (Eds.), *Anxiety and self-focused attention* (pp. 89–110). London: Harwood Academic Publishers.

Bandura, A. (1992). Exercise of personal agency through the self-efficacy mechanism. In R. Schwarzer (Ed.), *Self-efficacy: Thought control of action* (pp. 3–38). Washington, DC: Hemisphere.

Brähler, E. & Scheer, J. (1983). *Giessener Beschwerdefragebogen (GBB)* [Health Complaints Rating Scale]. Bern, Switzerland: Huber.

Brown, J. D., & Siegel, J. M. (1988). Attributions for negative life events and depression: The role of perceived control. *Journal of Personality and Social Psychology*, 54, 316–322.

Carver, C. S., & Scheier, M. F. (1988). A control-process perspective on anxiety. *Anxiety Research*, 1, 17–22.

Cohen, L. H. (Ed.) (1988). *Life events and psychosocial functioning: Theoretical and methodological issues*. London: Sage.

Dooley, C. D., & Catalano, R. A. (1988). Psychological effects of unemployment. *Journal of Social Issues*, 4.

Duck, S. (Ed.) (1990). *Personal relationships and social support*. London: Sage.

Feather, N. T. (1990). *The psychological impact of unemployment*. New York: Springer.

Hobfoll, S. E. (1989). Conservation of resources: A new attempt at conceptualizing stress. *American Psychologist*, 44, 513–524.

Hodapp, V., Schwarzer, R., Schwenkmezger, P., Laux, L., & Spielberger, C. D. (1988). *State-Trait Personality Inventory (STPI)*. Unpublished manuscript. Düsseldorf, Germany: Heinrich-Heine Universität Düsseldorf.

Jerusalem, M. (1990a). *Persönliche Ressourcen, Vulnerabilität und Stresserleben* [Personal resources, vulnerability, and stress]. Göttingen, Germany: Hogrefe.

Jerusalem, M. (1990b). Temporal patterns of stress appraisals for high- and low-anxious individuals. *Anxiety Research*, 3, 113–129.

Jerusalem, M. (1993). Personal resources, environmental constraints, and adaptational processes: The predictive power of a theoretical stress model. *Personality and Individual Differences*, 14, 15–24.

Jerusalem, M., & Schwarzer, R. (1986). Selbstwirksamkeit [Self-Efficacy Scale]. In R. Schwarzer (Ed.), *Skalen zur Befindlichkeit und Persönlichkeit* (pp. 15–28). Berlin: Freie Universität, Institut für Psychologie.

Jerusalem, M., & Schwarzer, R. (1989). Anxiety and self-concept as antecedents of stress and coping: A longitudinal study with German and Turkish adolescents. *Personality and Individual Differences*, 10, 785–792.

Jerusalem, M., & Schwarzer, R. (1992). Self-efficacy as a resource factor in stress appraisal processes. In R. Schwarzer (Ed.), *Self-efficacy: Thought control of action* (pp.195–213). Washington, DC: Hemisphere.

Johnson, J. H. (1986). *Life events as stressors in childhood and adolescence*. Beverly Hills, CA: Sage.

Kanfer, R., & Hulin, C. L. (1985). Individual differences in successful job searches following lay-off. *Personnel Psychology*, 38, 835–848.

Kelvin, P., & Jarrett, J. E. (1985). *Unemployment: Its social psychological effects*. Cambridge, MA: Cambridge University Press.

Lachmann, M.E. (1986). Personal control in later life: Stability, change, and cognitive correlates. In M. M. Baltes & P. B. Baltes (Eds.), *The psychology of control and aging* (pp. 207–236). Hillsdale, NJ: Erlbaum.

Lazarus, R. S. (1991). *Emotion and adaptation*. London: Oxford University Press.

Lazarus, R. S., & Folkman, S. (1987). Transactional theory and research on emotions and coping. *European Journal of Personality*, 1, 141–169.

Lin, N., Dean, A., & Ensel, W. (Eds.) (1986). *Social support, life events, and depression*. New York: Academic.

Mittag, W., & Schwarzer, R. (1993). Interaction of employment status and self-efficacy on alcohol consumption: A two-wave study on stressful life transitions. *Psychology and Health, 8*, 77–87.

Montada, L., Filipp, S.-H., & Lerner, M. J. (1992). *Life crises and experiences of loss in adulthood.* Hillsdale, NJ: Erlbaum.

Mortimer, J. T. (1991). Employment. In R. M. Lerner, A. C. Peterson, & J. Brooks-Gunn (Eds.), *Encyclopaedia of Adolescence* (pp. 311–318). New York: Garland.

Sarason, B. R., Sarason, I. G., & Pierce, G. R. (Eds.) (1990). *Social support: An interactional view.* New York: Wiley.

Sarason, I. G. (1988). Anxiety, self-preoccupation, and attention. *Anxiety Research, 1,* 3–8.

Schwarzer, R. (Ed.) (1986). *Self-related cognitions in anxiety and motivation.* Hillsdale, NJ: Erlbaum.

Schwarzer, R. (Ed.) (1992). *Self-efficacy: Thought control of action.* Washington, DC: Hemisphere.

Schwarzer, R., & Leppin, A. (1992). Social support and mental health: A conceptual and empirical overview. In L. Montada, S.-H. Filipp, & M. J. Lerner (Eds.), *Life crises and experiences of loss in adulthood* (pp. 435–458). Hillsdale, NJ: Erlbaum.

Schwefel, D., Svensson, P. G., & Zöllner, H. (Eds.) (1987). *Unemployment, social vulnerability, and health in Europe.* Berlin: Springer.

van Ryn, M., & Vinokur, A. D. (1992). How did it work? An examination of the mechanisms through which an intervention for the unemployed promoted job-search behavior. *American Journal of Community Psychology, 20,* 577–597.

Veiel, H. O. F., & Baumann, U. (Eds.) (1992). *The meaning and measurement of social support.* Washington, DC: Hemisphere.

Warr, P. B. (1987). *Work, unemployment, and mental health.* Oxford: Clarendon.

Wine, J. D. (1982). Evaluation anxiety: A cognitive-attentional construct. In H. W. Krohne & L. Laux (Eds.), *Achievement, stress, and anxiety* (pp. 207–219). Washington, DC: Hemisphere.

7. Self-efficacy and educational development

BARRY J. ZIMMERMAN

The ultimate goal of the educational system is to shift to the individual the burden of pursuing his [sic] own education. – John W. Gardner (1963, p. 21), former U.S. secretary of Health, Education, and Welfare

With few exceptions, the most demanding cognitive and motivational challenge that growing children face concerns their development of academic competencies. This formidable task, which begins for most youngsters even before they enter school, occupies most of their waking hours until adulthood. It is public, competitive, and self-defining in the sense that academic records predetermine public reactions and occupational paths. Within this educational crucible, children acquire their self-conceptions of academic agency. It is their growing sense of self-efficacy and purpose that serve as major personal influences in their ultimate level of accomplishment. To enable these youth to reach John Gardner's (1963) goal of self-education, schools must go beyond teaching intellectual skills – to foster students' personal development of the self-beliefs and self-regulatory capabilities to educate themselves throughout a lifetime.

Although the role of self-conceptions in academic performance has long been recognized (McCombs, 1989), their measurement and scientific study has been hampered historically by a variety of conceptual and psychometric problems (Wylie, 1968; Zimmerman, 1989b). This impasse was surmounted in 1977 with Bandura's seminal treatise that proposed a theory of the origins, mediating mechanisms, and diverse effects of beliefs of personal efficacy. It also provided guidelines for measurement of self-efficacy beliefs for different domains of functioning.

I would like to express my gratitude to Albert Bandura for his helpful comments on an earlier draft of this chapter.

This chapter reviews research regarding the *causal* or *mediational* role of perceived self-efficacy on students' educational development – that is, how efficacy beliefs affect motivation to learn, affective response to these efforts, and ultimate academic attainment. Special attention will be devoted to the acquisition of self-regulatory capabilities to preside over one's own learning activities (Zimmerman, 1989a, 1990). This analysis of causality will also include empirical evidence bearing on the distinctiveness of perceived self-efficacy from related theoretical constructs. Closely associated research on the effects of academic instruction on students' perceived efficacy and its impact on performance will not be addressed here unless the research sheds light on the issue of causality or predictiveness. The research literature on the impact of instruction on perceived efficacy has been reviewed elsewhere and will not be discussed here (e.g., Schunk, 1989, 1991). Also excluded from the present chapter is research on the role of teachers' personal and collective efficacy and students' self-efficacy for career choices, which has been treated elsewhere (Ashton & Webb, 1986; Bandura, 1993; Hackett, 1995).

Unique features of academic self-efficacy

Perceived academic self-efficacy is defined as personal judgments of one's capabilities to organize and execute courses of action to attain designated types of educational performances (see Bandura, 1977; Schunk 1989). Bandura (1977, 1986) developed scales to measure perceived academic efficacy as part of a microanalytic procedure to assess its level, generality, and strength across activities and contexts. In terms of academic functioning, self-efficacy *level* refers to variations across different levels of tasks, such as increasingly complex math problems; *generality* pertains to the transfer of self-efficacy beliefs across activities, such as different academic subject matters; *strength* of perceived efficacy is measured by degrees of certainty that one can perform given tasks.

A number of unique properties of the construct of self-efficacy are implicit in the assessment methodology. First, self-efficacy involves judgments of capabilities to perform activities rather than personal qualities such as one's physical characteristics or psychological traits. Students judge their capabilities to fulfill given task demands, not who they are as people or how they feel about themselves in general. Second, efficacy beliefs are multidimensional rather than a single disposition. Consequently, efficacy beliefs are linked to different domains of functioning. Thus, efficacy beliefs for mathematics may differ from efficacy beliefs for English composition or artistic production. Third, because many nonability influences can facilitate or impair the execution of skills, self-efficacy measures are context-dependent. For example, students may express a lower sense of efficacy to learn in competitive classroom structures than in cooperative ones.

A fourth feature of self-efficacy measures, related to their strength dimension, is their dependence on a mastery criterion of performance rather than normative or other criteria. For example, students rate their certainty that they can solve mathematical problems of varying difficulty, not how well they expect to do in comparison to other students (Bandura & Schunk, 1981). Finally, self-efficacy is measured before students perform the relevant activities. This antecedent property provides the temporal ordering for evaluating the role of self-efficacy beliefs in causal structures.

Self-efficacy and academic motivation

A key empirical issue concerns the validity of self-efficacy beliefs in predicting students' motivation. Bandura (1977) hypothesized that efficacy beliefs influence level of effort, persistence, and choice of activities. Students with a high sense of efficacy for accomplishing an educational task will participate more readily, work harder, and persist longer when they encounter difficulties than those who doubt their capabilities. Two measures of effort have been employed in research on self-efficacy. These include rate of performance and expenditure of energy. There is evidence that self-efficacy is associated with both indices of motivation. For example, perceived self-efficacy for learning correlates positively with students' rate of solution of arithmetic problems (Schunk & Hanson, 1985; Schunk, Hanson, & Cox, 1987). Self-efficacy is positively related to self-rated mental effort and achievement during students' learning from text material that was perceived as difficult (Salomon, 1984).

Considerable support has also been found regarding the effects of perceived self-efficacy on persistence. For example, Schunk (1981) found that modeling and didactic forms of arithmetic instruction increased students' self-efficacy beliefs, persistence during the posttest, and acquisition of arithmetic skills in students who were very low achievers in mathematics. Path analyses of causality revealed (see Figure 7.1) that the instructional treatments influenced children's arithmetic skills directly as well as indirectly, through their perceived efficacy beliefs. Students' perceived self-efficacy influenced their skill acquisition both directly and indirectly by heightening their persistence. The direct effect indicates that perceived

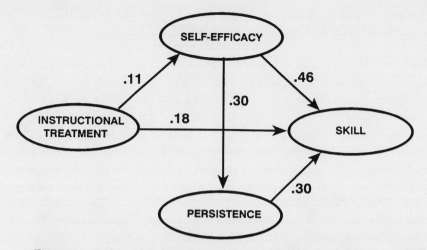

Figure 7.1. Path model showing effects of instructional treatment, self-efficacy, and persistence on subsequent skillful performance (Schunk, 1984). Adapted from "Self-efficacy perspective on achievement behavior" by D. H. Schunk, *Educational Psychologist, 19*, p. 51. Copyright 1984 by the American Psychological Association. Reprinted by permission.

self-efficacy influences students' learning through cognitive as well as motivational mechanisms.

Bandura (1993) has posited that perceived self-efficacy encompasses more than beliefs that effort determines performance. Judgments of one's knowledge, skills, strategies, and stress management also enter into the formation of efficacy beliefs. Berry (1987) similarly found that perceived efficacy contributes to memory performance both directly and by enhancing persistence. The role of efficacy beliefs in supporting persistence in the face of failure and in transferring this motivation to new tasks has also been investigated. Lyman and his associates studied the effects of success and failure on self-efficacy and persistence using a pattern-matching task with conduct-disordered children. Perceived self-efficacy was related to persistence in the face of negative feedback (Lyman, Prentice-Dunn, Wilson, & Bonfilio, 1984). Zimmerman and Ringle (1981) demonstrated the generalized effect of efficacy beliefs on persistence in research using unsolvable problem tasks. Elementary schoolchildren who had observed an optimistic model not only continued to be more self-efficacious and persistent during problem solving on a similar nonverbal task than youngsters who had viewed a pessimistic model; they also generalized their efficacy beliefs and motivation to different verbal problems. This evidence of transfer is of particular significance because it indicates that the motivational effects of efficacy beliefs are not limited to a specific task but extend to other tasks in the same context.

Efficacy beliefs have also been studied in relation to students' persistence and academic success in pursuing a major in college. Lent, Brown, and Larkin (1984) investigated self-efficacy for attaining each of 15 scientific and technical occupations. During a 1-year followup, students with strong belief in their ability displayed greater persistence and achieved significantly higher grades in science and engineering courses than those with low confidence. Perceived efficacy correlated positively with objective measures of mathematics aptitude and high school achievement. These findings were replicated in subsequent research (Lent, Brown, & Larkin, 1986), and additionally, self-efficacy was found to predict persistence and academic performance in the science/engineering major even when the variance attributable to other variables was controlled.

People's appraisal of their efficacy is strongly influenced by social comparisons (Bandura & Jourden, 1991). This is especially true in educational contexts where academic performances are subjected to a great deal of modeling and comparative evaluation. The successes and failures of others can affect one's own efficacy and motivation through perceived similarity. Brown and Inouye (1978) studied the role of perceived similarity in competence with a peer model. College students judged self-efficacy for solving anagrams and then attempted to solve them. Subjects were told they performed better than, or the same as, a model, who was observed to fail on this task. Observers maintained a high sense of efficacy and did not slacken their efforts, despite repeated failure, after exposure to a failing model whom they believed to be of lower ability. In contrast, observing a model of comparable ability fail had a detrimental effect on observers' self-efficacy and persistence. The more their self-efficacy was undermined by vicarious failure, the more readily they gave up when they encountered difficulty.

When tasks are solvable in persistence studies, self-efficacious children will solve them quicker (and have no need to persist) than those who doubt their capabilities. Such test conditions can yield the seemingly paradoxical finding that self-efficacious children are less persistent. The motivation effects of efficacy beliefs are, therefore, best tested on difficult or unsolvable problems. On such tasks, self-efficacious children tend to be more persistent than inefficacious youngsters.

The third measure of students' motivation that has been studied is their choice of activities. Bandura (1977) theorized that students with a high sense of efficacy will undertake difficult and challenging tasks readily, whereas youngsters who doubt their capabilities will avoid difficult tasks. This hypothesis has been investigated in several studies providing choice of activities and assessments of intrinsic interest. Bandura and Schunk (1981) studied the effects of proximal and distal goal setting on children's mastery of arithmetic operations through self-directed learning. Learning under proximal goals enhanced their perceived self-efficacy, rate of problem solving, and arithmetic attainments. Children were later given an opportunity to continue to do subtraction problems or to engage in a different type of task. The higher the children's sense of efficacy the greater their intrinsic interest in the arithmetic activity. Blom and Zimmerman (Zimmerman, 1985) also studied the influence of self-efficacy on choice behavior involving students' problem solving tasks. Providing feedback that conveyed competence to the youngsters increased not only their perceptions of self-efficacy but also their choice of this task in tests of intrinsic interest. Competence feedback also increased students' valuation of the task.

Perceived self-efficacy is also positively correlated with students' choice of majors in college, the success in course work, and perseverance in the field of study (Hackett & Betz, 1989; Lent, Brown, & Larkin, 1984). The relative roles of self-efficacy and math attitudes on students' achievement has been compared using structural modeling techniques. Randhawa, Beamer, and Lundberg (1993) found that perceived self-efficacy mediated the causal impact of math attitudes but not the reverse. Students' attraction toward the subject was insufficient to motivate them to achieve if they doubted their math capabilities.

The overall findings of cross-sectional, longitudinal, and experimental studies are quite consistent in showing that beliefs in personal efficacy enhance effort and persistence in academic activities. In a meta-analytic review, Multon, Brown, and Lent (1991) identified 68 published and unpublished studies of self-efficacy and academic outcomes during the period of 1977–1989. Measures of student motivation were employed in 18 of these studies: 7 studies involved time spent on task (persistence), 9 studies used number of tasks attempted (rate), and 2 studies focused on the number of academic semesters completed (activity choice). This meta-analysis revealed a significant positive effect size of $r = .34$. Students' self-efficacy beliefs accounted for 12% of the variance in their task persistence. Interestingly, students' self-efficacy judgments were more predictive of the rate measure ($r = .48$) and the semester measure ($r = .34$) than they were of the persistence time measures ($r = .17$). The lower effect size for persistence may reflect the fact that a high sense of efficacy may foster persistence on difficult tasks but low persistence through quick solution of moderately difficult tasks.

Self-efficacy and academic achievement

Because perceived self-efficacy fosters engagement in learning activities that promote the development of educational competencies, such beliefs affect level of achievement as well as motivation. Schunk (1989, 1991) and his coworkers have conducted a program of research in which children with major academic deficiencies engaged in self-directed learning of mathematical and language skills. The subject matter was structured for them in easily mastered steps in which they learned the basic principles and practiced applying the knowledge. Instructional influences were added that could alter children's perceptions of cognitive efficacy. These included modeling of cognitive strategiès, self-verbalization of cognitive operations and strategies, goal setting, self-monitoring, social comparison, and attributional feedback. The instructional programs and supplementary social experiences enhanced children's self-appraisal of their intellectual capabilities.

Low-achieving children who observe an adult model arithmetic operations while verbalizing the underlying cognitive strategies display greater acquisition of perceived efficacy and academic skills than youngsters who receive didactic instruction involving step-by-step descriptions of the operations (Schunk, 1981). Training students to verbalize the component steps of higher order strategies increases efficacy beliefs and learning even further because it enhances attention to important task features and the encoding of the information for retention (Schunk & Rice, 1984). Performance feedback has been studied by Schunk as another adjunct to strategy instruction. When feedback for prior performance successes is attributed to effort, students perceive greater progress, maintain higher motivation, and a stronger source of efficacy for further learning (Schunk, 1987). Another form of instructional feedback compares students' performance level to that of other students. Social comparative feedback revealing that other students can master the academic material increases beliefs of personal efficacy, skill acquisition, and performance (Schunk, 1983a). Clearly, social and evaluative feedback accompanying formal instruction influences self-efficacy beliefs, which in turn enhance development of academic competencies.

Schunk has shown that the frequency and immediacy of performance feedback also affect perceptions of personal efficacy. For example, regardless of whether daily progress in learning is monitored by a teacher or by students themselves, it creates higher perceptions of efficacy and arithmetic skill (Schunk, 1983b). When students adopt or personally set a learning goal, they experience an increase in efficacy for attaining it that is further strengthened by progress in learning. Setting proximal goals enhances self-efficacy and skill development more effectively than distal goals because the proximal attainments provide evidence of expanding capabilities (Bandura & Schunk, 1981). Schunk (1984) examined the joint effects of proximal goal setting and performance contingent rewards for progress made in learning. Although both instructional procedures were effective, their combination produced the highest level of self-efficacy and arithmetic skill. Providing students with a clear standard against which to gauge progress significantly enhanced their responsiveness to performance feedback. Finally, encouraging students to set their own goals improved not only their efficacy beliefs but their commitment to attaining them as well (Schunk, 1985).

In these investigations, Schunk and colleagues have demonstrated the impact of efficacy beliefs on engagement in learning and academic achievement (Schunk, 1989). Children's belief in their efficacy for learning predicts their rate of problem solutions during instructional sessions (range of r's = .33 to .42) and posttest level of self-efficacy and academic skill (range of r's = .46 to .90). Regression analyses reveal that efficacy beliefs made unique contributions to increment academic attainment over and above instruction (range of R^2 = .17 to .24). As previously noted, path analyses conducted by Schunk and others have established the causal role of efficacy beliefs in the development of academic competencies (Berry, 1987; Schunk, 1981).

This instructional research bears on the issue of causality in several important ways. Participants in these studies have little or no skill in the subject matter to provide a source of perceived efficacy. Instead efficacy beliefs are raised to differing levels by systematic variation in instructional treatment, removing ambiguity concerning causality. The acquisition of cognitive subskills is measured throughout the sessions so that the size of the independent contribution of perceived self-efficacy to academic performance can be gauged. These studies consistently demonstrate that efficacy beliefs are influenced by acquisition of skills but are not merely a reflection of them. Students with the same level of cognitive skill development vary in their intellectual performances depending on the strength of their perceived self-efficacy. Signs of progress are appraised cognitively in forming efficacy beliefs, which in turn affect the consistency and effectiveness with which students apply their skills. Moreover, the different types of psychosocial influences, such as evaluative feedback and social comparative information, contribute to efficacy beliefs independently of skills. Finally, the treatments build academic competencies in educational settings, which increases the generality of the results to everyday classroom learning.

In investigations by Schunk and colleagues as well as by others, three indices of academic achievement have been studied in relation to students' efficacy beliefs. These include basic cognitive skills, performance in academic course work, and standardized achievement tests. Efficacy beliefs have been shown to affect all three forms of academic performance.

In their meta-analysis, Multon, Brown, and Lent (1991) examined the effect of efficacy beliefs on students' academic achievement. They identified 38 published and unpublished studies that measured academic performance. Twenty-five studies assessed basic cognitive skills, 9 investigated performance in academic course work, and 4 studies used standardized achievement tests. The analyses yielded a positive effect size of .38, indicating that self-efficacy accounted for approximately 14% of the variance in students' academic performance across a variety of student samples, experimental designs, and criterion measures. The effect sizes were much larger when posttreatment efficacy beliefs serve as predictors (.58) than for pretreatment efficacy beliefs (.32). When children's perceived academic efficacy is raised by guided mastery experiences, instructional modeling, and supportive feedback, the altered efficacy beliefs rather than the pretest beliefs are the relevant predictors of subsequent academic attainments.

Multon and his colleagues reported several additional interesting findings. A stronger relationship between efficacy beliefs and student achievement was found among low-achieving students (.56) than among youth making good academic progress (.33). Whether this difference is partly due to ceiling effects among high-achieving students needs to be examined. The relationship between perceived self-efficacy and academic attainment was also higher for high school and college subjects (.41 and .35 respectively) than for elementary school youngsters (.21). Multon and his colleagues speculated that older students may be better able to assess their academic capabilities because of their greater experience in school. However, Assor and Connell (1992) found that level of accuracy did not diminish the validity of perceived efficacy measures in predicting their engagement on academic tasks and performance attainments beyond the second grade. A more plausible explanation for the differential effect size concerns the growing importance of self-directedness with advances in education.

Finally, Multon and colleagues noted that the relation between efficacy beliefs and achievement depended on the type of outcome measure selected, with the strongest effect size attained for basic cognitive skills (.52), an intermediate effect for performance in course work (.36), and the smallest effect by standardized tests (.13). This pattern of correlations is in accord with the domain relatedness of efficacy judgments. Most of the studies measure efficacy to perform basic cognitive operations. Were children to judge their efficacy for course grades or percentile ranks on standardized achievement tests, the correlations would probably be higher. The latter two measures not only tap cognitive functioning but other factors as well. Moreover, they are quantified in terms of relative standing rather than absolute performance.

Although gender differences in self-efficacy did not emerge across tasks and outcome measures in this meta-analysis (Multon et al., 1991), there is evidence they occur in research on mathematics. This issue was investigated because boys have often scored higher on standardized tests of mathematical achievement than girls (Kimball, 1989). Research revealed that boys surpass girls in perceived efficacy in math at elementary school (Schunk & Lilly, 1984), high school (Randhawa, Beamer, & Lundberg, 1993), and college levels (Betz & Hackett, 1983).

When the causal role of efficacy beliefs was compared with that of attitudes and anxiety about mathematics, efficacy beliefs were found to be the primary mediator of achievement outcomes (Meece, Wigfield, & Eccles, 1990; Randhawa, Beamer, & Lundberg, 1993). In fact, self-efficacy beliefs were a better predictor of college students' choice of a major than prior mathematical achievement (Hackett & Betz, 1989). Although no gender differences in the causal role of self-efficacy on math achievement emerged in path analyses (Meece, Wigfield, & Eccles, 1990; Randhawa, Beamer, & Lundberg, 1993), the higher perceived math efficacy of males was linked directly to their greater choice of math-related careers (Betz & Hackett, 1983). Moreover, a measure of a masculine sex role orientation (regardless of students' actual gender) was significantly related to students' math efficacy beliefs, whereas a feminine orientation was not. Because the superior achievement of boys in math cannot be attributed merely to differences in classroom behavior (Randhawa, 1991) and because girls do as well as boys according to teacher-assigned grades (Kimball, 1989), there is strong reason for educators to focus on improving girls' perceptions of efficacy in mathematics.

Self-efficacy and academic affect

Student's beliefs about their efficacy to manage academic task demands influence emotional states, such as stress, anxiety, and depression, as well as motivation and academic achievement (Bandura, 1993). In social cognitive theory, perceived ability to control potentially threatening events plays a central role in anxiety arousal and coping behavior. Because anxiety has both cognitive and physiological aspects (Morris & Liebert, 1970), it can intrude on and impair intellectual functioning.

There is evidence that students' performance in academically threatening situations depends more on efficacy beliefs than on anxiety arousal. Meece, Wigfield, and Eccles (1990) studied the role of math anxiety and two types of efficacy beliefs on students' math performance. The two efficacy beliefs – perceived mathematical ability and math performance expectancies – represented a domain-specific and a course-specific measure of efficacy, respectively. Meece and colleagues hypothesized that perceived math ability would affect math performance expectancies longitudinally because the former is less tied to specific performance contexts than the latter. Performance expectancies would, however, directly influence academic performance because of their contextual specificity. Both types of efficacy beliefs were hypothesized to affect math anxiety directly, whereas the effects of anxiety on academic performance should be mediated through math performance expectancies.

Path analyses revealed support for these hypotheses. Both perceived ability and performance expectations were predictive of math anxiety. A low sense of efficacy arouses anxiety over math rather than the other way around. In addition, students' perceptions of their math ability influenced their efficacy beliefs for math performance, which in turn affected their subsequent academic attainment. The effects of math anxiety were mediated through performance expectancies. These results clearly demonstrated the causal priority of self-efficacy: These beliefs influenced anxiety level and level of math performance, whereas the students' anxiety had no direct effect on academic performance.

Other studies confirm that efficacy beliefs are more predictive of math performance than is math anxiety (Siegel, Galassi, & Ware, 1985). When the effects of math ability were controlled statistically, the strength of efficacy beliefs accounted for more than 13% of the variance in their final math grades, whereas math anxiety did not prove to be a significant predictor. Together these studies support Bandura's (1993) recommendation that educators should focus on fostering a sense of personal efficacy rather than providing palliatives for scholastic anxiety.

Comparing self-efficacy and related constructs

A rather major issue regarding the causal or mediational function of beliefs of personal efficacy concerns its conceptual and empirical distinctiveness from closely related constructs. Many of these related constructs, such as academic ability, causal attributions, and perceived self-competence, have been emphasized in other theoretical accounts of educational development.

Academic ability

Students who have developed their abilities should perform well on standardized tests of achievement such as those in mathematics. Bandura (1993) has noted, however, that merely possessing knowledge and skills does not mean that one will necessarily use them effectively under difficult conditions. For example, students with the same level of ability may differ considerably in their perceived efficacy to manage academic demands because successful performance requires self-regulation of motivation, disruptive thought processes, and aversive emotional reactions. Efficacy beliefs, therefore, contribute to academic performance over and above actual ability (Bandura, 1993).

Empirical support for this view has been reported in several investigations. For example, Collins (1982) identified children of either high or low perceived math efficacy within each of three levels of mathematical ability. At each level of ability, students who were assured in their efficacy discarded faulty solution strategies more quickly, reworked more failed problems, and achieved higher performance than did children of equal ability who doubted their capabilities. Collins found that self-efficacy was a better predictor of positive attitudes toward mathematics than actual ability.

Bouffard-Bouchard (1989) selected children at two levels of ability and created different levels of perceived efficacy experimentally rather than by selection. This provides a strong basis for causal inference. Efficacy beliefs were systematically varied through arbitrary feedback that the children excelled or fell short of a comparison group on a novel problem-solving task. Although they did not differ in ability at pretest from students whose efficacy was lowered, those whose efficacy was raised used more effective strategies and were more effective in problem solving. The higher the efficacy beliefs, the more successfully the students performed. Clearly, perceived self-efficacy is distinguishable from actual academic ability.

Attributions

Efficacy beliefs are influenced by prior accomplishments, but performance experiences must be appraised cognitively when judging personal efficacy. Some of the factors used in the self-appraisal of efficacy are ones that are singled out in attribution theory, such as attributing performance attainments to high effort. In self-appraisal of efficacy, succeeding without having to exert much effort would signify higher efficacy than success achieved through laborious effort. According to attribution theorists (Nicholls, 1978; Weiner, 1985), students' judgments of the cause of their academic successes and failures will determine their expectancies for future performance: Attributions of failure to insufficient effort would heighten performance motivation, whereas attributions to inability would decrease it. Research reveals a bidirectional relation between causal attributions and beliefs of personal efficacy. Perceived self-efficacy influences causal attributions. Students of high efficacy attribute failure to insufficient effort, whereas those of low efficacy ascribe it to deficient ability (Collins, 1982; Silver, Mitchell, & Gist, 1989). Schunk and his colleagues (e.g., Schunk, 1981; Schunk & Cox, 1986) have shown that attributional feedback influences perceptions of efficacy.

A key issue is whether attributional feedback for learning successes enhances students' learning and motivation directly or indirectly as effects are perceived. Redlich, Debus, and Walker (1986) demonstrated through path analyses that attribution retraining in which children's successes were attributed to ability increased children's perceived self-efficacy and academic attainments. Perceived self-efficacy had a significant direct influence on children's math achievement, whereas attribution retraining exerted its effects through changes in efficacy beliefs. Schunk and his colleagues have also shown that causal attributions influence achievement through changes in perceived efficacy (Schunk & Gunn, 1986; Schunk & Rice, 1986).

Expectations and values

Expectancy-value theories (e.g., Atkinson, 1957; Feather, 1982) assume that human behavior is a joint function of people's expectations that a particular behavior will bring certain outcomes and the value of those outcomes. Clearly if an educational outcome is thought to be unattainable or worthless, students will not be motivated. Bandura (1991a) has argued that outcome expectations and values by themselves are insufficient to motivate high performance. Students may believe that social rewards and commendations are attainable and value those rewards but do not choose to pursue the academic activity because they believe they lack the capability to succeed. To predict behavior one must, therefore, measure people's efficacy beliefs as well. For activities in which outcomes are either inherent to the actions or tightly linked to them by social codes, people's beliefs about what they can do determine the outcomes they expect. In academic activities, quality of performance largely determines the outcomes one experiences.

The relation between self-efficacy and outcome expectancies was studied by Shell, Murphy, and Bruning (1989) in research on reading and writing achievement. Self-efficacy was measured in terms of perceived capability to perform various reading and writing activities, whereas outcome expectancies measured the importance of reading and writing skills in attaining various outcomes in employment, social pursuits, family life, education, and citizenship. Efficacy beliefs and outcome expectancies jointly predicted 32% of the variance in reading achievement with perceived efficacy accounting for virtually all the variance (28%). Only perceived self-efficacy was a significant predictor of writing achievement. The predictive primacy of efficacy beliefs is corroborated in other academic activities (Lent, Lopez, & Bieschke, 1991). The explanatory and predictive value of expectancy-value theories is substantially increased by including the self-efficacy factor (Ajzen & Madden, 1986; Dzewaltowski, Noble, & Shaw, 1990; McCaul, O'Neill, & Glasgow, 1988).

Perceived self-competence

Closely associated with the construct of self-efficacy is that of perceived self-competence. This construct emerged initially from White's (1959) theory of effectance motivation conceptualized as an intrinsic drive to feel competent. Harter (1978, 1985) extended this theory and devised generalized measures for cognitive, social, and physical perceived competence. Effectance theory and self-efficacy theory differ in several important respects (Bandura, 1986). In the latter theory, perceived efficacy reflects an acquirable self-belief system; in the former theory it is an expression of an innate drive. Beliefs of personal efficacy are measured in terms of per-

ceived capability to fulfill different levels of challenges in specified domains of functioning; perceived competence is measured in a general way
using normative criteria: Children are asked to compare themselves with
other children in their capabilities, for example, "How good in math are
you?"

Harter (1985) found developmental declines in perceived scholastic
competence from sixth through eighth grades, but not among younger
elementary school children. However, other researchers using self-competence scales for specific subject matters, such as reading and math, found
declines from the first through the fifth grades (Eccles, Wigfield, Harold, &
Blumenfeld, 1993; Nicholls, 1979). These diminished levels of perceived
competence were sustained or declined even further during adolescence
(Eccles, Midgely, & Adler, 1984). This developmental decline has been
attributed to unrealistically high perceptions of competence of young children relative to their peers. As the youngsters progressed through elementary school, however, their self-perceptions of competence became more
consonant with their teachers' normative assessments of them (Nicholls,
1978; Stipek & Hoffman, 1980).

In contrast to these developmental declines in perceived competence,
students display an increasing trajectory in perceived efficacy from the
fifth through the eleventh grades (Zimmerman & Martinez-Pons, 1990). In
this research, the children's perceived math and verbal efficacy was
assessed in terms of perceived capability to solve problems of increasing
complexity.

Development of academic and self-regulatory efficacy increases academic attainments. Other investigators (Pintrich & De Groot, 1990) have
found similarly that perceived self-efficacy was predictive of students' use
of cognitive and self-regulative learning strategies in classroom situations,
and that these strategies were in turn predictive of academic attainment.
Thus, self-efficacy is predictive of students' cognitive engagement during
learning as well as their academic accomplishments.

Perceived self-efficacy and perceived competence are concerned to
some extent with beliefs of personal capability. However, efficacy beliefs
are measured in greater depth and are differentiated across domains and
contexts of performance in recognition that the same skills may be differentially applied under different contextual conditions. In judging personal
efficacy to manage given task demands, individuals have to consider not
only their cognitive and behavioral skills but their skills in managing their
motivation and their stress and discouragement in the face of threats and
difficulties. Social cognitive theory describes the origins, mechanisms, and

differential effects of efficacy beliefs and provides guides on how to create and enhance them.

Perceived control

The construct of perceived control, which emerged from earlier research on locus of control (Rotter, 1966), is concerned with general expectancies that outcomes are controlled by one's behavior or by external forces. An internal locus of control would support directed courses of behavior, whereas an external locus of control would discourage them. In recent research, Skinner and her colleagues (Skinner, Wellborn, & Connell, 1990) distinguished among control beliefs that one can produce a given outcome, means-end strategy beliefs, and agency beliefs that one possesses the appropriate means beliefs. In order to be motivated to achieve, students must believe that (a) certain means are effective, (b) they possess the means, and (c) they can control the desired outcomes. Self-efficacy is most closely allied to agency beliefs, although obviously perceived control is also implicated.

Bandura (1986) has questioned the value of disembodied perceptions of control that are not tied to personal agency beliefs. People exercise control by using appropriate means. It is difficult to conceive of controlling outcomes without a person wielding influence though certain means. Interestingly, Skinner, Wellborn, and Connell (1990) found that the best predictor of student engagement in classroom learning and achievement was a combination of control beliefs *plus* an interaction term that includes agency and strategy beliefs. From a social cognitive perspective (Bandura, 1991a), beliefs that actions control outcomes, although important, are insufficient to motivate students to pursue academic activities. If students believe they lack the capability to master academic demands, they will tend to avoid them even through outcomes are academically achievable. For example, students might believe that they can control their learning setting, but they feel they lack the capacity or strategy to learn. In accord with this view, Smith (1989) reports that perceived efficacy but not locus of control predicted improvements in performance and reductions in anxiety in highly self-anxious students who underwent an intensive coping skills training program.

Self-concept

Although the conceptual distinction between self-efficacy and self-concept beliefs is often overlooked, Bandura (1986) has pointed out that the two constructs represent different phenomena. Self-efficacy is a context-related judgment of personal ability to organize and execute a course of action to attain designated levels of performance; whereas self-concept is a more general self-assessment that includes other self-reactions. Self-concepts do not focus on accomplishing a particular task but instead incorporate all forms of self-knowledge and self-evaluative feelings (English & English, 1958).

Historically, self-concept has been defined by phenomenologists as a global perception of oneself and one's self-esteem or self-worth reactions to that self-perception (McCombs, 1989). Measures of students' global self-concept have not been related consistently to their academic performance (Wylie, 1968). More recently, Shavelson, Huber, and Stanton (1976) have proposed a multidimensional view of students' self-concept that is differentiated by subject domain and organized hierarchically, with general self-concept at the apex and content area self-concepts at the bottom (e.g., for math or reading). They have developed course-particular evaluative questions, such as "Are you a good math student?" In contrast, self-efficacy questions minimize the evaluative dimension and focus on certainty about performing particular academic tasks successfully; for example "Can you solve this type of math problem?" Although Bandura (1986) has cautioned against global assessment of self-efficacy, his guidelines have not always been followed, and this has led to some misinterpretations of results.

Recently, the roles of self-efficacy beliefs and domain-particular self-concepts in students' academic performance have been compared. Parjares and Miller (1994) used path analysis procedures to examine the predictive and mediational roles of these two constructs in mathematical problem solving by college students. These researchers found that math self-efficacy was more predictive of problem solving than math self-concept, perceived usefulness of mathematics, prior experience with mathematics, or gender. Self-efficacy also mediated the effect of gender and prior math experience on self-concept, perceived usefulness, and problem solving. The poorer performance and lower self-concept of collegiate women in comparison with men were largely due to lower judgments of self-efficacy. Similarly, the effect of prior math experiences on math problem solving was mediated primarily by self-efficacy beliefs, not one's self-concept. Thus, when self-concept and self-efficacy beliefs are differentiated, self-efficacy beliefs are the principal predictor of math performance. These results underscore the need to distinguish between self-efficacy and even multifaceted measures of self-concept in academic learning and performance. In comparative tests of predictiveness, the self-concept of ability does not fare well.

Self-efficacy and educational self-regulation

According to Bandura (1986), "Self-regulatory capabilities require tools of personal agency and the self-assurance to use them effectively" (p. 435). In social cognitive theory, self-regulation operates through a set of psychological subfunctions (Bandura, 1986, 1991b). These include self-monitoring of one's activities, applying personal standards for judging and directing one's performances, enlisting self-reactive influences to guide and motivate one's efforts, and employing appropriate strategies to achieve success (Zimmerman & Martinez-Pons, 1986, 1988, 1990). It is one thing to possess self-regulatory skills but another thing to be able to get oneself to apply them persistently in the face of difficulties, stressors, or competing attractions. Students register the highest sense of efficacy to manage the content aspects of instruction, but a low sense of efficacy to manage themselves to get their academic activities done (Zimmerman, Bandura, & Martinez-Pons, 1992). Thus, the aspect of self-regulated learning that plays a central role – the capability to mobilize, direct, and sustain one's instructional efforts – has received relatively little attention in studies of academic self-directedness.

A number of studies have examined the causal role of self-efficacy beliefs in the operation of the various subfunctions of self-regulation.

Goal setting

Beliefs of personal capabilities affect the goals people select and their commitment to them. The more capable that people judge themselves to be, the more challenging goals they set for themselves (Bandura, 1986). Zimmerman, Bandura, and Martinez-Pons (1992) examined the impact of two facets of efficacy beliefs on goal setting and achievement. Self-efficacy for self-regulated learning measured students' perceived capability to use a variety of self-regulated learning strategies. Previous research on students' use of these learning strategies revealed a common self-regulation factor (Zimmerman & Martinez-Pons, 1988). Self-efficacy for academic achievement measured students' perceived capability to achieve in nine domains: mathematics, algebra, science, biology, reading and writing, computer use, foreign language proficiency, social studies, and English grammar. Efficacy beliefs as well as students' grade goals and the goal aspirations their parents had for them were measured at the beginning of the school year.

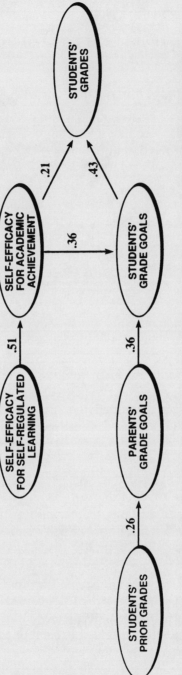

Figure 7.2. Path coefficients for significant paths between variables in the sociocognitive model of students' self-motivation and class grades (*p < .05). From "Self-motivation for Academic Attainment: The Role of Self-efficacy Beliefs and Personal Goal-setting" by B. J. Zimmerman, A. Bandura, & M. Martinez-Pons, *American Educational Research Journal, 29*, p. 671. Copyright 1992 by American Educational Research Association. Adapted by permission of the publisher.

The role played by efficacy beliefs in the causal structure was analyzed by path analysis. Perceived efficacy for self-regulated learning enhanced perceived efficacy for academic attainment (see Figure 7.2). Perceived academic self-efficacy in turn raised the academic goals students set for themselves and their final academic achievement at the end of the year. Students' prior grades were predictive of their parents' grade goals for them, which in turn were linked to the grade goals their children set for themselves. Efficacy beliefs and personal goal setting accounted for 31% of the variance in their final grades.

Self-evaluation

Self-efficacy beliefs not only influence the goals students set for themselves but also their evaluative reactions toward their own performances (Bandura, 1991a). Zimmerman and Bandura (1994) studied this aspect of self-regulation in a study of writing proficiency. Skill in formulating ideas and expressing them well in written form contributes importantly to success in all types of academic activities. However, writing presents special challenges to self-regulation (Bandura, 1986; Bereiter & Scardamalia, 1987; Wason, 1980). This is because writing activities are usually self-scheduled, performed alone, require creative effort sustained over long periods with all too frequent stretches of barren results, and what is eventually produced must be repeatedly revised to fulfill personal standards of quality.

Not surprisingly, even professional writers have to resort to varied techniques of self-discipline to promote their writing activities (Barzon, 1964; Gould, 1980; Wallace & Pear, 1977). A recent national assessment of the quality of students' writing revealed major deficits in this vital skill (De Witt, 1992). The processes governing the development of writing proficiency are, therefore, a matter of considerable import.

Instruction in writing strategies and verbal self-guidance have been shown to enhance perceived self-efficacy and to improve the schematic structure and quality of compositions (Graham & Harris, 1989a; Schunk & Swartz, 1993). The present study sought to clarify the self-regulatory mechanisms through which instruction in strategies for creative writing fosters the development of writing proficiency.

The role of self-efficacy beliefs concerning the academic attainment and regulation of writing, academic goals, and self-standards in the development of writing proficiency was studied with college freshmen using path analysis. These self-regulatory variables were measured at the beginning of a writing course and related to final writing proficiency. Students were tested for their perceived efficacy to regulate writing activities and perceived efficacy for academic attainment in the writing course. They were also assessed for their grade goals and their self-evaluative standards. These were measured in terms of the students' level of satisfaction and dissatisfaction for different levels of writing attainment. Students' verbal scholastic aptitude and level of instruction were included in the analysis.

Figure 7.3 presents the paths of influence in the development of writing proficiency. Enhancement of perceived self-efficacy for writing through instruction raised both perceived academic self-efficacy and personal standards for the quality of writing considered self-satisfying. High personal standards and perceived academic self-efficacy in turn fostered adoption of goals for mastering writing skills. Neither level of writing instruction nor verbal aptitude had any direct link to course grades. Verbal aptitude affected development of writing proficiency only indirectly by its influence on personal standards. Perceived academic self-efficacy influenced writing attainments both directly and through its impact on personal goal setting. The full set of predictive variables accounted for 35% of the variance in writing achievement.

Self-monitoring

Self-monitoring is not simply a mechanical audit of one's behavior but is rather a selective process in which self-beliefs influence which aspects of one's performance are given most attention, how they are perceived, and how the performance information is organized (Bandura, 1986). Bouffard-Bouchard, Parent, and Larivee (1991) studied the effects of efficacy beliefs on self-monitoring during concept learning with junior high and high school students at two levels of cognitive ability. Regardless of academic grade and level of cognitive ability, efficacy beliefs exerted significant effects on concept learning. Students of high perceived efficacy were better at monitoring their working time, were more persistent, were less likely to reject correct hypotheses prematurely, and were better at solving conceptual problems than students of equal ability but of low perceived efficacy. This study shed light on how efficacy beliefs influence self-monitoring processes. Perceived self-efficacy is not simply a reflection of cognitive ability because this factor was controlled.

Time planning and management

As a component of forethought, efficacy beliefs can motivate people to predict events and to develop ways to control those events that affect

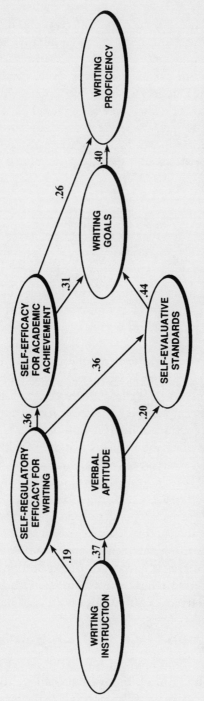

Figure 7.3. Path coefficients for the significant paths of influence between variables in the model of self-regulation and final academic grades (*ps* < .05). From "Impact on Self-regulatory Influences on Writing Course Attainment" by B. J. Zimmerman & A. Bandura, *American Educational Research Journal*, 1994. Copyright 1994 by the American Educational Research Association. Adapted by permission of the publisher.

them (Bandura, 1986, 1991a). Support for this hypothesis emerged in a longitudinal study of college students' management of their academic study time. Britton and Tesser (1991) identified a distinct self-efficacy factor in their scale, which concerned feelings of being in charge of one's time. Not only did efficacy beliefs predict academic achievement four years later, but it accounted for three times more variance than did a standardized scholastic aptitude test. Clearly, effective management of one's study time contributes importantly to academic self-development (see Zimmerman, Greenberg, & Weinstein, 1994).

Strategy use

In self-efficacy theory, efficacy beliefs affect human functioning through four intervening processes (Bandura, 1986). These include motivational, cognitive, affective, and choice processes. The motivational effects are rooted in goal setting and outcome expectations. The cognitive effects include among other things the anticipatory success and failure scenarios people generate and the acquisition and deployment of strategies for managing environmental demands. Zimmerman and Martinez-Pons (1990) investigated efficacy beliefs and use of various learning strategies for self-regulated learning by students in the fifth, eighth, and eleventh grades. Developmental increases in strategy use and perceived verbal and mathematical efficacy were observed. The study revealed a substantial relation (16% to 18% shared variance) between efficacy beliefs and strategy use across the three grade levels of schooling.

In an experimental study bearing on the issue of causality, Schunk and Swartz (1991) taught gifted fourth-grade students to use a five-step writing strategy. These youngsters were then encouraged to focus on either process or products of their writing and were given feedback of progress. Despite comparable training, only the students who monitored the process of strategy applications with feedback increased their perceived writing efficacy and writing achievement. The higher the students' perceived efficacy the better was their writing achievement. Students with an enhanced sense of efficacy to manage their writing activities continued to use the writing strategies effectively in followup assessments.

Social cognitive development of educational self-regulation

Virtually all theories of self-regulated learning acknowledge that skills in self-regulation alone are insufficient to ensure that they will be used well in particular conditions of learning (Zimmerman & Schunk, 1989). Issues of motivation and development of self-regulation are intimately inter-twined. Vygotskian sociocultural views of children's self-regulatory development emphasize reciprocal teaching and internalization. But this approach says little about the source of children's motivation except that they will be motivated when learning activities are embedded in a social system involving joint participation in learning with peers and/or teachers (Henderson & Cunningham, 1994).

In contrast, social cognitive theory (Bandura, 1993) provides a multifaceted approach to children's motivation and self-regulatory development. Within this conceptual framework, children's efficacy beliefs play a prominent role in regulating cognitive, affective, and motivational factors that operate in concert in the development of children's capabilities to manage their own learning and intellectual attainments. This body of research provides detailed knowledge on how instructional practices influence children's development of a sense of personal efficacy as well as their self-regulatory capabilities. Guided mastery is the main vehicle for the cultivation of intellectual competencies. In this approach, instructive aids and cognitive modeling are used to convey relevant knowledge and strategies in graduated steps. Opportunities are provided for guided practice with instructional feedback in when and how to use cognitive strategies in the solution of the new problems they face in different situations. Self-involving motivation and continued personal improvement is ensured by careful structuring of activities, incentives, and personal challenges. Self-directed mastery experiences are provided to strengthen and generalize children's growing sense of self-efficacy. Each of these sources of influence is organized to foster students' self-beliefs that they have what it takes to exercise control over their educational development.

The present body of research has implications for educational policy as well as for individual development: Students' improvements in perceived efficacy and self-regulation cannot be implemented fully unless there is greater flexibility in the curriculum. For example, if the time constraints for completion of academic assignments and test preparation were individualized, study time could be self-managed more effectively. This adaption in the school curriculum would not only increase students' perceptions of self-efficacy but also their motivation and academic success (Zimmerman, Greenberg, & Weinstein, 1994). Similar benefits would be obtained if other dimensions of academic learning could be altered to allow greater self-regulation, such as students' method of learning, type of motivation, and use of behavioral, environmental, and social supports (Zimmerman, 1994). When students have both the training and opportu-

226 Barry J. Zimmerman

nity to self-regulate their learning, they are more likely to assume responsibility for their academic achievement.

Conclusion

The research reviewed in this chapter lends validity to the causal role of students' perceived academic efficacy in different aspects academic functioning – their level of motivation, affective reactions to this process, performance achievements, and most important, their facility in regulating their own learning. The causal influence of efficacy beliefs on motivation and achievement is not only pervasive across experimental, cross-sectional, and longitudinal studies (Multon, Brown, & Lent, 1991), it is conceptually and empirically distinct from a wide array of related constructs.

Research establishing the role of efficacy beliefs in key self-regulatory processes is of importance to educational development. Efforts to promote self-directed learning must focus on self-referential processes, especially students' appraisal of their efficacy. Enhancing these key sources of personal agency, along with meta-cognitive skills, prepares students not only to gain new knowledge and cultivate new skills but to accept responsibility for their own education – John Gardner's (1963) ultimate educational goal.

References

Ajzen, I., & Madden, T. J. (1986). Prediction of goal-directed behavior: Attitudes, intentions, and perceived behavioral control. *Journal of Experimental Social Psychology, 22*, 453–474.

Ashton, P. T., & Webb, R. B. (1986). *Making a difference: Teachers' sense of efficacy and student achievement.* White Plains, NY: Longman.

Assor, A., & Connell, J. P. (1992). The validity of students: Self-reports as measures of performance affecting self-appraisals. In D. H. Schunk & J. Meece (Eds.), *Student perceptions in the classroom* (pp. 25–47). Hillsdale, NJ: Erlbaum.

Atkinson, J. W. (1957). Motivational determinants of risk-taking behavior. *Psychological Review, 64*, 359–372.

Bandura, A. (1977). Self-efficacy: Toward a unifying theory of behavior change. *Psychological Review, 84*, 191–215.

Bandura, A. (1986). *Social foundations of thought and action: A social cognitive theory.* Englewood Cliffs, NJ: Prentice-Hall.

Bandura, A. (1991a). Self-regulation of motivation through anticipatory and self-regulatory mechanisms. In R. A. Dienstbier (Ed.), *Perspectives on motivation: Nebraska symposium on motivation* (Vol. 38, pp. 69–164). Lincoln: University of Nebraska Press.

Bandura, A. (1991b). Social cognitive theory of self-regulation. *Organizational Behavior and Human Performance, 50*, 248–287.

Bandura, A. (1993). Perceived self-efficacy in cognitive development and functioning. *Educational Psychologist, 28,* 117–148.

Bandura, A., & Jourden, F. J. (1991). Self-regulatory mechanisms governing the impact of social comparison on complex decision making. *Journal of Personality and Social Psychology, 60,* 941–951.

Bandura, A., & Schunk, D. H. (1981). Cultivating competence, self-efficacy, and intrinsic interest through proximal self-motivation. *Journal of Personality and Social Psychology, 41,* 586–598.

Barzon, J. (1964). Calamaphobia, or hints towards a writer's discipline. In H. Hull (Ed.), *The writer's book,* (pp. 84–96). New York: Barnes & Noble.

Bereiter, C., & Scardamalia, M. (1987). *The psychology of written composition.* Hillsdale, NJ: Erlbaum.

Berry, J. M. (1987, September). *A self-efficacy model of memory performance.* Paper presented at the meeting of the American Psychological Association, New York.

Betz, N. E., & Hackett, G. (1983). The relationship of mathematics self-efficacy expectations to the selection of science-based college majors. *Journal of Vocational Behavior, 18,* 329–345.

Bouffard-Bouchard, T. (1989). Influence of self-efficacy on performance in a cognitive task. *Journal of Social Psychology, 130,* 353–363.

Bouffard-Bouchard, T., Parent, S., & Larivee, S. (1991). Influence of self-efficacy on self- regulation and performance among junior and senior high-school age students. *International Journal of Behavioral Development, 14,* 153–164.

Britton, B. K., & Tesser, A. (1991). Effects of time-management practices on college grades. *Journal of Educational Psychology, 83,* 405–410.

Brown, I., Jr., & Inouye, D. K. (1978). Learned helplessness through modeling: The role of perceived similarity in competence. *Journal of Personality and Social Psychology, 36,* 900–908.

Collins, J. L. (1982, March). *Self-efficacy and ability in achievement behavior.* Paper presented at the annual meeting of the American Educational Research Association, New York City.

De Witt, K. (1992, April 16). Survey shows U. S. children write seldom and not well. *New York Times,* p. A-1.

Dzewaltowski, D. A., Noble, J. M., & Shaw, J. M. (1990). Physical activity participation: Social cognitive theory versus the theories of reasoned action and planned behavior. *Journal of Sport & Exercise Psychology, 12,* 388–405.

Eccles, J. S., Midgely, C., & Adler, T. (1984). Grade-related changes in the school environment: Effects on achievement motivation. In J. G. Nicholls (Ed.), *The development of achievement motivation* (pp. 283–331). Greenwich, CT: JAI.

Eccles, J., Wigfield, A., Harold, R. D., & Blumenfeld, P. (1993). Age and gender differences in children self- and task perceptions during elementary school. *Child Development, 64,* 830–847.

English, H. B., & English, A. C. (1958). *A complete dictionary of psychological and psychoanalytic terms.* New York: McKay Co.

Feather, N. T. (Ed.). (1982). *Expectations and actions: Expectancy-value models in psychology.* Hillsdale, NJ: Erlbaum.

Gardner, J. W. (1963). *Self-renewal.* New York: Harper & Row.

Gould, J. (1980). Experiments on composing letters: some facts, some myths, and some observations. In L. Gregg & E. Steinberg (Eds.), *Cognitive processes in writing,* (pp. 97–127). Hillsdale, NJ: Erlbaum.

Graham, S., & Harris, K. R. (1989a). Components analysis of cognitive strategy instruction: Effects on learning disabled students' compositions and self-efficacy. *Journal of Educational Psychology, 81,* 353–361.

Graham, S., & Harris, K. R. (1989b). Improving learning disabled students' skills at composing essays: Self-instructional strategy training. *Exceptional Children, 56,* 210–214.

Hackett, G. (1995). Self-efficacy and career choices and development. In A. Bandura, (Ed.), *Self-efficacy in changing societies* (pp. 232–258). New York: Cambridge University Press.

Hackett, G., & Betz, N. E. (1981). A self-efficacy approach to career development of women. *Journal of Vocational Behavior, 18,* 326–339.

Hackett, G., & Betz, N. E. (1989). An exploration of the mathematics self-efficacy/mathematics performance correspondence. *Journal for Research in Mathematics Education, 20,* 263–271.

Harter, S. (1978). Effectance motivation reconsidered: Toward a developmental model. *Human Development, 21,* 34–64.

Harter, S. (1985). *Manual for the self-perception profile for children* (revision of the Perceived Competence Scale for Children). Denver, CO: University of Denver Press.

Henderson, R. W., & Cunningham, L. (1994). Creating interactive sociocultural environments for self-regulated learning. In D. H. Schunk & B. J. Zimmerman (Eds.), *Self-regulation of learning and performance: Issues and Educational Applications,* (pp. 255–281). Hillsdale, NJ: Erlbaum.

Kimball, M. M. (1989). A new perspective on women's math achievement. *Psychological Bulletin, 105,* 198–214.

Lent, R. W., Brown, S. D., & Larkin, K. C. (1984). Relation of self-efficacy expectations to academic achievement and persistence. *Journal of Counseling Psychology, 31,* 356–362.

Lent, R. W., Brown, S. D., & Larkin, K. C. (1986). Self-efficacy in the prediction of academic performance and perceived career options. *Journal of Counseling Psychology, 33,* 265–269.

Lent, R. W., Lopez, F. G., & Bieschke, K. J. (1991). Mathematics self-efficacy: Sources and relation to science-based career choice. *Journal of Counseling Psychology, 38,* 424–430.

Lyman, R. D., Prentice-Dunn, S., Wilson, D. R., & Bonfilio, S. A. (1984). The effect of success or failure on self-efficacy and task persistence of conduct-disordered children. *Psychology in the Schools, 21,* 516–519.

McCaul, K. D., O'Neill, K., & Glasgow, R. E. (1988). Predicting the performance of dental hygiene behaviors: An examination of the Fishbein and Ajzen model and self-efficacy expectations. *Journal of Applied Social Psychology, 18,* 114–128.

McCombs, B. L. (1989). Self-regulated learning and academic achievement: A phenomenological view. In B. J. Zimmerman & D. H. Schunk (Eds.), *Self-regulated learning and academic achievement: Theory, Research, and Practice,* (pp. 51–82). New York: Springer.

Meece, J. L., Wigfield, A., & Eccles, J. S. (1990). Predictors of math anxiety and its influence on young adolescents' course enrollment intentions and performance in mathematics. *Journal of Educational Psychology, 82,* 60–70.

Morris, L. W., & Liebert, R. M. (1970). Relationship of cognitive and emotional components of test anxiety to physiological arousal and academic performance. *Journal of Clinical and Consulting Psychology, 35,* 332–337.

Multon, K. D., Brown, S. D., & Lent, R. W. (1991). Relation of self-efficacy beliefs to academic outcomes: A meta-analytic investigation. *Journal of Counseling Psychology, 18,* 30–38.

Nicholls, J. (1978). The development of the concepts of effort and ability, perceptions of academic attainment, and the understanding that difficult tasks require more ability. *Child Development, 49,* 800–814.

Nicholls, J. (1979). Development of perception of own attainment and causal attributions for success and failure in reading. *Journal of Educational Psychology, 71,* 94–99.

Pajares, F., & Miller, M. D. (1994). Role of self-efficacy and self-concept beliefs in mathematical problem solving: A path analysis. *Journal of Educational Psychology, 86,* 193–203.

Pintrich, P. R., & De Groot, E. V. (1990). Motivational and self-regulated learning components of classroom academic performance. *Journal of Educational Psychology, 82,* 33–40.

Randhawa, B. S. (1991). Gender differences in academic achievement: A closer look at mathematics. *Alberta Journal of Educational Research, 37,* 241–257.

Randhawa, B. S., Beamer, J. E., & Lundberg, I. (1993). Role of mathematics self-efficacy in the structural model of mathematics achievement. *Journal of Educational Psychology, 85,* 41–48.

Redlich, J. D., Debus, R. L., & Walker, R. (1986). The mediating role of attribution and self-efficacy variables for treatment effects on achievement outcomes. *Contemporary Educational Psychology, 11,* 195–216.

Rotter, J. B. (1966). Generalized expectancies for internal versus external control of reinforcement. *Psychological Monographs, 80,* 148–154.

Salomon, G. (1984). Television is "easy" and print is "tough": The differential investment of mental effort in learning as a function of perceptions and attributions. *Journal of Educational Psychology, 76,* 647–658.

Schunk, D. H. (1981). Modeling and attributional feedback effects on children's achievement: A self-efficacy analysis. *Journal of Educational Psychology, 74,* 93–105.

Schunk, D. H. (1983a). Developing children's self-efficacy and skills: The roles of social comparative information and goal setting. *Contemporary Educational Psychology, 8,* 76–86.

Schunk, D. H. (1983b). Progress self-monitoring: Effects on children's self-efficacy and achievement. *Journal of Experimental Education, 51,* 89–93.

Schunk, D. H. (1984). Enhancing self-efficacy and achievement through rewards and goals: Motivational and information effects. *Journal of Educational Research, 78,* 29–34.

Schunk, D. H. (1985). Self-efficacy and classroom learning. *Psychology in the Schools, 22,* 208–223.

Schunk, D. H. (1987). Peer models and children's behavioral change. *Review of Educational Research, 57,* 149–174.

Schunk, D. H. (1989). Self-efficacy and achievement behaviors. *Educational Psychology Review, 1,* 173–208.

Schunk, D. H. (1991). Self-efficacy and academic motivation. *Educational Psychologist, 26,* 207–231.

Schunk D. H., & Cox, P. D. (1986). Strategy training and attributional feedback with learning-disabled students. *Journal of Educational Psychology, 78,* 201–209.

Schunk, D. H., & Gunn, T. P. (1986). Self-efficacy and skill development: Influence of task strategies and attributions. *Journal of Educational Research, 79,* 238–244.

Schunk, D. H., & Hanson, A. R. (1985). Peer models: Influence on children's self-efficacy and achievement behaviors. *Journal of Educational Psychology, 77,* 313–322.

Schunk, D. H., Hanson, A. R., & Cox, P. D. (1987). Peer model attributes and children's achievement behaviors. *Journal of Educational Psychology, 79*, 54–61.

Schunk, D. H., & Lilly, M. W. (1984). Sex differences in self-efficacy and attributions: Influence of performance feedback. *Journal of Early Adolescence, 4*, 203–213.

Schunk, D. H., & Rice, M. J. (1984). Strategy self-verbalization during remedial listening comprehension instruction. *Journal of Experimental Education, 53*, 49–54.

Schunk, D. H., & Rice, M. J. (1986). Extended attributional feedback: Sequence effects during remedial reading instruction. *Journal of Early Adolescence, 6*, 55–66.

Schunk, D. H., & Swartz, C. W. (1993). Goals and progress feedback: Effects on self-efficacy and writing achievement. *Contemporary Educational Psychology, 18*, 337–354.

Schunk, D. H., & Swartz, C. W. (1991). Writing strategy instruction with gifted students: Effects of goals and feedback on self-efficacy and skills. *Roeper Review, 15*, 225–230.

Shavelson, R. J., Hubner, J. J., & Stanton, G. C. (1976). Self-concept: Validation of construct interpretations. *Review of Educational Research, 46*, 407–441.

Shell, D. F., Murphy, C. C., & Bruning, R. H. (1989). Self-efficacy and outcome expectancy mechanisms in reading and writing achievement. *Journal of Educational Psychology, 81*, 91–100.

Siegel, R. G., Galassi, J. P., & Ware, W. B. (1985). A comparison of two models for predicting mathematics performance: Social learning versus math aptitude-anxiety. *Journal of Counseling Psychology, 32*, 531–538.

Silver, W. S., Mitchell, T. R., & Gist, M. E. (1989). *The impact of self-efficacy on causal attributions for successful and unsuccessful performance.* Unpublished manuscript, University of Washington.

Skinner, E. A., Wellborn, J. G., & Connell, J. P. (1990). What it takes to do well in school and whether I've got it: A process model of perceived control and children's engagement and achievement in school. *Journal of Educational Psychology, 82*, 22–32.

Smith, R. E. (1989). Effects of coping skills training on generalized self-efficacy and locus of control. *Journal of Personality and Social Psychology, 56*, 228–233.

Stipek, D. J., & Hoffman, D. (1980). Children's achievement related expectancies as a function of academic performance histories and sex. *Journal of Educational Psychology, 72*, 861–865.

Wallace, I., & Pear, J. (1977). Self-control techniques of famous novelists. *Journal of Applied Behavioral Analysis, 10*, 515–525.

Wason, P. C. (1980). Specific thoughts on the writing process. In L. W. Gregg & E. R. Steinberg (Eds.), *Cognitive processes in writing* (pp. 129–137). Hillsdale, NJ: Erlbaum.

Weiner, B. (1985). An attributional theory of achievement motivation and emotion. *Psychological Review, 92*, 548–573.

White, R. W. (1959). Motivation reconsidered: The concept of competence. *Psychological Review, 66*, 297–333.

Wylie, R. (1968). The present status of self-theory. In E. Borgotta & W. Lambert (Eds.), *Handbook of personality theory and research* (pp. 728–787). Chicago: Rand McNally.

Zimmerman, B. J. (1985). The development of "intrinsic" motivation: A social learning analysis. In G. J. Whitehurst (Ed.), *Annals of Child Development* (Vol. 2, pp. 117–160). Greenwich, CT: JAI.

Zimmerman, B. J. (1989a). A social cognitive view of self-regulated learning. *Journal of Educational Psychology, 82,* 297–306.

Zimmerman, B. J. (1989b). Models of self-regulated learning. In B. J. Zimmerman & D. H. Schunk (Eds.), *Self-regulated learning and academic achievement: Theory, research, and practice* (pp. 1–25). New York: Springer.

Zimmerman, B. J. (1990). Self-regulating academic learning and achievement: An overview. *Educational Psychology Review, 2,* 173–201.

Zimmerman, B. J. (1994). Dimensions of academic self- regulation: A conceptual framework for education. In D. H. Schunk & B. J. Zimmerman (Eds.), *Self-regulation of learning and performance: Issues and educational applications* (pp. 3–21). Hillsdale, NJ: Erlbaum.

Zimmerman, B. J., & Bandura, A. (1994). Impact of self-regulatory influences on writing course attainment. *American Educational Research Journal, 31,* 845–862.

Zimmerman, B. J., Bandura, A., & Martinez-Pons, M. (1992). Self-motivation for academic attainment: The role of self-efficacy beliefs and personal goal setting. *American Educational Research Journal, 29,* 663–676.

Zimmerman, B. J., Greenberg, D., & Weinstein, C. E. (1994). Self-regulating academic study time: A strategy approach. In D. H. Schunk & B. J. Zimmerman (Eds.), *Self-regulation of learning and performance: Issues and educational applications,* (pp. 181–199). Hillsdale, NJ: Erlbaum.

Zimmerman, B. J., & Martinez-Pons, M. (1986). Development of a structured interview for assessing student use of self-regulated learning strategies. *American Educational Research Journal, 23,* 614–623.

Zimmerman, B. J., & Martinez-Pons, M. (1988). Construct validation of a strategy model of student self-regulated learning. *Journal of Educational Psychology, 80,* 284–290.

Zimmerman, B. J., & Martinez-Pons, M. (1990). Student differences in self-regulated learning. *Journal of Educational Psychology, 82,* 51–59.

Zimmerman, B. J., & Ringle, J. (1981). Effects of model persistence and statements of confidence on children's self-efficacy and problem solving. *Journal of Educational Psychology, 73,* 485–493.

Zimmerman, B. J., & D. H. Schunk (Eds.). (1989). *Self-regulated learning and academic achievement: Theory, research, and practice.* New York: Springer-Verlag.

8. Self-efficacy in career choice and development

GAIL HACKETT

There are few other decisions that exert as profound an influence on people's lives as the choice of a field of work or career. Not only do most people spend considerably more time on the job than in any other single activity (save, arguably, sleep), but choice of occupation significantly affects one's lifestyle. Work adjustment is intimately associated with mental health and physical well-being. – Hackett & Betz, in press.

This chapter addresses the role of efficacy beliefs in the important area of human functioning concerning career decision making and career development.

Theories of career development

Some psychologists have always been concerned with work. However, career *development* has received less attention in the mainstream literature (Osipow, 1986). Career development, as opposed to training for job skills (e.g., vocational education), can be defined as the preparation for, choice of, entry into, and adjustment to work throughout the life span (Super, 1990). Although the demand for career guidance has long been high among adolescents and young adults, career counseling has not received the attention it warrants from most applied psychologists (Hackett, 1993; Spokane, 1991). In today's rapidly changing job markets the need for career services is only likely to increase.

The earliest forms of vocational guidance, now commonly termed career counseling or career intervention, were rooted in differential psychology (Crites, 1981). The approaches to career counseling based on trait and factor or "matching men [sic] and jobs" models, historically atheoreti-

I would like to acknowledge the influence of my colleagues Bob Lent, Nancy Betz, and Steve Brown on the ideas expressed herein. I am particularly appreciative of the support and invaluable assistance of Albert Bandura in the preparation of this chapter.

cal, have now been reconceptualized in the form of "person-environment (P-E) fit" theories (Hackett, Lent, & Greenhaus, 1991). Within the career development literature the dominant contemporary P-E fit theories are Holland's (1985) theory of careers and the theory of work adjustment (Dawis & Lofquist, 1984). Both theories posit that the degree of congruence between personality (in the form of interests, work values, ability, and other "person" variables) and the demands of an occupational environment determine occupational success, satisfaction, and tenure (Hackett & Lent, 1992). The P-E fit theories are concerned with the *content* of career choices, that is, *which* occupation is chosen.

In contrast, the other two dominant theories, developmental and social learning, focus on the *process* rather than the outcome of career choice. In his developmental theory, Super (1990) describes the tasks individuals negotiate in developing a vocational identity, exploring the world of work, making career choices, entering an occupation, changing career fields, and adjusting to work. Career maturity, or the effectiveness with which youth and adults handle the career development tasks they confront, has been a major focus of research within this theoretical tradition. The social learning perspective on career development also emphasizes the process of career decision making but eschews any sort of stage framework in favor of articulating the mechanisms whereby career interests, work values, career-related beliefs, and decision making skills are learned (Mitchell & Krumboltz, 1990).

Sociological theories have also strongly influenced the vocational literature (Hotchkiss & Borow, 1990; Osipow, 1983). However, they are not generally discussed among the major career development theories within the contemporary vocational psychology literature, largely because they have not been particularly useful in guiding career interventions. Moreover, social forces affecting career behavior (e.g., socioeconomic status, opportunity structures) have been incorporated to some degree within the most influential psychological and interactional theories of career development. For example, social learning theory specifically acknowledges the effects on career behavior of structural factors such as job and training opportunities, social policies, technological developments, family and community resources, the educational system, and various other environmental forces (Mitchell & Krumboltz, 1990).

Despite substantive differences across the dominant theories, the mainstays of the empirical literature on career development have been vocational interests, aptitudes and abilities, work values, personality traits of various sorts, and career decision making (Hackett et al., 1991). Cognitive perspectives have been conspicuously absent. The notion of the person as an active agent in shaping his or her career directions has always been acknowledged by career theorists, but only recently have the potential contributions of cognitive psychology to career development been formally acknowledged (Lent & Hackett, in press).

There is now persuasive empirical evidence for the role of cognitive mechanisms, perceived self-efficacy in particular, in career choice and development (Bandura, in press; Lent & Hackett, in press). Research findings strongly suggest that efficacy beliefs not only exert a strong, direct influence on career decision making and career choice, but self-efficacy also significantly affects the development of core vocational choice predictors such as interests, values, and goals (Bandura, 1986; Betz & Hackett, 1986; Hackett & Lent, 1992; Lent, Brown, & Hackett, in press).

In this chapter I will summarize the major findings from the research literature on career-related self-efficacy, explore some of the most salient issues within this literature, and identify promising trends in career self-efficacy theory and application. Investigations of perceived efficacy with respect to the career development tasks confronting youth and adolescents are featured, namely, self-efficacy for career decision making and career-related choices. The substantial body of research on educational self-efficacy (see Schunk, in press; Zimmerman, 1995) and the theoretical and empirical literature on the career self-efficacy of adult employees (see Hackett & Lent, 1992; Wood & Bandura, 1989) are also germane, but not central to the purposes of this review.

Applications of self-efficacy theory to careers

Explicit applications of Bandura's (1977, 1986, in press) self-efficacy theory to career development originated within the literature on women's career development. The problem of the underutilization of women's talents and abilities in career pursuits and the underrepresentation of women in higher-status (usually male-dominated)' positions and occupations has long been a concern of vocational theorists and researchers (Betz & Fitzgerald, 1987). Hackett and Betz (1981) hypothesized that career efficacy beliefs play a more powerful role than interests, values, and abilities in the restriction of women's career choices. Traditionally feminine sex-typed experiences in childhood often limit women's exposure to the sources of information necessary for the development of strong beliefs of efficacy in many occupational areas. Lowered perceived efficacy along important career-related dimensions could, in turn, unduly restrict the types of occupations considered (e.g., traditionally male or female dominated) and affect performance and persistence in the pursuit of a chosen occupation. Thus, Hackett and Betz (1981) argued that self-efficacy theory provides a heuristic framework for understanding the cognitive and affective mediators of women's gender-role socialization experiences, and the resulting gender differences in career choice patterns that can still be observed in the workforce.

Many of the earliest studies in this area therefore investigated gender differences in perceived self-efficacy for occupations, and the links between occupational or, more broadly, career self-efficacy, and the consideration of traditional (for women) and nontraditional (for women) career pursuits. In career theory parlance, most studies have examined the role of perceived efficacy in determining the *content* of career-related choices. More recently, researchers have turned to examining the role of efficacy beliefs in enhancing the *process* of career decision making, or how effectively one goes about exploring occupational options and deciding on a career.

Self-efficacy and career-related choices

Occupational self-efficacy of college students

In the initial empirical test of the usefulness of self-efficacy theory in understanding career choice, Betz and Hackett (1981) found no significant gender differences in overall self-efficacy across a wide range of occupational fields (Betz & Hackett, 1981). However, gender differences did emerge when nontraditional and traditional occupations were examined separately. College men's occupational self-efficacy was equivalent across occupations, but women's occupational self-efficacy was significantly lower than men's for traditionally male-dominated occupations, and significantly *higher* for traditionally female-dominated occupations. In addition, occupational self-efficacy, in combination with gender and vocational interests, was predictive of the range of occupations students considered as viable options.

Occupational self-efficacy also predicted occupational interests, and self-efficacy was a much more powerful predictor of the range of occupational alternatives considered than were objective achievement measures. The results from this investigation were strongly supportive of the role of efficacy beliefs in influencing the career choices of male and female college students, and the usefulness of self-efficacy theory in understanding women's career dilemmas. Basically, if female students prematurely close off viable (and overwhelmingly higher-status) nontraditional career options due to weak efficacy beliefs, their chances of ultimately choosing a satisfying, well-paid career path are significantly lowered.

Subsequent studies with college students have largely replicated, but also extended, the major findings from the Betz and Hackett (1981) investigation: (a) occupational self-efficacy is clearly predictive of career interests, occupational consideration, and career choice (Branch & Lichtenberg, 1987; Layton, 1984; Rooney & Osipow, 1992); (b) gender differences in occupational self-efficacy are common in diverse samples of college students (Betz & Hackett, 1981; Wheeler, 1983); (c) gender differences are manifested at an aggregate level (across a range of male- and female-dominated occupations); at the level of specific occupations (Church, Teresa, Rosebrook, & Szendre, 1992); and across job tasks and work activities (Matsui & Tsukamoto, 1991; Rooney & Osipow, 1992); and (d) gender differences are not usually found in homogenous samples, for example, with high-achieving students or students who have already embarked on advanced studies (Clement, 1987; Lent, Brown, & Larkin, 1984, 1986).

There also appear to be certain moderators of observed gender differences in self-efficacy. Gender differences are particularly likely to arise in response to gender-stereotypical tasks, activities, and careers, that is, in domains where women are unlikely to have efficacy-building experiences, or in which gender-role pressures may undermine perceived efficacy (Betz & Hackett, 1983; Hackett, Betz, O'Halloran, & Romac, 1990; Wheeler, 1983). There is a direct connection between gender differences in career self-efficacy and the percentages of males and females in varying occupations (Bores-Rangel, Church, Szendre, & Reeves, 1990; Church et al., 1992; Wheeler, 1983).

Relationships between occupational self-efficacy and other gender-related variables have also been found, supporting the hypothesis that past gender-role socialization and current gender-role beliefs are influential in producing gender differences in career self-efficacy (Matsui, Ikeda, & Ohnishi, 1989; Rotberg, Brown, & Ware, 1987). That is, traditional attitudes about gender roles and accompanying stereotypes about appropriate occupational roles for men and women undermine women's efficacy for pursuing nontraditional careers. Conversely, liberal gender-role attitudes and a variety of same-sex occupational role models enhance career efficacy beliefs and consequently expand the range of nontraditional careers women consider. Occupational self-efficacy also appears to be more strongly predictive of nontraditional career choices by women for whom a career is salient or important (Layton, 1984).

The findings from studies of white Americans appear to be generalizable to other Western countries (Clement, 1987; Matsui, Matsui, & Ohnishi, 1990; Matsui & Onglatco, 1991; Matsui & Tsukamoto, 1991; Wheeler, 1983), as well as to racial/ethnic minority groups within the United States (Bores-Rangel et al., 1990; Church et al., 1992; Rotberg et al., 1987). The interaction of gender and ethnicity, however, has not been explored to any great extent (Williams & Leonard, 1988). Post, Stewart, and Smith (1991), for example, found some important differences between African-American men and women in the relationship of career self-efficacy to career choice. Both occupational self-efficacy and occupational interests were predictive of the math/science occupations considered by African-American men, but interests were the only significant predictors of math/science occupational consideration for African-American women. For all African-American students, occupational self-efficacy was significantly predictive of interest in math/science occupations, indicating an indirect effect of self-efficacy, through interests, on the range of alternatives considered.

Measurement issues

Most of the studies of the occupational self-efficacy of college students have either used or slightly modified Betz and Hackett's (1981) instrument measuring efficacy for occupations. There are several studies, however, that have measured career self-efficacy quite differently. Wheeler (1983) operationalized occupational self-efficacy as "perceived ability match" and "ease of success" with respect to various occupations. Clement (1987) and Rotberg and colleagues (1987) provided occupational information along with job titles in their assessment of occupational self-efficacy, whereas Matsui and Tsukamoto (1991) and Rooney and Osipow (1992; Osipow, Temple, & Rooney, 1993) measured self-efficacy for discrete work activities and job tasks.

The influence of occupational information on the measurement of self-efficacy expectations has not been directly examined. Nevertheless, it is very likely that providing information is an intervention in itself. Therefore, providing job information may yield a misleading estimate of career self-efficacy, given that people generally make decisions about occupational pursuits on the basis of stereotypic information. Likewise, there are some serious problems with attempts to assess overall career efficacy beliefs via discrete work tasks. People simply do not make judgments about their ability to successfully pursue different lines of work by examining the discrete subskills required for effective job performance. Efficacy beliefs across clusters of work tasks are not equivalent to overall occupational self-efficacy. For example, perceived efficacy for job tasks and efficacy for occupational roles are only modestly interrelated (Ayers, 1980; Matsui & Tsukamoto, 1991; Rooney & Osipow, 1992).

Self-efficacy for multiple roles

A new and promising direction in research on career self-efficacy is represented by a few recent studies of efficacy for coping with multiple roles. Because women who work outside the home remain responsible for the lion's share of household and child-care responsibilities within families, the impact of multiple roles on women's work behavior and career development has received increasing attention (Hackett et al., 1991). Most of the research has examined the multiple role conflicts of adult workers. However, research has recently shifted to investigations of the influence of girls' anticipation of multiple role conflicts on their career choices. Girls and women often adopt "satisficing" strategies, choosing traditionally female occupations that are perceived to be easier to combine with home/family responsibilities rather than optimally translating their interests and abilities into career pursuits (Fitzgerald & Weitzman, 1992). Multiple role efficacy may play an important role in governing whether girls and women lower their aspirations and settle for a career that is "good enough" or attempt to pursue more challenging careers.

College women consistently report stronger efficacy for managing multiple roles in conjunction with traditional versus nontraditional careers (Bonett & Stickel, 1992; Lefcourt & Harmon, 1993; Stickel & Bonett, 1991). College-age women also report feeling more efficacious than men in balancing work/home demands with traditional career pursuits. Interestingly, the efficacy beliefs of college men and women are equivalent for combining nontraditional careers and home/family demands. Overall, college-age women report fairly high levels of confidence in their ability to manage multiple roles (Lefcourt & Harmon, 1993).

In addition to indicating that it is women rather than men whose career self-efficacy varies as a function of the traditionality of occupations, this work further underscores the complexity of women's career choices. It is not yet clear whether the data from these college samples, most of whom were single, can be generalized to working women actively confronted with multiple role conflicts. Nevertheless, self-efficacy theory and research on adult workers suggests that strong efficacy expectations should have a beneficial effect on coping with multiple role demands, and therefore on career choice and adjustment (Bandura, 1986; Ozer, 1992).

Occupational self-efficacy of younger students

The majority of the studies on occupational self-efficacy have been conducted with postsecondary students; a handful of investigations have examined occupational self-efficacy with younger students. In the first of these investigations, Post-Kammer and Smith (1985) replicated the Betz and Hackett (1981) study with eighth and ninth graders. Few differences in the occupational efficacy beliefs of boys and girls were found and vocational interests were more strongly related to the occupations being considered than self-efficacy. To explain their findings, the authors suggested that gender stereotyping may become more pronounced with age. What Post-Kammer and Smith (1985) did not consider is that their sample, drawn from a private suburban school, was uniformly above average in ability and undoubtedly quite homogeneous in other ways. There is a good chance that restriction in the range of ability and self-efficacy accounted for the relative absence of gender differences. Nor was the influence of self-efficacy on interests taken into account. We will return to these issues later in this chapter.

Contrary to Post-Kammer and Smith's (1985) findings, subsequent investigations demonstrated gender differences in the occupational self-efficacy of precollege students that were quite similar in magnitude to the gender differences observed in college samples (Hannah & Kahn, 1989; Lapan & Jingeleski, 1992; Lauver & Jones, 1991; Noble, Hackett, & Chen, 1992). In only one study was socioeconomic status (SES) found to be related to occupational self-efficacy; Hannah and Kahn (1989) reported that high SES 12th-grade girls were more efficacious than low SES girls, and also more likely to consider nontraditional, higher-status careers.

Both interests and occupational self-efficacy are significant predictors of occupational consideration for disadvantaged precollege students (Post-Kammer & Smith, 1986), and for 9th-, 10th-, and 11th-grade rural high school students of diverse racial/ethnic backgrounds (Lauver & Jones, 1991; Noble et al., 1992). Among students about to enter college, occupational self-efficacy was more predictive than interests of the consideration of math/science than non-math/science occupations (Post-Kammer & Smith, 1986). For all students, both strength of occupational self-efficacy and level of interest in different occupations was related to the extent to which students considered each occupation as an option for themselves

(Lauver & Jones, 1991; Noble et al., 1992). Interestingly, occupational effi-cacy beliefs were more important predictors for women than men in most of the research conducted with high school students.

Slight differences between racial/ethnic groups in occupational and academic self-efficacy were evident in these studies, attributable in the main to the lower self-efficacy of American Indian students (Lauver & Jones, 1991; Noble et al., 1992). Indian students living on reservations are far less likely than their non-Indian peers to be exposed to a range of effi-cacy-building experiences. Despite these minor group differences, neither gender nor ethnicity was strongly related, in isolation, to the range of careers students considered (Noble et al., 1992). That is, gender and ethnic-ity may influence the types of experiences contributing to the develop-ment of efficacy beliefs, but it is self-efficacy that is most strongly related to important career and educational attitudes and choices across groups. Students with higher levels of confidence in their ability to successfully complete high school and stronger beliefs in the relationship between aca-demic and occupational success were more likely, despite their ethnic background, to aspire to higher levels of education and consider occupa-tions requiring advanced training (Noble et al., 1992).

Self-efficacy and choice of college major

Some researchers have focused on the career-related choices of immediate concern and relevance to college students, namely, choosing a major. Because of the continuing problem of the underrepresentation of women in scientific and technical career fields, much of this research has focused on the power of math/science self-efficacy to predict choice of and achievement and persistence in scientific/technical college majors. In het-erogeneous samples (e.g., students in introductory college courses), col-lege men consistently report stronger math/science self-efficacy than do college women; higher levels of math self-efficacy are, in turn, directly related to the choice of math- and science-related college majors (Betz & Hackett, 1983; Hackett, 1985; Hackett & Betz, 1989). Research indicates that gender and gender role beliefs influence the selection of high school math courses, which in turn influence math self-efficacy and math achievement in college (Hackett, 1985). Further, perceived efficacy for mathematics and science is the immediate and strongest predictor of students' choice of math/science college majors (Hackett, 1985). Evidence also supports the theoretically based hypothesis that math self-efficacy is of greater importance than ability or past experience in predicting career-related choice behavior (Hackett & Betz, 1989).

Linkages between perceived efficacy for math/science and achievement, persistence in, and consideration of scientific college majors have also been conclusively supported (Brown, Lent, & Larkin, 1989; Lent et al., 1984, 1986; Williams & Leonard, 1988). Both self-efficacy for scientific occupations and self-efficacy for "academic milestones" (confidence in one's ability to negotiate major hurdles in an engineering/science program) are predictive of the range of scientific occupations students consider (Lent et al., 1984, 1986). Students who are confident of their abilities to succeed academically persist in demanding college majors and achieve higher levels of academic success than students with weaker efficacy beliefs. In virtually all of the studies on engineering majors men and women expressed equivalent levels of academic and occupational self-efficacy, undoubtedly due to comparable ability levels and efficacy-building experiences.

An investigation of science self-efficacy with ethnically diverse engineering students yielded similar results (Hackett, Betz, Casas, & Rocha-Singh, 1992). Majority students did express higher levels of self-efficacy for engineering careers than did Mexican-American students, but these differences in perceived efficacy were due primarily to differences in academic preparation. Hackett and colleagues (1992) found that neither gender nor ethnicity alone were related to the academic achievement of engineering majors. Ethnicity appears to be related to access to quality education, which in turn influences academic and career self-efficacy. Efficacy beliefs ultimately produce observed differences in academic achievement. However, in one study of African-American college students grades were found to be more predictive of academic persistence and achievement than occupational self-efficacy (Williams & Leonard, 1988). This finding does not negate the bulk of the evidence in this area; perceived occupational efficacy ought to be strongly predictive of career consideration, but not academic persistence and achievement. Academic self-efficacy was never measured in this investigation, seriously limiting the significance of the research.

Finally, Brown and colleagues (1989) reported findings in support of the role of self-efficacy in moderating the relationship between aptitude and academic achievement and persistence. Occupational self-efficacy was not a strong predictor of the achievement and persistence of high-ability students, who were already likely to do well academically. However, occupational self-efficacy did have a strong facilitative effect on students of moderate aptitude levels.

Occupational self-efficacy and career interests

Self-efficacy theory posits the causal role of efficacy judgments in the development of vocational interests (Bandura, 1986). Occupational self-efficacy and interests have consistently been found to be moderately related. Theoretically, strong career efficacy beliefs should give rise to enhanced occupational interests (Lent, Brown, & Hackett, in press). However, due to the historical emphasis on vocational interests as the primary determinant of career choice, some writers have questioned whether the two variables are conceptually distinct (e.g., Lapan & Jingeleski, 1992). Researchers have therefore attempted to grapple directly with the nature and extent of the self-efficacy/interest correspondence.

In several studies a simple relationship was found between interests and occupational self-efficacy: The stronger the efficacy beliefs, the more interest students expressed in a given occupational area (Betz & Hackett, 1981; Lapan, Boggs, & Morrill, 1989; Post-Kammer & Smith, 1985). In one of these studies causal modeling analyses supported theoretical predictions that occupational self-efficacy, influenced by past performance accomplishments, enhances occupational interests (Lapan et al., 1989). Lent, Larkin, and Brown (1989) also found that both variables uniquely contributed to the prediction of career-related behavior – career self-efficacy and career interests jointly predicted career choice. Conversely, Lapan and Jingeleski (1992) found that career self-efficacy, vocational interests, and expectations for occupational attainment (i.e., expectations about the job students felt they were likely to actually enter) were highly interrelated. They argued that these three variables are simply different manifestations of a single construct. In this latter study, however, theoretical propositions about cause and effect relationships between self-efficacy and interests were not directly tested. Actually, Lapan and Jingeleski's (1992) arguments run counter to most of the empirical evidence in the career self-efficacy literature.

The career self-efficacy model has been tested against two alternate models derived from competing career theories (Lent, Brown, & Larkin, 1987). Lent and colleagues (1987) reported that both interests and self-efficacy were significantly predictive of the range of career options students considered, but self-efficacy was the stronger predictor of academic achievement and persistence. That is, although efficacy beliefs and career interests will in combination determine whether a given occupation will be considered, stronger efficacy beliefs are more likely than high interest to predict persistence and achievement. Results from the Lent and colleagues (1987) study also suggested that when career-related behaviors other than occupational choice are being considered – for example, career decision making and career exploration (e.g., seeking out information about career options) – assessments tailored to the area under study are preferable to generic self-efficacy measures (Lent et al., 1987). This finding is consistent with the domain-specific nature of efficacy beliefs. Since efficacy beliefs concern personal capabilities for specific tasks, problems, and activities, assessments of efficacy for occupations should be predictive of the *content* of career choice – the fields students are considering – but would not necessarily be predictive of satisfactory career decision making (Lent & Hackett, 1987). The next section reviews investigations of the process of career development, in particular, efficacy for career decision making.

Self-efficacy and career decision-making processes

Career decision making and career indecision have received a great deal of attention in the career literature over the years (Hackett et al., 1991). Several elements of effective career decision making have been identified, including goal selection, career exploration, problem-solving capabilities, planning skills, and realistic self-appraisal skills (Crites, 1981). Taylor and Betz (1983) developed the Career Decision Making Self-efficacy (CDMSE) Scale to assess perceptions of efficacy with regard to these five dimensions of career decision making. One assumption guiding this research has been that effective career decision making involves not only the development of skills but also confidence in one's decision-making abilities. Taylor and Betz (1983) hypothesized that weak decision making self-efficacy could impede career exploratory behavior and the development of decision-making skills, and thus may be predictive of career indecision and other problems in career decision making.

Research findings have largely supported the usefulness of the CDMSE scale in predicting career indecision, particularly the aspects of indecision relating to lack of structure and lack of confidence in decisional outcomes (Robbins, 1985; Taylor and Betz, 1983). Few gender differences in CDMSE scores have been found. Career decision-making self-efficacy and occupational self-efficacy are only modestly interrelated, an anticipated and understandable finding (Taylor & Popma, 1990). The steps in the process of making a career decision are largely independent of which careers are being considered.

Other important results from research on self-efficacy for career decision making include the following: (a) weak self-efficacy for career decision making is associated with anxiety over the career choice process (Matsui & Onglatco, 1992); (b) flexible self-perceptions of gender roles facilitate stronger self-efficacy for career decision making (Arnold & Bye, 1989; Matsui & Onglatco, 1992); conversely, rigid, stereotypical attitudes about gender roles are associated with weaker efficacy for career decision making and higher levels of choice anxiety; and (c) more assertive women with stronger career decision-making efficacy are more willing to engage in nontraditional career activities (Nevill & Schlecker, 1988). All of these research findings are congruent with theoretical predictions.

Quite a bit of research has now been conducted on the relationships between decision-making self-efficacy and a variety of other career-related variables (Luzzo, 1993; Niles & Sowa, 1992; O'Hare & Beutell, 1987; O'Hare & Tamburri, 1986). Career decision-making self-efficacy appears to influence the extent of career exploratory behavior (Blustein, 1989); the more confidence people have in their decision-making capabilities, the more likely they will actively pursue information about their career options. It has also been found that efficacy beliefs with regard to career decision making can be enhanced through the use of computerized, self-directed career guidance programs (Fukuyama, Probert, Neimeyer, Nevill, & Metzler, 1988). Finally, college students' abilities to effectively process and integrate complex information enhance perceptions of efficacy for career decision making (Nevill, Neimeyer, Probert, & Fukuyama, 1986).

Sources of career self-efficacy

One of the benefits to counselors of career self-efficacy theory is that it provides guidelines for intervening to correct detrimental self-beliefs. That is, the four major sources of efficacy information – performance accomplishments, vicarious learning, physiological arousal and affective states, and verbal persuasion – all provide means whereby unrealistic efficacy beliefs can be modified. However, the direct, causal relationships between efficacy sources and career self-efficacy has only begun to receive sustained attention.

Causal influences of performance on self-efficacy

Several experimental analog studies have been conducted to test the hypothesis that performance accomplishments directly influence career-related efficacy beliefs. Studies have demonstrated that success on tasks tapping skills relevant to occupational pursuits enhances self-efficacy and, to a lesser extent, interest, whereas task failure weakens self-efficacy and interest (Campbell & Hackett, 1986; Hackett et al., 1990; Hackett & Campbell, 1987). Men consistently express stronger efficacy beliefs than women with respect to gender-stereotypical (e.g., math) tasks, but women's and men's level of self-efficacy is generally equivalent on gender-neutral (e.g., verbal) tasks. Women's efficacy beliefs appear to be more vulnerable to failure than men's (Hackett et al., 1990). College women also tend to ascribe success externally (e.g., to luck) and task failure internally (e.g., to lack of ability), whereas college men exhibit the opposite attributional pattern, with successful performance attributed to ability (internal attribution) and unsuccessful performance attributed to task difficulty (external attribution). Some authors have suggested that gender directly influences attributions, and attributions then mediate the effects of self-efficacy on future performance. That is, the tendency for women to attribute success externally and failure internally causes lowered efficacy beliefs, which in turn produces performance decrements (e.g., Zilber, 1988). However, social cognitive theory posits the converse – low or weak perceived efficacy causes maladaptive attributions, whereas strong efficacy percepts enhance appropriate attributional patterns.

The finding that self-efficacy judgments are more sensitive than interests to successes and failures provides indirect support for theoretical predictions that career self-efficacy influences vocational interests. This research also supports the notion of a temporal lag in the cultivation of interests in response to experience (Hackett et al., 1990). Successful performance enhances career-related efficacy beliefs; over time, interests may blossom in areas where efficacy is strong. Educators and psychologists must be particularly mindful of this process when working with students who exhibit low levels of intrinsic interest in academic and career pursuits.

Sources of math self-efficacy

Researchers have also used correlational methods to test the role of the four major sources of efficacy information in the cultivation of self-efficacy. Retrospective ratings of sources of efficacy information have been found to be predictive of current levels of math self-efficacy. Past performance accomplishments appear to be most strongly related to college students' math self-efficacy beliefs (Matsui et al., 1990). In one study, gender and past performance accomplishments, in interaction, were the strongest predictors of math self-efficacy; men who had a history of success in mathematics and science expressed the strongest math self-efficacy beliefs (Lent, Lopez, & Bieschke, 1991, 1993). Outcome expectations may also influence the relationship between self-efficacy and career-related choices. Students who both expressed strong efficacy beliefs and who perceived positive outcomes as a result of success in mathematics and science courses were more likely than other students to choose math/science college majors (Lent et al., 1991, 1993).

In these studies performance accomplishments were found to exert the most powerful effect on perceived efficacy; the perceived effects of the other sources of efficacy information accounted for less of the variance in self-efficacy (Lent et al., 1991; Lopez & Lent, 1992; Matsui et al., 1990). However, studies relying on recall of a lifelong series of influences are unlikely to reveal much about the actual processes affecting efficacy beliefs over time. Memories tapped in retrospective research of this type are heavily influenced by current attitudes. Further, individuals are far more likely to recall their own successes and failures than to remember comments by others or observational experiences. Thus, the results of this research on efficacy sources must be viewed with caution.

Methodological issues

In the research on career self-efficacy, as in any research area, there are examples of studies where the self-efficacy construct is inappropriately operationalized or weak research designs have been employed. However, in well-designed studies where self-efficacy is measured adequately, substantial support has been found for Bandura's (1977, 1986) theoretical propositions. Evidence exists, for example, for the direct and indirect contribution of perceived efficacy to career choice and development. Studies that have compared self-efficacy theory with alternate theoretical models convincingly demonstrate that self-efficacy is a powerful predictor of career choice, and a more important predictor than other career-related variables.

Researchers must now refocus their attention, moving beyond the basic questions that have been investigated to tackle some of the additional complexities regarding occupational pursuits. Investigations of efficacy-based career interventions are important, as are psychometric studies refining the measurement of career self-efficacy and examining the effects of different assessment procedures. Because career development occurs over extended periods of time, longitudinal research exploring the ongoing causal relationships among self-efficacy and other important variables influencing career choice and development is vital. The gender-related and cultural *dynamics* influencing observed gender and racial/ethnic differences in career self-efficacy likewise require attention. And finally, work has begun on the formulation of an explicit set of theoretical propositions derived from social cognitive theory, clarifying the interrelationships among career self-efficacy and other career-relevant variables, including social contextual factors (Lent, Brown, & Hackett, in press). This work may well guide future research that can importantly advance our understanding of how people's efficacy beliefs shape their career paths.

Summary of research findings

There are a number of conclusions that can be confidently drawn from the literature on the career self-efficacy of youth. Overall, it appears that career self-efficacy is strongly predictive of a wide range of career-related behaviors from early high school through college and beyond (Hackett & Lent, 1992; Lent & Hackett, 1987). Self-efficacy assessments tailored to particular domains of functioning yield more predictive utility than broad, generic measures (e.g., Betz & Hackett, 1983; Lent et al., 1986). As anticipated by theory, beliefs are most predictive of a given area of functioning if they are relevant to that domain. For example, occupational self-efficacy is strongly predictive of the fields students choose, whereas academic self-efficacy is a better predictor of academic persistence and achievement. Self-efficacy for career decision making is theoretically and empirically unrelated to the content of career choice, but is very useful in understanding the process of career decision making and the problems that may interfere with students' ability to make decisions (Taylor & Betz, 1983; Taylor & Popma, 1990).

Career efficacy beliefs causally mediate the effects of past performance on educational and occupational choices. Performance accomplishments contribute to the development of strong career self-efficacy, but perceived career efficacy is the more powerful predictor of career-related behavior (Hackett & Lent, 1992). Research on the sources of career self-efficacy suggests that mastery experiences are powerful contributors to the development of a strong sense of personal efficacy. The extent to which the other three efficacy sources influence career self-efficacy over and above the effects of past performance remains unclear from the research (Lent et al., 1991; Lopez & Lent, 1992; Matsui et al., 1990). As mentioned previously, research on sources of efficacy has been largely retrospective, and therefore cannot address the exact nature of the complex interrelationships among sources of efficacy information. It is likely, for example, that career-related modeling, encouragement, and lowered anxiety and arousal not only enhance efficacy directly, but also facilitate successful performance attempts in occupationally related areas. Performance accomplishments in turn further enhance perceived efficacy (Lent et al., in press).

Occupational self-efficacy is also related to other important predictors of career choice, in particular vocational interests (Lapan et al., 1989). Data support a social cognitive model wherein past experiences influence both interests and self-efficacy. However, career interests are not likely to develop in areas where perceived efficacy is weak (e.g., Lent et al., 1987, 1991). Career self-efficacy and interests are moderately related but past performance affects interests through career self-efficacy. Career self-efficacy consequently influences future performance and choice directly and indirectly through interests (Hackett & Lent, 1992).

Gender differences in academic and career self-efficacy are associated with past gender-role socialization, current gender-role pressures, and the perceptions of the gender-relatedness of tasks, activities, or occupations (e.g., Betz & Hackett, 1983; Hackett et al., 1990; Wheeler, 1983). The stronger the perceived gender linkage of an activity or occupation, the more likely it is that gender differences in self-efficacy will arise (Hackett et al., 1990). Within the career self-efficacy literature, however, investigations have not yet focused on the specific self-regulatory mechanisms governing gender-linked choices suggested by social cognitive theory (Bandura, 1986; Bussey & Bandura, 1992).

Finally, studies of career self-efficacy in Britain and Japan suggest that career self-efficacy has international applicability (e.g., Clement, 1987; Matsui et al., 1989, 1990). Investigations conducted in the United States with ethnic/minority populations likewise suggests that the findings from research on career self-efficacy are relevant across subcultures (Hackett et al., 1992; Noble et al., 1992; Post et al., 1991). Nevertheless, some ethnic differences have been reported and the topic requires further attention (e.g., Hackett et al., 1992; Noble et al., 1992). Not only are studies exploring cultural influences on career self-efficacy rare, but often they simply examine racial/ethnic differences rather than the effects of culture and ethnic identity on career self-efficacy and career development. While it is mildly interesting to describe cultural differences, it is of much greater import to explore the processes by which ethnicity affects career self-efficacy, to examine similarities across racial/ethnic groups, and to study intragroup variability.

Future directions

I would like to conclude with a few of the possible implications of career self-efficacy research for guiding services to youth in changing societies. The most obvious implication of this body of research is that, for all students, theory-based interventions designed to enhance academic *and* career efficacy beliefs are crucial. We currently have at our disposal an array of interventions to effectively enhance students' educational achievement and career decision making. Self-efficacy theory provides the conceptual scaffolding for organizing existing career interventions so that their impact on efficacy beliefs will be maximized. Efficacy for academic pursuits influences academic performance and has some spillover effects on career self-efficacy and work behavior. However, strong academic efficacy beliefs will not *necessarily* translate into career behavior without direct attention to career development and the enhancement of career efficacy.

As just one example of the problems with isolating academics from work, let us consider what is now occurring in the United States. Over the past several years highly controversial debates have revolved around the need for major educational reform in the United States. One of the chief catalysts for the calls for dramatic school reform has been the presumed erosion of the quality of the American workforce (National Commission on Excellence in Education, 1983). In particular, schools have been indicted for failing to prepare high school graduates to move directly into the workforce. In response to the demand to upgrade the workforce and prepare youth to respond effectively to ever-changing marketplaces, academic standards are being raised and job skills training and youth apprenticeship programs are being instituted (Olson, 1993).

The perception that our young people are poorly prepared for the labor market is at least partially a function of the structure and expectations of business and industry. For example, the fact that academic accomplishments in high school are rarely recognized as important in hiring decisions (despite the relationship between academic and work success) serves as a serious disincentive to many youth (Bandura, in press). However, the educational system bears some of the responsibility as well. School systems currently do very little to socialize students into the workforce save for vocational education programs. Moreover, what has not yet appeared in the proposals for reform issued by either business or education is a comprehensive and coordinated plan to facilitate the career development of youth.

In the 1970s educators and psychologists promoted comprehensive career development programs, in particular career education:

> Career education is an effort aimed at refocusing American education and the actions of the broader community in ways that will help individuals acquire and utilize the knowledge, skills, and attitudes necessary for each to make work a meaningful, productive and satisfying part of his or her way of living (Hoyt, 1977, p. 5).

Many students may never experience work as inherently meaningful – as more than a means of economic survival. Nevertheless, career development programs that *have* been instituted have been fairly successful in orienting students to work and enhancing career decision making (Isaacson & Brown, 1993). For example, some of the most important predictors of job success and satisfaction have more to do with work-related attitudes, habits, and interpersonal skills (all addressed in career education programs) than with the specific job skills emphasized in vocational training programs (Fitzgerald, 1986). Due to the back-to-basics movement in the 1980s, however, career education was all but abandoned by the schools (Isaacson & Brown, 1993). Contemporary emphases on the school-to-work transition have unaccountably lost sight of the context of career development, perhaps because the movement is being driven by the immediate demands of employers for skilled workers rather than by the educational and career development needs of students.

One of the demands of the educational reform movement is for the adoption of a German-style apprenticeship system. Overemphasis on apprenticeships, however, fails to account for the fundamental differences between American education and education in Germany and most other countries. In the United States much more emphasis has been placed on higher education, including the extensive community college system, for preparing students for work (Berliner, 1993). American students have the luxury of taking more time to complete their education, and the American educational system is also highly permeable; students can reenter the system for additional education and training fairly easily. The labor market in the United States is likewise fairly open compared to many other countries. Our young people have a much wider range of possible occupational options, and can delay their choice of a career for most fields much longer than their counterparts in Germany, Japan, and other countries. An apprenticeship system of the type that works so well in Germany may be problematic in the United States. Our pressing need is to provide systematic assistance in career exploration and decision making for our K–16 student population.

Thus, job training and apprenticeship programs are certainly important, but they ought to be but one component of comprehensive career exploration programs. It is especially vital that career exploration begin in the elementary years instead of in high school. Effective career education at the elementary level includes self-exploration (e.g., of interests and work values), cultivation of career decision-making skills, and information about and exposure to a wide range of occupations. In order to make informed and satisfying career decisions, students must understand both themselves and the world of work, and have the necessary skills to obtain information about relevant career pursuits (Herr & Cramer, 1988). Hierarchical exposure to the world of work, for example, through written materials and multimedia presentations, followed by interviews with adult workers and active exploratory activities such as job shadowing (following a worker for a day or week), are effective in clarifying the career directions of junior high and early high school students. Part-time and summer jobs, vocational education programs, and apprenticeships ought to occur later in the hierarchy of career exploratory experiences in high school, culminating in entry into jobs, advanced education, or training after high school graduation. Furthermore, although academic-track students usually receive some guidance in college selection, little *career* exploration occurs. College-bound students cannot indefinitely delay career choices. College course work does serve as a sort of mechanism for career exploration but does not usually provide the sorts of experiences that will maximally enhance career decision making and eventuate in satisfying career choices.

Although carefully planned career education programs can be effective in easing the school-to-work transition, they too have often been limited in crucial ways. Often career counselors assume that vocational interests are somehow innate, needing only to be "discovered" through exploratory activities. To the contrary, overwhelming evidence exists in support of the influence of efficacy in the cultivation of intrinsic interests and other work motivators (e.g., work values). We also know that academic and career self-efficacy are interrelated but not interchangeable. Educators and counselors must certainly be concerned with strengthening academic self-efficacy, but for most students such efforts will not translate directly into work/career self-efficacy without focused attention on career development.

Nowhere is the need for efficacy-based academic and career interventions more pressing than with students "at risk" for academic failure. The high dropout rate among disadvantaged, predominantly racial/ethnic minority students, has prompted compensatory programs aimed at bolstering academic skills (Richardson, Casanova, Placier, & Guilfoyle, 1989). The potential contributions of self-efficacy theory are untapped within this literature. For example, students labeled at risk for academic failure often lack interest, motivation, and a sense of purpose or life direction (Richardson et al., 1989). Academic remediation may foster a certain level of perceived efficacy, but sole emphasis on basic, low-level academic skills, as found in most compensatory programs, will not engender the types of mastery experiences and challenging goals prerequisite to the development of strong efficacy and inherent interests (Bandura, 1986). Programs that accelerate the pace of instruction for at-risk students are far more likely than compensatory programs to generate academic self-efficacy (Levin, 1987; Richardson et al., 1989). But such programs also require explicit attention to work/career efficacy beliefs.

Research on career self-efficacy also contains some noteworthy implications for work with girls and women, and with racial/ethnic minority students. Societies are increasingly in need of scientists, engineers, and workers with technological expertise. The changing demographics in American higher education and the U.S. workforce indicate a dramatic increase in the proportions of female and minority college students and workers. Yet both women and minorities have historically been, and continue to be, severely underrepresented in the ranks of scientific and technology training programs due to both external barriers and internal constraints such as unrealistically low efficacy beliefs (Betz, 1991). For example, stereotypical socialization experiences undermine girls' sense of efficacy for quantitative activities and leaves them unprepared to pursue quantitative and technical fields (Betz & Hackett, 1983; Hackett, 1985).

Empirical work on math/science self-efficacy clearly indicates that current inequities in the representation of men and women of color and white women in scientific and technological fields can be successfully addressed. Once again, however, the enhancement of academic achievement alone will not correct the problem. Multipronged interventions designed to cultivate strong math/science efficacy beliefs of women and racial/ethnic minorities are critical adjuncts to academic interventions. White women and women of color not only require special assistance in developing robust scientific efficacy beliefs, realistically high career aspirations, and a sense of agency in career pursuits, but they also need to develop strong efficacy for managing science-related and other demanding careers along with family responsibilities (Betz & Hackett, 1987; Lefcourt & Harmon, 1993).

Finally, as Bandura (in press) has argued, we must not forget the role of self-efficacy in generating options and creating opportunities. This proactive role of self-efficacy, and career efficacy beliefs in particular, is important in working with all youth. Cultivating a strong sense of agency is absolutely vital for assisting youth who may have particularly difficult circumstances to overcome or barriers to surmount.

References

Arnold, J., & Bye, H. (1989). Sex and sex role self-concept as correlates of career decision-making self-efficacy. *British Journal of Guidance and Counselling, 17,* 201–206.

Ayers, A. L. (1980). *Self-efficacy theory: Implications for the career development of women.* Unpublished doctoral dissertation, Ohio State University, Columbus.

Bandura, A. (1977). Self-efficacy: Toward a unifying theory of behavioral change. *Psychological Review, 84,* 191–214.

Bandura, A. (1986). *Social foundations of thought and action: A social cognitive theory.* Englewood Cliffs, NJ: Prentice-Hall.

Bandura, A. (in press). *Self-efficacy: The exercise of control.* New York: Freeman.

Berliner, D. (1993). Educational reform in an era of disinformation. *Educational Policy Analysis Archives, 1,* Listserv@asuacad.bitnet.

Betz, N. E. (1991). *What stops women and minorities from choosing and completing majors in engineering and science?* Washington, DC: Federation of Behavioral, Psychological, and Cognitive Sciences.

Betz, N. E, & Fitzgerald, L. F. (1987). *The career psychology of women.* San Diego: Academic.

Betz, N. E., & Hackett, G. (1981). The relationship of career-related self-efficacy expectations to perceived career options in college women and men. *Journal of Counseling Psychology, 28,* 399–410.

Betz, N. E., & Hackett, G. (1983). The relationship of mathematics self-efficacy expectations to the selection of science-based college majors. *Journal of Vocational Behavior, 23,* 329–345.

Betz, N. E., & Hackett, G. (1986). Applications of self-efficacy theory to understanding career choice behavior. *Journal of Social and Clinical Psychology, 4,* 279–289.

Betz, N. E., & Hackett, G. (1987). The concept of agency in educational and career development. *Journal of Counseling Psychology, 34,* 299–308.

Blustein, D. L. (1989). The role of goal instability and career self-efficacy in the career exploration process. *Journal of Vocational Behavior, 35,* 194–203.

Bonett, R. M., & Stickel, S. A. (1992). A psychometric analysis of the Career Attitude Scale. *Measurement and Evaluation in Counseling and Development, 25,* 14–25.

Bores-Rangel, E., Church, T. A., Szendre, D., & Reeves, C. (1990). Self-efficacy in relation to occupational consideration and academic performance in high school equivalency students. *Journal of Counseling Psychology, 37,* 407–418.

Branch, L. E., & Lichtenberg, J. W. (1987, August). *Self-efficacy and career choice.* Paper presented at the Annual Meeting of the American Psychological Association, New York City.

Brown, S. D., Lent, R. W., & Larkin, K. C. (1989). Self-efficacy as a moderator of scholastic aptitude–academic performance relationships. *Journal of Vocational Behavior, 35,* 64–75.

Bussey, K., & Bandura, A. (1992). Self-regulatory mechanisms governing gender development. *Child Development, 63,* 1236–1250.

Campbell, N. K., & Hackett, G. (1986). The effects of mathematics task performance on math self-efficacy and task interest. Journal of Vocational Behavior, 28, 149–162.

Church, A. T., Teresa, J. S., Rosebrook, R., & Szendre, D. (1992). Self-efficacy for careers and occupational consideration in minority high school equivalency students. *Journal of Counseling Psychology, 39,* 498–508.

Clement, S. (1987). The self-efficacy expectations and occupational preferences of females and males. *Journal of Occupational Psychology, 60,* 257–265.

Crites, J. O. (1981). *Career counseling: Methods, models and materials.* New York: McGraw-Hill.

Dawis, R., & Lofquist, L. (1984). *A psychological theory of work adjustment.* Minneapolis: University of Minnesota Press.

Fitzgerald, L. F. (1986). On the essential relations between education and work. *Journal of Vocational Behavior, 28,* 254–284.

Fitzgerald, L. F., & Weitzman, L. M. (1992). Women's career development: Theory and practice from a feminist perspective. In H. D. Lea & Z. B. Leibowitz (Eds.), *Adult career development: Concepts, issues and practices* (2nd ed., pp. 124–160). Alexandria, VA: National Career Development Association.

Fukuyama, M. A., Probert, B. S., Neimeyer, G. J., Nevill, D. D., & Metzler, A. E. (1988). Effects of DISCOVER on career self-efficacy and decision making of undergraduates. *Career Development Quarterly, 37,* 56–62.

Hackett, G. (1985). The role of mathematics self-efficacy in the choice of math-related majors of college women and men: A path analysis. *Journal of Counseling Psychology, 32,* 47–56.

Hackett, G. (1993). Career counseling and psychotherapy: False dichotomies and recommended remedies. *Journal of Career Assessment, 1,* 105–196.

Hackett, G., & Betz, N. E. (1981). A self-efficacy approach to the career development of women. *Journal of Vocational Behavior, 18,* 326–339.

Hackett, G., & Betz, N. E. (1989). An exploration of the mathematics self-efficacy/mathematics performance correspondence. *Journal for Research in Mathematics Education, 20,* 261–273.

Hackett, G., & Betz, N. E. (in press). Career choice and development. In J. E. Maddux (Ed.), *Self-efficacy, adaptation, and adjustment: Theory, research, and application.* New York: Plenum.

Hackett, G., Betz, N. E., Casas, J. M., & Rocha-Singh, I. (1992). Gender, ethnicity, and social cognitive factors predicting the academic achievement of students in engineering. *Journal of Counseling Psychology, 39,* 527–538.

Hackett, G., Betz, N. E., O'Halloran, M. S., & Romac, D. S. (1990). Effects of verbal and mathematics task performance on task and career self-efficacy and interest. *Journal of Counseling Psychology, 37,* 169–177.

Hackett, G., & Campbell, N. K. (1987). Task self-efficacy and task interest as a function of performance on a gender-neutral task. *Journal of Vocational Behavior, 30*, 203–215.

Hackett, G., & Lent, R. W. (1992). Theoretical advances and current inquiry in career psychology. In S. D. Brown & R. W. Lent (Eds.), *Handbook of Counseling Psychology* (2nd Ed., pp. 419–452). New York: Wiley.

Hackett, G., Lent, R. W., & Greenhaus, J. H. (1991). Advances in vocational theory and research: A 20-year retrospective. *Journal of Vocational Behavior, 38*, 3–38.

Hannah, J. S., & Kahn, S. E. (1989). The relationship of socioeconomic status and gender to the occupational choices of grade 12 students. *Journal of Vocational Behavior, 34*, 161–178.

Herr, E. L., & Cramer, S. H. (1988). *Career guidance and counseling through the lifespan: Systematic approaches* (3rd Ed.). Glenview, IL: Scott, Foresman/Little.

Holland, J. L. (1985). *Making vocational choices* (2nd Ed.). Englewood Cliffs, NJ: Prentice-Hall.

Hotchkiss, L., & Borow, H. (1990). Sociological perspectives on work and career development. In D. Brown, L. Brooks, and Associates, *Career choice and development* (2nd Ed., pp. 262–307). San Francisco: Jossey-Bass.

Hoyt, K. B. (1977). *A primer for career education*. Washington, DC: Office of Career Education.

Isaacson, L. E., & Brown, D. (1993). *Career information, career counseling, and career development* (5th Ed.). Boston: Allyn & Bacon.

Lapan, R. T., Boggs, K. R., & Morrill, W. H. (1989). Self-efficacy as a mediator of Investigative and Realistic General Occupational Themes on the Strong-Campbell Interest Inventory. *Journal of Counseling Psychology, 36*, 176–182.

Lapan, R. T., & Jingeleski, J. (1992). Circumscribing vocational aspirations in junior high school. *Journal of Counseling Psychology, 39*, 81–90.

Lauver, P. J., & Jones, R. M. (1991). Factors associated with perceived career options in American Indian, White, and Hispanic rural high school students. *Journal of Counseling Psychology, 38*, 159–166.

Layton, P. L. (1984). *Self-efficacy, locus of control, career salience, and women's career choice*. Unpublished doctoral dissertation, University of Minnesota, Minneapolis.

Lefcourt, L. A., & Harmon, L. W. (1993, August). *Self-efficacy expectations for role management (SEERM): Measure development*. Paper presented at the annual convention of the American Psychological Association, Toronto, Ontario.

Lent, R. W., Brown, S. D., & Hackett, G. (in press). Toward a unifying social cognitive theory of career and academic interest, choice, and performance. *Journal of Vocational Behavior*.

Lent, R. W., Brown, S. D., and Larkin, K. C. (1984). Relation of self-efficacy expectations to academic achievement and persistence. *Journal of Counseling Psychology, 31*, 356–362.

Lent, R. W., Brown, S. D., and Larkin, K. C. (1986). Self-efficacy in the prediction of academic performance and perceived career options. *Journal of Counseling Psychology, 33*, 165–169.

Lent, R. W., Brown, S. D., & Larkin, K. C. (1987). Comparison of three theoretically derived variables in predicting career and academic behavior: Self-efficacy, interest congruence, and consequence thinking. *Journal of Counseling Psychology, 34*, 293–298.

Lent, R. W., & Hackett, G. (1987). Career self-efficacy: Empirical status and future directions [Monograph]. *Journal of Vocational Behavior, 30*, 347–382.

Lent, R. W., & Hackett, G. (in press). Sociocognitive mechanisms of personal agency in career development: Pantheoretical prospects. In M. L. Savickas & R. W. Lent (Eds.), *Convergence in theories of career choice and development*. Palo Alto, CA: Consulting Psychologists Press.

Lent, R. W., Larkin, K. C., & Brown, S. D. (1989). Relation of self-efficacy to inventoried vocational interests. *Journal of Vocational Behavior, 34,* 279–288.

Lent, R. W., Lopez, F. G., & Bieschke, K. J. (1991). Mathematics self-efficacy: Sources and relation to science-based career choice. *Journal of Counseling Psychology, 38,* 424–430.

Lent, R. W., Lopez, F. G., & Bieschke, K. J. (1993). Predicting mathematics-related choice and success behaviors: Test of an expanded social cognitive model. *Journal of Vocational Behavior, 42,* 223–236.

Levin, H. M. (1987). New schools for the disadvantaged. *Teacher Education Quarterly, 14,* 60–83.

Lopez, F. G., & Lent, R. W. (1992). Sources of mathematics self-efficacy in high school students. *Career Development Quarterly, 41,* 3–12.

Luzzo, D. A. (1993). Value of career decision-making self-efficacy in predicting career-decision-making attitudes and skills. *Journal of Counseling Psychology, 40,* 194–199.

Matsui, T., Ikeda, H., & Ohnishi, R. (1989). Relations of sex-typed socialization to career self-efficacy expectations of college students. *Journal of Vocational Behavior, 35,* 1–16.

Matsui, T., Matsui, K., & Ohnishi, R. (1990). Mechanisms underlying math self-efficacy learning of college students. *Journal of Vocational Behavior, 37,* 225–238.

Matsui, T., & Onglatco, M. L. (1991). Instrumentality, expressiveness, and self-efficacy in career activities among Japanese working women. *Journal of Vocational Behavior, 39,* 241–250.

Matsui, T., & Onglatco, M. L. (1992). Career orientedness of motivation to enter the university among Japanese high school girls: A path analysis. *Journal of Vocational Behavior, 40,* 351–363.

Matsui, T., & Tsukamoto, S. (1991). Relation between career self-efficacy measures based on occupational titles and Holland codes and model environments: A methodological contribution. *Journal of Vocational Behavior, 38,* 78–91.

Mitchell, L. K., & Krumboltz, J. D. (1990). Social learning approach to career decision making: Krumboltz' theory. In D. Brown, L. Brooks, and Associates, *Career choice and development* (2nd Ed., pp. 145–196). San Francisco: Jossey-Bass.

National Commission on Excellence in Education (1983). *A nation at risk: The imperative of educational reform.* Washington, DC: U.S. Government Printing Office.

Nevill, D. D., Neimeyer, G. J., Probert, B., & Fukuyama, M. (1986). Cognitive structures in vocational information processing and decision making. *Journal of Vocational Behavior, 28,* 110–122.

Nevill, D. D., & Schlecker, D. I. (1988). The relation of self-efficacy and assertiveness to willingness to engage in traditional/nontraditional career activities. *Psychology of Women Quarterly, 12,* 91–98.

Niles, S. G., & Sowa, C. J. (1992). Mapping the nomological network of career self-efficacy. *Career Development Quarterly, 41,* 13–21.

Noble, A. J., Hackett, G., & Chen, E. C. (1992, April). *Relations of career and academic self-efficacy to the career aspirations and academic achievement of ninth and tenth grade at risk students.* Paper presented at the Annual Meeting of the American Educational Research Association, San Francisco.

O'Hare, M. M., & Beutell, N. J. (1987). Sex differences in coping with career decision making. *Journal of Vocational Behavior, 31*, 174–181.

O'Hare, M. M., & Tamburri, E. (1986). Coping as a moderator of the relation between anxiety and career decision making. *Journal of Counseling Psychology, 33*, 255–264.

Olson, L. (1993, June 23). Clinton to urge state systems for school-job link. *Education Week*, pp. 1, 36.

Osipow, S. H. (1983). *Theories of career development* (3rd Ed.). Englewood Cliffs, NJ: Prentice-Hall.

Osipow, S. H. (1986). Career issues through the life span. In M. S. Pallak & R. O. Perloff (Eds.), *Psychology and work: Productivity, change, and employment* (pp. 141–168). Washington, DC: American Psychological Association.

Osipow, S. H., Temple, R. D., & Rooney, R. A. (1993). The short form of the task-specific occupational self-efficacy scale. *Journal of Career Assessment, 1*, 13–20.

Ozer, E. M. (1992). *Managing work and family: The effects of childcare on perceived self-efficacy and the psychological health of new working mothers.* Unpublished doctoral dissertation, Stanford University, Stanford, California.

Post, P., Stewart, M. A., & Smith, P. L. (1991). Self-efficacy, interest, and consideration of math/science and non math/science occupations among college freshmen. *Journal of Vocational Behavior, 38*, 179–186.

Post-Kammer, P., & Smith, P. L. (1985). Sex differences in career self-efficacy, consideration, and interests of eighth and ninth graders. *Journal of Counseling Psychology, 32*, 551–559.

Post-Kammer, P., & Smith, P. L. (1986). Sex differences in math and science career self-efficacy among disadvantaged students. *Journal of Vocational Behavior, 29*, 89–101.

Richardson, V., Casanova, U., Placier, P., & Guilfoyle, K. (1989). *School children at risk.* London: Falmer.

Robbins, S. B. (1985). Validity estimates for the Career Decision-making Self-efficacy Scale. *Measurement and Evaluation in Counseling and Development, 18*, 64–71.

Rooney, R., & Osipow, S. H. (1992). Task-specific occupational self-efficacy scale: The development and validation of a prototype. *Journal of Vocational Behavior, 40*, 14–32.

Rotberg, H. L., Brown, D., & Ware, W. B. (1987). Career self-efficacy expectations and perceived range of career options in community college students. *Journal of Counseling Psychology, 34*, 164–170.

Schunk, D. H. (in press). Education and instruction. In J. E. Maddux (Ed.), *Self-efficacy, adaptation, and adjustment: Theory, research, and application.* New York: Plenum.

Spokane, A. R. (1991). *Career intervention.* Englewood Cliffs, NJ: Prentice-Hall.

Stickel, S. A., & Bonett, R. M. (1991). Gender differences in career self-efficacy: Combining a career with home and family. *Journal of College Student Development, 32*, 297–301.

Super, D. E. (1990). A life-span, life-space approach to career development. In D. Brown, L. Brooks, and Associates, *Career choice and development* (pp. 197–261). San Francisco: Jossey-Bass.

Taylor, K. M., & Betz, N. E. (1983). Applications of self-efficacy theory to the understanding and treatment of career indecision. *Journal of Vocational Behavior, 22*, 63–81.

Taylor, K. M., & Popma, J. (1990). An examination of the relationships among career decision-making self-efficacy, career salience, locus of control, and vocational indecision. *Journal of Vocational Behavior, 37*, 17–31.

Wheeler, K. G. (1983). Comparisons of self-efficacy and expectancy models of occupational preferences for college males and females. *Journal of Occupational Psychology, 56*, 73–78.

Williams, T. M., & Leonard, M. M. (1988). Graduating black undergraduates: The step beyond retention. *Journal of College Student Development, 29*, 69–75.

Wood, R., & Bandura, A. (1989). Social cognitive theory of organizational management. *Academy of Management Review, 14*, 361–384.

Zilber, S. M. (1988, August). *The effects of attributional styles, sex, and task performance on task and career self-efficacy expectations.* Paper presented at the Annual Convention of the American Psychological Association, Atlanta, Georgia.

Zimmerman, B. (1995). Self-efficacy and educational development. In A. Bandura (Ed.), *Self-efficacy in changing societies* (pp. 202–231). New York: Cambridge University Press.

9. Changing risk behaviors and adopting health behaviors: The role of self-efficacy beliefs

RALF SCHWARZER AND REINHARD FUCHS

Diseases can have a variety of causes, but a major cause is health-risk behaviors, such as smoking, alcohol consumption, poor nutrition, lack of physical exercise, risky sexual practices, and ignoring preventive health screenings. Moreover, many people try to cope with stress by regulating their emotions through health-impairing activities. For example, they might attempt to calm down by smoking or taking drugs. People often distract themselves from stressful encounters by resorting to behaviors that may alleviate discomfort in the short run, but at the expense of health in the long run. Public health efforts continually aim to reduce risk behaviors, which has produced some progress in this regard. There are many reasons – some personal, others social – why risk behaviors are attractive and persistent. Therefore, no single public health strategy can counteract them all effectively. This chapter will focus on individual determinants of behavioral change, although environmental conditions also deserve attention. A few introductory remarks will provide the context for this analysis.

Health behaviors in the context of macrosocial change

We live in a world that is characterized by rapid and uncertain macrosocial changes. In Europe, for example, the breakdown of the communist system, the economic recession, and the large influx of immigrants have created a great deal of social stress. The hardships of migration, unemployment, and poverty foster drug use, crime, and risky health habits. The growth of multiethnic and disadvantaged populations displaced from their native countries places additional strains on national and local public health systems.

One major health-risk behavior is smoking. It is more highly prevalent among lower social classes and in Eastern European countries than in the

West. Smoking as well as alcohol and drug abuse vary with level of education and social class, and with degree of westernization. Of all people over 14 years of age, 34% are smokers in the former East Germany, compared to 27% in the former West Germany. This gap widens when only heavy smokers are considered. Smoking significantly increases the risk of cancer, coronary heart disease, and other ailments. It not only has an independent effect on these health conditions but also interacts with other risk behaviors, such as drinking.

Sexual risk behaviors and intravenous drug use have become major health threats with the global spread of the AIDS epidemic (Ellickson & Hays, 1992; Pryor & Reeder, 1993). Drugs are now being shipped in massive quantities to Eastern Europe, which is submerged in severe instability, and within the European Community, with its now-open borders. In addition to political efforts to control drug trafficking, public health efforts aim at preventing individual drug use and at motivating the use of condoms. Although condoms provide protection against infection with sexually transmitted disease, they are used only by a minority of those at risk (DesJarlais, 1992; European Center, 1992; Jemmott, Jemmott, Spears, Hewitt, et al., 1992). Effective interventions are clearly needed (Abraham, Sheeran, Spears, & Abrams, 1992).

Adolescents represent an important group for health promotion. Many smoke, drink, experiment with drugs, drive recklessly, and practice unsafe sex, perhaps because they are not aware of the risks they are taking. Perceived invulnerability is one potential cause for risky behaviors. However, many young people do understand the risks they are taking but choose to ignore them because they weight other values more heavily (Bell & Bell, in press; Fischhoff, 1992; Jessor, 1993; Jessor, Donovan, & Costa, 1992). Recent research has shown that adolescents exhibit an optimistic bias in their perception of personal risks to the same degree as adults do. Thus, they do not constitute a unique age group that feels less vulnerable than adults (Jacobs Quadrel, Fischhoff, & Davis, 1993). If this is true, they need much more than risk information to motivate them to reduce their risk-taking behavior.

Smoking and sexual risks are salient examples of detrimental behaviors that can impair health. Poor eating habits, lack of physical exercise, and avoidance of recommended health screenings are other behaviors that contribute to health problems. Although some constraints exist, individuals in general have the freedom and capability to exercise influence over their health-related behavior. Public health campaigns can support this individual potential. However, unless well designed and appropriately tailored to particular audiences, such campaigns can waste a lot of resources. Psychologists have identified a number of factors that play an influential role in fostering motivation and adaptation of health-promoting habits. For example, goal setting and other decisional processes set the stage for personal change. However, good intentions are not sufficient to get people to adopt health practices or to refrain from risky ones. Self-referent thought intervenes at various stages of the initiation and maintenance of beneficial actions. Consideration of these processes in public health campaigns and in targeted interventions is of considerable importance. The present chapter analyzes these health-related cognitions and their impact on health behavior.

Optimistic self-beliefs as facilitators of health-related thought and action

Adopting health-promoting behaviors and refraining from health-impairing behaviors is difficult. Most people have a hard time making the decision to change, and an even harder time maintaining the adopted changes when they face inducements to revert to their prior habits. This chapter reviews evidence on social-cognitive factors that facilitate this process of change and presents new findings that increase understanding the role of self-beliefs. According to social cognitive theory (Bandura, 1986), human motivation and action are extensively regulated by forethought. This anticipatory control mechanism involves three types of expectancies: (a) situation-outcome expectancies, in which consequences are produced by environmental events independent of personal action; (b) action-outcome expectancies, in which outcomes flow from personal action; and (c) perceived self-efficacy, which is concerned with people's beliefs in their capabilities to perform courses of action required to attain a desired outcome.

The likelihood that people will adopt a valued health behavior (such as physical exercise) or give up a detrimental habit (such as smoking) may depend on three sets of cognitions: (a) the expectancy that one is at risk ("I have a high risk of getting cancer from smoking"); (b) the expectancy that behavioral change would reduce the threat ("If I quit smoking, I will reduce my risk"); and (c) the expectancy that one is sufficiently capable of exercising control over a risky habit ("I am capable of quitting smoking permanently"). Most people are optimistic when they assess situation-outcome relationships. They feel less vulnerable toward health threats than they should, but they believe that their reference group is at higher risk for diseases (Weinstein, 1982). Also, most people believe that their actions will produce positive outcomes and that they are personally capable to cope with their life demands. The former has been called defensive optimism, the latter functional optimism (Schwarzer, 1994; Taylor, 1989). Functional optimism relies not only on positive outcome expectancies but also on personal coping resources. To initiate and maintain health behaviors, it is not sufficient to perceive an action-outcome contingency. One must also believe that one has the capability to perform the required behavior. A large body of research has examined the role of optimistic self-beliefs as a predictor of behavior change in the health domain (for an overview see Bandura, 1992; O'Leary, 1992; Schwarzer, 1992). Behavioral change goals exert their effect through optimistic self-beliefs. These beliefs slightly overestimate perceived coping capabilities.

Both outcome expectancies and efficacy beliefs play influential roles in adoption of health behaviors, in elimination of detrimental habits, and in the maintenance of change. In adopting a desired behavior, individuals first form an intention and then attempt to execute the action. Outcome expectancies are important determinants in the formation of intentions but are less so in action control. Self-efficacy, on the other hand, seems to be crucial in both stages of the self-regulation of health behavior. Positive outcome expectancies encourage the decision to change one's behavior. Thereafter, outcome expectancies may play a lesser role as problems arise during the adoption of the behavior and its maintenance. At this stage, perceived self-efficacy continues to operate as a controlling influence.

Perceived self-efficacy represents the belief that one has the capability to change risky health behaviors by personal action. Behavior change is seen as dependent on one's perceived capability to cope with stress and boredom and to mobilize one's resources and courses of action required to meet the situational demands. Efficacy beliefs affect the intention to change risk behavior, the amount of effort expended to attain this goal, and the persistence to continue striving in spite of barriers and setbacks that may undermine motivation. Perceived self-efficacy has become a widely applied theoretical construct in models of addiction and relapse (e.g., Annis & Davis, 1988; Baer & Lichtenstein, 1988; Donovan & Marlatt, 1988; Marlatt & Gordon, 1985). These theories assume that success in coping with high-risk situations depends partly on people's beliefs that they operate as active agents of their own actions and that they possess the necessary skills to reinstate control should a slip occur.

Self-efficacy and specific health behaviors

A number of studies on adoption of health practices have measured self-efficacy to assess its potential influences in initiating behavior change. As people proceed from considering precautions in a general way toward shaping a behavioral intention, contemplating detailed action plans, and actually performing a health behavior on a regular basis, they begin to crystallize beliefs in their capabilities to initiate change. In an early study of adoptive behavior, Beck and Lund (1981) exposed dental patients to a persuasive communication designed to alter their beliefs about periodontal disease. Neither perceived disease severity nor outcome expectancy were predictive of adoptive behavior when perceived self-efficacy was controlled. Perceived self-efficacy emerged as the best predictor of the intention to floss ($r = .69$) and of the actual behavior, frequency of flossing ($r = .44$). Seydel, Taal, and Wiegman (1990) report that outcome expectancies as well as perceived self-efficacy are good predictors of intention to engage in behaviors to detect breast cancer (such as breast self-examination, see also Meyerowitz & Chaiken, 1987; Rippetoe & Rogers, 1987).

Perceived self-efficacy was found to predict outcomes of a controlled-drinking program (Sitharthan & Kavanagh, 1990). Perceived self-efficacy has also proven to be a powerful personal resource in coping with stress (Lazarus & Folkman, 1987). In addition, there is evidence that perceived self-efficacy in coping with stressors affects immune function (Wiedenfeld et al., 1990). Subjects with high efficacy beliefs are better able to tolerate pain than those of low self-efficacy (Litt, 1988; Manning & Wright, 1983). Self-efficacy has been shown to affect blood pressure, heart rate, and serum catecholamine levels in coping with challenging or threatening situations (Bandura, Cioffi, Taylor, & Brouillard, 1988; Bandura, Reese, & Adams, 1982; Bandura, Taylor, Williams, Mefford, & Barchas, 1985). Recovery of cardiovascular function in postcoronary patients is similarly enhanced by beliefs in one's physical and cardiac efficacy (Taylor, Bandura, Ewart, Miller, & DeBusk, 1985). Cognitive-behavioral treatment of patients with rheumatoid arthritis enhanced their efficacy beliefs, reduced pain and joint inflammation, and improved psychosocial functioning (O'Leary, Shoor, Lorig, & Holman, 1988). Perceived self-efficacy predicted degree of therapeutic change.

Smoking

Another area in the health field where perceived self-efficacy has been studied extensively is smoking. Quitting the habit requires optimistic self-beliefs, which can be instilled in smoking cessation programs (Baer & Lichtenstein, 1988; Carmody, 1992; Devins & Edwards, 1988; Haaga & Stewart, 1992; Ho, 1992; Karanci, 1992; Kok et al., 1992). Efficacy beliefs to resist temptation to smoking predict reduction in the number of cigarettes smoked (r = -.62), the amount of tobacco per smoke (r = -.43), and the nicotine content (r = -.30) (Godding & Glasgow, 1985). Pretreatment self-efficacy does not predict relapse, but posttreatment self-efficacy does (Kavanagh, Pierce, Lo, & Shelley, 1993). Mudde, Kok, and Strecher (1989) found that efficacy beliefs increase after treatment, and those who had acquired the highest levels of self-efficacy remained successful quitters as assessed in a one-year period (see also Kok, DeVries, Mudde, & Strecher, 1991).

Various researchers have verified relationships between perceived self-regulatory efficacy and relapse occurrence or time of relapse, with correlations ranging from -.34 to -.69 (Colletti, Supnick, & Payne, 1985; Condiotte & Lichtenstein, 1981; DiClemente, Prochaska, & Gibertini, 1985; M. E. Garcia, Schmitz, & Doerfler, 1990; Wilson, Wallston, & King, 1990). Hierarchies of instigating situations correspond to hierarchies of self-efficacy: The more a critical situation induces craving, the greater the perceived efficacy needed to prevent relapse (Velicer, DiClemente, Rossi, & Prochaska, 1990). In a program of research on smoking prevention with Dutch adolescents, Kok and colleagues (1991) conducted several studies on the influence of perceived self-efficacy on nonsmoking intentions and behaviors. Cross-sectionally, they could explain 64% of the variance of intentions as well as of behavior, which was due to the overwhelming predictive power of perceived self-efficacy (r = .66 for intention, r = .71 for reported behavior) (DeVries, Dijkstra, & Kuhlman, 1988). These relationships were replicated longitudinally, although with somewhat less impressive coefficients (DeVries, Dijkstra, & Kok, 1989). Also, studies of the onset of smoking in teenagers have shown that perceived self-efficacy mediates peer social influence on smoking (Stacy, Sussman, Dent, Burton, & Flay, 1992).

Physical exercise

Motivating people to engage in regular physical exercise depends on several factors, among them optimistic self-beliefs of being able to get oneself to do it in the face of many dissuading conditions. Perceived self-efficacy has been found to be a major influence in forming intentions to exercise and in maintaining the practice for an extended time (Dzewaltowski, Noble, & Shaw, 1990; Feltz & Riessinger, 1990; McAuley, 1992, 1993; Shaw, Dzewaltowski, & McElroy, 1992; Weinberg, Grove, & Jackson, 1992; Weiss, Wiese, & Klint, 1989). Various psychometric instruments have been developed to assess self-efficacy for physical activities, such as the Diving Efficacy Scale by Feltz, Landers, and Raeder (1979), the Physical Self-efficacy Scale by Ryckman, Robbins, Thornton, and Cantrell (1982), the Exercise Self-efficacy Scale by Garcia and King (1991), and others (Barling & Abel, 1983; Fruin, Pratt, & Owen, 1991; Godin, Valois, & Lepage, 1993; Marcus & Owen, 1992; Woolfolk, Murphy, Gottesfeld, & Aitken, 1985).

Dzewaltowski (1989) has compared the predictiveness of the theory of reasoned action (Fishbein & Ajzen, 1975), and social cognitive theory in the field of exercise motivation. The exercise behavior of 328 students was recorded for seven weeks and then related to prior measures of different cognitive factors. Behavioral intention was measured by asking the individuals the likelihood that they would perform exercise behavior. Attitude toward physical exercise, perceived behavioral control, and beliefs about the subjective norm concerning exercise were also assessed. The theory of reasoned action fit the data, as indicated by a path analysis. Exercise behavior correlated with intention (.22), attitude (.18), and behavioral control beliefs (.13). In addition, three social cognitive variables were assessed: (a) strength of self-efficacy to participate in an exercise program when faced with impediments, (b) 13 expected outcomes multiplied by the evaluation of those outcomes, and finally, (c) self-satisfaction or dissatisfaction with the participants' level of activities and with the multiple outcomes of exercise. Exercise behavior was correlated with perceived self-efficacy (.34), outcome expectancies (.15), and dissatisfaction (.23), as well as with the interactions of these factors. The higher the three social cognitive constructs were at the onset of the program, the more days they exercised per week. Persons who were confident that they could adhere to the strenuous exercise program were dissatisfied with their present level of physical activity and expected positive outcomes, and they were highly successful in adhering to a regular program of exercise. The variables in the theory of reasoned action did not account for any unique variance in exercise behavior after the influences of the social cognitive factor was controlled. These findings indicate that social cognitive theory provides powerful explanatory constructs.

The role of efficacy beliefs in initiating and maintaining a regular program of physical exercise has also been studied by Desharnais, Bouillon, and Godin (1986); Long and Haney (1988); Sallis and colleagues (1986); Sallis, Hovell, Hofstetter, and Barrington (1992); and Wurtele and Maddux (1987). Endurance in physical performance was found to be dependent on experimentally created efficacy beliefs in a series of experiments on competitive efficacy by Weinberg, Gould, and Jackson (1979); Weinberg, Gould, Yukelson, and Jackson (1981); and Weinberg, Yukelson, and Jackson (1980). In terms of competitive performance, tests of the role of efficacy beliefs in tennis performance revealed that perceived efficacy was related to 12 rated performance criteria (Barling & Abel, 1983).

Patients with rheumatoid arthritis were motivated to engage in regular physical exercise by enhancing their perceived efficacy in a self-management program (Holman & Lorig, 1992). In applying self-efficacy theory to recovery from heart disease, patients who had suffered a myocardial infarction were prescribed a moderate exercise regimen (Ewart, 1992). Ewart found that efficacy beliefs predicted both underexercise and overexertion during programmed exercise. Patients with chronic obstructive pulmonary diseases tend to avoid physical exertion due to experienced discomfort, but rehabilitation programs insist on compliance with an exercise regimen (Toshima, Kaplan, & Ries, 1992). Compliance with medical regimens improved after patients suffering from chronic obstructive pulmonary disease received a cognitive-behavioral treatment designed to raise confidence in their capabilities. Efficacy beliefs predicted moderate exercise ($r = .47$), whereas perceived control did not (Kaplan, Atkins, & Reinsch, 1984).

Nutrition and weight control

Dieting and weight control are health-related behaviors that have also been shown to be governed by self-efficacy beliefs (Bernier & Avard, 1986; Chambliss & Murray, 1979; Glynn & Ruderman, 1986; Hofstetter, Sallis, & Hovell, 1990; Shannon, Bagby, Wang, & Trenkner, 1990; Slater, 1989; Weinberg, Hughes, Critelli, England, & Jackson, 1984). Chambliss and Murray (1979) found that overweight individuals were most responsive to behavioral treatment when they had a high sense of efficacy and an internal locus of control. Other studies on weight control have been published by Bagozzi and Warshaw (1990) and Sallis, Pinski, Grossman, Patterson, and Nader (1988). Stotland, Zuroff, and Roy (1991) have developed a Situation-Based Dieting Self-efficacy Scale that presents 25 risk situations and measures adherence to a diet in these situations. Clark, Abrams, Niaura, Eaton, and Rossi (1991) developed a 20-item Weight Efficacy Life-style Questionnaire that includes five situational factors, namely negative emotions, availability of foods, social pressure, physical discomfort, and positive activities. It has been found that self-efficacy operates best in concert with general life-style changes, including physical exercise and provision of social support. Self-confident clients of intervention programs were less likely to relapse to their previous unhealthful diet.

Sexual risk behavior

Perceived self-efficacy has been studied with respect to prevention of unprotected sexual behavior, for example, the resistance of sexual coercions and the use of contraceptives to avoid unwanted pregnancies. For example, teenage women with a high rate of unprotected intercourse have been found to use contraceptives more effectively if they believed they could exercise control over their sexual activities (Levinson, 1986). Gilchrist and Schinke (1983) taught teenagers through modeling and role playing how to deal with pressures and ensure the use of contraceptives. This mode of treatment significantly raised their sense of perceived efficacy and self-protective skills. Sexual risk-taking behavior such as not using condoms to protect against sexually transmitted disease has also been studied among homosexual men with multiple partners and intravenous drug users. Beliefs in one's capability to negotiate safer sex practices emerged as the most important predictor of such behaviors (Basen-Engquist, 1992; Basen-Engquist & Parcel, 1992; Kasen, Vaughn, & Walter, 1992; McKusick, Coates, Morin, Pollack, & Hoff, 1990; O'Leary, Goodhart, Jemmott, & Boccher-Lattimore, 1992).

Influencing health behaviors that contribute to the prevention of AIDS has become an urgent matter. Perceived self-efficacy has been shown to play a role in such behaviors. Kok and colleagues (1991) reported a study from their Dutch laboratory that analyzed condom use and clean needle use by drug addicts. Intentions and behaviors were predicted by attitudes, social norms, and especially by efficacy beliefs. Perceived self-efficacy correlated with the intention to use clean needles (.35), with reported clean needle use (.46), with the intention to use condoms (.74), and with reported condom use (.67) (Paulussen, Kok, Knibbe, & Kramer, 1989). Bandura (1994) has summarized a large body of research relating perceived self-efficacy to the exercise of control over HIV infection.

Condom use requires not only some technical skills but interpersonal negotiation as well (Bandura, 1994; Brafford & Beck, 1991; Coates, 1990). Convincing a resistant partner to comply with safer sex practices calls for a high sense of efficacy to exercise control over sexual activities. Programs have been launched to enhance self-efficacy and to build self-protective skills in various segments of the population to prevent the spread of the HIV virus. In particular, studies with homosexual men have focused on their perceived efficacy to adopt safer sex (Ekstrand & Coates, 1990; McKusick et al., 1990). Jemmott and his associates have conducted a number of interesting intervention studies that successfully raised self-regulatory efficacy and intentions to adopt a safer sex practice (Jemmott, Jemmott, & Fong, 1992).

In sum, perceived self-efficacy has been found to predict intentions and health habits in different domains of health functioning. The intention to engage in a certain health behavior and the actual behavior itself are positively associated with beliefs in one's personal efficacy. Efficacy beliefs determine appraisal of one's personal resources in stressful encounters and contribute to the forming of behavioral intentions. The stronger people's efficacy beliefs, the higher the goals they set for themselves, and the firmer their commitment to engage in the intended behavior, even in the face of difficulties and setbacks (Locke & Latham, 1990).

Relationships between perceived self-efficacy, health behaviors, risk perceptions, and intentions to change

In the following section, perceived self-efficacy is explored within the broader context of health-related variables. Rather than evaluating efficacy beliefs and corresponding health behavior, the research examines how efficacy beliefs may operate within a more complex and theory-based network of health-related variables. According to modern health behavior approaches such as protection motivation theory (Rogers, 1983), the theory of planned behavior (Ajzen, 1988), and the health action process approach (Schwarzer, 1992), behavioral intentions are seen as important determinants of health behavior change. Intentions are themselves influenced by a number of antecedents such as risk status, risk perceptions, attitudes, outcome expectancies, and perceived self-efficacy. Some of these variables were studied within four health domains: smoking, physical exercise, nutrition, and condom use.

A questionnaire was developed that includes, among other factors, four sets of scales that assess the perceived self-efficacy to execute the four classes of health behaviors (cf. Schwarzer, 1993). Perceived self-efficacy to resist inducement to smoke is measured by eight four-point scales, such as "Even if I am exhausted or nervous, I can resist the urge to smoke" and "Even if I drink alcohol, I don't let myself be tempted to smoke" (Cronbach's alpha = .83). Perceived self-efficacy for physical exercise is measured by 12 seven-point scales, such as "I am confident that I can perform a planned exercise even if . . . 'friends are visiting' . . . 'I feel tense' . . . etc." (Cronbach's alpha = .82). Perceived self-efficacy to adhere to healthy eating behavior is measured by four 4-point scales, such as "I know for sure that I could adhere to a healthful diet if I really wanted to" and "I doubt that I could manage to really carry through a healthful diet" (reversed) (Cronbach's alpha = .65). Perceived self-efficacy to use condoms is measured by eight 4-point scales, such as "Even if I am extremely aroused sexually, I can still manage to use a condom" and "If my partner declines to use a condom, I cannot insist upon it" (reversed) (Cronbach's alpha = .80).

Past behaviors are assessed in terms of habitual activities, such as (a) "How often per week do you exercise? – *Hours – Minutes*" (b) "I am used to eating health foods (*not at all true, hardly true, almost true, exactly true*)." (c) "If I have had intimate contacts it is only with a condom (*not at all true, hardly true, almost true, exactly true*)." For smoking behavior, first the smoker status was determined by distinguishing between smokers, ex-smokers and never-smokers. For smokers only, three levels of risk behavior were designated: (a) frequent smoker (more than 10 cigarettes daily), (b) less frequent smoker (less than 10 cigarettes daily), (c) irregular smoker (smoking only at special occasions, e.g., at parties).

Behavioral intentions are measured by single items with a 4-point response format: (a) "I intend to practice more physical exercise in the near future," (b) "I intend to eat (even) more healthy foods in the near future," (c) "I intend to smoke less or to refrain from smoking," and (d) "I intend to use condoms in the future if I should engage in a new intimate relationship."

Risk perceptions are measured with 7-point scales where the median is anchored by the average risk for the reference group: "Compared to other persons of my age and sex, my risk to get lung cancer one day is . . . 1 = much smaller, 2 = smaller, 3 = somewhat smaller, 4 = the same as that of the others, 5 = somewhat higher, 6 = higher, 7 = much higher." In the same manner, the risks for myocardial infarct, HIV infection, pregnancy, and overweight were rated.

The instruments were administered to 970 university students in Costa Rica,[1] of whom 37% were male and 63% were female. Their average age was 21.2 years (*SD* = 6.64).

Predicting behavioral intentions

The research was designed to verify the predictors of intentions to execute health behaviors. Past behaviors, risk perceptions, and efficacy beliefs were used in a hierarchical regression analysis as predictors of nonsmoking, physical exercise, healthy eating, and condom use. Because the potential contribution of perceived self-efficacy is of main interest here, a conservative strategy was chosen by entering this variable as the last in the regression equation, after the other variables had been considered. The analyses were carried out separately for men and women.

Smoking

Table 9.1 presents the correlations of the predictors with intention to stop smoking or to smoke less, and the beta weights (standardized partial regression coefficients) that specify the contribution of each variable to the prediction when all the other variables are statistically controlled. Similar prediction patterns were found for females and males, but different amounts of variance were explained. Without self-efficacy, 17% of the variation in intention was explained in the female subsample. Self-efficacy explained an additional 7% of the variance. Past smoking behavior ($r = .37$), perceiving a personal risk of lung cancer ($r = -.39$), and perceived self-efficacy to quit ($r = .47$) were about equally correlated with the intention to smoke less or not at all. The less the young women smoked in the past and the stronger they believed they could control their smoking behavior, the more they intended to do so. Surprisingly, higher risk perception was associated with lower intention to quit. When all predictors are included in the regression equation, only self-efficacy remained as a significant contributor, making all others negligible. A similar pattern emerged for the males. Only 6% of the variation in intention was explained without the self-efficacy variable, and 11% was explained with it. Risk perceptions did not correlate significantly with intentions. Smoking infrequently ($r = -.22$) and belief in one's capability to stop smoking ($r = .25$) were correlated with intentions. But in the final regression equation, perceived self-efficacy again was the only significant predictor of behavioral intentions (beta = .31). For perceived risk of lung cancer (beta = .27), a borderline significant association could be identified ($p = .08$). In sum, for both males and females, perceived self-efficacy emerged as the best predictor of intention to smoke less or to quit smoking.

Physical exercise

Similar results were obtained for physical exercise. Table 9.2 shows that past level of exercise did not make a difference when it came to intentions to improve one's fitness. Also, the perceptions of risk for heart disease or for being overweight did not make a great difference (for women, the threat of heart disease was somewhat influential [beta = -.11]). Only perceived self-efficacy was positively associated with one's behavioral goals.

Table 9.1. *Prediction of the intention not to smoke or to smoke less*

	Females ($n = 96$)		Males ($n = 78$)	
	r	beta	r	beta
Smoking	.37	.03	.22	.17
Risk heart disease	−.15	−.02	−.07	−.11
Risk lung cancer	−.39	−.15	−.04	.27
Self-efficacy	.47	.36**	.25	.31*
Multiple R without self-efficacy		.41		.25
Multiple R with self-efficacy		.49		.33

* $p < .05$
** $p < .01$

Healthy eating

Only a small amount of variance in intention could be explained for healthy nutrition (see Table 9.3). Past eating patterns, body mass index, and risk perceptions were of negligible importance, whereas the zero-order correlations between efficacy beliefs and intention were significant ($r = .15$ for females, $r = .27$ for males). For females, efficacy beliefs yielded an increase from 2% to 4% explained variance. For males, an increase from 2% to 9% was obtained. In terms of beta weights, no other coefficient exceeded the one for perceived self-efficacy.

Condom use

The only health behavior where a different pattern of relationships emerged was condom use (see Table 9.4). Here, past behavior was the dominant predictor of intentions to use condoms in the future ($r = .55$ for females, $r = .46$ for males). Perceived self-efficacy was the second best predictor ($r = .25$ for females, $r = .37$ for males). Obviously, it was more important in the male subsample. Perceived risk for infection with the HIV virus or pregnancy did not play a significant role. A substantial amount of intention variance was explained (34% for females, 25% for males). Although there was only a 2% increase in explained variance by self-efficacy for females, the gain was significant.

Table 9.2. *Prediction of the intention to exercise*

	Females ($n = 529$)		Males ($n = 316$)	
	r	beta	r	beta
Exercise	.01	−.03	−.02	−.05
Risk heart disease	−.17	−.11[*]	−.06	−.01
Risk overweight	−.10	−.03	−.03	.01
Self-efficacy	.23	.21[**]	.21	.22[**]
Multiple R without self-efficacy		.17		.06
Multiple R with self-efficacy		.27		.22

[*] $p < .05$
[**] $p < .01$

In sum, past behavior predicted mainly the anticipated use of condoms with new partners. However, it did not predict other health behaviors when efficacy beliefs were also entered in the regression equations. *Risk perceptions* was the weakest predictor if at all for the factors. Perceived self-efficacy played a consistently significant role in all domains of health func-

Table 9.3. *Prediction of the intention to eat healthy foods*

	Females ($n = 517$)		Males ($n = 308$)	
	r	beta	r	beta
Eating	.10	.09[*]	.07	.07
Body mass index	.03	.03	−.05	.01
Risk heart disease	−.11	−.07	.01	.09
Risk overweight	−.03	.02	−.10	−.09
Self-efficacy	.15	.12[**]	.27	.27[**]
Multiple R without self-efficacy		.15		.15
Multiple R with self-efficacy		.19		.30

[*] $p < .05$
[**] $p < .01$

Table 9.4. *Prediction of the intention to use condoms with a new partner*

	Females (n = 295)		Males (n = 255)	
	r	beta	r	beta
Condom use	.55	.53**	.46	.37**
Risk HIV infection	.11	.08	−.09	−.05
Risk pregnancy	.05	.13*	n.a.	n.a.
Self-efficacy	.25	.14**	.37	.21**
Multiple R without self-efficacy		.57		.46
Multiple R with self-efficacy		.58		.50

* $p < .05$
** $p < .01$

tioning and was the dominant predictor except in condom use. These results, however, should be interpreted with caution because of the cross-sectional design of the research. However, a large body of experimental research verifying the causal contribution of efficacy beliefs to human motivation and behavior (Bandura, 1992) add some confidence to causal inference.

Relationship between self-efficacy and cancer screening behavior

The focus of another study was on predicting intention to participate in a medical cancer prevention examination. It was hypothesized that past behavior, perceived self-efficacy, and risk perceptions are important precursors of the intention to perform cancer screening behavior. In addition, outcome expectancies toward cancer screening were measured. Previous studies have shown that outcome expectancies of the type "If I participate in cancer prevention examinations, it is possible to detect cancer early enough to stop the disease" may be a strong predictor not only of the intention, but of the actual cancer screening behavior as well (Frazier & Cummings, 1990; Lerman, Rimer, Trock, Balshem, & Engstrom, 1990; Seydel et al., 1990). The present study investigated the possible synergetic and interactive effects of self-efficacy, outcome expectancies, and vulnerability cognitions in the motivational process that leads to a regular cancer screening behavior.

Participants were randomly selected citizens of Berlin. Complete data were obtained from 1,184 adults (age 18 to 70), who were asked to complete a self-administered questionnaire. Among other variables, the following were measured: Self-efficacy to engage in cancer screening behavior was assessed by three items: "There are barriers that make it difficult to attend a cancer screening. How confident are you that you could overcome the following barriers? . . . (1) I am able to overcome my aversion of an unpleasant medical examination. (2) I am able to cope with the fear that the physician might detect cancer. (3) I am able to find the time and patience necessary for undergoing cancer screening." Outcome expectancies regarding cancer screening behavior were measured by seven items, such as "If I attend cancer screenings on a regular basis (at least once a year) then I feel much safer" or ". . . then the doctoral visit takes me a lot of time and planning in advance." All outcome expectancies were summed up to an index reflecting the perceived benefits of cancer screening behavior. Perceived vulnerability to cancer was assessed by asking "Compared to other persons of my age and sex, my risk of getting cancer is . . . much smaller (1), smaller (2), somewhat smaller (3), the same as that of the others (4), somewhat higher (5), higher (6), much higher (7)." Past behavior was assessed with the item "How often have you had a cancer preventive examination during the last 5 years" and the response categories "several times per year," "once per year," "once every few years," and "never." The intention to engage in cancer screening behavior was measured by the item "I intend to have a cancer preventive examination done within the next 12 months."

Predicting the intention toward cancer screening

To predict intention to engage in cancer screening behavior, hierarchical regression analyses were performed with the past behavior as predictor in the first step; perceived self-efficacy, outcome expectancies, and vulnerability as predictors in the second step (main effects predictors); all possible two-way interactions in the third step; and the three-way interaction in the fourth step.

Table 9.5 summarizes the results of the regression analyses that were computed for four subgroups separately: younger men (age 18 to 40), younger women (age 18 to 40), older men (age 41 to 70), and older women (age 41 to 70). In all subgroups, past behavior was always the strongest predictor of the intention toward cancer screening in the future. After controlling for past behavior, only outcome expectancies emerged as a further

Table 9.5. *Four stepwise regression analyses (for four different sex × age groups) to predict the intention toward cancer screening behavior*

		Subgroups			
		18–40 years		41–70 years	
		Males $n = 222$	Females $n = 384$	Males $n = 286$	Females $n = 292$
Step	Predictor	beta	beta	beta	beta
1	Past cancer screening behavior	.25**	.47**	.43**	.47**
2	Outcome expectancies	.17*	.10*	.26**	.23**
	Perceived self-efficacy	.14	.18**	.19**	.21**
	Vulnerability (risk perception)	.05	.04	.03	.11*
3	Self-efficacy × outcome expectancies	−.06	−.13**	−.10	−.19**
	Vulnerability × self-efficacy	.07	.07	−.07	−.05
	Vulnerability × outcome expectancies	−.03	−.05	−.02	−.08
4	Self-efficacy × outcome expectancies × vulnerability	−.08	.04	.07	−.06

* $p < .05$
** $p < .01$

predictor that was significant in *all* subgroups. Self-efficacy turned out to be predictive in three of the four subgroups (it was no predictor in younger men), and perceived vulnerability to cancer contributed to the prediction only among older women.

A closer inspection of the coefficients shows that the intention toward cancer screening behavior is only weakly predictable in younger men, probably because "cancer prevention" is not yet an issue of great interest to this age group. Furthermore, the results suggest that in men (especially in older men) outcome expectancies may be more important for motivating cancer screening behavior than perceived self-efficacy. This is consistent with findings reported by Seydel and colleagues (1990), and it supports the general assumption that men's health-preventive actions are likely to be influenced more by outcome expectancies than by assessments of their own capabilities. In younger women, on the other hand, perceived self-efficacy seems to be the more decisive factor in predicting cancer prevention behavior; outcome expectancies here only play a marginal role.

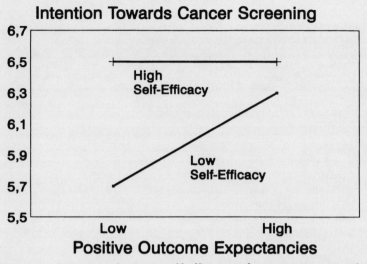

Figure 9.1. Interaction between self-efficacy and outcome expectancies in women.

The two-way interactions that were entered into the regression equation in the third step yielded a significant Self-Efficacy × Outcome Expectancies interaction in women of both age groups. The graphic display of this interaction is presented in Figure 9.1. The figure shows the result of an analysis of covariance (ANCOVA) based on all women (age 18 to 70) with intention as the dependent variable, self-efficacy and outcome expectancies as predictors, and past behavior as a covariate. For this analysis both predictors were dichotomized at the median. The significant interaction effect suggests that positive outcome expectancies may help to raise the intention to screen for cancer in women of lower self-efficacy. Women of high self-efficacy intend on engaging in screening activities regardless of outcome expectancies. This result sheds light on the interplay of health-related cognitions in the motivational process. The data suggest that a low sense of efficacy can be compensated by a high outcome expectancy. The behavioral intention seems to decline only if both self-efficacy and outcome expectancy are low.

Contrary to Rogers's (1983) motivation protection theory, risk perceptions (vulnerability) had virtually no effect in motivating cancer screening behavior. In particular, the hypothesized interaction effects of vulnerability by self-efficacy and vulnerability by outcome expectancies (see Wurtele & Maddux, 1987) did not emerge. Together with similar results of other studies (Seydel et al., 1990), the finding suggests that the role of vulnerability beliefs in the process of adoption and maintenance of preventive health behaviors needs to be seriously reexamined.

Theoretical status of perceived self-efficacy in health behavior changes: The health action process approach

There is overwhelming evidence that perceived self-efficacy is closely associated with behavioral intentions and health behavior change. However, the strength of relationships differs somewhat from domain to domain and from sample to sample. Adding efficacy beliefs to a set of predictors not only yields a significant gain in explained variance, but often self-efficacy turns out to become the most powerful single predictor. Beyond this evidence, it is desirable to identify the causal status of optimistic efficacy beliefs within a more comprehensive theoretical framework. Adopting precautions or changing risky habits must be seen as a self-regulation process that can be subdivided into a number of stages (see Prochaska, Norcross, Fowler, Follick, & Abrams, 1992; Weinstein & Sandman, 1992). Having formed an intention to change is the endpoint of the motivation phase, and subsequent events can be subsumed under the heading of volition processes (Gollwitzer, 1993; Kuhl & Beckmann, 1994).

In this section, a brief outline of the health action process approach is given (see Figure 9.2). Three groups of cognitions are influential in establishing a behavioral goal or intention: (a) risk perceptions, (b) outcome expectancies, and (c) perceived self-efficacy. Risk perceptions include one's perceived vulnerability and the perceived severity of a disease or other critical event. These risk perceptions are often distorted and reflect an "optimistic bias" that leads to underestimate the objective risk (Taylor, 1989; Weinstein, 1980; for an overview see Schwarzer, 1994). Nevertheless, some degree of threat is involved that may have motivational value in the decision-making process. In terms of causal order it is hypothesized that risk perceptions only set the stage for subsequent contemplations. Their effect on intentions is seen as being rather indirect than direct. Therefore, threat appraisal or risk perception often disappears as a determinant when entered into a regression equation to predict behavioral intentions. When stable outcome expectancies and self-beliefs are already formed, the motivational value of risk perceptions may become negligible.

Outcome expectancies represent specific contingency knowledge. Feeling threatened may stimulate the acquisition of such knowledge. People learn to see actions as causes of events and believe in the changeability of health risks and risky habits. But beliefs in action-dependent conse-

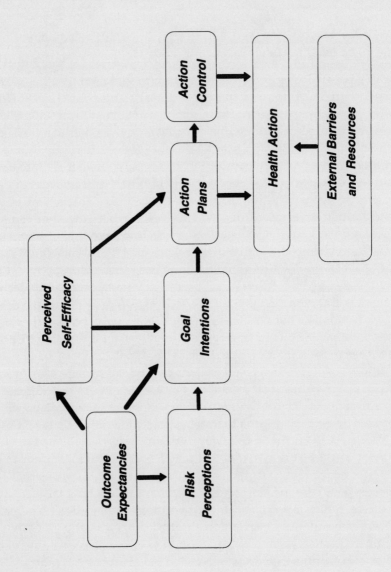

Figure 9.2. The health action process approach.

quences does not necessarily imply that people see themselves as agents of change. Perceptions of personal agency can be distinguished from means-ends beliefs (Skinner, 1992; Skinner, Chapman, & Baltes, 1988; Snyder et al., 1991) and refer to an internal attribution of actions. In the development of personal goals it is possible that agency comes later than means-ends beliefs. Thus, the hypothesized causal order in the motivation phase may proceed from threat to knowledge to agency, or in other words, from risk perceptions to outcome expectancies to perceived self-efficacy. However, a different causal order is also possible. If people believe they have no power to effect change, they do not waste time thinking about different means. Agency is then exercised through means. If people believe they can effect change, they consider the best means to do so. This confusion about causal order may have to do with the level of analysis. If people believe that general means to solve a problem must exist, they scrutinize their capability for appropriate actions and watch out for the best means available to them only if they feel capable. In cross-sectional research designs, all three groups of cognitions are confounded, and it can happen that risk perceptions not only fail to contribute to the intention, but can even have a reversed sign, indicating a counterintuitive influence: the lower the risk, the higher the goal. This may simply reflect the dominating force of optimistic self-beliefs because those who believe they have personal control over their future need no longer worry about critical health changes. The anticipated adoption of a health behavior leads to a reduction in current risk perception (Weinstein & Nicolich, 1993). From a different viewpoint, one could state that high-risk perception leads to low intentions to change because excessive fear leads to avoidance behavior.

Good intentions do not necessarily guarantee corresponding actions. Correlations between goals and behaviors vary greatly. Therefore, post-intentional self-regulation processes deserve more scientific attention. While in the motivation phase, it is described what people choose to do; in the subsequent action or volition phase it is described how hard they try and how long they persist. The right-hand part of Figure 9.2 consists of three levels: cognitive, behavioral, and situational. The focus is on cognitions that instigate and control the action, that is, a volitional or self-regulative process that is subdivided into action plans and action control.

When a preference for a particular health behavior has been shaped, the intention has to be transformed into detailed instructions on how to perform the desired action. If, for example, someone intends to lose weight, it has to be planned how to do it, that is, what foods to buy, when and how often to eat which amounts, when and where to exercise, and maybe even whether to cease smoking as well. Thus, a global intention can be specified by a set of subordinate intentions and action plans that contain proximal goals and algorithms of action sequences. The volition process seems not to be influenced by outcome expectancies, but more strongly by self-efficacy, as the number and quality of action plans have to be dependent on one's perceived competence and experience. Self-efficacy beliefs influence the cognitive construction of specific action plans, for example, by visualizing scenarios that may guide goal attainment. These postintentional preactional cognitions are necessary because otherwise the person would impulsively act in a trial-and-error fashion and would not know where to allocate the available resources.

Once an action has been initiated, it has to be controlled by cognitions in order to be maintained. The action has to be protected from being interrupted and from being given up prematurely due to incompatible competing intentions that may become dominant while a behavior is being performed. Meta-cognitive activity is needed to complete the primary action and to suppress distracting secondary action tendencies. Daily physical exercise, for example, requires self-regulatory processes in order to secure effort and persistence and to keep competing motivations – such as the desire to eat, socialize, or sleep – weak for the time being.

When the action is being performed, self-efficacy determines the amount of effort invested and the level of perseverance. People with self-doubts are more inclined to anticipate failure scenarios, worry about their possible performance deficiencies, and abort their attempts prematurely. People with an optimistic sense of self-efficacy, however, visualize success scenarios that guide the action and let them persevere in the face of obstacles. When they run into unforeseen difficulties they quickly recover.

Performing an intended health behavior is an action, just as is not performing a risk behavior. The control of health-detrimental actions also requires effort and persistence, and therefore is also guided by a volitional process that includes *action plans* and *action control*. If one intends to quit smoking or drinking alcohol, one has to plan how to do it. For example, it is important to avoid high-risk situations where the pressures to relapse are overwhelming (Marlatt, 1985). Attaining proximal subgoals contributes to increase in perceived efficacy to manage more difficult situations until one can resist under all possible circumstances. If someone is craving for a cigarette or a drink, action control helps to overcome the critical situation. For example, individuals can make favorable social comparisons, engage in competing actions, or seek social support to help resist smoking and drinking. The more these meta-cognitive skills and internal coping dialogues are developed and the better they are matched to specific risk situations, the easier the urges can be controlled. Self-efficacy helps to reestablish the perseverant efforts needed for the accomplishment of self-imposed goals.

Finally, situational barriers as well as opportunities have to be considered. If situational cues are overwhelming, meta-cognitive skills fail to protect the individual and the temptation cannot be resisted. Actions not only are a function of intentions and cognitive control but are also influenced by the perceived and the actual environment. A social network, for example, that ignores the coping process of a quitter by smoking in his presence creates a difficult stress situation which taxes the quitter's volitional strength. If, on the other hand, the spouse decides to quit too, then a social support situation is created that enables the quitter to remain abstinent in spite of lower levels of volitional strength.

In sum, the action phase can be described along three levels: cognitive, behavioral, and situational. The cognitive level refers to self-regulatory processes that mediate between the intentions and the actions. This volitional process contains action plans and action control and is strongly influenced by self-efficacy expectancies but also by perceived situational barriers and support.

Conclusions

Numerous studies have shown that health cognitions regulate adoption of health-promoting behaviors and elimination of health-impairing behaviors. Among them, perceived self-efficacy stands out as a major contributor that affects not only the decision-making process but also the initiation and maintenance process. Studies have been conducted to compare the role of perceived self-efficacy with that of risk perceptions and past behavior. The intention to use condoms with a new partner was best predicted by past behavior, although the intention to stop smoking, to eat healthy foods, and to exercise were mainly determined by self-efficacy. The intention to undergo cancer screening was also influenced by self-efficacy, but this effect was qualified by age, sex, and interactions with outcome expectancies. These findings have implications for the further development of a health behavior theory that comprises multiple stages of motivation and volition.

Note

1. The study was conducted by Judith Bässler (1993).

References

Abraham, C., Sheeran, P., Spears, R., & Abrams, D. (1992). Health beliefs and promotion of HIV-preventive intentions among teenagers: A Scottish perspective. *Health Psychology, 11,* 363–370.
Ajzen, I. (1988). *Attitudes, personality, and behavior.* Milton Keynes, CA: Open University Press.
Annis, H. M., & Davis, C. S. (1988). Assessment of expectancies. In D. M. Donovan & G. A. Marlatt (Eds.), *Assessment of addictive behaviors* (pp. 84–111). New York: Guilford.
Baer, J. S., & Lichtenstein, E. (1988). Classification and prediction of smoking relapse episodes: An exploration of individual differences. *Journal of Consulting and Clinical Psychology, 56,* 104–110.
Bagozzi, R. P., & Warshaw, P. R. (1990). Trying to consume. *Journal of Consumer Research, 17,* 127–140.
Bandura, A. (1986). *Social foundations of thought and action.* Englewood Cliffs, NJ: Prentice Hall.
Bandura, A. (1992). Self-efficacy mechanism in psychobiologic functioning. In R. Schwarzer (Ed.), *Self-efficacy: Thought control of action* (pp. 355–394). Washington, DC: Hemisphere.
Bandura, A. (1994). Social cognitive theory and exercise of control over HIV infection. In R. DiClemente & J. Peterson (Eds.), *Preventing AIDS: Theory and practice of behavioral interventions* (pp. 25–59). New York: Plenum.
Bandura, A., Cioffi, D., Taylor, C. B., & Brouillard, M. E. (1988). Perceived self-efficacy in coping with cognitive stressors and opioid activation. *Journal of Personality and Social Psychology, 55,* 479–488.
Bandura, A., Reese, L., & Adams, N. E. (1982). Micro-analysis of action and fear arousal as a function of differential levels of perceived self-efficacy. *Journal of Personality and Social Psychology, 43,* 5–21.
Bandura, A., Taylor, C. B., Williams, S. L., Mefford, I. N., & Barchas, J. D. (1985). Catecholamine secretion as a function of perceived coping self-efficacy. *Journal of Consulting and Clinical Psychology, 53,* 406–414.
Barling, J., & Abel, M. (1983). Self-efficacy and tennis performance. *Cognitive Therapy and Research, 7,* 265–272.
Basen-Engquist, K. (1992). Psychosocial predictors of "safer-sex" behaviors in young adults. *AIDS Education and Prevention, 4,* 120–134.
Basen-Engquist, K., & Parcel, G. S. (1992). Attitudes, norms, and self-efficacy: A model of adolescents' HIV-related sexual risk behavior. *Health Education Quarterly, 19,* 263–277.
Bässler, J. (1993). *Erprobung psychometrischer Skalen im Rahmen eines Kulturvergleichs zur diagnostischen Erfassung von allgemeinen und spezifischen Selbstwirksamkeitserwartungen* [Evaluation of psychometric scales within a cross-cultural study to measure general and specific self-efficacy]. Unpublished diploma thesis. Berlin, Freie Universität Berlin, Institut für Psychologie.
Beck, K. H., & Lund, A. K. (1981). The effects of health threat seriousness and personal efficacy upon intentions and behavior. *Journal of Applied Social Psychology, 11,* 401–415.

Bell, N. J., & Bell, R. W. (Eds.). (in press). *Perspectives on adolescent risk taking*. Newbury Park, CA: Sage.

Bernier, M., & Avard, J. (1986). Self-efficacy, outcome and attrition in a weight reduction program. *Cognitive Therapy and Research*, *10*, 319–338.

Brafford, L. J., & Beck, K. H. (1991). Development and validation of a condom self-efficacy scale for college students. *Journal of American College Health*, *39*, 219–225.

Carmody, T. P. (1992). Preventing relapse in the treatment of nicotine addiction: Current issues and future directions. *Journal of Psychoactive Drugs*, *24*, 131–158.

Chambliss, C. A., & Murray, E. J. (1979). Efficacy attribution, locus of control, and weight loss. *Cognitive Therapy and Research*, *3*, 349–353.

Clark, M. M., Abrams, D. B., Niaura, R. S., Eaton, C. A., & Rossi, J. S. (1991). Self-efficacy in weight management. *Journal of Consulting and Clinical Psychology*, *59*, 739–744.

Coates, T. J. (1990). Strategies for modifying sexual behavior for primary and secondary prevention of HIV disease. *Journal of Consulting and Clinical Psychology*, *58*, 57–69.

Colletti, G., Supnick, J. A., & Payne, T. J. (1985). The Smoking Self-Efficacy Questionnaire (SSEQ): Preliminary scale development and validation. *Behavioral Assessment*, *7*, 249–260.

Condiotte, M. M., & Lichtenstein, E. (1981). Self-efficacy and relapse in smoking cessation programs. *Journal of Consulting and Clinical Psychology*, *49*, 648–658.

Desharnais, R., Bouillon, J., & Godin, G. (1986). Self-efficacy and outcome expectations as determinants of exercise adherence. *Psychological Reports*, *59*, 1155–1159.

DesJarlais, D. C. (1992). The first and second decades of AIDS among injecting drug users. *British Journal of Addiction*, *87*, 347–353.

Devins, G. M., & Edwards, P. J. (1988). Self-efficacy and smoking reduction in chronic obstructive pulmonary disease. *Behaviour Research and Therapy*, *26*, 127–135.

DeVries, H., Dijkstra, M., & Kok, G. J. (1989). *Self-efficacy as a determinant of the onset of smoking and interventions to prevent smoking in adolescents*. Paper presented at the First European Congress of Psychology, Amsterdam.

DeVries, H., Dijkstra, M., & Kuhlman, P. (1988). Self-efficacy: The third factor besides attitude and subjective norm as a predictor of behavioural intentions. *Health Education Research*, *3*, 273–282.

DiClemente, C. C., Prochaska, J. O., & Gibertini, M. (1985). Self-efficacy and the stages of self-change of smoking. *Cognitive Therapy and Research*, *9*, 181–200.

Donovan, D. M., & Marlatt, G. A. (Eds.). (1988). *Assessment of addictive behaviors*. New York: Guilford.

Dzewaltowski, D. A. (1989). Toward a model of exercise motivation. *Journal of Sport & Exercise Psychology*, *11*, 251–269.

Dzewaltowski, D. A., Noble, J. M., & Shaw, J. M. (1990). Physical activity participation: Social cognitive theory versus the theories of reasoned action and planned behavior. *Journal of Sport & Exercise Psychology*, *12*, 388–405.

Ekstrand, M., & Coates, T. J. (1990). Maintenance of safer sexual behaviors and predictors of risky sex: The San Francisco Men's Health Study. *American Journal of Public Health*, *80*, 973–977.

Ellickson, P. L., & Hays, R. D. (1992). On becoming involved with drugs: Modeling adolescent drug use over time. *Health Psychology*, *11*, 377–385.

European Center for the Monitoring of AIDS. (1992). *AIDS surveillance in Europe* (Quarterly Report), *32*.

Ewart, C. K. (1992). The role of physical self-efficacy in recovery from heart attack. In R. Schwarzer (Ed.), *Self-efficacy: Thought control of action* (pp. 287–304). Washington, DC: Hemisphere.

Feltz, D. L., Landers, D. M., & Raeder, V. (1979). Enhancing self-efficacy in high-avoidance tasks: A comparison of modeling techniques. *Journal of Sport Psychology, 1*, 112–122.

Feltz, D. L., & Riessinger, C. A. (1990). Effects of in vivo emotive imagery and performance feedback on self-efficacy and muscular endurance. *Journal of Sport & Exercise Psychology, 12*, 132–143.

Fischhoff, B. (1992). Risk taking: A developmental perspective. In J. F. Yates (Ed.), *Risk taking behavior* (pp. 133–162). New York: Wiley.

Fishbein, M., & Ajzen, I. (1975). *Belief, attitude, intention, and behavior: An introduction to theory and research.* Reading, MA: Addison-Wesley.

Frazier, T. G., & Cummings, P. D. (1990). Motivational factors for participation in breast cancer screening. *Journal of Cancer Education, 5*, 51–54.

Fruin, D. J., Pratt, C., & Owen, N. (1991). Protection Motivation Theory and adolescents' perceptions of exercise. *Journal of Applied Psychology, 22*, 55–69.

Garcia, A. W., & King, A. C. (1991). Predicting long-term adherence to aerobic exercise: A comparison of two models. *Journal of Sport & Exercise Psychology, 13*, 394–410.

Garcia, M. E., Schmitz, J. M., & Doerfler, L. A. (1990). A fine-grained analysis of the role of self-efficacy in self-initiated attempts to quit smoking. *Journal of Consulting and Clinical Psychology, 58*, 317–322.

Gilchrist, L. D., & Schinke, S. P. (1983). Coping with contraception: Cognitive and behavioral methods with adolescents. *Cognitive Therapy and Research, 7*, 379–388.

Glynn, S. M., & Ruderman, A. J. (1986). The development and validation of an eating self-efficacy scale. *Cognitive Therapy and Research, 10*, 403–420.

Godding, P. R., & Glasgow, R. E. (1985). Self-efficacy and outcome expectations as predictors of controlled smoking status. *Cognitive Therapy and Research, 9*, 583–590.

Godin, G., Valois, P., & Lepage, L. (1993). The pattern of influence of perceived behavioral control upon exercising behavior: An application of Ajzen's Theory of Planned Behavior. *Journal of Behavioral Medicine, 16*, 81–102.

Gollwitzer, P. M. (1993). Goal achievement: The role of intentions. In M. Hewstone & W. Stroebe (Eds.), *European review of social psychology* (Vol. 4, pp. 141–185). Chichester, England: Wiley.

Haaga, D. A. F., & Stewart, B. L. (1992). Self-efficacy for recovery from a lapse after smoking cessation. *Journal of Consulting and Clinical Psychology, 60*, 24–28.

Ho, R. (1992). Cigarette health warnings: The effects of perceived severity, expectancy of occurence, and self-efficacy on intentions to give up smoking. *Australian Psychologist, 27*, 109–113.

Hofstetter, C. R., Sallis, J. F., & Hovell, M. F. (1990). Some health dimensions of self-efficacy analysis of theoretical specificity. *Social Science and Medicine, 31*, 1051–1056.

Holman, H. R., & Lorig, K. (1992). Perceived self-efficacy in self-management of chronic disease. In R. Schwarzer (Ed.), *Self-efficacy: Thought control of action* (pp. 305–323). Washington, DC: Hemisphere.

Jacobs Quadrel, M., Fischhoff, B., & Davis, W. (1993). Adolescent (in)vulnerability. *American Psychologist, 48*, 102–116.

Jemmott, J. B., Jemmott, L. S., & Fong, G. T. (1992). Reductions in HIV risk–associated sexual behaviors among black male adolescents: Effects of an AIDS prevention intervention. *American Journal of Public Health, 82*, 373–377.

Jemmott, J. B., Jemmott, L. S., Spears, H., Hewitt, N., et al. (1992). Self-efficacy, hedonistic expectancies, and condom use intentions among inner-city Black adolescent women: A social cognitive approach to AIDS risk behavior. *Journal of Adolescent Health, 13*, 512–519.

Jessor, R. (1993). Successful adolescent development among youth in high-risk settings. *American Psychologist, 48*, 117–126.

Jessor, R., Donovan, J. E., & Costa, F. M. (1992). *Beyond adolescence.* New York: Cambridge University Press.

Kaplan, R. M., Atkins, C. J., & Reinsch, S. (1984). Specific efficacy expectations mediate exercise compliance in patients with COPD. *Health Psychology, 3*, 223–242.

Karanci, N. A. (1992). Self-efficacy-based smoking situation factors: The effects of contemplating quitting vs. relapsing in a Turkish sample. *International Journal of the Addictions, 27*, 879–886.

Kasen, S., Vaughn, R. D., & Walter, H. J. (1992). Self-efficacy for AIDS preventive behaviors among tenth grade students. *Health Education Quarterly, 19*, 187–202.

Kavanagh, D. J., Pierce, J., Lo, S. K., & Shelley, J. (1993). Self-efficacy and social support as predictors of smoking after a quit attempt. *Psychology and Health, 8*, 231–242.

Kok, G., Den Boer, D., DeVries, H., Gerards, F., Hospers, H. J., & Mudde, A. N. (1992). Self-efficacy and attribution theory in health education. In R. Schwarzer (Ed.), *Self-efficacy: Thought control of action* (pp. 245–262). Washington, DC: Hemisphere.

Kok, G., DeVries, H., Mudde, A. N., & Strecher, V. J. (1991). Planned health education and the role of self-efficacy: Dutch research. *Health Education Research, 6*, 231–238.

Kuhl, J., & Beckmann, J. (Eds.). (1994). *Volition and personality: Action versus state orientation.* Göttingen, Germany: Hogrefe.

Lazarus, R. S., & Folkman, S. (1987). Transactional theory and research on emotions and coping. *European Journal of Personality, 1*, 141–170.

Lerman, C., Rimer, B., Trock, B., Balshem, A., & Engstrom, P. F. (1990). Factors associated with repeat adherence to breast cancer screening. *Preventive Medicine, 19*, 279–290.

Levinson, R. A. (1986). Contraceptive self-efficacy: A perspective on teenage girls' contraceptive behavior. *Journal of Sex Research, 22*, 347–369.

Litt, M. D. (1988). Self-efficacy and perceived control: Cognitive mediators of pain tolerance. *Journal of Personality and Social Psychology, 54*, 149–160.

Locke, E. A., & Latham, G. P. (1990). *A theory of goal setting and task performance.* Englewood, NJ: Prentice Hall.

Long, B. C., & Haney, C. J. (1988). Coping strategies for working women: Aerobic exercise and relaxation interventions. *Behavior Therapy, 19*, 75–83.

Manning, M. M., & Wright, T. L. (1983). Self-efficacy expectancies, outcome expectancies, and the persistence of pain control in childbirth. *Journal of Personality and Social Psychology, 45*, 421–431.

Marcus, B. H., & Owen, N. (1992). Motivational readiness, self-efficacy and decision-making for exercise. *Journal of Applied Social Psychology, 22*, 3–16.

Marlatt, G. A. (1985). Cognitive factors in the relapse process. In G. A. Marlatt & J. R. Gordon (Eds.), *Relapse prevention* (pp. 128–200). New York: Guilford.

286 Ralf Schwarzer and Reinhard Fuchs

Marlatt, G. A., & Gordon, J. R. (Eds.). (1985). *Relapse prevention*. New York: Guilford.

McAuley, E. (1992). The role of efficacy cognitions in the prediction of exercise behavior in middle-aged adults. *Journal of Behavioral Medicine, 15*, 65–88.

McAuley, E. (1993). Self-efficacy and the maintenance of exercise participation in older adults. *Journal of Behavioral Medicine, 16*, 103–113.

McKusick, L., Coates, T. J., Morin, S. F., Pollack, L., & Hoff, N. (1990). Longitudinal predictors of reductions in unprotected anal intercourse among gay men in San Francisco – The AIDS Behavioral Research Project. *American Journal of Public Health, 80*, 978–983.

Meyerowitz, B. E., & Chaiken, S. (1987). The effect of message framing on breast self-examination attitudes, intentions, and behavior. *Journal of Personality and Social Psychology, 52*, 500–510.

Mudde, A., Kok, G., & Strecher, V. (1989). *Self-efficacy and success expectancy as predictors of the cessation of smoking*. Paper presented at the First European Congress of Psychology, Amsterdam.

O'Leary, A. (1992). Self-efficacy and health: Behavioral and stress-physiological mediation. *Cognitive Therapy and Research, 16*, 229–245.

O'Leary, A., Goodhart, F., Jemmott, L. S., & Boccher-Lattimore, D. (1992). Predictors of safer sex on the college campus: A social cognitive theory analysis. *Journal of American College Health, 40*, 254–263.

O'Leary, A., Shoor, S., Lorig, K., & Holman, H. R. (1988). A cognitive-behavioral treatment for rheumatoid arthritis. *Health Psychology, 7*, 527–542.

Paulussen, T., Kok, G. J., Knibbe, R., & Kramer, T. (1989). AIDS en intraveneus druggebruik [AIDS and IV-drug use]. *Tijdschrift voor Sociale Gezondheitszorg, 68*, 129–136.

Prochaska, J. O., Norcross, J. C., Fowler, J., Follick, M. J., & Abrams, D. B. (1992). Attendance and outcome in a worksite weight control program: Processes and stages of change as process and predictor variables. *Addictive Behaviors, 17*, 35–45.

Pryor, J. B., & Reeder, G. D. (Eds.). (1993). *The social psychology of HIV infection*. Hillsdale, NJ: Erlbaum.

Rippetoe, P. A., & Rogers, R. W. (1987). Effects on components of protection motivation theory on adaptive and maladaptive coping with a health threat. *Journal of Personality and Social Psychology, 52*, 596–604.

Rogers, R. W. (1983). Cognitive and physiological processes in fear appeals and attitude change: A revised theory of protection motivation. In J. R. Cacioppo & R. E. Petty (Eds.), *Social psychology: A sourcebook* (pp. 153–176). New York: Guilford.

Ryckman, R. M., Robbins, M. A., Thornton, B., & Cantrell, P. (1982). Development and validation of a physical self-efficacy scale. *Journal of Personality and Social Psychology, 42*, 891–900.

Sallis, J. F., Haskell, W. L., Fortmann, S. P., Vranizan, K. M., Taylor, C. B., & Solomon, D. S. (1986). Predictors of adoption and maintenance of physical activity in a community sample. *Preventive Medicine, 15*, 331–341.

Sallis, J. F., Hovell, M. F., Hofstetter, C. R., & Barrington, E. (1992). Explanation of vigorous physical activity during two years using social learning variables. *Social Science and Medicine, 34*, 25–32.

Sallis, J. F., Pinski, R. B., Grossman, R. M., Patterson, T. L., & Nader, P. R. (1988). The development of self-efficacy scales for health-related diet and exercise behaviors. *Health Education Research, 3*, 283–292.

Schwarzer, R. (1992). Self-efficacy in the adoption and maintenance of health behaviors: Theoretical approaches and a new model. In R. Schwarzer (Ed.), *Self-efficacy: Thought control of action* (pp. 217–242). Washington, DC: Hemisphere.

Schwarzer, R. (1993). *Measurement of perceived self-efficacy: Psychometric scales for cross-cultural research.* Berlin: Freie Universität Berlin, Institut für Psychologie.

Schwarzer, R. (1994). Optimism, vulnerability, and self-beliefs as health-related cognitions: A systematic overview. *Psychology and Health, 9,* 161–180.

Seydel, E., Taal, E., & Wiegman, O. (1990). Risk-appraisal, outcome and self-efficacy expectancies: Cognitive factors in preventive behavior related to cancer. *Psychology and Health, 4,* 99–109.

Shannon, B., Bagby, R., Wang, M. Q., & Trenkner, L. (1990). Self-efficacy: A contributor to the explanation of eating behavior. *Health Education Research, 5,* 395–407.

Shaw, J. M., Dzewaltowski, D. A., & McElroy, M. (1992). Self-efficacy and causal attributions as mediators of perceptions of psychological momentum. *Journal of Sport & Exercise Psychology, 14,* 134–147.

Sitharthan, T., & Kavanagh, D. J. (1990). Role of self-efficacy in predicting outcomes from a programme for controlled drinking. *Drug and Alcohol Dependence, 27,* 87–94.

Skinner, E. (1992). Perceived control: Motivation, coping, and development. In R. Schwarzer (Ed.), *Self-efficacy: Thought control of action* (pp. 91–106). Washington, DC: Hemisphere.

Skinner, E. A., Chapman, M., & Baltes, P. (1988). Control, means-ends, and agency beliefs: A new conceptualization and its measurement during childhood. *Journal of Personality and Social Psychology, 54,* 117–133.

Slater, M. D. (1989). Social influences and cognitive control as predictors of self-efficacy and eating behavior. *Cognitive Therapy and Research, 13,* 231–245.

Snyder, C. R., Harris, C., Anderson, J. R., Holleran, S. A., Irving, L. M., Sigmon, S. T., Yoshinobu, L., Gibb, J., Langelle, C., & Harney, P. (1991). The will and the ways: Development and validation of an individual-differences measure of hope. *Journal of Personality and Social Psychology, 60,* 570–585.

Stacy, A. W., Sussman, S., Dent, C. W., Burton, D., & Flay, B. R. (1992). Moderators of peer social influence in adolescent smoking. *Personality and Social Psychology Bulletin, 18,* 163–172.

Stotland, S., Zuroff, D. C., & Roy, M. (1991). Situational dieting self-efficacy and short-term regulation of eating. *Appetite, 17,* 81–90.

Taylor, C. B., Bandura, A., Ewart, C. K., Miller, N. H., & DeBusk, R. F. (1985). Exercise testing to enhance wives' confidence in their husbands' cardiac capability soon after clinically uncomplicated acute myocardial infarction. *American Journal of Cardiology, 55,* 635–638.

Taylor, S. E. (1989). *Positive illusions: Creative self-deception and the healthy mind.* New York: Basic Books.

Toshima, M. T., Kaplan, R. M., & Ries, A. L. (1992). Self-efficacy expectancies in chronic obstructive pulmonary disease rehabilitation. In R. Schwarzer (Ed.), *Self-efficacy: Thought control of action* (pp. 325–354). Washington, DC: Hemisphere.

Velicer, W. F., DiClemente, C. C., Rossi, J. S., & Prochaska, J. O. (1990). Relapse situations and self-efficacy: An integrative model. *Addictive Behaviors, 15,* 271–283.

Weinberg, R., Grove, R., & Jackson, A. (1992). Strategies for building self-efficacy in tennis players: A comparative analysis of Australian and American coaches. *Sport Psychologist, 6,* 3–13.

Weinberg, R. S., Gould, D., & Jackson, A. (1979). Expectations and performance: An empirical test of Bandura's self-efficacy theory. *Journal of Sport Psychology, 1,* 320–331.

Weinberg, R. S., Gould, D., Yukelson, D., & Jackson, A. (1981). The effect of preexisting and manipulated self-efficacy on competitive muscular endurance task. *Journal of Sport Psychology, 4,* 345–354.

Weinberg, R. S., Hughes, H. H., Critelli, J. W., England, R., & Jackson, A. (1984). Effects of preexisting and manipulated self-efficacy on weight loss in a self-control program. *Journal of Research in Personality, 18,* 352–358.

Weinberg, R. S., Yukelson, D., & Jackson, A. (1980). Effects of public and private efficacy expectations on competitive performance. *Journal of Sport Psychology, 2,* 340–349.

Weinstein, N. D. (1980). Unrealistic optimism about future life events. *Journal of Personality and Social Psychology, 39,* 806–820.

Weinstein, N. D. (1982). Unrealistic optimism about susceptibility to health problems. *Journal of Behavioral Medicine, 5,* 441–460.

Weinstein, N. D., & Nicolich, M. (1993). Correct and incorrect interpretations of correlations between risk perceptions and risk behaviors. *Health Psychology, 12,* 235–245.

Weinstein, N. D., & Sandman, P. M. (1992). A model of the precaution adoption process: Evidence from home radon testing. *Health Psychology, 11,* 170–180.

Weiss, M. R., Wiese, D. M., & Klint, K. A. (1989). Head over heels with success: The relationship between self-efficacy and performance in competitive youth gymnastics. *Journal of Sport and Exercise Psychology, 11,* 444–451.

Wiedenfeld, S. A., O'Leary, A., Bandura, A., Brown, S., Levine, S., & Raska, K. (1990). Impact of perceived self-efficacy in coping with stressors on components of the immune system. *Journal of Personality and Social Psychology, 59,* 1082–1094.

Wilson, D. K., Wallston, K. A., & King, J. E. (1990). Effects of contract framing, motivation to quit, and self-efficacy on smoking reduction. *Journal of Applied Social Psychology, 20,* 531–547.

Woolfolk, R. L., Murphy, S. M., Gottesfeld, D., & Aitken, D. (1985). Effects of mental rehearsal of task motor activity and mental depiction of task outcome on motor skill performance. *Journal of Sport Psychology, 7,* 191–197.

Wurtele, S. K., & Maddux, J. E. (1987). Relative contributions of protection motivation theory components in predicting exercise intentions and behavior. *Health Psychology, 6,* 453–466.

10. Self-efficacy and addictive behavior

G. ALAN MARLATT, JOHN S. BAER, AND
LORI A. QUIGLEY

Perceived self-efficacy plays a unique role in the addictive behaviors field. Such beliefs influence both the initial development of addictive habits and the behavior change process involving the cessation of such habits and maintenance of abstinence. In both the acquisition and modification of smoking, for example, individuals are faced with a choice between starting to smoke or not (initiation), and for smokers, between attempting to quit or not. Most of the research reviewed in this chapter deals with the role of perceived self-efficacy in preventing the onset of addictive behavior (e.g., resistance self-efficacy) or in facilitating the quitting process (e.g., self-efficacy for coping with relapse crises). It is important to note, however, that self-efficacy can cut both ways at the choice point: In addition to resistance self-efficacy, self-efficacy is also involved in attempts to initiate an addictive habit, such as becoming a smoker.

As an illustration of this latter point, the senior author recalls his experience of taking up smoking at the age of 14 – a habit he unfortunately maintained for thirty years afterward. On vacation with his family in Hawaii, he met a 16-year-old boy who smoked. Wanting to impress his older friend, he lied and said that he too was a smoker. "Prove it!" he was told by the older boy, who offered him his first cigarette, a Cool menthol. In response to this challenge he wondered: "Can I do what it takes to be a smoker? Can I inhale without choking and giving away my lie?" He recalled his smoking grandmother and how she handled cigarettes as a model of what to do. He felt confident that he could pass as a seasoned smoker. Taking the cigarette, he lit it, taking his first drag. It tasted awful and he coughed, but by the second puff he managed to fake it by holding the smoke in his mouth and blowing it out later without inhaling. "Pretty cool, smoking Kools!" the older boy exclaimed, making his new friend feel confident and accepted in his first encounter with nicotine.

As this anecdote demonstrates, self-efficacy can lead one into addictive behavior as well as prevent its onset, depending on one's personal goals and outcome expectancies. If youngsters believe that smoking, drinking, or other drug use makes them look "cool" or provides other advantages, the question of efficacy is directed to the behaviors required to experiment with or initiate the habit. A conflict often develops between resistance self-efficacy (to "Just Say No") and peer pressures to indulge ("Just Say Yes"). A similar conflict arises concerning attempts to give up addictive habits. If the smoker believes that nicotine enhances one's level of functioning or helps keep excess weight off, efficacy concerning one's ability to quit is jeopardized. Conflicts of this kind, between starting and not starting or between stopping and not stopping, uniquely characterize the problem of addictive behavior.

This review explores the various ways in which self-efficacy theory applies to change in addictive behavior. We begin with an overview of how self-efficacy is involved in the initiation of or resistance to drug use (focus on prevention). The role of self-efficacy in changing addictive habits is then analyzed for both initiating a change and maintaining the change over time (relapse prevention). Recent research on the prevention and treatment of addictive behaviors and relapse prevention is selectively reviewed to illustrate various applications of self-efficacy theory. Most of the research to date on self-efficacy and addiction deals with the two most frequently consumed substances in the general population: tobacco and alcohol. The paper concludes with a discussion of emerging clinical issues and directions for future research.

Types of self-efficacy in addictive behavior change

In a recent paper on the role of perceived self-efficacy in addictive behaviors, DiClemente and colleagues (DiClemente, Fairhurst, & Piotrowski, in press) describe five different types of efficacy self-appraisals: (1) coping self-efficacy, referring to "belief in one's ability to cope successfully with specific situations such as resisting pressure from friends to use the substance or talking with someone when emotionally distressed instead of using the addictive substance"; (2) treatment behavior self-efficacy, pertaining to clients' beliefs in their ability to perform the tasks required to achieve personal change, such as self-monitoring; (3) recovery self-efficacy, concerning judgments of capability to recover from slips or lapses; (4) control self-efficacy, referring to perceived capability to control or moderate the target behavior (e.g., to avoid excessive drinking or eating); and

(5) abstinence self-efficacy, concerned with one's perceived capabilities to abstain from using the addictive substance.

Although a useful taxonomy, DiClemente's categories of self-efficacy are limited in the following ways. First, all five types of self-efficacy are tied to treatment and relapse prevention. Self-efficacy as a factor in the initial development of addictive behavior is not included in this list. As a second point, there seems to be considerable overlap among categories of beliefs: self-efficacy to master various therapeutic tasks would seem to subsume all the other types to the extent that treatment includes training in alternative coping skills, recovery from lapses, and resistance to urges to violate abstinence. The last two categories, control and abstinence self-efficacy, reflect different treatment goals – whether to seek abstinence or use the substance in controlled moderation. These forms of personal efficacy overlap with coping and self-efficacy to fulfill therapeutic tasks.

Building on and extending DiClemente's taxonomy, we propose the following five categories of efficacy beliefs. Our typology includes self-efficacy for both the initiation and subsequent change of addictive behaviors. In the initiation phase, a distinction is made between (1) *resistance self-efficacy*, judgments about one's ability to avoid use prior to first use, and (2) *harm-reduction self-efficacy*, risk reduction efficacy following initial use. In the behavior change stage, (3) *action self-efficacy*, or beliefs in one's capabilities to achieve the desired goal of abstinence or controlled use, is distinguished from self-efficacy for long-term maintenance of the achieved change. Maintenance efficacy is further differentiated into (4) *coping self-efficacy*, concerned with anticipatory efficacy to cope with relapse crises, and (5) *recovery self-efficacy*, involving restorative coping following lapse and relapse episodes. Each of these five types of efficacy is analyzed below in greater detail. A selective review of research pertaining to these types of efficacy is then presented.

Self-efficacy for primary and secondary prevention

The development of an addictive behavior pattern involves two phases. The first concerns the initial use or experimentation with a substance. Primary prevention programs have focused on enhancing resistance self-efficacy to deter initial drug use. Once the individual crosses the abstinence barrier, however, efficacy for remaining drug free is no longer at issue. The second phase concerns secondary prevention, namely the efficacy to reduce the amount of harm one experiences. Here self-efficacy is directed toward behaviors designed to minimize the risk or harm of ongoing drug use, including both moderate use, such as drinking in moderation, and/or abstinence.

Resistance self-efficacy

In the context of primary prevention, resistance self-efficacy refers to one's perceived ability to resist pressure to drink or use drugs (Hays & Ellickson, 1990; Rohrbach, Graham, Hansen, & Flay, 1987). Research has shown that low resistance self-efficacy coupled with prodrug social influences (e.g., exposure to drug offers) predicts both intentions and actual use of alcohol and tobacco by adolescents (Conrad, Flay, & Hill, 1992; Ellickson & Hays, 1991, 1992; Lawrence & Rubinson, 1986). As a result, many primary prevention programs focus on training children and adolescents to resist interpersonal pressures or intrapersonal temptations to experiment with drugs (e.g., Pentz, 1985).

Harm-reduction self-efficacy

Once drug use has been initiated, harm-reduction self-efficacy comes into play. Initial experimentation with drugs such as tobacco, alcohol, and marijuana frequently occurs in young people and does not necessarily lead to habitual drug abuse or dependence. Indeed, some authors have questioned whether drug experimentation should be considered normative rather than deviant, given the frequency with which it occurs in adolescence. According to Newcomb and Bentler (1988), "In fact, experimental use of various types of drugs, both licit and illicit, may be considered a normative behavior among contemporary United States teenagers in terms of prevalence" (p. 214).

In one influential longitudinal study, adolescents who did experiment with drugs were found to be psychologically more well adjusted than those who never used or those who progressed to drug abuse (Shedler & Block, 1990). According to these authors:

> When the psychological findings are considered as a set, it is difficult to escape the inference that experimenters are the psychologically healthiest subjects, healthier than either abstainers or frequent users (p. 614).

Other research clearly shows, on the other hand, that early experimentation with alcohol or other drugs may set the stage for future drinking or drug problems in later adolescence or early adulthood (Jessor, Donovan, & Costa, 1991). The goal of a harm-reduction approach to secondary prevention is to minimize the harm of ongoing drug use by reducing the amount of use or stopping further drug abuse. For alcohol use, moderate or social drinking is an acceptable harm-reduction goal (Marlatt, Larimer, Baer, & Quigley, 1993). For other drug use, including smoking, cutting back with an eventual goal of abstinence is also consistent with this goal (Marlatt & Tapert, 1993). As such, harm reduction offers an alternative goal for preventing drug abuse among initial alcohol or drug users. In a recent critical review of adolescent substance use prevention programs, Brown and Horowitz (1993) conclude:

> The harm reduction approach represents an alternative to the traditional AOD [alcohol and other drugs] prevention strategies examined here. This approach is not based on the view of the AOD user as deviant. Instead, the focus is on reducing the potential that an adolescent will go on to become an abuser of AODs and the harm to the individuals and society resulting from AOD abuse. (p. 549)

Self-efficacy for harm reduction is a new concept and will be discussed in greater detail later in this chapter.

Self-efficacy for change, treatment, and relapse prevention

Once an addictive behavior has become established, the individual may or may not embark on an attempt to change. In terms of the "stages of change" model proposed by Prochaska and DiClemente (1992), individuals who have moved from precontemplation (not considering change) into the contemplation stage are considering moving into the preparation and action stages of habit change. Self-efficacy for action involving reducing or eliminating an addictive behavior is a critical factor, beginning with a commitment to action (e.g., selection of a quit date for smoking). Both coping efficacy (confidence in one's ability to resist relapse) and recovery efficacy (confidence in one's ability to recover from a lapse or setback) are central to the maintenance stage of habit change. As Bandura (1991) has noted:

> Perceived efficacy can affect every phase of personal change – whether people even consider changing their health habits, whether they can enlist the motivation and perseverance needed to succeed should they choose to do so, and whether they adequately maintain the changes they have achieved. (p. 258)

Action self-efficacy

Many people with addictive behavior problems remain mired in the precontemplation or contemplation stages of behavior change. Precontemplators may remain stuck because they perceive themselves incapable of giving up drug use (e.g., smoking) and therefore do not even try to quit (Brod & Hall, 1984). Contemplators may postpone initial action because of doubts about their efficacy to change. DiClemente and Hughes (1990) assessed self-efficacy for abstinence in the context of the stages of change model for clients in an outpatient alcoholism treatment program. Both abstinence self-efficacy and temptations to drink were found to be related to the clients' stage of change. Among precontemplators or contemplators those classified as uninvolved or discouraged about changing had the lowest level of self-efficacy and the highest levels of temptation.

Although abstinence is a common goal for initial action, moderation or controlled use may be an alternative goal for changing addictive behavior. Although both abstinence and moderation may be target goals for behavior change, we prefer the term *action self-efficacy* to refer to the initiation of change. Action self-efficacy can be assessed both for individuals who attempt to change on their own and for those who join self-help groups or seek professional treatment.

Coping self-efficacy

Once an individual has passed through the action stage of personal change, long-term maintenance becomes the challenge. Relapse rates are high in the modification of addictive behavior. In the cognitive-behavioral model of relapse presented by Marlatt and Gordon (1985), self-efficacy plays a critical role. According to this model, individuals in the maintenance stage are frequently confronted with high-risk situations for relapse. These may take the form of negative emotional states, interpersonal conflicts, or social pressures to use the substance. Such situations may trigger an initial lapse unless the individual engages in effective coping strategies. Low self-efficacy for coping with high-risk situations often occurs in conjunction with positive outcome expectancies for substance use.

Relapse prevention techniques are designed to enhance self-efficacy for coping with high-risk situations, urges, and temptations (Chaney, O'Leary, & Marlatt, 1978). Research by Shiffman (Shiffman, 1984; Shiffman & Wills, 1985) demonstrates the critical role of behavioral and cognitive coping in the prevention of relapse in smoking cessation. Coping self-efficacy has also been found to be a predictor of treatment outcome for adolescent substance abuse (Myers, Brown, & Mott, 1993). Issues concerning the prediction of relapse based on self-efficacy assessed at pretreatment and posttreatment are discussed in greater detail later in this chapter.

Recovery self-efficacy

Individuals in the maintenance stage of habit change often experience lapses or slips as they progress. One's reactions to such setbacks may undermine efficacy for long-term maintenance, leading to relapse or even abandonment of the habit change attempt altogether. One such debilitating reaction to lapses is an attributional response known as the abstinence violation effect, or AVE (Collins & Lapp, 1991; Curry, Marlatt, & Gordon, 1987; Ross, Miller, Emmerson, & Todt, 1989). Individuals with this reaction attribute their lapses to internal, stable, and uncontrollable factors (e.g., lack of willpower or disease factors beyond one's individual control). Relapse prevention methods include procedures to enhance recovery efficacy, based on the assumption that mistakes are common in the process of habit change and should not be interpreted as a sign of personal failure. As Bandura (1991) has noted:

> Entrenched habits rarely yield to a single attempt at self-regulation. Success is usually achieved through renewed effort following failed attempts. Human attainments, therefore, necessitate a resilient sense of personal efficacy. To strengthen the staying power of self-beliefs, health communications should emphasize that success requires perseverant effort, so that people's sense of efficacy is not undermined by a few setbacks. (pp. 259–260).

We next review existing research programs that assess and test these types of efficacy in addictive behaviors.

Resistance self-efficacy: Primary prevention

Rates of drinking, smoking, and marijuana use are high among adolescents in the United States. A recent national study reported that by eighth grade, 70% of young adolescents acknowledged having tried alcohol and more than a quarter (27%) acknowledged having been drunk at least once. (National Institute on Drug Abuse [NIDA], 1992). This study also reports that almost half (44%) of eighth graders have tried smoking cigarettes and 14% have smoked in the previous month (NIDA, 1992). Twenty-eight percent of high school seniors reported smoking cigarettes in the previous month and 19% report daily smoking (NIDA, 1992). In addition, 10% of high school sophomores acknowledged that they have tried marijuana (NIDA, 1992).

Substance abuse programs that target adolescents and younger children as a whole are primary prevention efforts that seek to deter initiation to substance use. Studies of adolescent initiation to drug use focus primarily on the onset of alcohol consumption, cigarette smoking, and marijuana use because these are among the most commonly used substances and because they are considered to be potential "gateway drugs," which may lead to the use of more harmful substances (Jessor & Jessor, 1977; Kandel & Faust, 1975; Kandel, Yamaguchi, & Chen, 1992). Self-efficacy has been investigated as a potentially important factor in determining the onset of drug use among adolescents. This research has focused on *resistance self-efficacy*, or confidence in one's ability to resist using a substance despite social pressures to do so (Ellickson & Bell, 1990; Ellickson, Bell, & McGuigan, 1993; Ellickson & Hays, 1991; Hansen, Graham, Wolkenstein, & Rohrbach, 1991; Hays & Ellickson, 1990). A recent review of research in adolescent smoking onset reported that resistance self-efficacy emerged as a strong prospective predictor of smoking initiation (Conrad et al., 1992).

In a natural history study of adaptation to drug use, Ellickson and Hays (1991) evaluated the importance of prodrug social influence, perceptions of resistance self-efficacy, and beliefs about the prevalence of drug use in determining future substance use among 1,138 eighth and ninth graders in 10 junior high schools. This study tested a model that hypothesized that social pressures to use drugs, resistance self-efficacy, and perceived prevalence of substance use among peers would influence drug use nine months later, both directly and indirectly. Indirect influences were hypothesized to be mediated by expectations of future drug use. This model was tested separately for users and nonusers of alcohol, tobacco, and marijuana with structural equation modeling. For students who had never experimented with drugs, prodrug social influences, such as drug offers or exposure to people who use drugs, and low self-efficacy for drug resistance predicted drug involvement nine months later. Beliefs about the prevalence of drug use among peers did not predict future drug use, nor were expectations of future use a mediator for the other antecedents (Ellickson & Hays, 1991).

The model for students who had already initiated drug use differed from that of nonusers in that low resistance self-efficacy did not have a direct effect on future drug use but rather exerted an indirect effect through the mediation of expected drug use. Social influences toward drug use predicted subsequent use both directly and indirectly through the cognitive mediator of expected use. It should be noted that in both models social influence was a stronger predictor than resistance self-efficacy. For adolescent drug users, social pressures toward drug use and low perceptions of efficacy in resisting drug use both enhanced expectations of future use, which in turn led to drug taking behavior (Ellickson & Hays, 1991). Although the mechanisms affecting drug use differ for substance users and nonusers, both social influences and judgments about resistance self-efficacy play an important role in future drug use (Ellickson & Hays, 1991).

Stacy and his colleagues (Stacy, Sussman, Dent, Burton, & Flay, 1992), evaluated potential moderators of peer social influence in predicting smoking among 1,245 southern California high school students. Not surprisingly, the social influence of friends was determined to have the largest effect in predicting smoking. However, this effect was moderated by students' judgments of their perceived self-efficacy to resist smoking. For students with low self-efficacy, peer influence was the better predictor of tendency to smoke. However, high self-efficacy served as a protective factor against social pressures to smoke. The authors concluded that, "greater belief in the ability to resist social influences reduces the strength of friends social influence on smoking" (p. 170).

One study compared the relative effectiveness of two alcohol prevention programs for fifth grade students (Hansen et al., 1991). The first program, Normative Education, sought to correct erroneous beliefs about the rates and peer acceptability of adolescent alcohol consumption. The second program, Resistance Training, provided training in alcohol refusal skills. The Resistance Training program was hypothesized to have a greater impact on resistance self-efficacy and on instructor ratings of alcohol refusal skills. Although resistance training enhanced refusal skills, it did not increase self-efficacy to avoid alcohol consumption. However, quality of program had a moderating effect. Classes that implemented the resistance training well, as rated by observers, enhanced resistance self-efficacy. Thus, the quality of program implementation affects the success of the self-efficacy intervention. Interestingly, the Normative Education program did increase resistance self-efficacy even though observer's ratings of refusal skills remained unchanged (Hansen et al., 1991). Apparently, efficacy for resistance can be increased with interventions that do not specifically target resistance skills.

Perceived social pressure and resistance self-efficacy have been shown to generalize across substances for alcohol, cigarettes, and marijuana (Hays & Ellickson, 1990). However, contrary to studies which have found self-efficacy evaluations to generalize across situations (Baer & Lichtenstein, 1988a; DiClemente, Prochaska, & Gibertini, 1985), adolescents' judgments of their ability to avoid drug use did not transfer across dating and party situations thus reflecting distinct although moderately correlated domains of efficacy (Hays & Ellickson, 1990). Although these findings suggest the need for situation-specific efficacy enhancement, substance specific training may not be needed because the resistance skills transfer across substances (Hays & Ellickson, 1990). Not surprisingly, there was an inverse relationship of prodrug pressure and feelings of efficacy to avoid drug use. Hence, adolescents reported feeling less able to resist drug use when they felt social pressures to conform.

Because of the strong association between resistance self-efficacy and future drug use, some researchers have designed interventions that focus specifically on enhancing students' self-efficacy to resist drugs (Ellickson et al., 1993; Ellickson & Bell, 1990; Hansen et al., 1991; Pentz, 1985). In one such study, Ellickson and her associates (Ellickson et al., 1993; Ellickson & Bell, 1990) directed and evaluated a junior high school drug prevention program designed to enhance both the motivation to resist drug use and the skills required to do so. The Project ALERT program was delivered to 6,527 students in 20 junior high schools. Eight lessons were taught one week apart to the seventh grade and three booster lessons were taught when the children reached the eighth grade. The purpose of these lessons was to help students identify and resist internal and external pressures to use drugs, to identify reasons and benefits of refraining from drug use, and to provide accurate normative information about the prevalence of drug use. The programs were presented in an interactive format that included role modeling, small group exercises, skills practice, and question-and-answer periods. In half of the intervention schools the programs were taught by older teens with assistance from adult teachers; in the other half programs were taught by adult health educators. Ten additional schools, which did not receive the Project ALERT program, served as comparison schools. Although this program was designed primarily to prevent drug use, some students were experimenters or regular drug users at baseline, while students were in the seventh grade. The impact of the Project ALERT program on early initiators was evaluated and reported as well as for the nonusers.

Early results for students at end of the seventh grade indicated that this program reduced drinking rates for all students. These beneficial effects were due primarily to the teen-led programs, underscoring the strong impact of peers. Initiation to drinking was reduced by 28% for baseline nondrinkers. By eighth grade, the gains regarding alcohol use were lost so that students in the intervention and comparison schools did not differ.

Project ALERT did not affect cigarette smoking in initial nonusers. More smoking experimenters, or those who had previously used tobacco, quit smoking and those who continued to smoke reduced their cigarette use. However, smoking levels increased by 20% to 30% for students who were smokers at the beginning of the study. This unexpected boomerang effect may have implications for differential targeting of students at risk for heavy smoking. Program effects for marijuana use included substantial decreases in initiation for nonusers who were also not tobacco smokers, and decreases in levels of use for those who had already initiated marijuana use or were thought to be at higher risk for use due to baseline smoking status.

A long-term follow-up assessment yielded disappointing findings (Ellickson et al., 1993). By 10th and 12th grades the general treatment effects for drug use were no longer significant. It should be noted that there was a temporary increase in drinking frequency among baseline drinkers who had received the Project ALERT program from teen leaders. This boomerang effect faded by 12th grade. Significant effects on the enhancement of resistance self-efficacy had been demonstrated in the 7th through 9th grades but disappeared by 10th grade. Program effects on normative perceptions of drug use and consequences of use remained significant in 10th grade primarily in teen-led groups. However, even these effects declined by 12th grade (Ellickson et al., 1993).

Other programs designed both to build resistance skills for cigarette smoking and to present accurate normative smoking information have had more favorable long-term outcomes (Perry, Kelder, Murray, & Klepp, 1992; Telch, Killen, McAlister, Perry, & Maccoby, 1982). Perry (Perry et al., 1992) reported a 40% reduction in smoking prevalence over a six-year period for adolescents who received the school-based program as part of a larger community preventive effort. Telch (Telch et al., 1982) reported similar reductions in smoking prevalence for adolescents who had received a school-based intervention 33 months earlier. Both of these programs involved resistance skills training within a broader social effort. Although resistance efficacy expectations may have been enhanced by these programs, perceived self-efficacy was not assessed.

Harm reduction self-efficacy: Secondary prevention

As reviewed above, most programs designed to prevent substance initiation or abuse indiscriminately target adolescents with messages designed to help them refrain from using drugs. Limited effectiveness over time (Ellickson et al., 1993) as well as the inevitability of youthful experimentation suggest the need for secondary prevention programs designed for

adolescents who have already said yes and are at risk for problems of substance abuse. These programs target adolescents who have already initiated smoking, drinking, or using other drugs. One goal of this harm-
reduction approach is to avoid the escalation of drug use by alienating
early initiators who have thus far not learned how to "just say no" or have
been unwilling to do so. The emphasis with this subgroup is on enhancing
self-efficacy to exercise control over the escalation of drug use into drug
abuse or dependency.

The High Risk Drinkers Project (Baer, 1993; Baer et al., 1992; Fromme,
Kivlahan, & Marlatt, 1986; Kivlahan, Marlatt, Fromme, Coppel, & Williams, 1990) conducted at the Addictive Behaviors Research Center at the
University of Washington is an example of such a secondary prevention
program. In the first of these programs (Kivlahan et al., 1990), college students were recruited who were interested in learning more about or
changing their drinking and who reported a pattern of heavy drinking,
but with few or no signs of physical dependency. They were randomly
assigned to either a cognitive-behavioral program that taught skills on
how to maintain moderation in drinking, an alcohol information class that
focused on negative consequences of drinking, or an assessment-only control group. The cognitive-behavioral program included interventions
designed to enhance self-efficacy to maintain moderation through decision making and exercise of personal control (Fromme et al., 1986). Follow-up assessments conducted at 4, 8, and 12 months posttreatment revealed significant reductions in alcohol consumption for all three groups
but that the moderation-oriented skills training group achieved the greatest decrease in consumption in retrospective reports of drinking (Kivlahan
et al., 1990).

Lower efficacy beliefs at pretreatment to control overdrinking during
negative emotional states were associated with higher dependency on
alcohol and more alcohol-related consequences (Fromme et al., 1986).
Curiously, high baseline beliefs of efficacy to avoid overdrinking in social
influence situations were associated with more frequent monthly drinking
and higher weekly consumption, but with fewer dependency symptoms.
Efficacy beliefs to avoid overdrinking under social pressure and negative
affect assessed at baseline, posttreatment, and 4 months posttreatment
increased over time for all groups. However, changes in efficacy level from
pretreatment to posttreatment and follow-up did not correspond to
changes in alcohol consumption from baseline to posttreatment and follow-up (Fromme et al., 1986).

In summary, peer influence is a primary factor in initiation to drug use among adolescents (Ellickson & Hays, 1991; Hays & Ellickson, 1990; Stacy et al., 1992). Indeed, adolescents appear to make distinctions in the relative difficulty of avoiding drug use in different social settings (Hays & Ellickson, 1990). Perceived self-efficacy generalizes across substances, such that those who judge that they are able to avoid smoking cigarettes would also feel confident in their ability to refuse pressure to use marijuana (Hays & Ellickson, 1990).

The impact of social influence appears to be moderated by beliefs in personal efficacy to resist pressure to use substances (Stacy et al., 1992). Programs have been designed specifically to enhance resistance self-efficacy across substances and have shown promising results in the short term (Ellickson et al., 1993; Ellickson & Bell, 1990). The long-term results for school-based programs alone are mixed and suggest the need to integrate school-based programs in a broader community-oriented effort. Special interventions are also needed to reduce escalation of drug use to problematic levels for those who have already initiated drug use. Secondary prevention programs may help individuals manage risks associated with continued substance use (Baer, 1993; Baer et al., 1992; Fromme et al., 1986; Kivlahan et al., 1990), although the role of efficacy for harm reduction has yet to be demonstrated in behavioral changes (Fromme et al., 1986). Self-management of substance use fluctuates over time. This requires more sensitive investigatory designs in which ongoing covariation in changes in efficacy beliefs or level of substance use are continuously measured rather than only at arbitrary discrete points in time. Other complex motivational factors need to be addressed within programs aimed at risk reduction as well (Baer, 1993).

Self-efficacy for treatment and relapse prevention

A review of the treatment literature reveals that self-efficacy is consistently and significantly associated with attempts to stop addictive behaviors (action self-efficacy), success in initial cessation attempts (coping self-efficacy), and relapse (recovery self-efficacy). Self-efficacy judgments reflect treatment gains, and such judgments are often significant predictors of subsequent behavior even when other predictors are statistically controlled. Studies vary, however, in the use of different efficacy scales, in the time frame of behavioral prediction, the type of behavioral prediction, and in the magnitude of observed relationships. The application of efficacy

theory across different addictive substances (i.e., alcohol and smoking) is
just beginning.

Assessment of self-efficacy

Self-efficacy scales for drug use vary from single items (Erickson, Tiffany,
Martin, & Baker, 1983) to scales with 100 items or more (Annis, 1982). The
most common scale for assessing coping self-efficacy measures strength of
confidence to avoid substance use in specific situations (e.g., Annis, 1982;
Colletti, Supnick, & Payne, 1985; Condiotte and Lichtenstein, 1981;
DiClemente et al., 1985). The development of these scales was guided by
the assumption that relapses are triggered by specific situational influences (Marlatt & Gordon, 1985), and that beliefs in coping efficacy are situ-
ationally specific (Bandura, 1977). Thus, if beliefs about one's ability to
resist addictive behavior in specific situations predict coping success, clients could be taught how to manage high-risk situations to prevent
relapse.

Factor analytic studies of coping self-efficacy scales reveal a strong principle component (Baer & Lichtenstein, 1988b; DiClemente et al., 1985).
This finding had led to the view that efficacy beliefs may not be specific to
situations. However, more recent studies have revealed both a higher
order factor and situational efficacy beliefs (Velicer, DiClemente, Rossi, &
Prochaska, 1990). Efficacy scales have also been developed to assess perceived ability to restrict use of substances (Fromme et al., 1986; Godding &
Glasgow, 1985; Sitharthan & Kavanaugh, 1990; Young, Oei, & Crook, 1991)
and to remain abstinent over given periods of time (Rychtarik, Prue, Rapp,
& King, 1992).

Haaga (1989; Haaga & Stewart, 1992) has more recently assessed efficacy beliefs using an articulated thoughts technique. Subjects are asked to
verbalize thoughts about coping and the outcome of tempting situations
for addictive behaviors (smoking in this case). These verbalized or articulated thoughts are transcribed and then coded by trained raters for
expressed confidence in ability to either resist smoking or to continue cessation efforts after a temptation. Although potentially useful in testing
theoretical aspects of relapse and the role of self-efficacy, the articulated
thoughts technique does not lend itself to convenient clinical application.

Action and coping self-efficacy and smoking cessation

Efficacy beliefs are generally associated with motivation and readiness to
make attempts to quit smoking (action self-efficacy). DiClemente et al.

(1991) have shown that complex relationships exist between efficacy beliefs and change processes at different points in time. The types of efforts toward change vary as a function of the individual's stage of change. Action self-efficacy predicts attempts to quit smoking in a wide range of studies, from professionally led worksite programs (Sussman et al., 1989) to self-initiated New Year's resolutions (Marlatt, Curry, & Gordon, 1988).

Within smoking treatment programs self-efficacy consistently has been predictive of abstinence (Baer, Holt, & Lichtenstein, 1986; Coehlo, 1984; Condiotte & Lichtenstein, 1981; DiClemente, 1981; McIntyre, Lichtenstein, & Mermelstein, 1983; Wojcik, 1988). Pretreatment efficacy ratings (action self-efficacy) – one's confidence in one's ability to quit – generally are not related to eventual success in treatment (Baer & Lichtenstein, 1988b). This is to say that if treatment raises an individual's sense of efficacy, behavior will be regulated by current efficacy beliefs rather than by past efficacy beliefs. Presumably, efficacy judgments made prior to quitting are based on fears or optimism about quitting, but not based on prior performance experience in actually avoiding cigarettes and are thus not relevant. In contrast, efficacy ratings made *after* cessation is attempted (coping self-efficacy) are more likely to be based on recent experience (resistance of smoking) as well as program effects, and are thus better predictors of difficulty in the future.

The prediction of successful abstinence with posttreatment efficacy has been demonstrated in several studies (Baer et al., 1986; Condiotte & Lichtenstein, 1981; Coehlo, 1984; McIntyre et al., 1983). It is noteworthy that in at least two of these studies, efficacy retains statistically significant predictive power when only successful quitters are examined (Baer et al., 1986; McIntyre et al., 1983), thus demonstrating unique predictive capacity beyond that of behavioral attainment. Haaga and Stewart (1992), using an articulated thoughts technique described above, have further suggested that subjects with moderate efficacy ratings fared somewhat better than those with the highest efficacy scores. Although this result is only of marginal statistical significance, it is the first suggestion of an "overconfidence" effect in smoking cessation. Overconfidence is a clinical issue common in addictions (see discussion below regarding alcohol treatment). In theory, persons who do not fear a relapse are likely to test themselves by using the substance. Bandura (1991) has recently argued that successful abstinence requires high resistance or coping efficacy but moderate recovery efficacy, so as not to lead to trials of substance use. Future research in smoking (and other addictions) will need to utilize measures that assess different components of efficacy, as well as scales that provide a range of difficulty of efficacy so that overconfidence might be assessed. Although in need of replication, the articulated thoughts technique may provide greater variability to assess differences at a high end of confidence.

The study of smoking cessation efficacy has further been associated with processes thought to be important in the maintenance of cessation long after initial and successful attempts to quit. Marlatt and Gordon (1985) in a cognitive-behavioral model of relapse, propose that coping self-efficacy plays a critical role in managing urges and temptations to use substances. After a slip, recovery self-efficacy for continued abstinence drops (Shiffman, 1984). McDermut, Haaga, & Shayne (1991) have further demonstrated that persons who rate negative affect situations as more difficult than social situations were more likely to lapse during a 12-month follow-up period. Such individual differences in efficacy for managing different types of situations, if reliable, could be used to tailor treatments (see discussion below). It is noteworthy that the relationship between situation-specific efficacy and actual coping in situations has been difficult to demonstrate using other methodologies (Baer & Lichtenstein, 1988a).

Action and coping self-efficacy: Studies of alcohol and other drug addiction

Research applying the self-efficacy theory to alcohol and other drug problems is less well developed than that for research on smoking (see DiClemente et al., in press, for a review). Given the similarities between addictive problems and the application of the same cognitive-behavioral model (Marlatt & Gordon, 1985), most of the theoretical and practical issues are similar to those in smoking cessation. Annis and Davis (1988, 1989), in fact, have developed a complete treatment program for alcohol problems based on an assessment of self-efficacy across situations.

Studies on self-efficacy theory and application have only recently appeared in the research literature on drug addiction. For example, Heller and Krauss (1991) report on the development of an efficacy scale with 63 polysubstance abusers enrolled in an inpatient detoxification center. Subjects rated their confidence in their ability to perform behaviors necessary to enter aftercare, and a 17-item scale was developed with high internal reliability. The scale did correlate modestly ($r = .28$) with eventual entrance into aftercare. Stephens, Wertz, and Roffman (1993) examined self-efficacy as a predictor of success in an outpatient marijuana treatment program. Using a 19-item scale assessing confidence in avoiding marijuana use in different situations, self-efficacy was prospectively predictive of rates of use up to 1 year after treatment, but was unrelated to the experience of marijuana-related problems.

Coping self-efficacy has also been studied in an opiate drug treatment program. Gossop, Green, Phillips, and Bradley (1990) studied 80 opiate addicts immediately after discharge and again 6 months later. Self-efficacy was assessed by asking subjects to rate their ability to stay off opiates over six different periods of time ("from the evening after leaving hospital through six months after discharge" to "for the rest of your life"). A summary score from these six responses was found to significantly and prospectively predict drug use at both 2 and 6 months after discharge.

More data pertaining to self-efficacy are available for treatments of alcohol abuse. Individuals who have successfully abstained from drinking after treatment report markedly higher efficacy for resisting alcohol than individuals who are just entering treatment (Miller, Ross, Emmerson, & Todt, 1989). Self-efficacy for controlling drinking is associated with fewer problems and lower rates of consumption (Collins & Lapp, 1991). Self-efficacy is also related to readiness to change behavior. DiClemente and Hughes (1990) found that patients appearing for treatment who were uninvolved or discouraged about changing expressed the lowest efficacy for abstinence compared to patients who showed a greater readiness to change. These authors recommend assessment of other constructs in relation to self-efficacy (e.g., temptation to drink) to provide a complete picture of clients' motivational states.

Within alcohol treatment, Sitharthan and Kavanaugh (1990) found that efficacy beliefs predicted drinking in a controlled drinking program even after removing the possible influence of demographic variables, alcohol dependence history, and level of consumption during treatment. Annis and Davis (1988) reported with a small sample ($n = 41$) that efficacy beliefs increase dramatically over treatment, and that specific situational efficacy scores predicted drinking lapses during treatment. Predictable situations were those of heavier drinking; occasions of lighter drinking during treatment were not associated with situational efficacy ratings. Solomon and Annis (1990) reported that efficacy ratings taken prior to treatment were strongly associated with the extent of drinking during follow-up, but failed to distinguish those who drank from those who did not.

Two studies have examined the role of coping efficacy in more traditional drug and alcohol treatment programs. Burling, Reilly, Moltzen, and Ziff (1989) evaluated coping self-efficacy among 419 male substance abuse inpatients at an American Veteran's Administration hospital. The inpatient treatment facility utilized a therapeutic community for self-governance, and the program utilized cognitive and behavioral skills training, education, didactic classes, and group therapy. Self-efficacy was assessed using the Situational Confidence Questionnaire (SCQ; Annis, 1982, modified to allow ratings of both drugs and alcohol) monthly during treatment. A number of methodological issues plague this study. First, the patient population reported abuse of a number of many different substances, most commonly alcohol (43%) and cocaine (23%). Further, only 81 of 419 patients were available for interview approximately 6 months after discharge to determine drug use posttreatment. "Any drug use" was considered "relapse," a criterion that may mask important differences in outcome. Nevertheless, results revealed a number of interesting relationships between efficacy and addictive treatment. Consistent with research in smoking cessation, judgments of ability to refrain from substance use were low on admission, and rose dramatically during treatment. Further, low self-efficacy was associated with longer stays in treatment, and discharge under more negative circumstances.

In this study, prediction of relapse from self-efficacy scores revealed a pattern not previously reported: although pretreatment and posttreatment SCQ scores were not related to relapse, the *change* in efficacy over the treatment period was predictive of outcome (Burling et al., 1989). More specifically, although patients who maintained sobriety reported lower efficacy ratings at treatment entry, they changed more during treatment than those who relapsed during follow-up. Further, the situational efficacy of patients who had generally low sense of efficacy at entry to treatment was related to actual relapse situations. The authors suggest that patients in drug and alcohol treatment can be "overconfident," particularly those forced into treatment, less motivated for treatment, or in denial about the severity of their difficulties. These patients are less likely to expend energy in treatment or appraise accurately their abilities to avoid relapse. In contrast, those lower in efficacy initially are more accurate in judging their efficacy in high-risk situations, tend to gain more from treatment, and do better during follow-up. The authors suggest that this may be one important way in which patients in treatment for alcohol or other drug problems are different from smokers. The large number of methodological problems noted above, of course, caution interpretations of findings.

Rychtarik and colleagues (1992) reported a similar study with somewhat different results. This study of 87 male alcoholics also took place at a Veterans' Affairs Treatment Unit. Patients completed a version of the Confidence Questionnaire (Condiotte & Lichtenstein, 1981) modified to reflect beliefs about "what percentage of time they believed they would be able to resist the urge to drink in that situation." Considerably more method-ological rigor was present in the Rychtarik and colleagues study than that of Burling and colleagues. The self-efficacy questionnaire was completed at intake, discharge, 2 weeks, and 1, 2, 3, 6, and 12 months postdischarge from a 28-day inpatient treatment program; 80% of the sample was suc-cessfully followed. Consistent with Burling and colleagues (1989) and many other studies, self-efficacy was generally low at treatment entry and increased significantly during treatment. In contrast to the Burling and colleagues study, and the literature from smoking, pretreatment efficacy was associated with relapse: Those with higher confidence at treatment entry were less likely to relapse. In no analysis did posttreatment scores predict relapse, nor did change in efficacy judgments predict relapse.

Rychtarik and colleagues (1992) note a number of differences between their results and those reported by Burling and colleagues (1989). The two studies used different scales to measure self-efficacy, and their popula-tions were somewhat different. In particular, the Rychtarik study included only those who completed a 28-day inpatient alcoholism treatment pro-gram, whereas Burling and colleagues (1989) attempted to follow drop-outs from a long residential community (although proportionally few were found). Rychtarik and colleagues further express concerns about ceiling effects in self-efficacy scales, particularly at posttreatment assess-ments. These investigators note that such ceiling effects could be method-ological. Restricting the study to the cases who successfully completed the treatment would curtail this range of scores and restrict the magnitude of relationships. Rychtarik and colleagues further question if efficacy rating scales might reflect unrealistic expectations or impression management by patients at discharge. Nevertheless, high and invariant ratings preclude any predictive capacity of posttreatment ratings among these populations.

Other studies, noted above, particularly those with moderation goals (Sitharthan & Kavanaugh, 1990), have shown good predictive relation-ships from posttreatment efficacy, and no evidence of an overconfidence effect. It may be that overconfidence is a psychological state that creates risk for relapse, particularly for abstinence goals. Only Haaga and Stewart (1992) have data to suggest this relationship in smoking cessation; such a finding is in great need of replication. In the alcoholism treatment studies reviewed, both Burling and colleagues (1989) and Rychtarik and col-leagues (1992) adopt such an interpretation, albeit with very different scales, methods, and results (in Rychtarik and colleagues' case to explain why posttreatment scores are too high and nonpredictive, and for Burling and colleagues to explain why high pretreatment scores predict difficulty in treatment). As noted above, overconfidence is a common concern in addictions treatment associated with attributions of "denial." Given available research, we can only conclude that the data for overconfidence are, at best, weak. Clearly, only continued research, using measures of efficacy with a full range of difficulty and that assess different components of confidence (coping, recovery) can evaluate this issue (Bandura, 1991). Furthermore, all of the research reviewed above tends to treat efficacy something like a personality trait. Bandura (1977) has proposed that efficacy is most appropriately considered a state that changes over time with experience. Research programs need to address how efficacy beliefs regulate addictive behavior in an ongoing manner as emotional experiences, coping successes, and situational influences change. Issues such as "overconfidence" could perhaps be best tested with a methodology that assessed efficacy closer in time to the behavior it is hypothesized to influence.

Recovery self-efficacy

Both coping self-efficacy and recovery self-efficacy are central concepts in relapse prevention (Marlatt & Gordon, 1985; Shiffman & Wills, 1985). Whereas coping self-efficacy relates to the maintenance of action-stage goals (e.g., abstinence or moderate use), recovery self-efficacy is concerned with the individual's confidence in reinstating control should a relapse occur. The distinction between coping and recovery self-efficacy is similar to the distinction proposed earlier between resistance self-efficacy (maintaining abstinence prior to first use) and harm-reduction self-efficacy (risk reduction following first use).

Little research has been conducted on the role of self-efficacy following an initial lapse or setback. In most of the coping self-efficacy research reviewed above, self-efficacy is assessed prior to relapse, at pretreatment or posttreatment. As such, these measures assess anticipatory coping self-efficacy. Recovery self-efficacy refers to restorative coping or confidence that one can successfully recover from lapses.

Research has, however, assessed attributional processes following a lapse. Studies have documented a helplessness reaction to the first slip or setback (among subjects committed to abstinence) termed the abstinence violation effect (Collins & Lapp, 1991; Marlatt & Gordon, 1985; Ross et al., 1989). Individuals experiencing this reaction tend to attribute the cause of initial lapses (e.g., after smoking the first cigarette after a quit attempt) to internal, stable, and uncontrollable factors such as lack of willpower or biological craving/withdrawal. Such an attributional pattern is associated with greater relapse rates compared to individuals who attribute lapses to deficient coping with changing situational demands that are perceived to be under personal control (Curry, Marlatt, & Gordon, 1987).

In the relapse prevention literature a number of intervention techniques have been described to bolster and restore self-efficacy following setbacks. Since clients often experience a motivational crisis in the midst of a lapse and are in danger of giving up or dropping out of treatment, enhancing recovery efficacy is a critical challenge. Curry and Marlatt (1987) offer a number of clinical methods to help clients cope with slips and the abstinence violation effect, including consulting a reminder card that details specific restorative coping instructions. Clients are advised to immediately stop the addictive behavior and recognize the triggering situation and their emotional reactions. By reviewing the situation leading up to the lapse, clients can enlist coping strategies that reverse the course of behavior. Recovery efficacy is also enhanced by invoking a plan for recovery (e.g., seeking help, renewing initial commitment to change, developing a relapse recovery contract). Structuring reactions to setbacks that restore efficacy and enhance coping help clients to prevent being overwhelmed with a sense of failure. Relapse prevention programs attempt to reframe relapse as a natural part of the recovery learning process. Future research should clarify the role of recovery self-efficacy and should pave the way for the development of additional relapse prevention methods.

Clinical implications of coping self-efficacy

The findings concerning the modification of smoking and drinking behavior only show that what is already being done effectively changes self-efficacy. More conceptually, self-efficacy theory could be useful in structuring treatments in at least three ways. First, self-efficacy theory can guide the development of treatments that better facilitate a sense of personal efficacy, and hence lead to better outcomes (Curry & Marlatt, 1987). For example, self-efficacy is altered by performance mastery experience, social modeling, verbal persuasion, and from emotional states. Treatment should be structured and implemented in ways that capitalize on these different sources of influence. For example, Fairhurst (1990, cited in DiClemente et al., in press) suggests that performance attainments are a major contributor to perceived efficacy to control smoking behavior (see also, Baer & Lichtenstein, 1988b; Tiffany, Martin, & Baker, 1986). Most treatment programs seek to reduce substance use through mastery experience. Future performance attainments alone do not necessarily instill a high sense of efficacy. Witness the variation in perceived efficacy among individuals who have all quit smoking by the end of treatment. It is not performance attainments, per se, but what is made of them that determines perceived efficacy. Self-efficacy theory suggests ways of structuring experience to maximize their impact on beliefs in one's capability to control addictive behavior.

Second, self-efficacy ratings are used to identify clients at greatest risk for difficulty. This includes identifying which persons are unprepared to change at the current time and those most at risk for relapse. The timing of treatment steps could also be based on level of perceived self-efficacy. People may not be ready to make specific changes without more time or training. Such a treatment scheme naturally requires that efficacy judgments prospectively predict success in the change process. Given the variability of scales measuring different facets of self-efficacy at different phases of change and for different addiction problems, more research is needed to specify which efficacy scales for what problems will best direct treatment decisions and different phases of change.

Third, efficacy judgments could be used to assess which particular places or times pose high risk for given individuals. Theoretically, beliefs about coping capabilities in specific situations could guide tailoring of treatment and developing specific coping strategies for specific situations (i.e. Annis & Davis, 1988). Although attempts at situational predictions have not always met with success, recent studies using different analytic methods (Annis & Davis, 1988; Burling et al., 1989; McDermut et al., 1991; Velicer et al., 1990) suggest that efficacy beliefs may vary across different classes of situational and emotional conditions that tax coping capabilities. It remains a problem of future research to determine how best to identify the patterning of risks for given individuals based on the structure of their efficacy beliefs.

"The swimming hole": A final comment

On a hot, slow, summer day, a 15-year-old boy happens upon a quiet, cool pond. At the edge of the pond is a large sign that reads "no swimming." It is reasonable to assume that such a situation would place this boy in a motivational dilemma. How can perceptions of self-efficacy be applied to this situation? One might ask the boy about his confidence in his ability to resist the urge to dive in. Yet such a question and such a response likely involve a number of different types of motivational states and efficacy beliefs. We might also ask the youngster about his confidence in his ability to have a good time or cool off without diving in. On further analysis one might ask the boy about his confidence in his ability to swim! Or about his ability to cool off and enjoy himself without getting caught. All of these judgments, of course, are relative to the heat of the day, the coolness of the pond, the size of the sign, and the social norms for this kind of activity. Imagine the young man's conflict if, immediately beyond the large sign, he sees three of his friends frolicking about in the water experiencing no apparent negative consequences. Perhaps most realistically, still others are present, many who do not jump in but heed the sign.

This analogy, we believe, demonstrates the self-regulatory complications involved in the study of addictive behaviors. The goals for behavior (and efficacy) are often unclear. Despite a behavior pattern that creates considerable health risks, the goal of any individual client can vary considerably along a continuum from "go" to "no go." Such mixed motivations must be carefully assessed, in our view, because they indicate what types of self-efficacy beliefs are most relevant for predicting and explaining addictive behaviors.

References

Annis, H. M. (1982). Inventory of drinking situations. Ontario: Addiction Research Foundation.

Annis, H. M., & Davis, C. S. (1988). Self-efficacy and the prevention of alcoholic relapse: Initial findings from a treatment trial. In T. B. Baker & D. S. Cannon (Eds.), *Assessment and treatment of addictive disorders* (pp. 88–112). New York: Praeger.

Annis, H. M., & Davis, C. S. (1989). Relapse Prevention. In R. K. Hester & W. R. Miller (Eds.), *Handbook of alcoholism treatment approaches: Effective alternatives* (pp. 170–182). Needham Heights, MA: Allyn & Bacon.

Baer, J. S. (1993). Etiology and secondary prevention of alcohol problems with young adults. In J. S. Baer, G. A. Marlatt, & R. J. McMahon (Eds.), *Addictive behaviors across the lifespan: Prevention, treatment, and policy issues* (pp. 111–137). Newbury Park, CA: Sage.

Baer, J. S., Holt, C. S., & Lichtenstein, E. (1986). Self-efficacy and smoking reexamined: Construct validity and clinical utility. *Journal of Consulting and Clinical Psychology, 54,* 846–852.

Baer, J. S., & Lichtenstein, E. (1988a). Classification and prediction of smoking relapse episodes: An exploration of individual differences. *Journal of Consulting and Clinical Psychology, 56,* 104–110.

Baer, J. S., & Lichtenstein, E. (1988b). Cognitive assessment in the treatment of smoking addiction. In D. M. Donovan & G. A. Marlatt (Eds.), *Assessment of addictive behaviors: Behavioral, cognitive, and physiological procedures* (pp. 198–213). New York: Guilford.

Baer, J. S., Marlatt, G. A., Kivlahan, D. R., Fromme, K., Larimer, M. E., & Williams, E. (1992). An experimental test of three methods of alcohol risk reduction with young adults. *Journal of Consulting and Clinical Psychology, 60,* 974–979.

312   G. Alan Marlatt, John S. Baer, and Lori A. Quigley

Bandura, A. (1977). Self-efficacy: Toward a unifying theory of behavior change. *Psychological Review, 84*, 191–215.
Bandura, A. (1991). Self-efficacy mechanism in physiological activation and health-promoting behavior. In J. Madden, IV (Ed.), *Neurobiology of learning, emotion and affect* (pp. 229–269). New York: Raven.
Brod, M. I., & Hall, S. M. (1984). Joiners and non-joiners in smoking treatment: A comparison of psychosocial variables. *Addictive Behaviors, 9*, 217–221.
Brown, J. H., & Horowitz, J. E. (1993). Deviance and Deviants: Why adolescent substance use prevention programs can't work. *Evaluation Review, 17*, 529–555.
Burling, T. A., Reilly, P. M., Moltzen, J. O., & Ziff, D. C. (1989). Self-efficacy and relapse among inpatient drug and alcohol abusers: A predictor of outcome. *Journal of Studies on Alcohol, 50*, 354–360.
Chaney, E. F., O'Leary, M. R., & Marlatt, G. A. (1978). Skill training with alcoholics. *Journal of Consulting and Clinical Psychology, 46*, 1092–1104.
Coelho, R. J. (1984). Self-efficacy and cessation of smoking. *Psychological Reports, 54*, 309–310.
Colletti, G., Supnick, J. A., & Payne, T. J. (1985). The Smoking Self-Efficacy Questionnaire (SSEQ): Preliminary scale development and validation. *Behavioral Assessment, 7*, 249–260.
Collins, R. L., & Lapp, W. M. (1991). Restraint and attributions: Evidence of the abstinence violation effect in alcohol consumption. *Cognitive Therapy and Research, 15*, 69–84.
Condiotte, M. M., & Lichtenstein, E. (1981). Self-efficacy and relapse in smoking cessation programs. *Journal of Consulting and Clinical Psychology, 49*, 648–658.
Conrad, K. M., Flay, B. R., & Hill, D. (1992). Why children start smoking cigarettes: Predictors of onset. *British Journal of Addiction, 87*, 1711–1724.
Curry, S., & Marlatt, G. A. (1987). Building self-confidence, self-efficacy, and self-control. In W. M. Cox (Ed.), *Treatment and prevention of alcohol problems* (pp. 117–138). New York: Academic.
Curry, S., Marlatt, G. A., & Gordon, J. R. (1987). Abstinence violation effect: Validation of an attributional construct with smoking cessation. *Journal of Consulting and Clinical Psychology, 55*, 145–149.
DiClemente, C. C. (1981). Self-efficacy and smoking cessation maintenance: A preliminary report. *Cognitive Therapy and Research, 5*, 175–187.
DiClemente, C. C., Fairhurst, S. K., & Piotrowski, N. A. (in press). The role of self-efficacy in the addictive behaviors. In J. Maddux (Ed.), *Self efficacy, adaptation and adjustment: Theory, research and application*. New York: Plenum.
DiClemente, C. C., & Hughes, S. O. (1990). Stages of change profiles in alcoholism treatment. *Journal of Substance Abuse, 2*, 217–235.
DiClemente, C. C., Prochaska, J. O., Fairhurst, S. K., Velicer, W. F., Velasquez, M. M., & Rossi, J. S. (1991). The process of smoking cessation: An analysis of pre-contemplation, contemplation and preparation stages of change. *Journal of Consulting and Clinical Psychology, 59*, 295–304.
DiClemente, C. C., Prochaska, J. O., & Gibertini, M. (1985). Self-efficacy and the stages of self-change of smoking. *Cognitive Therapy and Research, 9*, 181–200.
Ellickson, P. L., & Bell, R. M. (1990). Drug prevention in junior high: A multisite longitudinal test. *Science, 247*, 1299–1305.
Ellickson, P. L., Bell, R. M., & McGuigan, K. (1993). Preventing adolescent drug use: Long-term results of a junior high program. *American Journal of Public Health, 83*, 856–861.

Ellickson, P. L., & Hays, R. D. (1991). Beliefs about resistance self-efficacy and drug prevalence: Do they really affect drug use? *International Journal of the Addictions, 25*, 1353–1378.

Ellickson P. L., & Hays, R. D. (1992). On becoming involved with drugs: Modeling adolescent drug use over time. *Health Psychology, 11*, 377–385.

Erickson, L. M., Tiffany, S. T., Martin, E. M., & Baker, T. B. (1983). Aversive smoking therapies: A conditioning analysis of therapeutic effectiveness. *Behaviour Research and Therapy, 21*, 595–611.

Fairhurst, S. K. (1990). Predictors of smoking abstinence self-efficacy. Unpublished master's thesis.

Fromme, K., Kivlahan, D. R., & Marlatt, G. A. (1986). Alcohol expectancies, risk identification, and secondary prevention with problem drinkers. *Advances in Behavior Research and Therapy, 8*, 237–251.

Godding, P. R., & Glasgow, R. E. (1985). Self-efficacy and outcome expectations as predictors of controlled smoking status. *Cognitive Therapy and Research, 9*, 583–590.

Gossop, M., Green, L., Phillips, G., & Bradley, B. (1990). Factors predicting outcome among opiate addicts after treatment. *British Journal of Clinical Psychology, 29*, 209–216.

Haaga, D. A. F. (1989). Articulated thoughts and endorsement procedures for cognitive assessment in the prediction of smoking relapse. *Psychological Assessment: A Journal of Consulting and Clinical Psychology, 1*, 112–117.

Haaga, D. A. F., & Stewart, B. L. (1992). Self-efficacy for recovery from a lapse after smoking cessation. *Journal of Consulting and Clinical Psychology, 60*, 24–28.

Hansen, W. B., Graham, J. W., Wolkenstein, B. H., & Rohrbach, L. A. (1991). Program integrity as a moderator of prevention program effectiveness: Results for fifth-grade students in the adolescent alcohol prevention trial. *Journal of Studies on Alcohol, 52*, 568–579.

Hays, R. D., & Ellickson, P. L. (1990). How generalizable are adolescents' beliefs about pro-drug pressures and resistance self-efficacy? *Journal of Applied Social Psychology, 20*, 321–340.

Heller, M. C., & Krauss, H. H. (1991). Perceived self-efficacy as a predictor of aftercare treatment entry by the detoxification patient. *Psychological Reports, 68*, 1047–1052.

Jessor, R., Donovan, J. E., & Costa, F. M. (1991). *Beyond adolescence: Problem behavior and young adult development.* Cambridge, England: Cambridge University Press.

Jessor, R., & Jessor, S. L. (1977). *Problem behavior and psychosocial development: A longitudinal study.* New York: Academic.

Kandel, D. B., & Faust, R. (1975). Sequences and stages in patterns of adolescent drug use. *Archives of General Psychiatry, 32*, 923–932.

Kandel, D. B., Yamaguchi, K., & Chen, K. (1992). Stages of progression in drug involvement from adolescence to adulthood: Further evidence for the gateway theory. *Journal of Studies on Alcohol, 53*, 447–457.

Kivlahan, D. R., Marlatt, G. A., Fromme, K., Coppel, D. B., & Williams, E. (1990). Secondary prevention with college drinkers: Evaluation of an alcohol skills training program. *Journal of Consulting and Clinical Psychology, 58*, 805–810.

Lawrence, L., & Rubinson, L. (1986). Self-efficacy as a predictor of smoking behavior in young adolescents. *Addictive Behaviors, 11*, 367–382.

Marlatt, G. A., Curry, S., & Gordon, J. R. (1988). A longitudinal analysis of unaided smoking cessation. *Journal of Consulting and Clinical Psychology, 56*, 715–720.

Marlatt, G. A., & Gordon, J. R. (Eds.). (1985). *Relapse prevention: Maintenance strategies in the treatment of addictive behaviors.* New York: Guilford.

Marlatt, G. A., Larimer, M. E., Baer, J. S., & Quigley, L. A. (1993). Harm reduction for alcohol problems: Moving beyond the controlled drinking controversy. *Behavior Therapy, 24,* 461–504.

Marlatt, G. A., & Tapert, S. F. (1993). Harm reduction: Reducing the risks of addictive behaviors. In J. S. Baer, G. A. Marlatt, & R. McMahon (Eds.), *Addictive behaviors across the lifespan* (pp. 243–273). Newbury Park, CA: Sage.

McDermut, W., Haaga, D. A. F., & Shayne, V. T. (1991). Schemata and smoking relapse. *Behavior Therapy, 22,* 423–434.

McIntyre, K. O., Lichtenstein, E., & Mermelstein, R. J. (1983). Self-efficacy and relapse in smoking cessation: A replication and extension. *Journal of Consulting and Clinical Psychology, 51,* 632–633.

Miller, P. J., Ross, S. M., Emmerson, R. Y., & Todt, E. H. (1989). Self-efficacy in alcoholics: Clinical validation of the Situational Confidence Questionnaire. *Addictive Behaviors, 14,* 217–224.

Myers, M. G., Brown, S. A., & Mott, M. A. (1993). Coping as a predictor of adolescent substance abuse treatment outcome. *Journal of Substance Abuse, 5,* 15–29.

National Institute on Drug Abuse. (1992). Smoking, drinking, and illicit drug use among American secondary school students, college students, and young adults, 1975–1991 (Volume II). Rockville, MD: National Institute on Drug Abuse.

Newcomb, M., & Bentler, P. (1988). *Consequences of adolescent drug use: Impact on the lives of young adults.* Newbury Park, CA: Sage.

Pentz, M. A. (1985). Social competence and self-efficacy as determinants of substance abuse in adolescence. In S. Shiffman & T. A. Wills (Eds.), *Coping and substance abuse* (pp. 117–139). Orlando, FL: Academic.

Perry, C. L., Kelder, S. H., Murray, D. M., & Klepp, K. (1992). Communitywide smoking prevention: Long-term outcomes of the Minnesota Heart Health Program and the class of 1989 study. *American Journal of Public Health, 82,* 1210–1216.

Prochaska, J. O., & DiClemente, C. C. (1992). Stages of change in the modification of problem behaviors. In M. Hersen, R. M. Eisler, & P. M. Miller (Eds.), *Progress in behavior modification* (Vol. 28, pp. 184–214). Sycamore, IL: Sycamore Publishing.

Rohrbach, L. A., Graham, J. W., Hansen, W. B., & Flay, B. R. (1987). Evaluation of resistance skills training using multitrait-multimethod role play skill assessments. *Health Education Research, 2,* 401–407.

Ross, S. M., Miller, P. J., Emmerson, R. Y., & Todt, E. H. (1989). Self-efficacy, standards and abstinence violation: A comparison between newly sober and long-term sober alcoholics. *Journal of Substance Abuse, 1,* 221–229.

Rychtarik, R. G., Prue, D. M., Rapp, S. R., King, A. C. (1992). Self-efficacy, aftercare and relapse in a treatment program from alcoholics. *Journal of Studies on Alcohol, 53,* 435–440.

Shedler, J., & Block, J. (1990). Adolescent drug use and psychological health: A longitudinal inquiry. *American Psychologist, 45,* 612–630.

Shiffman, S. (1984). Cognitive antecedents and sequelae of smoking relapse crises. *Journal of Applied Social Psychology, 14,* 296–309.

Shiffman, S., & Wills, T. A. (1985). *Coping and substance abuse.* New York: Academic.

Sitharthan, T., & Kavanagh, D. J. (1990). Role of self-efficacy in predicting outcomes from a programme for controlled drinking. *Drug and Alcohol Dependence, 27,* 87–94.

Solomon, K. E., & Annis, H. M. (1990). Outcome and efficacy expectancy in the prediction of post-treatment drinking behaviour. *British Journal of Addiction, 85,* 659–665.

Stacy, A. W., Sussman, S., Dent, C. W., Burton, D., & Flay, B. R. (1992). Moderators of peer social influence in adolescent smoking. *Personality and Social Psychology Bulletin, 18,* 163–172.

Stephens, R. S., Wertz, J. S., & Roffman, R. A. (1993). Predictors of marijuana treatment outcomes: The role of self-efficacy. *Journal of Substance Abuse, 5,* 341–354.

Sussman, S., Whitney-Saltiel, D. A., Budd, R. J., Spiegel, D., Brannon, B. F., Hansesn, W. B., Johnson, C. A., and Flay, B. R. (1989). Joiners and non-joiners in worksite smoking treatment: Pretreatment smoking, smoking by significant others, and expectation to quit as predictors. *Addictive Behaviors, 14,* 113–119.

Telch, M. J., Killen, J. D., McAllister, A. L., Perry, C. L., & Maccoby, N. (1982). Long-term follow-up of a pilot project on smoking prevention with adolescents. *Journal of Behavioral Medicine, 5,* 1–8.

Tiffany, S. T., Martin, E. M., & Baker, T. B. (1986). Treatment for cigarette smoking: An evaluation of the contributions of aversion and counseling procedures. *Behaviour Research and Therapy, 24,* 437–452.

Velicer, W. F., DiClemente, C. C., Rossi, J. S., & Prochaska, J. O. (1990). Relapse situations and self-efficacy: An integrative model. *Addictive Behaviors, 15,* 271–283.

Wojcik, J. V. (1988). Social learning predictors of the avoidance of smoking relapse. *Addictive Behaviors, 13,* 177–180.

Young, R. M., Oei, T. P. S., & Crook, G. M. (1991). Development of a drinking self-efficacy questionnaire. *Journal of Psychopathology and Behavioral Assessment, 13,* 1–15.

Name index

Abel, M., 265, 266
Abidin, R. R., 119
Aboud, F. E., 13
Abraham, C., 260
Abrams, D., 260
Abrams, D. B., 266, 277
Abramson, L. Y., 12, 85, 96, 156
Achermann, E., 117
Adams, N. E., 263
Adler, A., 2
Adler, T., 216
Ainsworth, M. D. S., 91
Aitken, D., 265
Ajzen, I., 7, 215, 265, 268
Alden, L., 7
Alloy, L. B., 12, 85, 96
Alpern, D., 121
Altmaier, E. M., 7, 20
Amato, P. R., 121
Ames, C., 153, 168
Amrhein, J., 96
Anderson, C. S., 22
Annis, H. M., 262, 302, 304, 305, 306, 310
Antoni, M. H., 27
Appels, A., 27
Ardelt, M., 15, 53, 56, 60
Arkowitz, H., 12
Armstrong, S., 88
Arnold, J., 244
Aronfreed, J., 88
Asendorpf, J., 118
Ashton, P. T., 20, 203
Assor, A., 210
Atkins, C. J., 266
Atkinson, J. W., 80, 214
Ausubel, D., 89
Avard, J., 266
Ayers, A. L., 238
Azar, S. T., 129

Bachmann, M., 93
Baer, J. S., xii, 32, 262, 263, 293, 297, 300, 301, 302, 303, 304, 309

Bagby, R., 266
Bagozzi, R. P., 266
Bahr, S. J., 132
Bakan, D., 114
Baker, T. B., 302, 309
Baldwin, J. M., 69, 73
Balshem, A., 273
Baltes, M. M., 81, 93, 94
Baltes, P. B., xiii, 48, 70, 79, 81, 86, 88, 89, 116, 118, 149, 161, 165, 166, 167, 168, 279
Baltes-Goetz, B., 84
Band, E. B., 82
Bandura, A., vii, viii, ix, 2, 3, 5, 6, 7, 8, 9, 10, 18, 19, 21, 26, 28, 31, 32, 33, 50, 70, 75, 83, 85, 89, 116, 149, 150, 156, 162, 165, 169, 178, 181, 202, 203, 204, 205, 206, 207, 209, 212, 213, 215, 217, 218, 219, 221, 222, 224, 225, 234, 239, 242, 246, 248, 252, 261, 262, 263, 267, 273, 293, 295, 302, 303, 308
Bank, L., 19
Barchas, J. D., 263
Barker, G., 92
Barker, K. M., 17
Barling, J., 265, 266
Barlow, D. H., 8
Barrington, E., 265
Bartholomew, K., 117
Barton, R., 12
Barzon, J., 221
Basen-Engquist, K., 267
Bates, J. E., 118, 128
Baum, A., 26, 27
Baumann, U., 180
Beady, C., 22
Beaman, J., 131
Beamer, J. E., 207, 211
Beck, K. H., 263, 267
Beckmann, J., 277
Beckmann, M., 124, 125
Bell, N. J., 260
Bell, R. M., 296, 298, 301
Bell, R. W., 260

317

Subject index

Made in the USA
Lexington, KY
13 June 2011